Charlotte

TRADE MARK USE

TRADE MARK USE

Edited by

JEREMY PHILLIPS

Intellectual Property Consultant
Slaughter and May

Visiting Professorial Fellow
Queen Mary Intellectual Property Research Institute

Professor, Magister Lucentinus
University of Alicante

Editor
European Trade Mark Reports

and

ILANAH SIMON

Doctoral Associate
Queen Mary Intellectual Property Research Institute

Deputy Editor
European Trade Mark Reports

OXFORD
UNIVERSITY PRESS

OXFORD
UNIVERSITY PRESS

Great Clarendon Street, Oxford OX2 6DP

Oxford University Press is a department of the University of Oxford.
It furthers the University's objective of excellence in research, scholarship,
and education by publishing worldwide in

Oxford New York

Auckland Cape Town Dar es Salaam Hong Kong Karachi
Kuala Lumpur Madrid Melbourne Mexico City Nairobi
New Delhi Shanghai Taipei Toronto

With offices in

Argentina Austria Brazil Chile Czech Republic France Greece
Guatemala Hungary Italy Japan South Korea Poland Portugal
Singapore Switzerland Thailand Turkey Ukraine Vietnam

Oxford is a registered trade mark of Oxford University Press
in the UK and in certain other countries

Published in the United States
by Oxford University Press Inc., New York

© the various contributors 2005

British Library Cataloguing in Publication Data

Data available

Library of Congress Cataloging in Publication Data

Data available

ISBN 0–19–928033–9   978–0–19–928033–9

1 3 5 7 9 10 8 6 4 2

Typeset by RefineCatch Limited, Bungay, Suffolk
Printed in Great Britain
on acid-free paper by
Biddles Ltd, King's Lynn

To our parents, with love

FOREWORD

This is a fascinating book. It is not often possible to say that about books on esoteric subjects such as intellectual property law, nor, within intellectual property law, about trade marks. Certainly you would not expect to find a fascinating book on trade mark *use*. But what the editors have done here is to look at the concept of use, the utility of use, the necessity of use, the requirement to use, and all other possible aspects of use of trade marks and how the law deals with these uses. Since, over the years, I have found that intellectual property, and especially trade mark, problems throw up quite an extraordinary number of philosophical issues, I found this approach by the authors quite captivating, and I was not at all surprised to find a philosopher among the contributors! And all this from the point of view of TRIPs, of the German courts, the English courts, from the point of view of OHIM, as well as the European Court of Justice, including the Court of First Instance.

This is a book not just for the academic, or the practitioner, nor just for the judge or the legislator, but for all of those, and indeed for any others who might find trade marks of some interest—especially in the context in which we now find the developing law at Community level so critically positioned.

I was particularly impressed by the way in which the topics on use are divided. It makes a great deal of sense, in examining the role of use of a trade mark, to look at use in discrete segregated sections, notwithstanding the often overlapping roles which that use may enjoy. So, for example, the chapter on use and non-use is a marvellous general chapter which lays the groundwork for the remaining chapters. Use in context of registration, more particularly to establish distinctive character, or use by third parties, or in infringement cases, all merit different arguments, even if sometimes related, so that the particular role of use in the various individual contexts in which it is found, or required, is clear.

I look forward to seeing, in future editions of the work—which I am sure will certainly come—a continuation of the debate on the interesting topic of 'The Need to Leave Free for Others' and the way in which this may develop at national level, as well as in the ECJ. And I am sure we shall see, as greater numbers of cases, especially those on exotic marks, come to the ECJ, further developments in the debate on the boundaries between the requirement for a sign to have the necessary capacity to distinguish before it can constitute a trade mark and the requirement that a trade mark, in turn, be distinctive for the purposes of registration, especially in light of the excellent exposé of the manner in which English law on this issue has evolved during the past 100 years.

Among the other very interesting topics I found was the chapter entitled 'Infringement', and especially the section on 'Permitted Infringement', which I think could lead to quite a heated exchange between those who consider that there can be no such thing as a 'permitted infringement', and those who take the opposite view. It is not surprising that the author of this particular section takes the view that Article 6 of the Directive (Article 12 of the Regulation) 'yields several surprises'. It is wonderful to find such a debate about a part of the European trade mark legislative scheme which addresses the real difficulties which can arise in commerce, and I think that this, and others among the several excellent contributions, will be of enormous assistance to those charged with interpreting Community legislation, whether at national or at Community level.

It would be unforgivable to conclude this foreword without a special recognition of the enormously valuable contribution which the two editors have made to this book. It is true of course that the individual contributions are very interesting, arresting at times, and controversial even. But the ability of the editors, Jeremy Phillips and Ilanah Simon, to assemble such an interesting group of contributors is quite admirable, and the choice of contributors inspired. And with such inspired choices are found views from quite different perspectives from those we might normally be exposed to; that is no bad thing, for it helps avoid the trap, so readily fallen into, of believing that what we are used to or familiar with must be right!

If there is an area in which I would like to see some further research, it is one in which there appears to date to be very little written material. It is the status of the jurisprudence of the ECJ developed in the period when trade mark rights, including use of a trade mark, were embedded exclusively in the free movement of goods between Member States context; in particular, those rights existing under the then Article 36, vis-à-vis the position since the adoption of the Community Trade Mark Regulation and (less so) the Directive. If it is accepted that the Regulation legislates for the actual *grant of rights*, as opposed to controlling or permitting the exercise of trade mark rights granted at national level, as was the case, does this make a difference? I leave this question for the editors to consider, and wait to see whether, in a future edition of this excellent book, it might be tackled!

For the moment, the task which they undertook has been superbly accomplished.

Fidelma Macken
The High Court
Dublin
February 2005

ACKNOWLEDGEMENTS

We owe an enormous debt of gratitude to many people, without whom we could never have put this work together:

First and foremost, our contributors: these good folk, consisting of enthusiasts, workaholics and/or insomniacs, gave freely of their time and effort again and again in their attempts to satisfy the ever-growing demands made upon them by the editors.

Charlotte Knights, Sharon Watson and Sharon Mitchell for their invaluable administrative assistance.

Our friends and colleagues at Queen Mary Intellectual Property Research Institute, University of London and at Slaughter and May, for their intellectual stimulation and professional insights.

Katarina Wihlborg, Chris Rycroft, Geraldine Mangley and the team at OUP, whose sleek professionalism in turning this book from dream to reality, from nightmare to object of desire, in so short a time cannot be bettered.

Finally, Matthew Reed, whose drive and initiative ensured that we and our contributors had something to write about.

Jeremy Phillips and Ilanah Simon
London, August 2004

CONTENTS—SUMMARY

Biographies   xxvii
Tables of Cases   xxxv
Tables of Legislation   lvii

A. INTRODUCTION

1. Introduction   3
   Jeremy Phillips and Ilanah Simon

B. THE CONCEPT OF USE

2. Use and Non-Use in Trade Mark Law   11
   Bojan Pretnar

3. The Need to Leave Free for Others to Use and the Trade
   Mark Common   29
   Jennifer Davis

C. REGISTRATION

4. Distinctive Character Acquired through Use: The Law and
   the Case Law   49
   Arnaud Folliard-Monguiral

5. Distinctive Character Acquired through Use: Establishing
   the Facts   71
   Anna Carboni

6. Distinguishing Use versus Functional Use: Three-
   Dimensional Marks   93
   Thomas Hays

D. EXPLOITATION

7. Third Party Use of Trade Marks 111
   Neil J Wilkof

8. Trade Mark Use and Denominative Trade Marks 125
   Massimo Sterpi

9. Use, Certification and Collective Marks 147
   Jeffrey Belson

E. INFRINGEMENT

10. Infringing 'Use in the Course of Trade': Trade Mark Use and
    the Essential Function of a Trade Mark 163
    Robert Sumroy and Carina Badger

11. Permitted Infringing Use: The Scope of Defences to an
    Infringement Action 181
    Ashley Roughton

12. Infringing Use of a Trade Mark as a Criminal Offence 203
    Andreas Rahmatian

F. DEATH OF A TRADE MARK

13. Use for the Purpose of Resisting an Application for Revocation
    for Non-Use 223
    Belinda Isaac

14. The Requirement for Evidence of Use of Earlier Trade Marks
    in Opposition and Invalidation Proceedings 239
    Allan James

G. BROADER PERSPECTIVES

15. Trade Mark Use on the Internet 263
    Spyros Maniatis

16. TRIPs and Trade Mark Use 279
    G E Evans

17. Use, Intent to Use and Registration in the USA 313
    Graeme B Dinwoodie and Mark D Janis

18. The Role of Trade Mark Use in US Infringement, Unfair
    Competition and Dilution Proceedings 329
    Sheldon H Klein and N Christopher Norton

H. POST MORTEM

19. Conclusion: What Use is Use? 343
    Jeremy Phillips and Ilanah Simon

Index 355

CONTENTS

Biographies   xxvii
Tables of Cases   xxxv
Tables of Legislation   lvii

A. INTRODUCTION

1. Introduction   3
Jeremy Phillips and Ilanah Simon

  A. Eine Kleine Rechtlichs Problem   1.01

  B. The Importance of Use in Trade Mark Law   1.04

  C. Use: A Global Concern   1.06

  D. The Essential Function   1.07

  E. Methodology   1.08
    (1) Identifying the contexts within which the word 'use' required
       analysis   1.10
    (2) Arranging those contexts into a format in which they could be
       cogently explained to a specialist readership of trade mark
       practitioners and theoreticians   1.11
    (3) Identifying authors capable of providing the degree of analysis
       required   1.12
    (4) Identifying a working definition of the word 'use'   1.13
    (5) Finding a publisher   1.14

  F. A Word of Warning   1.19

  G. Feedback   1.20

B. THE CONCEPT OF USE

2. Use and Non-Use in Trade Mark Law   11
Bojan Pretnar

   A. Introduction: The Scope and Purpose of this Chapter   2.01

   B. Why must Trade Marks be Used?   2.06

   C. The Meaning of the Notion of Use   2.12

   D. The Impact of the Requirement of Use on Rights in
Trade Marks   2.26

   E. Exceptions from the Use Requirement   2.36

   F. Concluding Remarks   2.45

**3. The Need to Leave Free for Others to Use and the Trade
Mark Common**   29
Jennifer Davis

   A. The Development and Nature of the Trade Mark Common
in English Law   3.06

   B. The ECJ Doctrine that Signs should be Kept Free for Others
to Use   3.12

   C. The ECJ and 'Need to Keep Free': Why has the Court not
Developed a Commons Theory?   3.18

   D. Conclusion: The Balance Between Leaving Marks Free for
Others to Use and Recognizing Distinctiveness Acquired
through Use   3.25

C. REGISTRATION

**4. Distinctive Character Acquired through Use: The Law and
the Case Law**   49
Arnaud Folliard-Monguiral

   A. Introduction   4.01

B. The Sign for which Acquired Distinctiveness is Claimed   4.12
   (1) The sign for which acquired distinctiveness is claimed is
       juxtaposed with other signs   4.15
   (2) The sign for which acquired distinctiveness is claimed is
       merged into a broader ensemble   4.18
   (3) The acquisition of distinctiveness for signs having a function   4.24

C. The Time of the Acquisition of Distinctiveness and When to
   Claim it   4.34
   (1) When must distinctiveness have been acquired?   4.35
   (2) When can distinctiveness be claimed?   4.42

D. The Geographical Extent of the Use Conferring
   Distinctiveness   4.45

E. The Persuasive Elements as to Acquired Distinctiveness   4.51

F. Conclusion   4.57

5. **Distinctive Character Acquired through Use: Establishing
   the Facts**   71
   Anna Carboni

A. Introduction   5.01

B   Understanding the objection   5.04

C. Remembering the Objective   5.05

D. Legal and Regulatory Guidance   5.06

E. Contents of the Evidence   5.13
   (1) Direct Evidence of Use   5.14
   (2) Evidence of Recognition   5.29

F. Relevant Date for Proving Acquired Distinctiveness   5.41

G. Proving Acquired Distinctiveness of CTMs   5.45

H. Language Issues for CTMs   5.53

I. Deciding When to Argue for Acquired Distinctiveness   5.55

J. Making the Most of the Evidence   5.57

K. Publication   5.59

L. Concluding Remarks   5.60

6. **Distinguishing Use versus Functional Use: Three-
    Dimensional Marks**   93
    Thomas Hays

    A. The Nature of the Problem   6.01

    B. Distinguishing Trade Marks from Functional Features   6.07

    C. *Philips Electronics v Remington Consumer Products*   6.12

    D. Marks with Less than Complete Technical Functions   6.22

    E. Peculiarities of Use of Three-Dimensional Marks   6.31

D. EXPLOITATION

7. **Third Party Use of Trade Marks**   111
    Neil J Wilkof

    A. Introduction   7.01

    B. Is Authorized Use by a Third Party Legally Possible?   7.06
        (1) The classic position of trade mark use by a licensee 7.06
        (2) The present situation   7.17

    C. Use by Licensees and Revocation   7.27
        (1) Attribution of use   7.27
        (2) Use by a distributor or contract manufacturer   7.33

    D. Conclusion   7.45

8. **Trade Mark Use and Denominative Trade Marks**   125
    Massimo Sterpi

    A. Introduction   8.01

B. Unauthorized Use of Trade Marks Referring to Fictional
   Characters in the Music Industry   8.04
   (1) The *Barbie Girl* case   8.07
   (2) The *NELLIE THE ELEPHANT* cases   8.17

C. Unauthorized Use of Trade Marks Referring to Fictional
   Characters in a Website   8.21
   (1) *Paramount Pictures* and *Time Warner*: the policy adopted by
      media companies   8.23
   (2) *Elvis Presley Enterprises*: the protection of a real character's
      name and places referring to him   8.27

D. Unauthorized Reference to Fictional Characters in Retailing   8.30
   (1) The *TARZAN* case   8.32
   (2) The *BIANCANEVE* case   8.36

E. Unauthorized Reference to Real and Fictional Names in
   Business Names   8.38
   (1) The *Daily Planet* case   8.40
   (2) The *CACAO MERAVIGLIAO* case   8.42
   (3) The *Lane Capital Management* case   8.46
   (4) The *Nichols* case   8.48

F. Unauthorized Use of a Trade Mark in Press Products and
   Merchandising   8.53
   (1) The *Swatchissimo* case   8.55
   (2) The *Super Inter* case   8.57
   (3) The *Juventissima* case   8.59
   (4) The *Arsenal* case   8.62

G. Conclusion   8.68

9. **Use, Certification and Collective Marks**   147
   Jeffrey Belson

A. Introduction   9.01

B. What are Certification and Collective Marks Used for?   9.02

C. Registration of Certification Marks   9.07
   (1) Is there a use requirement for a certification mark to be
      registered?   9.08

D. Ownership and Use of Certification Marks   9.11
   (1) Who can use a certification mark?   9.12
   (2) Authorized use of a certification mark versus trade mark use by
       a licensee   9.17
   (3) Licensee estoppel   9.22

E. Registration of Collective Marks   9.24

F. Ownership and Use of Collective Marks   9.28

G. Summary   9.34

E. INFRINGEMENT

10. Infringing 'Use in the Course of Trade': Trade Mark Use and the Essential Function of a Trade Mark   163
Robert Sumroy and Carina Badger

A. Introduction   10.01

B. Merchandising and the Importance of Brands   10.04

C. The *Arsenal* Litigation   10.12
   (1) The First High Court decision   10.14
   (2) The ECJ ruling   10.16
   (3) The Second High Court decision   10.20
   (4) The Court of Appeal decision   10.22

D. Infringing Use in the English Courts after *Arsenal*   10.23
   (1) *R v Johnstone*   10.24
   (2) *Reed Executive v Reed Business Information*   10.29

E. Reasons for the Inertia   10.31
   (1) The 1938 Act   10.32
   (2) Broadening of the monopoly   10.35

F. Infringing Use Under the 1994 Act   10.37
   (1) Implementation of the Trade Mark Directive   10.37
   (2) The Defences to Trade Mark Infringement   10.40
   (3) Anti-competitive practices   10.45

G. Concluding Thoughts   10.47

11. Permitted Infringing Use: The Scope of Defences to an Infringement Action   181
Ashley Roughton

A. Infringement and Defences in Context   11.01
  (1) Infringing use   11.01
  (2) The 'owner' and the 'user', the 'mark' and the 'sign'   11.02
  (3) Three kinds of infringement   11.03
  (4) Types of defence   11.04

B. The Scope of This Chapter   11.05

C. Defences: The Legislation   11.06

D. Honesty   11.11
  (1) The *Gerolsteiner* case: of fairness and plodding horses   11.12
  (2) A use-related definition of honesty?   11.13
  (3) Non-use related definitions of honesty   11.20
  (4) Does honesty equate to a duty not to cause prejudice to another's trade mark?   11.23
  (5) The concept of honesty in UK criminal law   11.26
  (6) Does *Gerolsteiner* import an objective or subjective definition of honesty?   11.33
  (7) Pure objective sense   11.36

E. Objective and Subjective   11.39

F. Article 6(1)(a): Own Name and Address   11.41

G. Article 6(1)(b): Other Indications   11.42

H. Comparative Advertising   11.49

I. Article 6(1)(c): Other Indications   11.50

K. Article 6(2): Prior Marks   11.52

L. Conclusion   11.58

12. Infringing Use of a Trade Mark as a Criminal Offence   203
Andreas Rahmatian

A. Introduction   12.01

B. Criminal Offences in Relation to Trade Mark Infringement   12.02

C. An Outline of the House of Lords' Decision in *R v Johnstone*   12.08

D. Infringing Trade Mark Use in Criminal Proceedings as
Interpreted by *R v Johnstone*   12.13

E. Criminal Infringement of Trade Marks in Other European
Jurisdictions   12.27

F. Conclusion   12.35

F. DEATH OF A TRADE MARK

**13. Use for the Purpose of Resisting an Application for Revocation
for Non-Use**   223
Belinda Isaac

A. What is Meant by 'Genuine Use'?   13.06

B. What Level of 'Use' is Required?   13.14

C. The Intentions of the Proprietor   13.24

D. Conclusion   13.29

**14. The Requirement for Evidence of Use of Earlier Trade Marks
in Opposition and Invalidation Proceedings**   239
Allan James

A. The Purpose of the Provisions   14.01

B. The Community Trade Mark Regulation   14.09

C. The Timing and Nature of the Request for the Earlier
Conflicting Mark to be Shown to have been put to Genuine
Use   14.12

D. What Form must the Evidence Take at OHIM?   14.16

E. When must the Evidence of Use be Filed at OHIM?   14.23

F. The Period within which Genuine Use must be Shown   14.27

G. The Territorial Extent of the Use   14.30

H. What must be Shown   14.38

I. The UK Trade Marks Act 1994   14.45

J. The Applicant or Proprietor of the National Trade Mark does
not have to Make a Request   14.48

K. The Preliminary Indication in Opposition Proceedings   14.52

L. The Time for an Opponent to File Supporting Evidence   14.54

M. The Time for an Applicant for Invalidation to File
Supporting Evidence   14.56

N. What Form must the Evidence Take?   14.57

O. What must be Shown   14.61

P. The Period within which Genuine Use must be Shown   14.64

Q. The Notional Specification   14.69

R. Conclusion   14.74

G. BROADER PERSPECTIVES

15. Trade Mark Use on the Internet   263
Spyros Maniatis

A. Introduction   15.01

B. Trade Marks and Domain Names   15.03

C. 'New' Types of Infringement   15.12
(1) Adapting trade mark law principles   15.13

D. Warehousing   15.28

E. Enforcement and Territoriality Questions   15.31

F. Conclusion   15.35

Contents

16. **TRIPs and Trade Mark Use**   279
    G E Evans

    A. Trade Mark Use and the Bounds of Property   16.13

    B. Expansionary Pressure on Descriptive Marks: Leaving Marks
       Free for Others to Use Contrasted with Registrability
       Acquired through Use   16.23

    C. Trade Mark Use and the Impact of WTO Jurisprudence   16.31
       (1) Article 20: unjustifiable encumbrances involving trade mark
           use   16.32
       (2) National treatment and MFN   16.40
       (3) Article 8: exceptions for economic development and the
           public interest   16.44

    D. Expansionary Pressure and Trade Mark Infringement   16.51
       (1) Well-known marks and anti-dilution protection: protection
           for unused marks and use requirements for infringement by
           dilution   16.55

    E. Towards a Holistic Approach to the Interpretation of TRIPs   16.62
       (1) Ordinary meaning: beyond the dictionary   16.65

    F. Conclusion   16.72

17. **Use, Intent to Use and Registration in the USA**   313
    Graeme B Dinwoodie and Mark D Janis

    A. Introduction   17.01

    B. Use as a Condition for Acquiring Rights   17.03
       (1) Actual use   17.05
       (2) Constructive use   17.17

    C. Use as a Condition for Maintaining Rights   17.22

    D. Use and the Geographical Scope of Rights   17.26

    E. Conclusion   17.33

18. **The Role of Trade Mark Use in US Infringement, Unfair**
    Competition and Dilution Proceedings   329
    Sheldon H Klein and N Christopher Norton

    A. 'Use' in the Establishment of Rights   18.02

    B. 'Use' in Infringement and Unfair Competition Actions   18.05

    C. 'Use' in Defences to Infringement and Unfair Competition
       Claims   18.07
       (1) Defences attacking the claimant's rights in the mark   18.08
       (2) Defences based on the defendant's priority   18.14
       (3) Defences based on lack of likelihood of confusion   18.19
       (4) Fair use defence   18.22

    D. 'Use' in Trade Mark Dilution Actions   18.25

    E. Conclusion   18.29

H. POST MORTEM

19. **Conclusion: What Use is Use?**   343
    Jeremy Phillips and Ilanah Simon

    A. The Danger of Drawing Conclusions   19.01

    B. Is There Just One Type of Trade Mark Use?   19.02
       (1) Backwards and forwards   19.04

    C. Further Issues for Investigation   19.05
       (1) Use and the Community trade mark   19.06
       (2) The role of old law   19.07
       (3) The interface between trade mark rights and other intellectual
           property rights   19.09

    D. Use: The Battle Lines are Drawn   19.11

    E. Is Use the Centre of the Trade Mark System?   19.14

    F. The Essential Function: The Linchpin of the System?   19.17

    G. The Future of Use   19.22

H. Eine Kleine Answer . . . or five   19.26
    (1) Answer 1   19.27
    (2) Answer 2   19.29
    (3) Answer 3   19.31
    (4) Answer 4   19.33
    (5) Answer 5   19.34

Index   355

BIOGRAPHIES

THE EDITORS

Professor Jeremy Phillips

Intellectual Property Consultant to London-based solicitors Slaughter and May, Jeremy previously held a variety of academic posts. He is currently Visiting Professorial Fellow, Queen Mary Intellectual Property Research Institute, as well as a visiting professor at University College London, Bournemouth University and the University of Alicante.

Jeremy edits the *European Trade Mark Reports* and has been consultant editor of the *Butterworths Intellectual Property Law Handbook* since its inception. His most recent book, *Trade Mark Law: a Practical Anatomy*, was published in 2003 by Oxford University Press. He is a joint director of the IPKat intellectual property weblog.

Ilanah Simon

A Doctoral Associate of the Queen Mary Intellectual Property Research Institute, Ilanah holds two degrees from University College London. Her doctoral thesis is a comparative study of trade mark dilution in the USA and the European Union. She has published numerous articles in recent years, particularly within the field of trade mark law.

A regular contributor of cases for the MARQUES case law database, Ilanah is Deputy Editor of the *European Trade Mark Reports* and the contributory editor for trade mark law in the *European Union Law Reporter*. She is also joint director of the IPKat, the first intellectual property based weblog to be based in Europe.

THE CONTRIBUTORS

Carina Badger

Carina, a philosophy graduate from the University of Cambridge, is an assistant solicitor in the Intellectual Property group of the London-based firm of Slaughter and May.

Carina's experience includes a spell in Sweden, where she worked with a leading intellectual property practice. She has also worked in-house in the trade mark department of a company that owns many leading internationally renowned brands of alcoholic beverage.

Dr Jeffrey Belson

The author of *Certification Marks* (Sweet & Maxwell London 2002) and various articles in the field of trade mark law, Jeffrey is Regulatory and Intellectual Property Manager for the Indigo Division of Hewlett-Packard. He has served on various committees and on the Board of Directors of the International Trademark Association.

Before joining HP-Indigo, Jeffrey was advanced technologies manager in the Israel microelectronics sector. He is a recipient of the Israel Government's Kaplan Prize for distinguished service to industry. Jeffrey holds a B.Sc. (Hons) and Ph.D. in physics from the University of Reading, England.

Anna Carboni

Anna Carboni is a barrister at Wilberforce Chambers in London. The first seventeen years of her legal career were spent as a solicitor at Linklaters, latterly as a partner in the Intellectual Property Department. However, having qualified as a Solicitor-Advocate in 2000, she made her move to the Bar three years later in order to concentrate on court and advisory work.

Trade mark law is Anna's favourite field. She has done the full range of trade mark filing and prosecution, advising on brand clearance and protection and standing up in court for her trade mark clients. She has conducted litigation for numerous well-known brand owners, including adidas, Gucci, Microsoft and 3M—to name a few. Anna is on the panel of experts for Nominet's domain name dispute resolution service. She is an active member of numerous industry and professional associations and she also regularly speaks and writes on trade mark and other intellectual property topics.

Dr Jennifer Davis

Jennifer Davis is a Newton Trust Lecturer in Intellectual Property Law in the Law Faculty, University of Cambridge. She is also a Fellow of Wolfson College, Cambridge, where she is Director of Studies in Law. She lectures in various areas of intellectual property and has a particular interest in trade marks and the theoretical underpinnings of intellectual property law.

Before joining the Faculty, Jennifer practised as a lawyer in the area of intellectual property litigation. She is the author of *Intellectual Property*

(Butterworths London 2001; 2nd edn 2003) and her recent articles on trade marks include 'To Protect or Serve? European Trade Mark Law and the Decline of the Public Interest' [2003] European Intellectual Property Review 180–187 and 'European Trade Mark Law and the Enclosure of the Commons' [2002] Intellectual Property Quarterly 342–367.

Professor Graeme B Dinwoodie

Professor Dinwoodie is a Professor of Law and Director of the Program in Intellectual Property Law at Chicago-Kent College of Law, having previously taught at the University of Cincinnati College of Law and the University of Pennsylvania School of Law. He teaches and writes on intellectual property law, with an emphasis on the international and comparative aspects of the discipline. A prolific writer in the field, he is the co-author of the casebooks *Trademarks and Unfair Competition: Law and Policy, International Intellectual Property Law* and *International and Comparative Patent Law.*

Graeme has served as a consultant to the World Intellectual Property Organization on matters of private international law, as the Independent Academic Expert on the ICANN Names Council's Task Force reviewing the Uniform Domain Name Dispute Resolution Policy and as an Adviser to the American Law Institute Project on Principles on Jurisdiction and Recognition of Judgments in Intellectual Property Matters. Before entering academe, Graeme was an associate with Sullivan and Cromwell, New York.

Dr G E Evans

Gail Elizabeth Evans is Reader in Intellectual Property Law at Queen Mary, University of London, and Head of the Intellectual Property Unit. She has held academic positions in Australia and the USA, teaching various commercial law subjects including international intellectual property and cyberlaw. She is the author of *Lawmaking under the Trade Constitution: A Study in Legislating by the World Trade Organization* (Kluwer Law International The Hague 2000), which traces the making of the TRIPs Agreement and its impact on the domestic trade mark legislation of nation states.

Gail has published numerous articles in the fields of international trade, intellectual property law and electronic commerce. Recent publications include: 'Comment on the Second WIPO Internet Domain Name Process' [2001] EIPR 1 and 'Online Contracts' in *The Handbook of Informational Security,* edited by H. Bidgoli (Wiley New York 2005).

Arnaud Folliard-Monguiral

Arnaud Folliard-Monguiral was admitted to the Paris Bar and is qualified as a trade mark and design professional representative. Having joined the Office for Harmonisation in the Internal Market (OHIM) in 2000, Arnaud is a member of the Industrial Property Litigation Unit (IPLU). As such, he is appointed agent of the Office in proceedings before the Court of First Instance and the European Court of Justice.

Arnaud writes a monthly review of Community trade mark-related case law for the French intellectual property review *Propriété Industrielle* (published by JurisClasseur). In addition to his commentaries, Arnaud is the author of articles, the latest of which are dedicated to three-dimensional trade marks (*Prop. Ind.* March 2003, *EIPR* April 2003), procedural issues before the CFI (*Prop. Ind.* May 2003, *Prop. Ind.* January 2004), and the impact of EU enlargement on Community trade marks and designs (*Prop. Ind.* September 2003, *EIPR* February 2004).

Dr Thomas Hays

Thomas Hays is Senior Lecturer in Intellectual Property Law at the University of Aberdeen and a Research Fellow, Centrum voor Intellectueel Eigendomsrecht (CIER), the Molengraaff Institute for Private Law Research, Utrecht, The Netherlands.

An attorney qualified to practise in the District of Columbia, Thomas has recently published *Parallel Importation under European Union Law* (Sweet & Maxwell London 2003) and *Intellectual Property Law and Practice* (W Green & Co Edinburgh 2004). He has a Ph.D. from the University of Cambridge.

Dr Belinda Isaac

Belinda Isaac is a partner and Head of Intellectual Property at the Oxford office of Morgan Cole, solicitors. She has a Doctorate in intellectual property law from London University. Belinda has many years of experience advising on a broad range of intellectual property issues, especially trade mark protection and enforcement. She has acted for numerous international businesses in connection with the protection of their well-known brands. More recently her practice has spread to include biotechnology and research governance advising both private and public sector organizations.

Belinda writes extensively on intellectual property subjects in leading academic journals and in the newspapers. She is author of *Brand Protection Matters* (Sweet & Maxwell London 2001) and a contributory author of *Pharmaceutical Medicine Biotechnology and European Law* (CUP Cambridge

2000). Belinda sits on the Editorial Advisory Board of the *European Trade Mark Reports* and is the UK correspondent for the *Entertainment Law Review*. A member of several trade mark organizations including the International Trade Mark Association and the Pharmaceutical Trade Mark Group, Belinda has also taught intellectual property in Oxford and is a regular speaker at international intellectual property conferences.

Allan James

Allan James is Head of Practice for trade marks and designs at the UK Patent Office. He entered the field of intellectual property in 1988 when he joined the Patent Office and became one of the Office's Hearing Officers in 1991. He still regularly hears opposition and invalidation cases in the Patent Office.

In addition, Allan has been the author of the Patent Office's examination guidelines since 1994 and, for the past six years, he has served as a member of the team responsible for the drafting of the UK's submissions to the European Court of Justice on those trade mark cases which have come before that Court.

Professor Mark D Janis

Professor Mark Janis is Professor of Law and H Blair & Joan V White Intellectual Property Law Scholar at the University of Iowa College of Law in Iowa City. Mark teaches and writes in the fields of patents, trade marks/ unfair competition and intellectual property/antitrust. He has published numerous law review articles on intellectual property law and is co-author of both *IP and Antitrust* (Aspen Publishers New York 2001) and *Trademarks & Unfair Competition: Law and Policy* (Aspen Publishers New York 2004).

Mark has been named a University of Iowa Faculty Scholar for 2002–2005 to conduct research on intellectual property rights in plant biotechnology. A registered patent attorney, prior to joining the Iowa law faculty in 1995 Mark practised patent law with Barnes & Thornburg in Indianapolis, Indiana.

Sheldon H Klein

Sheldon Klein, of Washington, DC, law firm Arent Fox, handles trade mark, copyright, unfair competition, advertising and internet law matters, includ-ing client counselling, litigation, registration and licensing. Well known in the intellectual property bar, he has been quoted on significant cases by the *Wall Street Journal*, the *Los Angeles Times*, the *Philadelphia Inquirer*, *Corporate Legal Times* and many other publications.

Sheldon, a frequent lecturer at major intellectual property conferences, is the author of numerous scholarly articles for intellectual property law publications such as the *Trademark Reporter, Trademark World, Managing Intellectual Property* and the *AIPLA Quarterly Journal,* and for general legal publications such as the *National Law Journal* and *Legal Times.* He is currently on the Editorial Board of *Trademark World* and is a past member of the Editorial Board of the *Trademark Reporter.*

Dr Spyros Maniatis

Spyros Maniatis is a Senior Lecturer in Intellectual Property Law and a Senior Research Fellow at the Queen Mary Intellectual Property Research Institute, University of London. His research interests include trade mark and unfair competition law, the history of intellectual property rights and innovation, and innovation theory.

An active author and lecturer in the field of trade marks and related areas of law, Spyros has written extensively for UK and US journals on the subject of domain names and other trade mark issues. He has been co-author of *Trade Marks, Trade Names and Unfair Competition: World Law and Practice* (Sweet & Maxwell London) since 1996 and is also co-author of *Domain Names: Global Policy and Procedure* (West and Sweet & Maxwell London 2000).

N Christopher Norton

N Christopher Norton is an Associate in the Intellectual Property Practice of Washington, DC, law firm Arent Fox. His practice includes preparing and prosecuting domestic and international trade mark applications, representing clients before the US Patent and Trademark Office in trade mark cancellation and opposition proceedings, litigating disputes involving claims of trade mark infringement and unfair competition, advising clients on issues pertaining to copyright law and licensing and drafting intellectual property agreements and licences.

Prior to attending law school, Christopher worked with the Columbia Institute for Political Research in Washington, DC, and the University of California, San Francisco's Center for AIDS Prevention Studies in Albuquerque, New Mexico.

Professor Bojan Pretnar

Born in Ljubljana, Slovenia, Bojan Pretnar is a graduate of Ljubljana University where he holds a degree in mechanical engineering as well as M.Sc. and Ph.D. degrees from the Faculty of Economics. He has taught courses on innovation and intellectual property at Ljubljana University since 1990. He is a founding Member of the World Intellectual Property Organization Policy Advisory Commission and a member of the Editorial Board of the *European Trade Mark Reports*. He is also the author of two books and numerous articles in the field of intellectual property.

The first Director of the newly established Slovenian Intellectual Property Office, Bojan is the main architect of advanced and original intellectual property legislation of Slovenia. He has been a senior staff member of the World Intellectual Property Organization in Geneva since March 2000.

Dr Andreas Rahmatian

Andreas Rahmatian's first degrees are in law and in musicology and history (University of Vienna). He completed an LL M in comparative and intellectual property law at the University of London (1995) and a Ph.D. in private law at the University of Vienna (1996).

Andreas has worked as an Associate Attorney at Law in a law firm in Vienna, where he specialized in intellectual property law, before training as a solicitor with a City firm in London. During that time, and after qualification as a solicitor (2001), he taught property and trust law part-time at the University of London, then took the post of Lecturer in Law at the University of Stirling in February 2002. He currently teaches commercial law subjects and intellectual property law.

Andreas' main research interests are (apart from intellectual property law) property law, contract law, private and commercial law, comparative law, civil law systems and their relationship with Scots law and legal history.

Dr Ashley Roughton

Ashley Roughton, a barrister, practises at Hogarth Chambers. He is a co-author of *The Modern Law of Trade Marks* (second edition under preparation) and is also a co-author and joint editor of the forthcoming book *The Modern Law of United Kingdom and European Patents* (both published by LexisNexis, London).

Before becoming a barrister in 1992 Ashley was an engineer with Mercedes Benz. He took his Ph.D. at Cambridge and B.Sc. at King's College, London. He also has an M.Sc. in economics from City University and is a member of the Department of Economics at City University. Ashley practises in all aspects of intellectual property law.

Massimo Sterpi

Massimo Sterpi is a partner in the law firm Studio Legale Jacobacci e Associati of Turin (Italy), having studied at the University of Turin and King's College, London. He is a member of the Editorial Board of the *European Copyright and Design Reports*, he also serves as a Council Member of MARQUES, the organization of European trade mark proprietors. Massimo chairs MARQUES' IP Outer Borders Team, which deals with the limits of intellectual property protection and social reaction to latest intellectual property trends.

A frequent speaker in conferences on intellectual property topics, Massimo practises mainly in the areas of technology, famous brands and art-related issues. He is co-author of *The Community Trademark Handbook* (Turin 1995). He has authored several articles, in various languages, on copyright, patent and trade mark law as well as intellectual property litigation issues.

Robert Sumroy

Since 2003 Robert Sumroy has been a partner in the Intellectual Property Group of London-based solicitors Slaughter and May, which he joined in 1994. The areas in which he practises are intellectual property, information technology, data protection and electronic commerce.

Robert is the author of the intellectual property aspects of the 'International joint ventures' chapter of the *PLC* practice manual.

Dr Neil J Wilkof

Neil Wilkof is a partner and head of the IP and Information Technology department at the law firm of Herzog, Fox & Neeman (Tel Aviv, Israel). An active member of the International Trademark Association, he is also a member of the Editorial Board of the *European Trade Mark Reports* and the *European Copyright and Design Reports*.

Neil is the author of numerous articles in the field of trade mark, copyright and computer law. He is the author of *Trade Mark Licensing* (Sweet & Maxwell London 1995), the second edition of which will be published in 2005 and is also co-editor (with Mel Simensky and Lanning Bryer) of *Intellectual Property in the Global Marketplace* (Wiley New York 1999). He has taught intellectual property and computer law since 1991, first at Bar-Ilan University and more recently at the University of Haifa.

TABLES OF CASES

Australia
Koninklijke Philips Electronics NV v Remington Products
  Australia Pty Ltd [1999] FCA 816 (Fed Ct) 6.21

Canada
All Canada Vac Ltd v Lindsay Manufacturing Inc [1990]
  2 CPR (3d) 385 . . . . 7.35
Remington Rand Corp and Remington Products (Canada) Inc v Philips
  Electronics NV [1996] 2 CF 15 (Fed Ct App) 6.21

European Court of Human Rights

Golder v The United Kingdom (4451/70) [1975] ECHR 1 . . . 16.65, 16.69

European Court of Justice and Court of First Instance

Alphabetical
Adidas-Salomon AG and Adidas Benelux BV v Fitnessworld Trading Ltd
  (Case C–408/01) [2004] ETMR 10 . . . . 11.03, 16.61
Alcon Inc v OHIM (BSS) (Case T–237/01) [2004] ETMR 6 . . . 4.41, 4.46,
                                                                    4.55, 5.23
Anklagemyndigheden v Peter Michael Poulsen and Diva Navigation Corp
  (Case C–286/90) [1992] ECR I–6019 . . . . 16.08
Ansul BV v Ajax Brandbeveiliging BV (MINIMAX) (Case C–40/01)
  [2003] ECR I–2439; [2003] ETMR 85 . . . . 8.18, 13.06, 13.12,
                                                   13.14, 13.22, 13.23, 13.27, 13.28,
                                                   14.33, 14.37, 14.40, 14.61, 16.16
Arsenal Football Club plc v Matthew Reed (Case C–206/01)
  [2002] ECR I–10273; [2003] ETMR 19;
  [2003] 1 CMLR 345 . . . . 3.27, 8.54, 8.63, 8.68, 10.01, 10.02,
                                               10.12, 10.16, 10.23, 10.26, 10.28, 10.43,
                                               10.44, 10.49, 11.15, 11.16, 11.17,

11.58, 12.11, 12.14, 12.15, 12.17,
12.19, 12.20, 12.21, 12.22, 12.35,
16.10, 16.52, 19.02, 19.13, 19.20,
19.23, 19.24, 19.25, 19.33, 19.37

Audi AG v OHIM (TDI) (Case T–16/02) [2004] ETMR 59 .... 4.36,
4.44, 4.46, 4.53

Bayerische Motorenwerke AG (BMW) and BMW Nederland BV v Ronald
  Karel Deenik (Case C–63/97) [1999] All ER (EC) 235;
  [1999] ECR I–905; [1999] 1 CMLR 1099; [1999] CEC 159;
  [1999] ETMR 339 .... 10.19, 11.23, 11.25, 19.02
BioID v OHIM (Case T–91/01) [2002] ECR II–5159;
  [2003] ETMR 60 .... 4.26

Canon Kabushiki Kaisha v Metro-Goldwyn-Mayer Inc (Case C–39/97)
  [1998] ECR I–5507; [1999] ETMR 1 .... 4.05, 19.25
Centrafarm v American Home Products (Case 3/78) [1978] ECR 1823;
  [1979] 1 CMLR 326 .... 6.17

DaimlerChrysler v OHIM (Grille) (Case T–128/01)
  [2003] ETMR 87 .... 4.27, 5.56
Davidoff & Cie and Zino Davidoff SA v Gofkid Ltd (Case C–292/00)
  [2003] 1 WLR 1714; [2003] All ER (EC) 1029; [2003] ECR I–389;
  [2003] 1 CMLR 1039; [2003] CEC 208; [2003] ETMR 42;
  [2003] ETMR 534; [2003] FSR 490;
  The Times 22 January 2003 .... 11.03, 16.61, 16.68
DKV Deutsche Krankenversicherung AG v OHIM (COMPANYLINE)
  (Case C–104/00P) [2002] ECR I–7561; [2003] ETMR 20 ...... 16.28
Dyson Ltd v OHIM (Case T–278/02) 4.30
Dyson Ltd v The Registrar of Trade Marks (Case C–321/03) 4.29

eCopy v OHIM (ECOPY) (Case T–247/01) [2003] ETMR 99 .... 4.36,
4.37, 4.44, 5.41
Eurocermex SA v OHIM (Long neck bottle) (Case T–399/02)
  [2004] ETMR 95 .... 4.17, 4.44, 4.50

Ford Motor Company v OHIM (OPTIONS) (Case T–91/99)
  [2000] ETMR 554 .... 4.46, 4.48, 5.46, 5.49

General Motors Corporation v Yplon SA (CHEVY) (Case C–375/97)
  [1999] ETMR 950; [2000] RPC 572 .... 4.46, 16.21
Gerolsteiner Brunnen GmbH & Co v Putsch GmbH (Case C–100/02)
  [2004] ETMR 559 .... 11.12, 11.13, 11.18, 11.19, 11.23, 11.25,
                                11.33, 11.34, 11.36, 11.45
Goulbourn v OHIM–Redcats (SILK COCOON) (Case T–174/01)
  [2003] ECR II–789 .... 14.41

Heidelberger Bauchemie GmbH (Case C–49/02)
  [2004] ETMR 99 .... 3.17, 16.23, 16.71
Henkel KGaA v OHIM (3-dimensional marks) (Joined Cases C–456/01P
  and C–457/01P) [2004] 3.16, 3.17, 6.24, 6.31, 6.33,
                                           6.34, 16.28
Henkel KGaA v OHIM (KLEENCARE) (Case T–308/01)
  not yet reported 4.43
Hermès International and FHT Marketing Choice BV (Case C–53/96)
  [1998] ECR I–3603 .... 16.09
Hoffmann-La Roche & Co AG v Centrafarm Vertriebsgesellschaft
  Pharmazeutischer Erzeugnisse mbH (Case 102/77) [1978] ECR 1139;
  [1978] 3 CMLR 217 .... 3.27, 10.19, 16.15, 19.17
Hölterhoff (Michael) v Ulrich Freiesleben (Case C–2/00)
  [2002] ETMR 66; [2002] FSR 362; [2002] ECR I–4187;
  [2002] ETMR 917 .... 10.41, 10.42, 10.43, 11.44, 11.49

Institut für Lernsysteme GmbH v OHIM (Case T–388/00)
  [2004] ETMR 17 .... 14.21, 14.24

Kabushiki Kaisha Fernandes v OHIM (HIWATT) (Case T–39/01)
  [2003] ETMR 98 .... 5.57, 13.06, 13.17, 13.18, 13.19, 13.21,
                                           14.31, 14.43
Koninklijke KPN Nederland NV v Benelux Trade Mark Office
  (POSTKANTOOR) (Case C–363/99) [2004] ETMR 57 .... 4.06, 5.02
Koninklijke Philips Electronics NV v Remington Consumer Products Ltd
  (Case C–299/99) [2001] ETMR 38, 81; [2001] RPC 48;
  [2002] 2 CMLR 52, 1329; [2002] ECR I–5475;

[2002] ETMR 955 . . . . 3.16, 3.18,
3.19, 3.28, 4.03, 4.09, 4.25, 4.32,
4.45, 6.05, 6.12, 6.15, 6.16, 6.18,
6.19, 6.20, 6.22, 6.32, 10.30

Libertel Groep BV v Benelux-Merkenbureau (Case C–104/01)
[2003] ECR I–3793; [2003] ETMR 63 . . . . 3.02, 3.03, 3.04, 3.17,
3.20, 3.23, 4.57, 16.23
Linde AG, Windward Industries Inc and Radio Uhren AG v Deutsches
Patent- und Markenamt (Joined Cases C–53/01 to C–55/01)
[2003] RPC 45; [2003] ETMR 78, 963 ... 3.14, 3.16, 3.17, 3.20, 4.06,
5.02, 6.23, 6.24, 6.25, 6.27, 6.32
Lloyd Schuhfabrik Meyer & Co GmbH v Klijsen Handel BV
(Case C–342/97) [1999] ETMR 690 . . . . 5.38

Marleasing SA v La Comercial Internacional de Alimentacion SA
(Case C–106/89) [1990] ECR I–4135 . . . . 10.32
Merz & Krell GmbH & Co's Trade Mark Application (Case C–517/99)
[2002] ETMR 21 . . . . 3.12
Messe München v OHIM (Electronica) (Case T–32/00)
[2000] ETMR 135 . . . . 4.56
MFE Marienfelde GmbH v OHIM (Case T–344/01),
8 July 2004 . . . . 14.25, 14.41, 14.44

Nakajima All Precision Co Ltd v Council (Case C–69/89)
[1991] ECR I–2069 . . . . 16.08
Nestlé Waters France v OHIM (Case T–305/02) [2004] ETMR 41 ... 6.34
Nichols (Case C–404/02) [2004] ETMR 48 . . . . 8.48, 8.49
Nordmilch eG v OHIM (Case T–295/01), [2004] ETMR 70 . . . . 3.13

OHIM v Wm Wrigley Jr Company (DOUBLEMINT) (Case C–191/01)
[2004] ETMR 9; [2004] RPC 18 . . . . 3.15, 3.21, 16.28
Opinion 1/75 [1975] ECR 1355 . . . . 16.08

Parfums Christian Dior SA v Tuk Consultancy BV (Case C–300/98)
[2001] ETMR 277 . . . . 16.08
Parfums Dior SA v Evora BV (Case C–337/95) [1998] ETMR 26 ... 10.19
Procter & Gamble Company v OHIM (shaped soap) (Case T–122/99)
[1999] 2 CMLR 1142; [2000] ETMR 580 . . . . 6.10

Procter & Gamble v OHIM (baby-dry) (Case C–383/99P)
   [2001] ECR I–6251; [2002] ETMR 3 . . . . 3.21, 3.22, 3.23, 5.02,
                                                                   5.56, 16.28
Procter & Gamble v OHIM (baby-dry) (Case T–163/98)
   [1999] ETMR 767 . . . . 4.42, 4.44, 5.56
Procter & Gamble v OHIM (Case C–383/99) [2001] ETMR 75 . . . . . 3.10
Procter & Gamble v OHIM (Soap bar shape) (Case T–63/01)
   [2003] ETMR 43 . . . . 4.42

SA CNL-Sucal NV v HAG GF (Case C–10/89) [1990] ECR I–3711;
   [1990] 3 CMLR 571 . . . . 10.19, 16.02
SAT.1 Satelliten Fernsehen GmbH v OHIM (Case T–323/00)
   [2003] ETMR 49 . . . . 4.07
Société des Produits Nestlé SA v Marks UK Ltd (Case C–353/03) 4.19
Sunrider Corp v OHIM (Case T–203/02),
   8 July 2004 . . . . 14.17, 14.19, 14.72
Sykes Enterprises Inc v OHIM (real people, real solutions)
   (Case T–130/01) [2003] ETMR 57 . . . . 4.18

Toshiba Europe GmbH v Katun Germany GmbH (Case C–112/99)
   [2002] ETMR 26 . . . . 8.10

Wm Wrigley Jr Company v OHIM (doublemint) (Case C-191/01)
   2004 [ETMR] 9; [2004] RPC 18 . . . . 3.15, 3.21, 16.28
Windsurfing Chiemsee Produktions- und Vertriebs GmbH v Boots- und
   Segelzubehör Walter Huber and Franz Attenberger (Joined Cases
   C–108/97 and C–109/97) [1999] ECR I–2799;
   [1999] ETMR 585 . . . . 3.13, 3.14, 3.17, 3.20, 3.21,
                             3.28, 4.05, 4.07, 4.45, 4.51, 5.06, 5.07, 5.38, 6.19,
                                               11.44, 11.45, 16.23, 19.08

Zino Davidoff SA v A&G Imports Ltd and Levi Strauss & Co v Tesco Stores
   and Costco Wholesale UK Ltd (Joined Cases C–414/99 to C–416/99)
   [2002] ETMR 9 1/75 Opinion [1975] ECR 1355 . . . . 10.37, 16.08

Chronological

1/75 Opinion [1975] ECR 1355 . . . . 16.08
102/77 Hoffmann-La Roche & Co AG v Centrafarm Vertriebsgesellschaft
   Pharmazeutischer Erzeugnisse mbH [1978] ECR 1139;
   [1978] 3 CMLR 217 . . . . 3.27, 10.19, 16.15, 19.17

3/78 Centrafarm v American Home Products [1978] ECR 1823;
　　[1979] 1 CMLR 326 .... 6.17
C–10/89 SA CNL-Sucal NV v HAG GF [1990] ECR I–3711;
　　[1990] 3 CMLR 571 .... 10.19, 16.02
C–69/89 Nakajima All Precision Co Ltd v Council [1991]
　　ECR I–2069 .... 16.08
C–106/89 Marleasing SA v La Comercial Internacional de
　　Alimentacion SA [1990] ECR I–4135 .... 10.32
C–286/90 Anklagemyndigheden v Peter Michael Poulsen and Diva
　　Navigation Corp [1992] ECR I–6019 .... 16.08
C–337/95 Parfums Dior SA v Evora BV [1998] ETMR 26 .... 10.19
C–53/96 Hermès International and FHT Marketing Choice BV
　　[1998] ECR I–3603 .... 16.09
C–39/97 Canon Kabushiki Kaisha v Metro-Goldwyn-Mayer Inc
　　[1998] ECR I–5507; [1999] ETMR 1 .... 4.05, 19.25
C–63/97 Bayerische Motorenwerke AG (BMW) and BMW
　　Nederland BV v Ronald Karel Deenik [1999] All ER (EC) 235;
　　[1999] ECR I–905; [1999] 1 CMLR 1099; [1999] CEC 159;
　　[1999] ETMR 339 .... 10.19, 11.23, 11.25, 19.02
C–108/97 and C–109/97 Windsurfing Chiemsee Produktions- und
　　Vertriebs GmbH v Boots- und Segelzubehör Walter Huber and Franz
　　Attenberger [1999] ECR I–2799;
　　[1999] ETMR 585 .... 3.13, 3.14, 3.17, 3.20, 3.21, 3.28,
　　　　　　　　　　　　　　　　　　　4.05, 4.07, 4.45, 4.51, 5.06, 5.07,
　　　　　　　　　　　　　　　　　　5.38, 6.19, 11.44, 11.45, 16.23, 19.08
C–342/97 Lloyd Schuhfabrik Meyer & Co GmbH v Klijsen Handel BV
　　[1999] ETMR 690 .... 5.38
C–375/97 General Motors Corporation v Yplon SA (CHEVY)
　　[1999] ETMR 950; [2000] RPC 572 .... 4.46, 16.21
C–300/98 Parfums Christian Dior SA v Tuk Consultancy BV
　　[2001] ETMR 277 .... 16.08
T–163/98 Procter & Gamble v OHIM (BABY-DRY)
　　[1999] ETMR 767 .... 4.42, 4.44, 5.56
C–112/99 Toshiba Europe GmbH v Katun Germany GmbH
　　[2002] ETMR 26 .... 8.10
C–299/99 Koninklijke Philips Electronics NV v Remington Consumer
　　Products Ltd [2001] ETMR 38, 81; [2001] RPC 48;
　　[2002] 2 CMLR 52, 1329; [2002] ECR I–5475;

[2002] ETMR 955 .... 3.16, 3.18, 3.19,
3.28, 4.03, 4.09, 4.25, 4.32,
4.45, 6.05, 6.12, 6.15, 6.16, 6.18, 6.19,
6.20, 6.22, 6.32, 10.30
C–363/99 Koninklijke KPN Nederland NV v Benelux Trade Mark
Office (POSTKANTOOR) [2004] ETMR 57 .... 4.06, 5.02
C–383/99 Procter & Gamble v OHIM [2001] ETMR 75 .... 3.10
C–383/99P Procter & Gamble v OHIM (BABY-DRY)
[2001] ECR I–6251; [2002] ETMR 3 .... 3.21, 3.22, 3.23, 5.02,
5.56, 16.28
C–414/99 to C–416/99 Zino Davidoff SA v A&G Imports Ltd and
Levi Strauss & Co v Tesco Stores and Costco Wholesale UK Ltd
[2002] ETMR 9 .... 10.37
C–517/99 Merz & Krell GmbH & Co's Trade Mark Application
[2002] ETMR 21 .... 3.12
T–91/99 Ford Motor Company v OHIM (OPTIONS)
[2000] ETMR 554 .... 4.46, 4.48, 5.46, 5.49
T–122/99 Procter & Gamble Company v OHIM (shaped soap)
[1999] 2 CMLR 1142; [2000] ETMR 580 .... 6.10
C–2/00 Hölterhoff (Michael) v Ulrich Freiesleben [2002] ETMR 66;
[2002] FSR 362; [2002] ECR I–4187;
[2002] ETMR 917 .... 10.41, 10.42, 10.43,
11.44, 11.49
C–104/00P DKV Deutsche Krankenversicherung AG v OHIM
(COMPANYLINE) [2002] ECR I–7561; [2003] ETMR 20 ..... 16.28
C–292/00 Davidoff & Cie and Zino Davidoff SA v Gofkid Ltd
[2003] 1 WLR 1714; [2003] All ER (EC) 1029; [2003] ECR I–389;
[2003] 1 CMLR 1039; [2003] CEC 208; [2003] ETMR 42;
[2003] ETMR 534; [2003] FSR 490;
The Times 22 January 2003 .... 11.03, 16.61, 16.68
T–32/00 Messe München v OHIM (Electronica)
[2000] ETMR 135 .... 4.56
T–323/00 SAT.1 Satelliten Fernsehen GmbH v OHIM
[2003] ETMR 49 .... 4.07
T–388/00 Institut für Lernsysteme GmbH v OHIM
[2004] ETMR 17 .... 14.21, 14.24
C–40/01 Ansul BV v Ajax Brandbeveiliging BV (MINIMAX)
[2003] ECR I–2439; [2003] ETMR 85 .... 8.18, 13.06, 13.12,

13.14, 13.22, 13.23, 13.27, 13.28,
14.33, 14.37, 14.40, 14.61, 16.16

C–53/01 to C–55/01 Linde AG, Windward Industries Inc and
Radio Uhren AG v Deutsches Patent- und Markenamt [2003] RPC 45;
[2003] ETMR 78, 963 . . . . 3.14, 3.16, 3.17, 3.20,
4.06, 5.02, 6.23, 6.24, 6.25, 6.27, 6.32

C–104/01 Libertel Groep BV v Benelux-Merkenbureau
[2003] ECR I–3793; [2003] ETMR 63 . . . . 3.02, 3.03, 3.04, 3.17,
3.20, 3.23, 4.57, 16.23

C–191/01 OHIM v Wm Wrigley Jr Company (DOUBLEMINT)
[2004] ETMR 9; [2004] RPC 18 . . . . 3.15, 3.21, 16.28

C–206/01 Arsenal Football Club plc v Matthew Reed
[2002] ECR I–10273; [2002] ETMR 82; [2003] ETMR 19;
[2003] 3 ETMR 227; [2003] 10 ETMR 895; [2003] 1 CMLR 345;
[2003] RPC 9 . . . . . . 3.27, 8.54, 8.63, 8.68, 10.01, 10.02, 10.12, 10.16,
10.23, 10.26, 10.28, 10.43, 10.44, 10.49, 11.15, 11.16, 11.17, 11.58,
12.11, 12.14, 12.15, 12.17, 12.19, 12.20, 12.21, 12.22, 12.35, 16.10,
16.52, 19.02, 19.13, 19.20, 19.23, 19.24, 19.25, 19.33, 19.37

C–408/01 Adidas-Salomon AG and Adidas Benelux BV v Fitnessworld
Trading Ltd [2004] ETMR 10 . . . . 11.03, 16.61

C–456/01P and C–457/01P Henkel KGaA v OHIM (3-dimensional
marks), 29 April 2004 . . . . 3.16, 3.17, 6.24, 6.31, 6.33, 6.34, 16.28

T–39/01 Kabushiki Kaisha Fernandes v OHIM (HIWATT)
[2003] ETMR 98 . . . . 5.57, 13.06, 13.17, 13.18, 13.19, 13.21,
14.31, 14.43

T–63/01 Procter & Gamble v OHIM (Soap bar shape)
[2003] ETMR 43 . . . . 4.42

T–91/01 BioID v OHIM [2002] ECR II–5159; [2003] ETMR 60 . . . 4.26

T–128/01 DaimlerChrysler v OHIM (Grille)
[2003] ETMR 87 . . . . 4.27, 5.56

T–130/01 Sykes Enterprises Inc v OHIM (REAL PEOPLE, REAL SOLUTIONS)
[2003] ETMR 57 . . . . 4.18

T–174/01 Goulbourn v OHIM–Redcats (SILK COCOON)
[2003] ECR II–789 . . . . 14.41

T–237/01 Alcon Inc v OHIM (BSS) [2004] ETMR 6 . . . . 4.41, 4.46,
4.55, 5.23

T–247/01 eCopy v OHIM (ECOPY) [2003] ETMR 99 . . . . 4.36, 4.37,
4.44, 5.41

T–295/01 Nordmilch eG v OHIM, 15 October 2003 .... 3.13
T–308/01 Henkel KGaA v OHIM (KLEENCARE) not yet reported 4.43
T–344/01 MFE Marienfelde GmbH v OHIM, 8 July 2004 .... 14.25,
                                                           14.41, 14.44
C–49/02 Heidelberger Bauchemie GmbH, 24 June 2004 .... 3.17,
                                                           16.23, 16.71
C–100/02 Gerolsteiner Brunnen GmbH & Co v Putsch GmbH
    [2004] ETMR 559 .... 11.12, 11.13, 11.18, 11.19, 11.23, 11.25,
                                         11.33, 11.34, 11.36, 11.45
C–404/02 Nichols [2004] ETMR 48 .... 8.48, 8.49
T–16/02 Audi AG v OHIM (TDI) [2004] ETMR 59 ..... 4.36, 4.44, 4.46,
                                                                   4.53
T–203/02 Sunrider Corp v OHIM, 8 July 2004 ...... 14.17, 14.19, 14.72
T–278/02 Dyson Ltd v OHIM 4.30
T–305/02 Nestlé Waters France v OHIM [2004] ETMR 41 .... 6.34
T–399/02 Eurocermex SA v OHIM (Long neck bottle)
    [2004] ETMR 95 .... 4.17, 4.44, 4.50
C–321/03 Dyson Ltd v The Registrar of Trade Marks 4.29
C–353/03 Société des Produits Nestlé SA v Marks UK Ltd 4.19

Commission Decisions
Charles Jourdan [1989] EC 94 .... 7.04

France
Esprit International v INPI and Chaumet International, 14 March 2003
    (Cour d'Appel de Paris) 4.43

Indonesia
Prefel SA v Fahmi Babra (Case no 200/PDT.G/1998/PN.JKT.PST)
    1998–1999 (S Ct) 16.56

International Court of Justice
Case Concerning Maritime Delimitation and Territorial Questions
    Between Quatar and Bahrain (Qatar v Bahrain) ICJ Reps 2001 ... 16.64

Italy
Brecciaroli (Giovanni) v Astoria 73 Srl (BIANCANEVE case),
    29 December 1981 (Court of Rome) 8.36, 8.37

Edgar Rice Burroughs Inc v Candygum SpA (TARZAN case), 12 November
  1976 (CA Milan) 8.32, 8.34
FC Internazionale Milano Spa, Nerazzurra Srl and A Paleari Srl v Forte
  Editore Srl (Super inter case), 29 May 1995
  (Court of Milan) 8.57, 8.58
Inditex SA v Compagnia Mercantile Srl
  [2002] ETMR 2 Trib (Turin) 15.13
Juventus FC Spa v Forservice Srl (Juventissima case), 5 November 1999
  (Court of Turin) 8.59, 8.60
RAI-Radio Televisione Italiana v Old Colonial Sas and Regina Srl (CACAO
  MERAVIGLIAO case), 10 January 1990 (Court of Rome) 8.42, 8.44
Swatch SA v Antiquorum Italia Srl and Grimoldi Srl (Swatchissimo case),
  30 March 1998 (Court of Milan) 8.55, 8.56

New Zealand
Levi Strauss & Co and Levi Strauss (New Zealand) Ltd v Kimbyr
  Investments Ltd [1994] FSR 335 HC 5.22

OHIM
Animal Foodstuffs Device (Case R 927/2001–2), 12 December 2002
  (Second Board of Appeal) 4.17

BABY-DRY (Case R 531/2001–2), 1 July 2003
  (Second Board of Appeal) 4.42
Black & Decker Corporation (Case R 350/1991–2)
  (Second Board of Appeal) 5.56

Case R 704/1999–3 (Third Board of Appeal) 4.49
Caterham Car Sales & Coachworks Ltd's Application (7)
  (Case R 63/ 1999–3), 22 June 1999, [2000] ETMR 14
  (Third Board of Appeal) 4.13

Decision no 601/2000 (Opposition Division) 14.18
Disney Enterprises Inc v Francis Fitzpatrick (WINNIE THE POOH/
  PIGGLEY POOH) (Opposition Division Decision 951/2001),
  11 April 2001 . . . . 8.20
Dyson Ltd (Case R 665/01–1), 2 July 2002
  (First Board of Appeal) 4.30, 4.31

FLAGSHIP (Case R 229/1999–3), 14 February 2000
(Third Board of Appeal) 4.16

Harcourt Brace & Co's Application (Case R 130/1999–1)
[2000] ETMR 382 (First Board of Appeal) 5.56

Laboratorios Menarini SA v Takeda Chemical Industries Ltd
[2002] ECR II–2879; [2002] 3 CMLR 8; [2002] ETMR 93
(Opposition Division) 14.14
Leupold & Stevens Inc (Case R 947/2001–2) 5.40

M & R Marking Systems Inc's Application (IDEAL) (Case R 1163/2000–1)
[2002] ETMR 28 (First Board of Appeal) 5.20
MEDLINE (Case R 230/2003–1), 19 December 2003 (First Board of
Appeal) 4.48
MEMBER OF THE SOCIETY OF FINANCIAL ADVISERS (Case R 865/1999–3),
12 March 2001 (Third Board of Appeal) 4.13

NETSTORE (Case R 142/2001–4), 12 May 2003
(Fourth Board of Appeal) 4.54

Payless Car Rental System Inc's Application: Opposition of Canary Islands
Car SA [2000] ETMR 1136 .... 5.58
PLASMALAB (Case R 751/2001–2), 17 December 2002 (Second Board of
Appeal) 4.16

QS/QUALITY STANDARD (Case R 131/1999–2), 1 February 2000
(Second Board of Appeal) 4.13

Salvatore Ferragamo Italia SpA's Application (Case R 254/1999–1)
(First Board of Appeal) 4.54
Shape of a Golden Ring (Case R 947/2001–2), 28 November 2003
(Second Board of Appeal) 4.16, 4.53
Shape of a Triangle (Case R 1025/2000–2), 17 December 2002
(Second Board of Appeal) 4.49
Shape of a Tyre (Case R 126/2001–2) (Second Board of Appeal) 4.49

THE GREATEST SHOW ON EARTH (Case R 111/2000–2), 23 May 2001
(Second Board of Appeal 4.16
THE WORLD BUSINESS ORGANIZATION (Case R 413/2002–3), 4 June 2003
(Third Board of Appeal) 4.16

Ty Nant Spring Water Ltd's Application (blue bottle) (Case R 5/1999–3)
[1999] ETMR 974 (Third Board of Appeal) 5.46

WORLD MASTERS GAMES (Case R 428/2000), 21 March 2001
(Third Board of Appeal) 4.13

Sweden
System 3R International Aktiebolag v Erowa Aktiengesellschaft and
Erowa Nordic Aktiebolag (Case T 14711–01)
[2003] ETMR 916 .... 11.13

United Kingdom
American Greeting Corp's Application (HOLLY HOBBIE)
[1984] FSR 199 .... 10.34
Amp Inv v Utilux Pty Ltd [1972] RPC 103 .... 6.08, 6.13
Animal Trade Mark [2004] FSR 19 .... 14.71, 14.72
Aristoc Ltd v Rysta Ltd [1945] 62 RPC 65 .... 16.67
Arsenal Football Club plc v Matthew Reed [2001] ETMR 77;
[2002] EWHC 2695 (Ch); [2003] EWCA Civ 696;
[2003] RPC 39 .... 1.08, 8.62, 8.64, 8.66, 10.01, 10.02,
10.14, 10.20, 10.22, 10.23, 10.24, 10.26,
10.30, 10.31, 10.47, 10.49, 11.58,
12.15, 12.21, 12.23, 12.25, 12.26,
12.34, 17.35, 19.07, 19.31
Arsenal Football Club plc v Matthew Reed (No 2)
[2003] ETMR 73 (CA) 16.15

BON MATIN Trade Mark [1989] RPC 537 .... 13.13, 13.16
BOSTITCH Trade Mark [1963] RPC 183 .... 7.13
Bowden Wire v Bowden Brake (1913) 30 RPC 45 (CA);
(1914) 31 RPC 385 (HL) 7.08
Bravado Merchandising Services Ltd v Mainstream Publishing
(Edinburgh) Ltd [1996] FSR 205 .... 19.35
British Sugar Plc v James Robertson & Sons Ltd (TREAT)
[1996] RPC 281 .... 3.25, 5.30, 6.19, 10.30, 10.31

Cable & Wireless Plc v British Telecommunications Plc
[1998] FSR 383 .... 11.22

Claritas (UK) Ltd v The Post Office and Post Preference Service Ltd
  [2001] ETMR 63 .... 10.46
Coca Cola Trade Marks [1986] RPC 421 (HL) 3.04, 3.09, 3.16
Compass Publishing BV v Compass Logistics Ltd [2004] EWHC 520;
  (2004) 101(17) LSG 32; *The Times* 29 April 2004 .... 11.53, 11.55

Decon Laboratories Ltd v Fred Baker Scientific Ltd [2001] RPC 17 ... 14.70
Domenico Tanzarelle v Stella Products Ltd BL O/104/03 .... 14.68
Dualit Ltd's Application [1999] RPC 304 .... 6.10
Dualit Ltd's (Toaster Shapes) Trade Mark Applications
  [1999] RPC 890 (Ch) 5.35
Dyson Ltd v Registrar of Trade Marks EWHC 1062 (Ch);
  [2003] ETMR 77 .... 5.21

Easyjet Airline Co Ltd v Dainty (t/a EasyRealestate)
  [2002] FSR 6 (ChD) 15.30
Electrocoin v Coinworld [2005] ETMR 31 .... 19.24
Elvis Trade Marks [1997] RPC 543 .... 3.11
Emaco Ltd and Aktiebolaget Electrolux v Dyson Appliances Ltd
  [1999] ETMR 903; (1999) 96(7) LSG 36;
  The Times 8 February 1999 .... 11.20, 11.41
Euromarket Designs Inc v Peters and Crate & Barrel Ltd
  [2000] ETMR 1025; [2001] FSR 20 (ChD) 15.33, 19.29

French Connection Ltd v Sutton [2001] ETMR 341 (ChD) 15.30

Imperial v Philip Morris [1984] RPC 293 (Ch) 5.35, 5.37
Imperial Group v Philip Morris (NERIT) [1982] FSR 72 (CA) 13.02,
                                                       13.12, 13.15
International Business Machines Corporation and another v
  Web-Sphere Ltd and others [2004] EWHC 529 (Ch);
  [2004] All ER (D) 328 (Mar) 11.36, 15.15
Invermont Trade Mark, Re [1997] RPC 125 .... 13.27, 13.29

Joseph Crosfield & Sons Ltd's Application (PERFECTION)
  (1909) 26 RPC 837 .... 3.06, 3.10

KODAK Trade Mark [1990] FSR 49 .... 10.33

La Mer Technology Inc v Laboratoires Goemar [2002] FSR 51;
     [2002] ETMR 34, 47 (Ch); [2004] ETMR 640 .... 5.57, 13.01, 13.02,
                              13.06, 13.09, 13.14, 13.16, 13.22,
                              13.24, 13.26, 13.27, 13.30, 14.40, 14.61

Marks & Spencer plc (& Ladbrokes plc & J Sainsbury plc & Virgin
     Enterprises Ltd & British Telecommunications plc) v One In a Million
     [1998] FSR 265; [1999] FSR 1 (CA) 15.30
Massland NV's Application [2000] RPC 893 .... 6.10
Mecklermedia Corp v DC Congress [1997] FSR 627 (ChD) 15.34
Minerva Trade Mark [2000] FSR 734 .... 14.70
Mothercare (UK) Ltd v Penguin Books Ltd [1988] RPC 113 .... 10.25,
                                        10.36, 12.13

NAD Electronics Inc v NAD Computer Systems Ltd
     [1997] FSR 380 .... 11.21
Nestlé SA's Trade Mark Application [2003] FSR 37;
     [2002] EWHC 2533 (Ch); [2003] ETMR 101 .... 5.19
Nichols plc, Re [2003] RPC 16 .... 3.10, 3.11, 3.22
1–800 Flowers Inc v Phonenames Ltd [2000] ETMR 369 (ChD);
     [2002] FSR 12 (CA) 15.07, 15.33

Philips Electronics NV v Remington Consumer Products
     [1998] RPC 283; [1999] ETMR 816;
     [1999] RPC 809 (CA) 6.02, 6.05, 6.13, 6.14,
                              6.15, 6.36, 10.14, 10.31
Pringle plc v Prince Sports Group Inc [1998] FSR 21 (ChD) 15.34

R v Deb Baran Ghosh [1982] QB 1053; [1982] 3 WLR 110;
     [1982] 2 All ER 689; [1982] 75 Crim App Rep 154;
     [1982] 126 SJ 429 (CA) 11.29, 11.30, 11.31
R v Isaac [2004] EWCA Crim 1082 .... 10.27
R v Johnstone [2003] UKHL 28; [2003] 10 FSR 748;
     [2003] 3 All ER 884; [2003] 1 WLR 1736;
     [2004] ETMR 2 (HL) 10.24, 10.27, 10.28,
                              10.36, 12.01, 12.04, 12.05, 12.07,
                              12.08, 12.10, 12.11, 12.12, 12.13,
                              12.15, 12.18, 12.19, 12.20, 12.22,
                              12.23, 12.24, 12.25, 12.26, 12.35,
                              16.22, 19.07, 19.09, 19.24, 19.25

R v Zaman [2003] FSR 230 (CA) 12.06

Radiation, Re (1930) 47 RPC 37 .... 7.09

Reed Executive plc and another v Reed Business Information Ltd
and others [2004] EWCA Civ 159; [2004] ETMR 56;
(2004) 148 SJLB 298;
The Times 9 March 2004 (CA) 10.29, 11.36, 11.41, 15.19,
15.23, 15.30, 19.24

Roadtech Computer Systems Ltd v ManData (Management and Data
Services) Ltd [2000] ETMR 870 ChD 15.18

Royal Brunei Airlines Sendirian Berhad v Philip Tan Kok Ming
[1995] 2 AC 378; [1995] 3 WLR 64; [1995] 3 All ER 97;
[1995] BCC 899; (1995) 92(27) LSG 33; (1995) 145 NLJ 888;
(1995) 139 SJLB 146; *The Times* 29 May 1995;
The Independent 22 June 1995 (PC) 11.31

Rugby Football Union and Nike European Operations Netherlands BV v
Cotton Traders Ltd [2002] EWHC 467 .... 10.10

Scandecor Developments AB v Scandecor Marketing AB et al [1998]
FSR 500; (1998) 95(12) LSG 28: *The Times* 9 March 1998;
[2001] ETMR 74; [2001] UKHL 21;
[2001] 2 CMLR 30 (HL) 7.18, 7.25, 7.26,
7.28, 7.29, 7.32, 7.36, 7.38,
7.39, 7.47, 9.19, 11.21, 11.41

Shetland Times Ltd v Dr Jonathan Wills & Another
[1997] FSR 604 OH 15.26

The European Ltd v The Economist Newspaper Ltd
[1996] FSR 431 .... 11.21

Thomson Holidays Ltd v Norwegian Cruise Line Ltd
[2003] RPC 32 .... 14.70

Unidoor Ltd v Marks & Spencer plc [1988] RPC 275 .... 10.33

W & G du Cros Ld's Application (1913) 30 RPC 661 ... 3.01, 3.03, 3.04,
3.08, 3.11, 3.13, 3.16, 3.17, 3.24

Wagamama v City Centre Restaurants [1995] FSR 713 .... 10.35

YORK Trade Mark [1984] RPC 231 .... 3.01

Yorkshire Copper Works Ltd's Application for a Trade Mark, Re (1953)
71 RPC 150 .... 3.01, 3.07, 3.08, 3.11, 3.28

ZIPPO Trade Mark, Re [1999] RPC 173 .... 13.29

Trade Marks Registry
Animated Music Ltd's Trade Mark; Application for a Declaration of
    Invalidity by Dash Music Co Ltd (NELLIE THE ELEPHANT case)
    (Case O–391–03) 15 December 2003 .... 8.17, 8.45
Animated Music Ltd's Trade Mark; Application for Revocation by Dash
    Music Co Ltd (NELLIE THE ELEPHANT case) (Case O–392–03)
    15 December 2003 .... 8.17, 8.45
Application of R Delamore to Register CHARLIE'S ANGELS; Opposition
    of Columbia Pictures Industries Inc, 8 April 2004 .... 8.20
Ashwood Grove Trade Marks, Re (Case O–015–04)
    14 January 2004 .... 13.28

United States of America
Abercrombie & Fitch Co v Hunting World Inc 461 F2d 1040
    (2nd Cir 1972) 16.22
Allard Enterprises Inc v Advanced Programming Resources Inc
    146 F 3d 350 (6th Cir 1998) 13.01, 17.07
American Steel Foundries v Robertson 269 US 372 (Sup Ct 1926) .. 16.02
Anheuser-Busch Inc v Balducci Publications 28 F3d 769
    (8th Cir 1994) 16.17, 16.20
August Storck KG v Nabisco Inc 59 F3d 616 (7th Cir 1995) 18.24

B F Goodrich Company v National Cooperatives Inc
    114 USPQ 406 (1957) 9.33
Barcelona.com Inc v Excelentisimo Ayuntamiento de Barcelona
    189 F Supp 2d 367, 63 USPQ 2d 1189 (ED Va 2002); 330 F 3d 617,
    67 USPQ 2d 1025 (4th Cir Va 2003) 15.34
Bayer Co v United Drug Co 272 F 505 (SDNY 1921) 16.51
Bihari v Gross 119 F Supp 2d 309, 56 USPQ 2d 1489
    (SDNY 2000) 15.18
Boogie Kings v Guillory 188 So2d 445 (La App 1966) 17.12
Bourjois & Co v Katzel 275 F 539 (2nd Cir 1921) rev'd 260 US 689
    (Sup Ct 1923) 16.24
British-American Tobacco Co v Philip Morris Inc 55 USPQ 2d 1585
    (TTAB 2000) 17.19
Brookfield Communications Inc v West Coast Entertainment Corp
    174 F3d 1036, 50 USPQ 2d 1545 (9th Cir Cal 1999) 15.16, 15.22

Brother Records Inc v Jardine 319 F3d 900 (9th Cir 2003) 17.01
Buti v Impressa Perosa 139 F3d 98 (2d Cir 1998) 17.31

Cable News Network LP, LLLP v CNNews.com 162 F Supp 2d 484,
    61 USPQ 2d 1323 (ED Va 2001) aff'd in part 56 Fed Appx 599,
    66 USPQ 2d 1057 (4th Cir 2003) 15.34
Chance v Pac-Tel Teletrac Inc 242 F3d 1151 (9th Cir 2001) 17.06
Circuit City Stores Inc v CarMax Inc 165 F3d 1047
    (6th Cir 1995) 17.30, 18.04
Coca Cola Bottling Co v Coca-Cola Co 269 F 796 (D Del 1920) 7.09
Coca Cola Co v Busch 44 F Supp 405 (ED Pa 1942) 17.13
Columbia Mill Co v Alcorn 150 US 460 (1893) 17.03
Cosmetically Sealed Indus Inc v Cheesebrough-Pond's USA Co
    125 F3d 28 (2d Cir 1997) 18.23
Crocker National Bank v Canadian Imperial Bank of Commerce
    223 USPQ (BNA) 909 (TTAB 1984) 17.19
Cumulus Media Inc v Clear Channel Communications Inc
    304 F3d 1167 (11th Cir 2002) 17.23

Data Concepts Inc v Digital Consulting Inc 150 F3d 620,
    47 USPQ 2d 1672 (6th Cir Mich 1998) 15.13
Dawn Donut Co Inc v Hart's Food Stores Inc 267 F2d 358
    (2d Cir 1959) 17.25, 17.30, 18.18, 18.20
DC Comics Inc v Powers (Daily Planet case) 482 F Supp 494
    (SD NY 1979) 8.40, 8.41, 8.45

E & J Gallo Winery v Spider Webs Ltd 286 F3d 270
    (5th Cir Tex 2002) 15.28
EI Du Pont de Nemours & Co, In re 476 F2d 1357 (CCPA 1973) .. 18.19
El Greco Leather Products Company Inc v Show World Inc
    224 USPQ 921 (ED NY 1984); 1 USPQ 2d 1016
    (2d Cir 1986) 7.42, 7.43
Emergency One Inc v American Fireeagle Ltd 228 F3d 531
    (4th Cir 2000) 17.23, 18.11
Estee Lauder Inc v The Fragrance Counter Inc 189 FRD 269,
    52 USPQ 2d 1786 (SDNY 1999) 15.22
Exon Corp v Humble Exploration Co Inc 695 F2d 96
    (5th Cir 1983) 17.23

Ferrari SpA Esercizio Fabbriche Automobili e Corse v McBurnie
11 USPQ 2d (BNA) 1843 (SD Cal 1989) 17.24
Fila Sport SpA v Diadora America Inc 141 FRD 74 (ND Ill 1991) .. 18.18
First Savings Bank FSB v First Bank System Inc 101 F3d 645
(10th Cir 1996) 18.21
Ford Motor Co v 2600 Enterprises 177 F Supp 2d 661,
61 USPQ 2d 1757 (ED Mich 2001) 15.18
Freedom Savings and Loan Association v Way 757 F2d 1176
(11th Cir 1985) 18.21
Frehling Enter Inc v International Select Group Inc 192 F3d 1330
(11th Cir 1999) 18.06
Futuredontics Inc v Applied Anagramics Inc 45 USPQ 2d 2005
(CD Cal 1997) aff'd 152 F3d 925 (9th Cir Cal 1998) 15.26

Garden of Life Inc v B Letzer S Letzer and Garden of Life
LLC 2004 WL 1151593 (CD Cal 2004) 15.28
General Health Care Ltd v Qashat 364 F3d 332 (1st Cir 2004) 17.23
GoTo.com Inc v Walt Disney Co 202 F3d 1199
(9th Cir 2000) 18.06, 18.19

Hanover Star Milling Co v Metcalf 240 US 403 (1916) 17.24, 17.27
Harley-Davidson Inc v Grottanelli 164 F3d 806 (2d Cir 1999) 17.14
Hasbro Inc v Cloue Computing Inc 66 F Supp 2d 117,
52 USPQ 2d 1402 (D Mass 1999) 15.21
Hasbro Inc v Internet Entertainment Group Ltd 40 USPQ 2d 1479
(WD Wash 1996) 15.21
Heinemann v General Motors Corp 342 F Supp 203 (ND Ill 1972)
aff'd 478 F2d 1405 (7th Cir 1973) 17.09
Herbko International Inc v Kappa Books Inc 308 F3d 1156
(Fed Cir 2002) 17.15
Holiday Inns Inc v 800 Reservation Inc 86 F3d 619
(6th Cir 1996) 17.01, 17.34

Idaho Potato Commission v M&M Produce Farms and Sales
335 F3d 130 (2d Cir 2003) 9.17, 9.23
Illinois High School Association v GTE Vantage Inc 99 F3d 244
(7th Cir 1996) 17.14
Imperial Tobacco Ltd Assignee of Imperial Group PLC v Philip Morris Inc
899 F2d 1575 (Fed Cir 1990) 18.11

Interactive Products Corp v A2Z Mobile Offices Solution 326 F3d 687,
    66 USPQ 2d 1321 (6th Cir Ohio 2003) 15.17
International Bancorp v Société des Bains de Mer et du Cercle des
    Etrangers à Monaco 329 F3d 359 (4th Cir 2003) 17.31, 18.04

Johnny Blastoff Inc v Los Angeles Rams Football Co 188 F3d 427
    (7th Cir 1998) 17.13

Kremen v Cohen 325 F3d 1035 67, USPQ 2d 1502
    (9th Cir Cal 2003) 15.07

L & JG Stickley Inc v Canal Dover Furniture Co Inc 79 F3d 258
    (2d Cir 1996) 17.24
Lane Capital Management Inc v Lane Capital Management
    Inc Docket no 98–9173 (2nd Cir 1999) 8.46
Larry Harmon Pictures Corp v Williams Restaurant Corp 929 F2d 662
    (Fed Cir 1991) 17.01
Le Cordon Bleu Sa v BPC Pub Ltd 451 F Supp 63
    (DC NY 1978) 18.13
Lear Inc v Adkins 395 US 653, 23 L Ed 2d 610,
    89 S Ct 1902 (1969) 9.23
Lindy Pen Co v Bic Pen Corp 796 F2d 254, 230 USPQ 791
    (9th Cir 1986) 15.16
Linville v Rinard 23 USPQ 2d (BNA) 1508 (TTAB 1993) 17.19

Macmahan Pharmacol Co v Denver Chemical Mfg Co 113 F 468
    (8th Cir 1908) 7.08, 7.21
McNeil–PPC v Guardian Drug Co 984 F Supp 1066, 45 USPQ 2d 1437
    (ED Mich 1997) 15.16
Mattel Inc v Barbie-Club.com 310 F3d 293, 64 USPQ 2d 1879
    (2nd Cir NY 2002) 15.07
Mattel Inc v MCA Records Inc ('Barbie Girl') DC No 97–06791;
    296 F3d 894 (9th Cir 2002) 8.07, 8.08, 8.11, 8.12, 8.28
May Dept Stores Co v Prince 200 USPQ (BNA) 803 (TTAB 1978) ..17.12
Medinal Ltd v Neuro Vasc Inc 67 USPQ 2d 1205
    (TTAB 2003) 18.12, 18.13
Mobil Oil Corp v Pegasus Petroleum Corp 818 F2d 254,
    2 USPQ 2d 1677 (2nd Cir 1987) 15.16
Monte Carlo Shirt Co Inc v Daewoo International (America) Corp
    707 F2d 1054 (9th Cir 1982) 7.44

Moseley v V Secret Catalogue Inc 537 US 418 (Sup Ct 2003) 16.18,
                                                                   18.28

National Federation of the Blind Inc v Loompanics Enterprises Inc
    936 F Supp 1232 (D Md 1996) 18.24
New Kids on the Block v News America Publishing Inc 971 F2d 302
    (9th Cir 1992) 16.21, 18.24
New West Corp v NYM Co of Cal 595 F2d 1194 (9th Cir 1979) ... 17.08
Nike Inc v Marc Kasky 539 US (Sup Ct 2003) 16.21
Nissan Motor Co Ltd v Nissan Computer Corp 204 FRD 460
    (CD Cal 2001) 15.24

Orient Express Trading Co v Federated Department Stores Inc
    842 F2d 650 (2d Cir 1988) 18.12

Packman v Chicago Tribune Co 267 F3d 628
    (7th Cir 2001) 18.06, 18.23
Panavision International LP v Toeppen 141 F3d 1316,
    46 USPQ 2d 1511 (9th Cir Cal 1998) 15.29
People for Ethical Treatment of Animals v Doughney 263 F3d 359,
    60 USPQ 2d 1109 (4th Cir Md 2001) 15.18
Pfaff v Wells Electronics 525 US 55 (1998) 17.05
Planetary Motion Inc v Techplosion Inc 261 F3d 1188
    (11th Cir 2001) 17.05, 17.09, 18.04
Planned Parenthood Federation of America Inc v Bucci
    42 USPQ 2d 1430 (SDNY 1997) 15.16
Playboy Enterprises Inc v Netscape Communications Corp
    52 USPQ 2d 1162 (CD Cal 1999) 15.21
Playboy Enterprises Inc v Netscape Communications Corp
    354 F3d 1020, 69 USPQ 2d 1417 (9th Cir 2004) 15.22
Playboy Enterprises Inc v Welles 47 USPQ 2d 1186 (SD Cal 1998)
    aff'd 279 F3d 796, 61 USPQ 2d 1508 (9th Cir Cal 2002) .. 15.18, 18.26

Qualitex Co v Jacobson Products Co 514 US 159 (Sup Ct 1995) 16.23

Rock and Roll Hall of Fame and Museum Inc v Gentile Productions
    134 F3d 749 (6th Cir 1998) 18.04
Rogers 8.12, 8.15

Sallen v Corinthians Licenciamentos LTDA 273 F3d 14,
    60 USPQ 2d 1941 (1st Cir Mass 2001) 15.13

San Juan Products Inc v San Juan Pools of Kansas Inc 849 F2d 468
  (10th Cir 1988) 18.12
Sands Taylor & Wood Co v Quaker Oats Co 987 F2d 947
  (7th Cir 1992) 18.23
Schafer Co v Innco Management Corp 797 F Supp 477
  (ED NC 1992) 18.23
SCM Corp v Long's Foods Ltd 539 F2d 196 (DC Cir 1976) 17.20
Search King Inc v Google Technology Inc 2003 WL 21464568
  (WD Okla 2003) 15.24
Silverman v CBS Inc 870 F2d 40 (2d Cir 1989) 17.23
Soweco Inc v Shell Oil Co 617 F2d 1178 (5th Cir 1980) 18.06
Stanfield v Osborne Industries Inc 52 F3d 867 (10th Cir 1995) 17.25
State of New York v Network Associates Inc D/B/A Mcafee Software
  (SC NY 2002) 16.19
Sterling Drug Inc v Bayer AG 14 F3d 763, 29 USPQ 2d 1321
  (2d Cir NY 1994) 15.34

TAB Systems v Pactel Telectrac 77 F3d 1372 (Fed Cir 1996) 17.15
Tally-Ho Inc v Coast Community College Dist 889 F2d 1018
  (11th Cir 1989) 17.28
Taubman Co v Webfeats 319 F3d 770 (6th Cir Mich 2003) 15.29
Thrifty Rend-a-car Sys v Thrift Cars Inc 831 F2d 1177
  (1st Cir 1987) 17.30
Ticketmaster Corp v Tickets.com Inc 54 USPQ 2d 1344
  (CD Cal 2000) 15.25
TMI Inc v JM Maxwell 368 F3d 433, 70 USPQ 2d 1630
  (5th Cir Tex 2004) 15.29
Torres v Cantine Torresella Srl 808 F2d 46 (Fed Cir 1986) 18.12
Trade-Mark Cases 100 US 82 (Sup Ct 1879) 16.02
Two Pesos Inc v Taco Cabana Inc; Wal-Mart Stores Inc v Samara Brothers
  Inc 529 US 205 (2000) 18.05

U-Haul International Inc v WhenU.com Inc 279 F Supp 2d 723,
  68 USPQ 2d 1038 (ED Va 2003) 15.24, 17.34
United Drug Co v Theodore Rectanus Co 248 US 90 (1918) 17.27,
                                                        17.29, 17.30
United States Jaycees v Philadelphia Jaycees 639 F2d 134
  (3d Cir 1981) 17.12

United We Stand America Inc v United We Stand America NY Inc
128 F3d 86 (2d Cir 1997) 17.01
University Bookstore v University of Wisconsin Board of Regents
33 USPQ 2d (BNA) 1385 (TTAB 1994) 17.13, 17.25

Virtual Works Inc v Volkswagen of Am Inc 238 F3d 264,
57 USPQ 2d 1547 (4th Cir Va 2001) 15.28
WarnerVision Ent Inc v Empire of Carolina 101 F3d 259
(2d Cir 1996) 17.18
Wells Fargo & Co v WhenU.com Inc 293 F Supp 2d 734
(ED Mich 2003) 15.24
West Florida Seafood Inc v Jet Restaurants Inc 31 F3d 1122
(Fed Cir 1994) 17.08
Wrist-Rocket Mfg Co Inc v Saunders Archery Co 183 USPQ 117
(CD Neb 1974) 7.38

Zazu Designs v L'Oréal SA 979 F2d 499 (7th Cir 1992) 17.08

WTO

Canada—Patent Protection of Pharmaceutical Products
(Canada—Pharmaceuticals) WT/DS114/R, 7 April 2000 .... 16.48
Canada—Term of Patent Protection AB–2000–7 WT/DS170/AB/R,
18 September 2000 .... 16.49, 16.66

EU—Protection of Trade-marks and Geographical Indications for
Agricultural Products and Foodstuffs, 24 February 2004,
Constitution of the Panel Established at the Requests of the US and
Australia WT/DS174/21, WT/DS290/19, 23 April 2004 .. 16.03, 16.66

Indonesia—Certain Measures affecting the Automobile Industry
WT/DS54/R, WT/DS55/R, WT/DS59/R, WT/DS64/R,
2 July 1998 .... 16.37, 16.39, 16.41
US—Section 110(5) Copyright Act WT/DS160/R, 27 July 2000 ... 16.48
US—Section 211 Omnibus Appropriations Act 1998 (US–Havana Club)
WT/DS176/AB/R, 2 January 2002 .... 16.06, 16.07, 16.16, 16.24,
16.29, 16.42, 16.62

TABLES OF LEGISLATION

Australia
Corporations Law 9.32

Trade Marks Act 1995
   reg 16.3 .... 9.14
   s 162 .... 9.32
   s 169 .... 9.13
   s 175 .... 9.14

Austria
Criminal Code 1975
   § 7 .... 12.33

Trade Marks Protection Act 1970 (*Markenschutzgesetz*) 12.30
   § 60 .... 12.30
   § 60a(1) 12.30

Benelux
Uniform Benelux Law implementing the Trade Mark
      Directive 1971 .... 13.07

Canada
Patent Act 16.48

Trade-marks Act
   s 23(2) 9.17
   s 34(1) 9.08

European Union

Treaties
EC Treaty 10.15
   Art 81 .... 10.15
   Art 82 .... 10.15, 10.46

Art 113 .... 16.08
Art 234 .... 4.20

European Convention on Human Rights
Art 6(2) 12.11

Decisions
Council Decision 94/800/EC of 22 December concerning the conclusion
    on behalf of the EC, as regards matters within its competence,
    of the agreements reached in the Uruguay Round multilateral
    negotiations (1986–1994) 1994 OJ L 336/1 .... 16.08, 16.09

Directives
Directive 84/450/EEC concerning misleading advertising (Advertising
    Directive) 11.49

First Council Directive 89/104/EEC of 21 December 1988 to
    approximate the laws of the Member States relating to trade marks
    (Trade Marks Directive) OJ 1989 L 40/1 .... 2.09, 2.11, 2.16,
                    2.21, 2.23, 3.02, 3.11, 3.18, 3.21, 4.01, 4.03, 4.07,
                4.15, 5.02, 6.01, 6.06, 6.07, 6.10, 6.12, 7.17, 8.52, 9.29,
            10.01, 10.02, 10.03, 10.12, 10.21, 10.23, 10.26, 10.27, 10.32,
        10.37, 10.38, 10.40, 10.48, 10.49, 11.04, 11.49, 12.02, 12.20,
                                            14.03, 14.40, 16.17, 19.07
Preamble 2.09
Recital 5 .... 14.05
Recital 8 .... 13.01, 13.02, 13.11, 14.04, 16.15
Recital 10 .... 10.19, 19.18
Art 2 .... 3.23, 4.31, 6.01, 6.04, 6.13, 6.16, 6.17, 6.19, 9.29
Art 3 .... 3.02, 3.13, 3.15, 3.18, 3.23, 6.06, 6.07, 6.19, 6.37
Art 3(1) 3.16, 6.06, 6.12, 6.35
Art 3(1)(a) 3.19, 6.06
Art 3(1)(b) ... 3.02, 3.12, 3.17, 3.19, 3.20, 4.06, 4.07, 4.09, 4.35, 4.36,
                    4.41, 6.07, 6.13, 6.19, 6.31, 6.34, 6.35, 6.36, 8.48
Art 3(1)(c) ... 3.12, 3.13, 3.14, 3.19, 3.20, 4.06, 4.07, 4.09, 4.35, 4.36,
                    4.41, 6.06, 6.13, 6.19, 6.25, 6.26, 6.27, 6.28, 8.49
Art 3(1)(d) 3.12, 3.19, 3.20, 4.06, 4.07, 4.09, 4.35,
                                            4.36, 4.41, 6.19, 6.23

Art 3(1)(e) ... 3.12, 4.08, 4.09, 4.10, 4.24, 6.05, 6.06, 6.07, 6.10, 6.12,
6.13, 6.18, 6.19, 6.20, 6.25, 6.26, 6.27, 6.31, 6.34,
6.35, 6.36, 6.37
Art 3(1)(f) 4.08, 4.09
Art 3(1)(g) 4.08, 4.09
Art 3(1)(h) 4.09
Art 3(3) 3.02, 3.12, 3.13, 3.14, 3.19, 3.20, 3.21, 3.22, 3.26,
4.01, 4.03, 4.05, 4.06, 4.12, 4.20, 4.21, 4.28, 4.30,
4.32, 4.40, 4.41, 4.46, 5.02, 5.42, 6.19, 6.25
Art 3a 11.47
Art 4(2)–(4) 11.52
Art 5 .... 2.19, 10.03, 10.32, 10.37, 10.44, 11.08,
11.44, 11.47, 12.29, 16.16
Art 5(1) 10.38, 10.41, 10.43, 12.20, 16.02
Art 5(1)(a) 8.63, 10.13, 11.03, 12.15, 16.10, 19.14,
19.23, 19.25, 19.31, 19.33, 19.34
Art 5(1)(b) 10.13, 11.03, 19.25
Art 5(2) 2.19, 11.03, 12.25, 16.02, 16.61, 16.68, 19.25, 19.30
Art 5(3) 2.19, 11.03, 11.49
Art 6 .... 10.38, 10.40, 10.41, 10.42, 10.44, 11.05, 11.08, 11.09,
11.10, 11.11, 11.13, 11.23, 11.25, 11.26, 11.33, 11.43, 16.20
Art 6(1) 11.06, 11.07, 11.46, 11.47, 12.22, 19.28
Art 6(1)(a) 11.07, 11.10, 11.25, 11.41
Art 6(1)(b) 3.22, 10.42, 11.07, 11.10, 11.25, 11.42,
11.44, 11.45, 11.47, 11.48
Art 6(1)(c) 11.07, 11.10, 11.50, 11.51
Art 6(2) 11.52, 11.53, 11.54, 11.56, 11.57
Art 7 .... 10.38, 16.17
Art 7(1)(c) 3.21
Art 10 .... 2.17, 13.03, 14.04, 14.29, 14.38
Art 10(1) 2.17, 2.29, 16.16
Art 10(2)(a) 4.12
Art 11 .... 2.35
Art 11(1) 2.35, 14.04
Art 11(2) 2.35, 14.04, 14.05
Art 12 .... 2.35, 13.03, 13.04, 13.06, 14.38
Art 12(1) 2.31, 13.05, 13.08
Art 61 .... 12.02

Directive 97/55/EC of European Parliament and of the Council of
    6 October 1997 amending Directive 84/450/EEC concerning
    misleading advertising so as to include comparative advertising OJ
    L 290/18
  Recital 15 . . . . 11.47
  Art 1(4) 11.47

Regulations
Council Regulation 2081/92 on the protection of geographical indications
    and designations for agricultural products and foodstuffs (GI
    Regulation) 4.08, 16.03
Council Regulation 2082/92 on Certificates of Specific Character for
    agricultural products and foodstuffs 16.03
Council Regulation (EC) No 40/94 of 20 December 1993 on the
    Community trade mark (Community Trade Mark/CTM
    Regulation/CTMR) OJ 1994 L 11/1 . . . . 3.04, 3.11, 4.02, 4.03,
                                        4.07, 4.15, 5.02, 6.06, 6.35, 9.30, 11.04,
                    11.06, 11.49, 11.54, 13.08, 14.03, 14.07, 14.12, 14.29, 14.32,
                                    14.34, 14.37, 14.46, 14.47, 14.48
  Art 1(2) 5.46
  Art 4 . . . . 4.31, 6.01, 6.04, 6.06
  Art 5(1)(b)–(d) 3.12
  Art 7 . . . . 3.15
  Art 7(1) 4.47, 6.06
  Art 7(1)(a) 6.06
  Art 7(1)(b) 4.04, 4.06, 4.07, 4.26, 4.35, 4.36, 4.39, 4.40,
                                        4.41, 4.46, 5.11, 5.46, 6.34
  Art 7(1)(c)–(d) 4.04, 4.06, 4.07, 4.35, 4.36, 4.39, 4.40, 4.41, 4.46
  Art 7(1)(e) 4.08, 4.09, 4.10, 4.24, 6.10
  Art 7(1)(f)–(j) 4.08, 4.09
  Art 7(1)(k) 4.08
  Art 7(2) 4.47, 5.45
  Art 7(3) 4.02, 4.05, 4.06, 4.12, 4.13, 4.20, 4.21, 4.28, 4.39,
                                        4.42, 4.46, 5.02, 5.05, 5.41, 5.56
  Art 8(2) 4.39
  Art 8(2)(a) 4.37, 14.09
  Art 8(2)(b) 4.37
  Art 8(4) 11.53

Art 9(1)(a)–(c) 11.03
Art 9(2) 11.49
Art 9(2)(d) 11.49
Art 12 .... 11.05, 11.06
Art 13 .... 14.34
Art 15 .... 13.08, 14.38
Art 15(2)(a) 4.12
Art 15(2)(b) 14.36
Art 26 .... 4.37
Art 31 .... 4.38
Art 40 .... 4.02
Art 43 .... 14.09, 14.14, 14.40
Art 43(2) 13.18, 14.09, 14.15, 14.23, 14.30, 14.38
Art 43(3) 14.09, 14.14, 14.15, 14.38
Art 50 .... 13.08, 14.38
Art 51(1)(a) 4.41, 4.43
Art 51(2) 4.04, 4.40
Art 56 .... 14.09, 14.40
Art 56(2) 14.09, 14.15, 14.30, 14.38
Art 56(3) 14.09, 14.15, 14.38
Art 61(1) 4.42
Art 62(1) 4.42, 4.43
Art 64 .... 9.30
Art 74(2) 4.42
Art 76(1) 5.09
Art 76(1)(f) 14.16
Art 84 .... 5.25
Art 106 .... 14.37
Art 107 .... 11.55
Art 107(1) 11.54, 11.57
Art 107(3) 11.55, 11.56, 11.57
Art 108 .... 5.52
Art 108(2) 14.31
Arts 109–110 .... 5.52
Art 115(4) 5.53
Art 142a 5.51

Regulation No 3288/94 of 22 December 1994, OJ 1994 L 349/83 ... 4.02

Commission Regulation 2868/95 implementing the CTMR (IR) 14.12
  Rule 3(2) 4.31
  Rule 11(2) 5.04
  Rule 12(i) 4.02
    Art 1 .... 5.59
  Rule 19(1) 14.13
  Rule 22 .... 13.19
  Rule 22(1) 13.18, 14.23
  Rule 22(2)–(3) 14.16
  Rule 22(4) 14.22
  Rule 40(1) 14.13
  Rule 40(5) 14.16
  Rule 84(2)(k) 4.02
  Rule 88(c)
    Art 1 .... 5.26
  Rule 96(1)
    Art 1 .... 5.54
  Rule 96(2)
    Art 1 .... 5.54

Council Regulation (EC) 1383/2003 of 22 July 2003 concerning customs
    action against goods suspected of infringing certain intellectual
    property rights and the measures to be taken against goods found
    to have infringed such rights (Regulation against counterfeit and
    pirated goods) OJ L 196 .... 12.02
  Recital 8 .... 12.02
  Art 2 .... 12.02

Commission Regulation 874/2004 laying down public policy rules
    concerning the implementation and functions of the .eu Top
    Level Domain OJ 2004 L 162/40 .... 15.32

Council Regulation 2081/92 .... 16.03

France
Intellectual Property Code 1992 (Law No 92–597 of 1 July 1992)
  Art L716–9 .... 12.32
  Art L716–10 .... 12.32

Law No 2004–204 of 9 March 2004
  Art 34 . . . . 12.32

Penal Code
  Art 121–3 . . . . 12.33

Germany
Criminal Code 1871
  § 15 . . . . 12.33

Trade Marks Act 1994 (*Markengesetz*) 2.35
  §§ 14–15 . . . . 12.29
  § 143 . . . . 12.29, 12.33

International
GATT 1947 . . . . 16.40, 16.65
GATT 1994 . . . . 16.04, 16.06, 16.08, 16.37, 16.40, 16.44
  Art XX(d) 16.44
  Arts XXII–XXIII 16.06

Madrid Agreement Concerning the International Registration of Marks
  1891 (revised 1979) 2.27, 16.24
  1989 Protocol 2.27, 16.24, 17.19, 18.03, 18.13, 18.20
Marrakech Agreement Establishing the World Trade Organization 1994
  (WTO Agreement) 16.06, 16.07, 16.40, 16.72
  Art XVI:1 . . . . 16.65
  Annex 1C—Agreement on Trade-Related Aspects of Intellectual
  Property Rights, Including Trade in Counterfeit Goods
  (TRIPs Agreement) 2.06, 2.07, 2.16, 2.27, 2.28, 2.40,
      6.01, 7.31, 7.32, 9.08, 9.29, 9.34, 12.02, 16.04, 16.06,
    16.07, 16.08, 16.09, 16.10, 16.11, 16.12, 16.16, 16.18, 16.24,
    16.31, 16.34, 16.39, 16.46, 16.47, 16.48, 16.50, 16.57, 16.61,
          16.62, 16.63, 16.65, 16.66, 16.73, 17.17
    Preamble 16.16
    Art 1 . . . . 16.04, 16.06
    Art 1(2) 16.62
    Art 2 . . . . 9.34
    Art 2(1) 2.28, 16.62

Art 3 .... 16.04, 16.30, 16.35, 16.40, 16.41
Art 4 .... 16.04, 16.30, 16.35, 16.40, 16.42
Art 8 .... 16.29, 16.30, 16.44, 16.45, 16.46, 16.47, 16.49
Art 15 .... 2.28, 16.05, 16.24, 16.30, 16.32, 16.47
Art 15(1) 2.07, 4.01, 6.01, 16.23, 16.26, 16.27
Art 15(3) 2.07, 2.27, 2.32, 9.08, 16.16, 16.33, 17.17
Art 16 .... 16.16, 16.17, 16.24, 16.52
Art 16(1) 16.10, 16.51, 16.52, 16.54, 16.62, 16.66
Art 16(2) 2.39, 2.40, 16.57
Art 16(3) 2.39, 16.12, 16.18, 16.57, 16.58, 16.59, 16.60
Art 17 .... 16.20
Art 18 .... 16.05
Art 19 .... 2.28, 2.33
Art 19(2) 7.31
Art 20 .... 16.30, 16.32, 16.33, 16.35, 16.36, 16.37, 16.38, 16.39
Art 21 .... 16.05, 16.16
Art 24(5) 16.03
Art 27(1) 2.22
Art 28 .... 16.49
Art 30 .... 16.48, 16.49
Art 64 .... 16.06, 16.63
Art 65(1)–(2) 16.07
Art 65(4) 16.07
Subsidies and Countervailing Measures (SCM) Agreement 16.37,
                                                              16.39
Trade Related Investment Measures (TRIMs) Agreement 16.37

Paris Convention for the Protection of Industrial Property (Paris
        Convention) ... 2.04, 2.06, 2.16, 2.42, 16.04, 16.23, 16.24, 16.25,
                16.40, 16.42, 16.55, 17.20, 18.03, 18.13, 18.15, 18.20
Arts 1–3 .... 16.05
Art 4 .... 16.05, 16.24, 17.20
Arts 4(A)–4(B) 4.38
Art 5 .... 16.05
Art 5(C) 2.28
Art 5(C)(1) 2.06
Art 6 .... 2.37, 2.39, 2.40, 2.42, 2.43, 4.08, 16.05, 16.23, 16.24,
                16.25, 16.26, 16.55, 16.56, 16.57, 16.58, 16.60, 17.19

Art 6(1) 16.25
Art 6(2) 2.43
Art 6(B) 16.26
Art 6(C)(1) 16.27
Art 7 .... 9.29, 9.34, 16.05
Art 7(1) 9.28
Art 7(3) 9.34
Art 8 .... 16.05, 16.62
Arts 9–12 .... 16.05
Art 19 .... 16.05

Official Acts of the Revision Conference of the Paris Convention 1925
    (*Actes de la Haye*) 2.04

Pan American Convention 17.19

Statute of the International Court of Justice
    Art 38 .... 16.71
    Art 38(1)(c) 16.71

Vienna Convention on the Law of Treaties 1969 .... 16.63
    Art 31 .... 16.62, 16.63, 16.69
    Art 31(1) 16.63
    Art 32 .... 16.64
    Art 84(1) 16.62

WTO Understanding on Rules and Procedures Governing the
    Settlement of Disputes (DSU) 16.06
    Art 1 .... 16.06
    Art 1.1 .... 16.06
    Art 17 .... 16.06
    Art 3.2 .... 16.63

Slovenia
Law on Industrial Property 2.35

Switzerland
Trade Marks Protection Act 1992 (*Markenschutzgesetz*)
    Art 61 .... 12.31, 12.33
    Art 62 .... 12.31

United Kingdom

Competition Act 1998 .... 10.46

Copyright, Designs and Patents Act 1988

    s 107 .... 12.08

    s 198 .... 12.08

Registered Designs Act 1949 .... 6.08

Theft Act 1968

    s 1 .... 12.24

Trade Mark Act 1875 .... 3.01

Trade Mark Act 1905 .... 3.01

    s 9 .... 3.01

    s 9(5) 3.01

Trade Marks Act 1938 .... 2.14, 6.12, 7.13, 7.20, 10.25, 10.26, 10.31,
                             10.32, 10.33, 10.34, 10.35, 10.36, 10.40, 13.16,
                                   19.07, 19.08, 19.11, 19.25

    s 4 .... 10.32

    s 9 .... 3.08

    s 9(2)–(3) 3.08

    s 9(3)(a)–(b) 3.08

    s 10 .... 3.08

    s 26 .... 13.13, 13.15

    s 28(6) 10.34

Trade Marks Act (TMA) 1994 .... 3.01, 3.25, 6.12, 7.17, 7.19,
                             7.21, 7.24, 7.27, 9.10, 9.28, 9.29, 10.14,
           10.25, 10.26, 10.27, 10.32, 10.35, 10.40, 11.04, 12.01, 12.16,
                                  13.01, 13.15, 14.45

    s 1 .... 6.01

    s 1(1) 6.04

    s 2 .... 16.16

    s 3(1) 4.30

    s 3(1)(a) 4.30, 6.06

    s 3(1)(b) 4.20, 4.30

    s 3(1)(c) 4.30

    s 3(2) 6.06

    s 5(3) 8.20

    s 6A(2) 14.48

s 6A(3)(a)(a) 14.48
s 9 .... 10.30, 12.04, 12.09, 12.10, 12.16, 12.20, 12.24
s 10 .... 10.14, 10.24, 10.26, 10.30, 10.32, 10.40,
                         12.04, 12.09, 12.10, 12.16, 12.20, 12.24, 12.34
s 10(1) 10.13, 10.36, 11.03, 12.15, 16.53, 19.24, 19.25
s 10(2) 10.36, 11.03, 12.15, 19.24, 19.25
s 10(2)(b) 10.13
s 10(3) 10.36, 11.03, 12.02, 12.15, 12.25, 19.24, 19.25
s 10(4) 1.19
s 10(6) 11.05, 11.20
s 11 .... 10.40, 11.05, 12.04, 12.09, 12.24
s 11(2) 11.06, 11.21, 12.22
s 11(2)(b) 12.08
s 22 .... 16.16
s 29 .... 12.04
s 29(1) 12.04
s 30 .... 7.17, 12.04
s 30(2)–(3) 12.04
s 31 .... 7.17, 12.04
s 31(1) 12.04
s 46 .... 12.02, 14.68
s 46(1) 13.01, 16.16
s 46(1)(a) 7.30, 14.64
s 46(3) 13.27
s 46(6)(b) 11.04
s 47 .... 12.02
s 47(2A)(c) 14.48
s 47(2B) 14.66
s 49 .... 9.24, 9.28, 9.30
s 67 .... 5.25
s 92 .... 10.24, 10.27, 12.02, 12.04, 12.05, 12.06, 12.07,
            12.08, 12.09, 12.10, 12.13, 12.16, 12.17, 12.18, 12.19, 12.20,
                   12.22, 12.23, 12.24, 12.25, 12.26, 12.34, 12.35
s 92(1)–(2) 12.02, 12.03, 12.04, 12.05, 12.06, 12.07, 12.18
s 92(3) 12.02, 12.03, 12.04, 12.05, 12.06, 12.18, 12.26
s 92(4)(a) 12.02
s 92(4)(b) 12.02, 12.25
s 92(5) .. 12.02, 12.04, 12.09, 12.10, 12.11, 12.17, 12.19, 12.24, 12.26

s 92(6) 12.01, 12.02
s 92A 12.02
ss 93–98 .... 12.02
s 100 .... 14.62
s 101 .... 12.02
s 104 .... 12.17, 12.24
Sch 1 .... 9.24
   para 2 .... 9.25
   para 5 .... 9.24
   para 13 .... 9.24
Sch 2 .... 9.17
   para 7(1)(b) 9.10
   para 13 .... 9.17
Sch 3
   para 2(2) 6.12

Statutory Instruments
Trade Mark Rules 2000 .... 14.47
   Rule 13(2)(e) 14.48
   Rule 13C(1)(b)(ii) 14.50
   Rule 13C(2) 14.55
   Rule 33 .... 14.51
   Rule 33(7) 14.56
   Rule 33A 14.51
   Rule 33A(1) 14.56
   Rule 33A(1)(b)(iii) 14.56
   Rule 55 .... 14.58
Trade Marks (Amendment) Rules 2004 .... 14.47
Trade Marks (Proof of Use, etc) Regulations 2004, SI 2004 No 946 .. 14.45

United States of America
Anticybersquatting Consumer Protection Act 1999 (ACPA) 15.07,
   15.31, 15.32, 15.34
Appropriations Act 1999
   s 211 .... 16.42
   s 211(a)(2) 16.42
   s 211(b) 16.42
   37 CFR §2.56(b)(3) 9.33

Constitution 16.02

Art I §8, cl 8 .... 16.02
Commerce Clause 16.02, 17.01
First Amendment 8.08, 8.13, 15.24
Intellectual Property Clause 16.02

Federal Trademark Dilution Act 1995 (FTDA) 8.08, 8.10, 16.18
s 43(c) 16.18

Lanham Act 2.20, 2.21, 2.27, 7.14, 9.09, 9.16, 9.27, 9.33,
                    13.24, 15.34, 17.01, 17.04, 17.05, 17.12, 17.13, 17.17,
                            17.18, 17.19, 17.22, 18.20, 18.25, 18.26
s 1 .... 16.02
s 1(a) 17.01
s 1(b) 17.01, 17.17
s 1(d) 17.18
s 2(d) 17.15, 18.20
s 5 .... 17.12
s 7(b) 18.08
s 7(c) 17.17, 17.30, 18.14, 18.18
ss 8–9 .... 18.13
s 14 .... 18.09
s 15 .... 18.08
s 22 .... 17.30
s 32 .... 18.05
s 32(1)(a) 17.01
s 32(2)(D)(iv) 15.31
s 33(a)—(b) 18.08
s 33(b)(1) 18.12
s 33(b)(2) 18.11
s 33(b)(4) 18.22
s 33(b)(5) 18.18
s 43(a) 18.05, 18.06
s 43(c) 18.25
s 43(c)(1) 18.27
s 43(c)(4) 18.26
s 44 .... 15.34, 18.03, 18.13
s 44(d) 17.20, 18.15
s 44(d)(4) 18.15

s 44(e) 17.19
s 45 .... 2.20, 7.14, 13.01, 13.24, 17.01, 17.05, 17.12, 17.22, 18.04,
18.11
s 45 (1) 2.20
s 45 (1)(A)–(B) 2.20
s 45 (2) 2.20
ss 60–74 .... 17.19
s 66 .... 18.03, 18.13, 18.16
s 67 .... 18.16
s 71 .... 18.13

Restatement (Third) of Unfair Competition
s 25 .... 15.03

TMEP 1303.02(b) 9.33
Trademark Law *see* Lanham Act
Trademark Law Revision Act 1988 *see* Lanham Act

15 USC §1051 .... 16.02, 18.04
15 USC §1051(a) 17.01
15 USC §1051(b) 17.01, 17.17
15 USC §1051(d) 17.18
15 USC §1052(d) 17.15
15 USC §1054 .... 9.16
15 USC §1055 .... 17.12
15 USC §1057(c) 17.17, 17.30
15 USC §1072 .... 17.30
15 USC §1114 .... 9.16
15 USC §1114(1)(a) 17.01
15 USC §1116 .... 9.16
15 USC §1125(c) 16.18
15 USC §1125(d)(2)(A) 15.07
15 USC §1126(d)(4) 17.20
15 USC §1127 .... 2.20, 9.09, 9.33, 17.01, 17.05, 17.12, 17.22
15 USC §§1141–1141n 17.19
15 USCA 1005 .... 7.14
15 USCA 1127 .... 7.14

WIPO

Joint Recommendation concerning Provisions on the Protection of
    Well-Known Marks 1999 .... 2.41
    Art 2(2) 2.41
    Art 2(2)(a) 2.41
    Art 2(2)(a)(iii) 2.41
    Art 2(2)(b) 2.41

Part A

INTRODUCTION

1

INTRODUCTION

Jeremy Phillips and Ilanah Simon

A. Eine Kleine Rechtlichs Problem   1.01
B. The Importance of Use in Trade Mark Law   1.04
C. Use: A Global Concern   1.06
D. The Essential Function   1.07
E. Methodology   1.08
  (1) Identifying the contexts within which the word 'use' required analysis   1.10
  (2) Arranging those contexts into a format in which they could be cogently explained to a specialist readership of trade mark practitioners and theoreticians   1.11
  (3) Identifying authors capable of providing the degree of analysis required   1.12
  (4) Identifying a working definition of the word 'use'   1.13
  (5) Finding a publisher   1.14
F. A Word of Warning   1.19
G. Feedback   1.20

A. Eine Kleine Rechtlichs Problem

1.01 Imagine the following (not entirely fictitious) situation. Brigadier plc manufactures heavy vehicles, including buses. Since 1926 it has been the proprietor of the BRIGADIER trade mark in Class 12 of the Nice Classification for vehicles, including buses. Mr and Mrs Jones purchase a second-hand bus and in their spare time convert it into a 'bus bar', from which they intend to sell beer and other refreshments when they visit the sites of local fetes throughout England.

1.02 Mr and Mrs Jones receive an offer of sponsorship from Tomkins & Sons, who have been brewing fine ales under the BRIGADIER trade mark since 1950. As a condition of their sponsorship, they require the Joneses to paint their bus bar in the blue and yellow livery of Tomkins & Sons and to display the BRIGADIER trade mark in large letters on both sides of the bus. Mr and Mrs

Jones seek your advice as to whether, if they accept the sponsorship deal, they run the risk of infringing Brigadier plc's trade mark.

1.03 This question illustrates just one of the many problematic facets of the law concerning trade mark use. Although the factual scenario is simple, the law is less so. A selection of answers, given by some of our (anonymized) contributors, can be found at the end of the Conclusion to this book.

B. The Importance of Use in Trade Mark Law

1.04 The concept of use goes to the very heart of trade mark law. For example:

- use justifies protection of trade marks—they are not property rights *per se*. They are only deemed worthy of protection as property rights in so far as some commercial use is made of them
- use or intent to use is a requirement for registration as a trade mark
- use transforms signs that would not otherwise be worthy of trade mark registration when, because of that use, the public perceives them as indicating the origin of the goods or services with regard to which they are used
- use is an implicit or explicit requirement in most, if not all, forms of trade mark infringement
- use is the means by which trade marks are profitably exploited in the market
- use is a necessary condition for the continuation of trade mark registration.

1.05 There is no significant aspect of trade mark law that does not require an understanding of the concept of use. There is however no single cogent and authoritative definition of use. Nor, to our knowledge, has any publication been specifically dedicated to an analysis of the concept of use. In this publication, with the aid of our contributors, we therefore attempt to examine the concept of use at every stage of a trade mark's life cycle.

C. Use: A Global Concern

1.06 This book focuses principally on European trade mark law. It was conceived and edited by a pair of European lawyers writing within the legal and cultural milieu of the European Union. Additionally, it was a development in European law which suggested the subject-matter. However, we invited Sheldon

Klein, N. Christopher Norton, Graeme Dinwoodie and Mark Janis to write on aspects of use in the United States and Gail Evans to consider the place of use in international trade mark law. This goes to show that, while much of the recent debate on use has taken place in the EU, use is a global concern.

D. The Essential Function

To the extent that it addresses European law, we will examine the concept of **1.07** use through the prism of the essential function:

> to guarantee the identity of origin of the marked goods or services to the consumer or end user by enabling him, without any possibility of confusion, to distinguish the goods or services from others which have another origin.

It is the contention of one of the editors that the essential function is the linchpin of EU trade mark law. It would therefore have been remiss of us not to pay particular attention to it and to urge our contributors to do the same.

E. Methodology

This book was conceived on the back of a heated discussion between its **1.08** editors about the meaning of the word 'use', and the concept of 'use'. The context of this discussion was the reference by Laddie J to the European Court of Justice of the trade mark infringement action of *Arsenal v Reed*.[1] It soon become became apparent to us not only that the word 'use' was employed in several different contexts within modern European trade mark law but that our respective commitments left us with insufficient time to pursue this weasel word ourselves. Accordingly the idea of a multi-contributor book was conceived.

We initially faced a number of challenges: **1.09**

(1) Identifying the contexts within which the word 'use' required analysis

Our first attempts at taxonomy yielded just six or seven contexts, but the final **1.10** arrangement of chapters in this book shows that we had previously seriously

---

[1] *Arsenal Football Club v Matthew Reed* [2001] ETMR 77 (Ch).

underestimated the ubiquity and flexibility of the 'use' concept. Serious omissions in this book include the absence of chapters on (a) trade mark use and exhaustion of rights, (b) unused marks and trade mark use, (c) trade mark use in the context of dilution (a subject alluded to in more than one of our chapters) and (d) decorative use and embellishments. Should this volume run to a second edition, all of these omissions will be rectified.

(2) Arranging those contexts into a format in which they could be cogently explained to a specialist readership of trade mark practitioners and theoreticians

1.11 Having worked closely together on a number of projects over the previous two years, we ran the danger that our ideas—though generally instantly comprehensible to each other—were not necessarily self-explanatory to anyone else. The exercise of explaining what we wanted to do with the 'use' concept to others was actually valuable in that, through calculating how to present it to others, we were able to refine and enhance our own understanding of it.

(3) Identifying authors capable of providing the degree of analysis required

1.12 Trade mark law is a subject that has generated a large amount of printed material in the form of books, articles, case notes, web pages and promotional leaflets. It was therefore easy for us to identify authors in the field of trade mark law. What narrowed our field was the need to find a team of writers who fulfilled the following criteria: they had to be (i) practising or academic lawyers, or trade mark administrators (ii) who were respected within the trade mark community and by us (whether we agreed with their position on trade mark use or not) (iii) with an ability to express themselves clearly and concisely. They had to be (iv) familiar with issues relating to trade mark use and (v) prepared to engage in our peculiarly interactive form of chapter editing; they also had to be (vi) available to write their chapters during a brief and busy window of opportunity that spread effectively from March to July 2004.

(4) Identifying a working definition of the word 'use'

1.13 We could not ask our contributors to write on the subject of trade mark use without at least being able to indicate what we ourselves meant by 'use'. Even now we are not entirely sure that we agree on the definition between our-selves. However, to put together a coherent work, we adopted a working hypothesis, influenced by our previous readings on the matter, that use as a trade mark involves use to denote the origin of the goods or services on or in respect of which the mark is used. This abstract definition turned out to be no more than a *de minimis* position, since we have identified at least one form of use that does not conform to it. Our working hypothesis turned out to be only a starting-point: it transpires that more must be done in order to con-vince a court or other relevant authority that trade mark use has taken place.

(5) Finding a publisher

Having prepared ourselves for the responsibility of publishing this book **1.14** ourselves, we were relieved when Oxford University Press committed itself to supporting this venture. Among those whose contribution to literature is the purchase and perusal of books, it may not be known how greatly OUP participates in the development of the intellectual content of its titles as well as in the production process. A further contribution of OUP was to enforce upon us a production schedule that was so tight as to concentrate the minds of chapter authors and editors alike.

Having identified and commissioned our authors, we then enjoyed a brief **1.15** period of peace and tranquillity before our chapters started coming in. Our plan was for each of us to read each chapter and then discuss them, following which we would add our comments (where serious issues of content required debate), tracked changes (for textual amendments that were open to discus-sion) and silent changes (for amendments relating largely to conformity and cross-referencing between chapters, house style and punctuation). By and large we adhered to this plan, though in some cases the discussion between the editors took place more after the editorial process than in the course of it.

Our authors responded quite differently to our comments and changes. **1.16** Some embarked upon a spirited defence of their *ipsissima verba*; others took an almost *laissez-faire* attitude towards our criticisms. In all cases, however, the interactive process that ensued and which continued until the text of each chapter was finally agreed turned out to be an educative process, for us as editors if not also for our contributors. Several of our authors who were practitioners commented that the subject of trade mark use seemed to have become very lively while they were writing their chapters. This may well have been so; it may also have been the result of their own increasing awareness of and sensitivity to trade mark use issues over the past months.

1.17 On the subject of contributors, there is nothing quite as efficacious as working with other people as a means of getting to know them. Among our contributors were early birds and night owls, inspirational poets and methodical plodders; among them too were those who vested in the abstract concept of the word 'deadline' a remarkable degree of concreteness and unforgiving finality, as well as those who, if they comprehended the concept at all, viewed it as one which was distant, abstruse and of no application to them personally. Our team of experts also contained many fine people who reasoned that, if they (but no one else) wrote twice as many words in their chapter as the quantity which their editors advised, this book would be scarcely any longer.

1.18 At this juncture we should point out that we do not necessarily agree with either the legal propositions advanced by our contributors or with the conclusions that they have drawn from them. Nor indeed do our contributors necessarily agree with each other. It goes without saying that there were many points of disagreement between the two editors themselves. There is no one true path to enlightenment in trade mark law and during the editing process, though we did make our positions on the various subjects (sometimes painfully) clear to our contributors, we were happy to tolerate differing opinions in the interest of scholarly discourse.

F. A Word of Warning

1.19 When considering the meaning of the word 'use', the fact that it bears a colloquial meaning should not be forgotten. The plain meaning of 'use' includes merely fixing a sign on to goods, as is exemplified by section 10(4) of the Trade Marks Act 1994. The context will generally determine the type of use to which we and our contributors refer. Note also that the terms 'trade mark use' and 'use as a trade mark' are synonymous.

G. Feedback

1.20 The editors would greatly appreciate comments and responses from readers of this book. Any such responses should be directed at first instance to the editors, care of the IPKat (theipkat@yahoo.co.uk).

PART B

THE CONCEPT OF USE

2

USE AND NON-USE IN TRADE MARK LAW

Bojan Pretnar

A. Introduction: The Scope and
   Purpose of this Chapter   2.01
B. Why must Trade Marks be Used? 2.06
C. The Meaning of the Notion of
   Use   2.12

D. The Impact of the Requirement
   of Use on Rights in Trade Marks   2.26
E. Exceptions from the Use
   Requirement   2.36
F. Concluding Remarks   2.45

A. Introduction: The Scope and Purpose of this Chapter

Trade marks significantly differ from most of other intellectual property **2.01** rights in two respects. First, their protection can be renewed indefinitely, which means that there is no ultimate 'falling into public domain' imposed by law in a manner similar to the patent law, copyright, or industrial design law. However, the lasting protection of a trade mark can be maintained and enforced only if the requirement of its *actual and genuine use* is fulfilled. This is the second distinctive principle of trade mark law, the application of which can be found virtually everywhere in the world. Fezer says that the 'obligation of use' (in German, *Benutzungszwang*) of a trade mark represents the basic principle (*Grundprinzip*) of (German) trade mark law, which in the last decades has been adopted with proven effectiveness in almost all jurisdictions.[1] Cornish underlines this fact, stating that:

[T]he conception of a trade mark registration as an entitlement dependent

---

The views expressed in this chapter are personal and do not necessarily reflect the views of the World Intellectual Property Organization, of which the author is currently a staff member.

[1] K-H Fezer *Markenrecht* (CH Beck Munich 2001) 1191.

upon need—which has always underpinned the British approach to the subject, has become the major element in the EU system.[2]

2.02 The same principle has been also followed in the United States, where it has been said that:

> [A] fundamental common law tenet is that trademark property rights arise from a manufacturer or merchant's actual adoption and use of a mark . . . Adoption and use creates ownership rights . . .[3]

2.03 All intellectual property rights are meant to be used in commerce and trade in one way or another. Yet the strict dependence of protection and enforcement of an intellectual property right upon its actual and genuine use is nowhere so explicitly set out as in trade mark law. This fact begs a fundamental question: what actually constitutes such use of a trade mark that meets the legal requirements for its registration, maintenance, enforcement etc?

2.04 Intuitively, one may assume that the use of a trade mark in trade and commerce is so self-evident in daily life that not much ink could be spent on the issue. Indeed, such reasoning has apparently prevailed in the past; Bodenhausen, for example, in his authoritative commentary on the Paris Convention observes that, according to the *Actes de la Haye* (1925),[4] 'use of the mark is generally understood as meaning the sale of goods bearing such mark'.[5] However, a closer look at the issue reveals that the concept of use and, for that matter, non-use, is a complex legal issue: the more we delve into it, the more complex it gets.

2.05 Given the modest scope of this chapter, only the tip of the iceberg can be explored. Therefore, the main purpose of this chapter is threefold: (i) to explore whether the concepts of use and non-use are defined and, if so, how, (ii) to present the conceptual relationship of use and non-use, respectively, in

---

[2] W Cornish and D Llewelyn *Intellectual Property: Patents, Copyright, Trade Marks and Allied Rights* (Sweet & Maxwell London 2003) 689.

[3] DS Chisum and MA Jacobs *Understanding Intellectual Property Law* (Matthew Bender New York 1992) 5–114.

[4] Official Acts of the Revision Conference of the Paris Convention held in The Hague in 1925.

[5] GHC Bodenhausen *Guide to the Application of the Paris Convention for the Protection of Industrial Property* (BIRPI Geneva 1969, reprinted as WIPO Publication no 611 (Geneva 1991)) 75.

regard to the protectability of trade marks and (iii) to discuss an important exception to the use requirement where the protection of well-known trade marks are concerned.

B. Why must Trade Marks be Used?

The fact that the fate of trade marks so crucially depends upon their use **2.06** obviously raises the question, why has the use requirement found worldwide acceptance? An inspection of the two most relevant international treaties, the Paris Convention for the Protection of Industrial Property (Paris Convention) and the more recent Agreement on Trade-Related Aspects of Intellectual Property Rights (TRIPs Agreement) reveals that the use requirement is optional, not obligatory. Article 5 paragraph C (1) of the Paris Convention provides that:

> [I]f, in any country, use of the registered trade mark is compulsory, the registration may be cancelled . . . if the person concerned does not justify his inaction.

The TRIPs Agreement is even more straightforward. Article 15(3) provides **2.07** that:

> Members may make registrability depend on use. However, actual use of a trademark shall not be a condition for filing an application for registration.

In addition, paragraph 1 of the same Article contains, *inter alia*, the following provision:

> Where signs are not inherently capable of distinguishing the relevant goods or services, Members may make registrability depend on distinctiveness acquired through use.

Although these provisions do not compel use, they make it plain that use is a **2.08** means of both obtaining some trade marks and also for maintaining the registration of all trade marks. But why has use become so fundamental a concept in trade mark law? In this regard, Bodenhausen says the following:

> The working of a patent in a country may be in the public interest but this is not necessarily true with respect to the use of a trademark in such country, because it is, in principle, a matter of indifference whether goods are sold under a certain trademark or not. Nevertheless, many countries require in their national legislation that trademarks be used, in order to prevent the trademark register becoming clogged with unused marks which preclude the valid

registration of identical or similar marks which are used or intended to be used.[6]

2.09 Much the same logic was followed more than sixty years later[7] in EC Directive 89/104, in which one of the recitals in the preamble reads as follows:

> Whereas in order to reduce the total number of trade marks registered and protected in the Community and, consequently, the number of conflicts which arise between them, it is essential to require that registered trade marks must actually be used or, if not used, be subject to revocation . . .[8]

2.10 In short, there are two main arguments in favour of the obligatory use of trade marks. The first is of a predominantly administrative nature: unused trade marks should not unnecessarily burden trade-mark-granting authorities in the maintenance of their registers. The second argument, mentioned by Bodenhausen, is of a more substantive value from the economic standpoint: unused trade marks should not be allowed because they ought to be available for those who would be actually willing to use them. The availability of words and other distinctive symbols that are potentially useful as trade marks plays an important role in enhancing consumer decision-making, as has been convincingly shown in Landes and Posner's economic analysis of trade marks.[9] Clearly, the requirement of use reduces the number of registered trade marks and thus results in significantly more trade marks being available for others.

2.11 While this logic can be accepted, the claim made in the recital of the EC Directive 89/104 cited above, i.e. that the use requirement may reduce the number of conflicts, does not seem to be convincing. Signs may, of course, be in use without being registered as trade marks; such practice is indeed widespread. However, the fact that signs are not examined in the registration procedure does not necessarily imply a reduction in the number of conflicts.

---

[6] ibid.

[7] As noted above, the provision cited above was introduced into the Convention at the Revision Conference in The Hague in 1925; ibid.

[8] First Council Directive (89/104/EEC) of 21 December 1988 to approximate the laws of the Member States relating to trade marks, OJ 1989 L 40.

[9] WM Landes and RA Posner *The Economic Structure of Intellectual Property Law* (Belknap Press Cambridge 2003) 172ff.

C. The Meaning of the Notion of Use

Having clarified the background to the justification of the obligation to use a **2.12** trade mark, the next question to be logically addressed is how the notion of 'use', or its counterpart, 'non-use', is actually defined.

Before considering this issue, however, it is necessary to make two remarks. **2.13** First, the terms 'requirement of use' and 'obligation to use' are used here as synonyms and thus interchangeably. However, neither the 'requirement' nor the 'obligation' implies a kind of a mandatory use; a trade mark owner is not actually obliged to use his trade mark although he may face sanctions, typically the revocation of his trade mark, if he has not used it for a certain period, which is five years in most countries. The fact that sanctions actually occur in the case of non-use has led some authors to conclude that the expression 'requirement of use' is to some extent misleading.[10]

Second, and more fundamental, is a point concerning the earlier discussion **2.14** of reasons behind making use a condition of registrability. It is already clear at this point that the registration of trade marks solely with the aim of preventing competitors from registering them is not deemed to constitute 'use' within the proper meaning of this term, regardless of how 'use' is defined. In other words, so-called 'stockpiling' is not permitted, though it is difficult to eliminate it,[11] especially in EU and other countries, where trade mark owners get an initial period, usually of five years after their registration, within which to commence the use of their trade marks. Moreover, stockpiling may lead to the making of registrations in bad faith; in Germany, for example such unused marks, known as *defensive* marks, are considered to be a restraint of competition and are thus deemed to be filed in bad faith, though bad faith must be proved on a case-by-case basis.[12] Much the same is true for United Kingdom.[13] On the other hand, Canada and the USA are fighting stockpiling by requiring the evidence on actual use of a registered trade mark whenever it

---

[10] JJ Bugge and PEP Gregersen 'Requirement of Use of Trade Marks' [2003] EIPR 309.
[11] Cornish and Llewelyn (n 2) 689.
[12] Fezer (n 1) 1506ff. In contrast, defensive registration of well-known marks, for classes of goods in which the proprietor did not intend to use them, was provided for under the United Kingdom's Trade Marks Act 1938. See Cornish and Llewelyn (n 2) 578.
[13] ibid 641ff.

ought to be renewed; this measure was initially proposed for the Community Trade Mark system, but was eventually abandoned.[14]

2.15 Returning to the notion of use, we will now seek to find out how the term 'use' is defined in trade mark law. Generally speaking, several types of definitions are available. A *positive definition* (roughly, a 'what is' type of definition) ought to be the most preferred, because it is usually very precise and thus least ambiguous. On the opposite side there is a *descriptive definition* (i.e. 'which comprises the following . . .'); the *negative definition* ('what is not') may be placed somewhere between them. Finally, there is of course also a possibility of having no definition at all, presumably whenever the subject matter of the definition is sufficiently elementary and/or self-explanatory.

2.16 Given the sheer importance of the obligation to use a trade mark, one could with good reason expect a clear, unambiguous *positive definition* of the *use* concept to prevail in trade mark law. However, it soon becomes apparent that this is not the case. In international law, such as the Paris Convention and the TRIPs Agreement, the term *use* is not defined at all; at national, and in Europe at the regional (Community) level, the *descriptive* approach clearly dominates the scene. Bearing in mind that Directive 89/104 has shaped the trade mark laws of all current twenty-five EU Member States, it makes sense to have a more detailed look at it.

2.17 Noticing that Article 10 of the Directive is entitled *Use of trade marks*, it seems plausible to expect that at least some guidance may be found in the provisions of this Article. In paragraph 1, it says that

> [I]f, within a period of five years . . . the proprietor has not put the trade mark into genuine use . . .

The next paragraph then, in essence, repeats provisions from the Paris Convention, i.e. that

> use of the trade mark in a form differing in elements which do not alter the distinctive character of the mark in the form in which it was registered,

as well as

> affixing the trade mark to goods or to the packaging thereof in the Member State concerned solely for export purposes

also constitute use within the meaning of paragraph 1.

---

[14] ibid 689ff.

This provision is curious. Despite the fact that some scholars consider it to be **2.18** *the* definition of use,[15] *use* is defined as taking place if there is *genuine use* of the trade mark by the proprietor (within the period of five years, counted from the date of completion of registration procedure). In plain language, the notion of use is defined by the word 'use', to which only the adjective 'genuine' is added. This is little help, if any.

It is thus necessary to look elsewhere. Indeed Article 5 of the Directive, **2.19** entitled *Rights conferred by a trade mark*, gives more useful guidance. According to paragraph 3 of this Article, the following may be, *inter alia*, prohibited whenever a sign which is identical or confusingly similar to the registered trade mark is used for identical or similar goods or services (and occasionally also for dissimilar goods or services, provided that certain further conditions set out in paragraph 2 are met):

  (a) affixing the sign to the goods or to the packaging thereof;
  (b) offering the goods, or putting them on the market or stocking them for these purposes under that sign, or offering or supplying services thereunder;
  (c) importing or exporting the goods under that sign;
  (d) using the sign on business papers and in advertising.

If these and other related acts constitute the unauthorized 'use in the course **2.20** of trade' necessary for infringement, it is reasonable to predict that the very same acts and dealings undertaken by any owner of a trade mark must be considered as a genuine use as well. Such an approach, using a positive type of description, is followed in the US Trademark Law:

> The term 'use in commerce' means the bona fide use of a mark in the ordinary course of trade, and not merely to reserve a right in a mark. For purposes of this Act, a mark shall be deemed to be in use in commerce—
>
> (1) on goods when—
>
>   (A) it is placed in any manner on the goods or their containers or the displays associated therewith or on the tags or labels affixed thereto, or if the nature of the goods makes such placement impracticable, then on documents associated with the goods or their sale, and
>   (B) the goods are sold or transported in commerce, and

---

[15] Compare Fezer (n 1) 1207.

> (2) on services when it is used or displayed in the sale or advertising of services and the services are rendered in commerce, or the services are rendered in more than one State or in the United States and a foreign country and the person rendering the services is engaged in commerce in connection with the services.[16]

2.21 Yet despite all these provisions, it is apparent that there is still some ambiguity, especially as far as Directive 89/104 is concerned. Recall that the acts listed above which may be prohibited by the owner of a trade mark is not exhaustive, as is indicated by the expression *inter alia*. On the other hand, considerable differences may exist in the way in which a particular trade mark is actually used. This naturally implies that some flexibility in this respect may even be desirable, as the overly strict definition could be too rigid for the rapidly evolving economy. Therefore it is hardly surprising that the issue of flexibility was explicitly raised in the USA during the discussions concerning the Trademark Law Revision Act of 1988 (the Lanham Act). The Senate and the Judiciary Committee stated in this respect that use was to be interpreted

> with flexibility so as to encompass various genuine but less traditional trademark uses, such as those made in test markets, infrequent sales of large or expensive items, or ongoing shipments of a new drug to clinical investigation by a company awaiting FDA approval and to preserve ownership rights in a mark, if, absent an intent to abandon, use of a mark is interrupted due to special circumstances.[17]

2.22 In the light of this, the most plausible conclusion seems to be that there is actually no special need to define the expression 'use' in a precise manner by reference to a positive type of definition. In fact, such an approach is nothing new in the area of intellectual property law. For example, there is no universal definition of what constitutes a well-known trade mark; the same is true, say, for the absence of a definition of what constitutes a patentable invention— only the main criteria which must be met in order to obtain patent protection, are listed.[18]

---

[16] §45 (15 USC §1127) of the US Trademark Law available at http://www.uspto.gov/web/offices/tac/tmlaw2.html.

[17] Bugge and Gregersen (n 10) fn 21 at 311.

[18] Compare art 27(1) of the TRIPs Agreement, according to which '. . . patents shall be available for any inventions, whether products or processes, in all fields of technology, provided that they are new, involve an inventive step and are capable of industrial application'.

Before concluding this section, a few words should be said about the concept **2.23** of non-use. As before, at first impression it appears that there is very little to say in this respect: non-use apparently reflects the simple fact that a trade mark is not, or has not been, used. However, the discussion above shows that the concept of use is ambiguous, which enables it to be sufficiently flexible. Recall that Directive 89/104 says that, roughly speaking, 'use means genuine use'. Now, what can be considered 'genuine use'? Imagine that only advertising of a certain product bearing a registered trade mark takes place, but sales of the advertised product are negligible for a period of, say, more than five years; do the described circumstances warrant the conclusion that genuine use, rather than non-use, has taken place? Alternatively, is there any minimum quantity of a product in question that needs to be sold in order to be able to claim genuine use?

In other words, if we want to know what constitutes non-use, we have first to **2.24** clarify what constitutes 'genuine use'. The concept of 'genuine use' has been discussed to some detail by Bugge and Gregersen.[19] They first note that 'genuine use' may well be a narrower concept than 'usual marketing activities', the latter being used in Denmark to determine what constitutes the former. Next, while pointing to the fact that there is little material that could support such a restrictive interpretation,[20] they suggest that

> [W]hen assessing use, consideration should be given to customers, products and . . . usual marketing activities. As regards the intensity of use for the purpose of complying with the requirement concerning genuine use, this will depend on the nature of the goods and services in question. The product market may be very narrowly defined so that the demand for the sales intensity of, e.g., a special alcoholic liquor is moderate as compared to usual sales.[21]

The most likely conclusion then seems to be the following: unless there is a **2.25** clear-cut situation of absolute non-use of a trade mark, when not even a single act of any trading or marketing activity is taking place, non-use can be established only by assessing whether the acts undertaken constitute 'genuine use'.

---

[19] Bugge and Gregersen (n 10) 311ff.
[20] ibid.
[21] ibid.

D. The Impact of the Requirement of Use on Rights in Trade Marks

2.26 The next set of questions to consider concerns the conceptual relationship between use (or non-use) and what can be generally termed as the protectability (though some scholars find this an awkward word)[22] of trade marks.

2.27 In this respect, the first issue at hand is whether use may be stipulated as a condition for registration of a trade mark. At least since the TRIPs Agreement entered into force, the answer to this question is without any doubt negative. The relevant provision of Article 15(3) is more than clear: 'However, actual use of a trademark shall not be a condition for filing an application for registration.' This provision, which however does not rule out requiring use as a condition for *continued* existence of trade mark protection, was of particular relevance in the USA because its position was, until 1988, unique among the industrialized countries, since the use of a trade mark had been required as a condition for registration.[23] The reform of the Lanham Act in 1988 then generally permitted the filing of trade mark applications for unused signs provided, however, that an Intent to Use declaration is filed together with the application.[24] This declaration must also be filed where an application is made under the provisions of the Madrid Protocol Agreement, to which the USA has been a Contracting Party since 2 November 2003. Bearing in mind the problems of possible stockpiling, discussed above, one may indeed wonder why the practice in the USA has not found a more widespread acceptance, especially when considering yet another provision in Article 15(3) of the TRIPs Agreement, i.e. that at least three years must elapse from the filing date before an application can be refused 'solely on the ground that the intended use has not taken place'.

2.28 Next, there is the issue of maintaining the validity of the trade mark registration. Again taking the TRIPs Agreement as the yardstick, a distinction between the provisions in Articles 15 and 19 needs to be observed. Article 15, quoted above, deals with the *intent to use* a trade mark: at least three years

---

[22] Chisum and Jacobs (n 3) 5–11.
[23] A Kur 'The International Trademark System Before and After TRIPs', in F-K Beier and G Schricker (eds), *From GATT to TRIPs* (VCH Weinheim 1996) 102ff.
[24] ibid.

must elapse before an *application* for a trade mark may be refused solely on the grounds that this has not taken place. As explained above, this provision has been applied only in the USA. On the other hand, Article 19 deals with the *maintenance of registration*, and in essence repeats the provisions of Article 5, Section C of the Paris Convention, which is itself incorporated into the TRIPs Agreement by virtue of its Article 2(1). Article 19 says that:

> [I]f use is required to maintain a registration, the registration may be cancelled only after an interrupted period of at least three years of non-use, unless valid reasons based on the existence of obstacles to such use are shown by the trademark owner.

This term is in the EU Member States (and also in many other countries) set **2.29** to five years, and is universally applicable from the 'completion of the registration procedure'.[25] In other words, in Europe there is no distinction made between the period related to the *intent to use*, and the period related to the *maintenance of registration*. It is not easy to find out why this approach has been chosen; while it is certainly less complex than the US approach, it is not necessarily equally effective in preventing stockpiling and possible applications in bad faith.

Whatever the reasons are, another question arises as to how to calculate the **2.30** date from which the five-year period begins to run. In other words, it is important to determine what is meant by the phrase 'completion of the registration procedure' in the Directive. The general rule seems to be that the period runs from the date of the registration of a trade mark, or as of the date of final decision, if an opposition against registration has been filed. This is the approach taken, for example, in Germany[26] and the United Kingdom,[27] and also by the Office for Harmonization in the Internal Market (OHIM), but not necessarily in Denmark, where an opposition can be filed up to two months after registration.[28]

Another issue relating to the calculation of the five-year period is whether **2.31** there is a deadline before which the genuine use must be started in order to prevent possible sanctions for non-use. Article 12(1) of the Directive

---

[25] Council Directive 89/104 art 10(1).
[26] Fezer (n 1) 1268.
[27] Cornish and Llewelyn (n 2) fn 46 on p 690.
[28] Bugge and Gregersen (n 10) 310.

unambiguously requires a *continuous* period of use of five years, provided that there are no legitimate reasons for non-use. This implies that, in principle, the genuine use may commence, or resume, as the case may be, just before the expiry of the five-year period. In fact, this period is extended by the following provision, which is also part of the first paragraph of Article 12 of the Directive:

> However, no person may claim that the proprietor's rights in a trade mark should be revoked where, during the interval between expiry of the five-year period and filing of the application for revocation, genuine use of the trade mark has been started or resumed; the commencement or resumption of use within a period of three months preceding the filing of the application of the revocation which began at the earliest on expiry of the continuous period of five years of non-use, shall, however, be disregarded where preparations for the commencement or resumption occur only after the proprietor becomes aware that the application for revocation may be filed . . .

2.32 While this provision may obviously be justified in case of resumed use, it is less convincing in the case of the first commencement of a trade mark use, given all the above discussed problems of stockpiling and registrations made in bad faith. At least, the initial period for beginning the use could be shorter. This is the case in the USA, where this period can be at maximum three years, in accordance with the provision of Article 15(3) of the TRIPs Agreement.[29]

2.33 The last question in this context is: which reasons may be considered to be legitimate for excusing non-use? This is clearly a highly relevant issue in calculating the actual period of non-use. Some guidance in this respect can be found in Article 19 of the TRIPs Agreement:

> Circumstances arising independently of the will of the owner of the trademark which constitute an obstacle to the use of the trademark, such as import restrictions on or other government requirements for goods or services protected by the trademark, shall be recognized as valid reasons for non-use.

2.34 However, the reader must again be warned that this seemingly logical and self-explanatory provision is actually not so simple, as it allows different interpretations. For example the Portuguese Industrial Property Office accepts a wide interpretation, that any matter not directly attributable to the trade mark owner is considered to be a proper reason for non-use. In contrast

---

[29] Kur (n 23) 102.

is the narrower approach followed in most other European countries, where a proper reason is an act or event beyond control or influence of the trade mark owner, such as fire, acts of God, war or a governmental intervention, but not, say, a reorganization of a company, according to one Swedish case.[30]

The last issue worthy of mention, albeit briefly, concerns the impact of **2.35** (genuine) use on enforcement issues. If a registered trade mark is genuinely used, this issue is not an issue at all. However, the story is different where there is non-use. The mere fact that a non-used trade mark is not revoked under the provisions of Article 12 (which may quite often be the case) and thus remains on the register, does not automatically allow its owner to undertake a legal action against a later conflicting mark. This is the subject-matter of Article 11 of Directive 89/104. Paragraph 1 of this Article is mandatory and thus has had to be incorporated into the national legislation of all of the EU Member States. In essence, this paragraph provides that a later trade mark may not be declared invalid on the ground that there is an earlier conflicting trade mark if the latter does not fulfill the requirements of use. Paragraph 2 further provides that the registration of a later trade mark may not be refused on the ground that there is an earlier conflicting trade mark if the earlier mark does not fulfil the requirements of use. However, this second provision is not mandatory and it is left to each Member State to decide whether to adopt it as part of its national law. Germany, for example, adopted it in its *Markengesetz*[31] while Slovenia, an EU Member State since 1 May 2004, has not adopted it in its Law on Industrial Property.[32]

E. Exceptions from the Use Requirement

While the requirement of use has spread into virtually all jurisdictions **2.36** worldwide, there is an exception to the rule as far as well-known and famous trade marks are concerned. To be sure, this exception is rapidly becoming more and more relevant in a modern global economy in which an increasing number of trade marks can be considered to be well known.

---

[30] Bugge and Gregersen (n 10) 316.
[31] Fezer (n 1) 1439.
[32] The English translation of the Slovene Law on Industrial Property may be found at the website of the Slovenian Intellectual Property Office, available at http://www.uil-sipo.si.

2.37 In principle it is not difficult to justify the exception. If a foreign trade mark is at a certain point in time already known, but not yet genuinely used, then its registration by a person other than its true (foreign) owner would be an act of misappropriation of a trade mark having a reputation abroad;[33] and it would also amount to a restraint of competition, which would negatively affect potential foreign competitors.[34] This undoubtedly justifies Article 6*bis* of the Paris Convention,[35] which accords additional protection to well-known marks by refusing or cancelling their registration and by prohibiting the use of a trade mark

> which constitutes a reproduction, an imitation, or a translation, liable to create confusion, of a mark considered by the competent authority of the country of registration or use to be well known in that country . . .

2.38 Bodenhausen makes clear that:

> A trademark may be well known in a country before its registration there and, in view of the possible repercussions of publicity in other countries, even before it is used in such country.[36]

The fact that protection must be accorded, even when an actual use has not taken place, has been recently strongly emphasized by Mostert:

> There is a strong body of opinion that a well-known mark need not actually have been used in the jurisdiction in which protection is sought.[37]

The author supports the statement with an impressive list of documents and judgments in a footnote of almost two pages in length which is attached to it.

2.39 Given the basic justification expounded above, the exception from the use requirement is, *prima facie*, a logical and inseparable part of the additional protection as accorded to well-known marks under Article 6*bis* of the Paris Convention and its extension in paragraphs 2 and 3 of Article 16 of the TRIPs Agreement. However, two important, and mutually related, questions are still left open in this respect.

---

[33] Compare Cornish and Llewelyn (n 2) 641ff.
[34] Compare Fezer (n 1) 1508ff.
[35] This Article was introduced into the Convention at the Revision Conference in The Hague in 1925. See Bodenhausen (n 5) 91.
[36] ibid.
[37] FW Mostert, *Famous and Well-Known Marks* (INTA New York 2004) §§1–33 to 1–34.

First, it should be remembered that well-known marks (in much the same **2.40** way as there is not straightforward definition of the notion of 'use') are not defined in a straightforward manner. Rather, only a number of criteria are available. Mostert says that:

> [S]ets of guidelines which can assist trademark authorities and courts in deter-mining whether a mark is famous or well-known have emerged in regional and national legislation, case law, and trademark procedures.

He again offers a solid body of evidence that supports his view.[38] Article *6bis* of the Paris Convention contains a simple yet extremely vague guideline: a mark is a well-known mark if it is so considered by the competent authorities. It is then no wonder that the TRIPs Agreement went a bit further, by adding, *inter alia*, the following provision in Article 16(2):

> In determining whether a trademark is well-known, Members shall take into account of the knowledge of the trademark in the relevant sector of the public, including knowledge in the Member concerned which has been obtained as a result of the promotion of the trademark.

Apart from noting *in passim* that promotion would most probably be con- **2.41** sidered as a normal type of 'use', the added criterion is also ambiguous unless the meaning of 'relevant sector of the public' is also known. This issue was addressed by WIPO in its Joint Recommendation concerning Provisions on the Protection of Well-Known Marks of 1999.[39] According to Article 2(2) of this Recommendation,

> (a) Relevant sectors of the public shall include, but shall not necessarily be limited to . . . (iii) business circles dealing with the type of goods and/or services to which the mark applies . . . (b) Where a mark is determined to be known in at least one relevant sector of the public in a Member State, the mark shall be considered by the Member State to be a well-known mark.

In the modern world of the internet and global trade, there is little doubt that **2.42** almost every mark for a given type of goods or services may be known to business circles dealing with the goods in question. Accordingly, if the above criteria are strictly applied, all trade marks may sooner or later qualify as well-known marks. In other words, what was clearly meant to be an exception in 1925, when Article *6bis* was introduced into the Paris Convention, may

---

[38] ibid §1–13.
[39] WIPO Publication no 833 (Geneva 2000).

under recent additional criteria become a rule. If so, then literally any conclusion about possible consequences can be drawn, even the most extreme that the requirement of use may, at least on the international level, become completely irrelevant, despite playing a central role in (national) trade mark law.

2.43 It would make little sense to predict implications that could be imagined on the basis of this admittedly speculative reasoning; however, it should not be misinterpreted as an argument that the exception concerning the use of well-known marks has no justification. Rather, the main message is that significantly more work needs to be done towards further clarification and elaboration of a number of aspects of well-known marks and, on this basis, to strive for a harmonization of relevant law on the international level. For example, one could consider the idea of introducing a time limit necessary for a well-known trade mark to be put to a 'genuine use' in any country, where one or more attempts have been made by third parties to register it, but have (fortunately) failed through the proper application of Article 6*bis* of the Paris Convention. Currently, there is only the provision for the time limit of at least five years, during which the cancellation of the conflicting trade mark may be requested;[40] however, no time limit is set for the period during which the 'genuine use' of the well-known mark should commence. In fact, the absence of such or similar type of provision in the relevant international law is the second question that seems appropriate to be addressed.

2.44 In short, the exception to the use requirement for well-known marks is certainly justified and consistent with the basic rationale for protecting them, as embedded in the international law. The problem, however, is how the notion of well-known mark itself is going to evolve. Despite all the emerging guidelines, there is still a lot to be said about well-known marks and their impact, first, on international trade and global competition, and then on trade mark law on both national and international levels.

F. Concluding Remarks

2.45 The notion of use and non-use is not only an essential feature of trade mark law: it is *the* feature of trade mark law. Although at first what constitutes use

---

[40] para 2 of art 6*bis* of the Paris Convention.

may seem simple and unambiguous, the basic conclusion that may be drawn from this chapter is that the situation is just the opposite. The concepts of use, non-use and genuine use are complex and highly sophisticated legal topics for which no precise definition is available. Equally, such a definition is not necessarily desirable as it may easily become too rigid and/or obsolete in a rapidly changing world where every day new ways of sales, marketing and commerce are developed and applied. This means that the issue must be left to its own dynamics of further development and refinement. Given the global nature of the modern world, most future activities in this respect should preferably take place at the international level, so that the uniformity of developed concepts, rules and standards will prevail worldwide.

3

THE NEED TO LEAVE FREE FOR OTHERS TO USE AND THE TRADE MARK COMMON

Jennifer Davis

A. The Development and Nature of the Trade Mark Common in English Law   3.06

B. The ECJ Doctrine that Signs should be Kept Free for Others to Use   3.12

C. The ECJ and 'Need to Keep Free': Why has the Court not Developed a Commons Theory?   3.18

D. Conclusion: The Balance Between Leaving Marks Free for Others to Use and Recognizing Distinctiveness Acquired through Use   3.25

In 1913 the 'motor car dealers and motor car proprietors' W. and G. du Cros **3.01** Ltd sought to register the letters W&G both in fancy script and in block capitals as trade marks in the United Kingdom.[1] The applicants had carried on business for many years both as car dealers and cab proprietors: indeed, they had 1300 cabs which were in use in and round London. The script mark was carried on doors, radiators and on the caps of the company's drivers. It was used in advertisements and the company was known to 'police and public' as W&G. The applications eventually reached the House of

---

[1] *W. & G. du Cros Ld's Application* (1913) 30 RPC 661. Trade mark registration was introduced into England by the 1875 Trade Mark Act. Letters became registrable for the first time under the Trade Mark Act 1905, provided they were 'adapted to distinguish' (s 9(5)); that is, 'adapted to distinguish the goods of the applicant for the registration from the goods of other persons'. However, under a Proviso to s 9, a mark which was adjudged not initially adapted to distinguish could be registered 'to the extent to which actual user has rendered the mark in fact distinctive'.

Lords, where they were refused on the grounds that they lacked the initial distinctiveness required for registration. In his famous speech, Lord Parker set out the grounds upon which his decision was based:

> The applicant's chance of success in this respect must, I think, largely depend upon whether other traders are likely, in the ordinary course of their business and without any improper motive, to desire to use the same mark, or some mark nearly resembling it, upon or in connection with their own goods. It is apparent from the history of Trade Marks in this country that both the Legislature and the Courts have always shown a natural disinclination to allow any person to obtain by registration under the Trade Marks Act a monopoly in what others may legitimately desire to use.[2]

In this case, he noted:

> There seems to be no doubt that any individual or firm may legitimately desire in the ordinary course of trade to use a mark consisting of his or their own initials upon, or in connection with, his or their goods.

As a result, according to Lord Parker,

> I cannot think that the mark 'W. and G.,' whether in script or in block type, is in itself distinctive within the meaning of the Act.[3]

3.02 Almost a century later, Libertel applied to the Benelux-Merkenbureau (the Benelux Trade Marks Office) to register the colour orange as a trade mark for telecommunications equipment, without proof of acquired distinctiveness.[4] A key question which was eventually posed to the European Court of Justice (ECJ) was whether a colour was precluded from registration under Article

---

[2] *W. & G. du Cros* (n 1) 671–672.

[3] *W. & G. du Cros* (n 1) 672. Before the passage of the 1994 Trade Marks Act, the English courts drew a distinction between marks which were capable in fact of distinguishing the goods of one trader from those of another and could be registered and trade marks which while they might be distinctive in fact, were incapable of distinguishing in 'law'. Marks which were incapable in law of distinguishing, included certain descriptive marks, and other marks which the courts believed, as in the case of *W. & G. du Cros*, other traders might 'desire' to use without 'improper motive'. Later cases, such as *Re Yorkshire Copper Works Ltd's Application for a Trade Mark* (1953) 71 RPC 150 and *YORK Trade Mark* [1984] RPC 231 as per Lord Wilberforce at 254, elaborate this distinction more fully. This principle as it was developed by the English courts will be considered later in this article. For a fuller discussion, see J Davis 'European Trade Mark Law and the Enclosure of the Commons' [2002] IPQ 342–367.

[4] *Libertel Groep BV v Benelux-Merkenbureau* Case C-104/01 [2003] ETMR 63.

3(1)(b) of the Trade Marks Directive on the grounds that it lacked distinctive character.[5] The ECJ noted that:

> As regards the registration as trade marks of colours per se, not spatially delimited, the fact that the number of colours actually available is limited means that a small number of trade mark registrations for certain services or goods could exhaust the entire range of colours available. Such a monopoly would be incompatible with a system of undistorted competition, in particular because it could have the effect of creating an unjustified competitive advantage for a single trader.[6]

It went on that, in the case of a colour *per se*,

> distinctiveness without prior use is inconceivable save in exceptional circumstances[7]

and concluded that:

> In assessing the potential distinctiveness of a colour as a trade mark, regard must be had to the general interest in not unduly restricting the availability of colours for other traders who offer for sale goods or services of the same type as those in respect of which registration is sought.[8]

The symmetry between these two cases, decided in vastly different political **3.03** and economic climates, and under entirely different legal regimes, is more than superficial. In both cases, the courts were asked to decide whether the marks at issue had sufficient inherent distinctiveness to be registrable. In both cases the marks, letters and a colour, belonged to a category of signs which, because of their limited availability, the courts decided should be left available for other traders to use. On that basis both courts determined that such marks should not ordinarily be registered without acquired distinctiveness: in effect that they lacked 'inherent' distinctive character. But there were also, not surprisingly, crucial differences between the reasoning in the two cases. In *W. & G. du Cros*, Lord Parker added that there were, by the same reasoning,

---

[5] First Council Directive 89/104/EEC of 21 December 1988 to approximate the laws of the Member States relating to trade marks. Article 3 of the Directive concerns grounds for refusal or invalidity. Article 3(1)(b) refuses registration to 'trade marks which are devoid of distinctive character' unless, under Article 3(3), such marks have acquired distinctive character through use.

[6] *Libertel* (n 4) para 54.

[7] *Libertel* (n 4) para 66: for instance where the number of goods or services for which the mark is claimed is very restricted and the relevant market very specific.

[8] *Libertel* (n 4) para 78.

certain signs which, even if they acquired distinctiveness through use, would never be registrable. The courts or the Registrar may be influenced by the acquired distinctiveness of a mark to allow its registration, but 'distinctiveness in fact is not conclusive'[9] of its entitlement to be registered. Lord Parker's reasoning may be contrasted with the conclusion of the ECJ in *Libertel*, where the ECJ held that colour marks may be found to possess distinctive character provided that they are perceived by the public as capable of identifying the goods and services for which registration is sought as originating from a particular undertaking.[10]

3.04 The decision in *W. & G. du Cros* marked an important milestone in the development of two overriding principles of English trade mark law that maintained their status until the implementation of the Directive. The first was that the public interest demanded that certain signs should be left free for others to use unless there was evidence of acquired distinctiveness. The second was the definition of a more limited category of signs which should never be registered, even with evidence of distinctiveness: this was what the courts came to define as an 'English language common'.[11] *Libertel* itself marks the culmination of a number of cases in the course of which the ECJ has developed an interpretation of the Directive[12] which also recognizes a public interest in leaving certain signs free for others to use. But, at the same time, it has rejected the notion that there should remain a protected 'common' of signs that are too valuable to be monopolized by a single trader, preferring instead to reward use that results in an otherwise unregistrable sign being perceived as an indication of origin with its registration as a trade mark.

3.05 The first part of this chapter will briefly examine the development and nature of the trade mark 'common' in English law. The second part will examine how the ECJ came to develop the idea of signs which should be left free. The third part of this chapter will identify the apparent conflict between the need to protect such signs and the fact that, under the Directive, signs with

---

[9] *W. & G. du Cros* (n 1) 673.

[10] *Libertel* (n 4) para 69.

[11] The English language common as it was shaped by the English courts also came to include shapes. For example, *Coca Cola Trade Marks* [1986] RPC 421 (HL). Davis (n 3) 351–356, and see below.

[12] The law regulating the Community Trade Mark (CTM) has been interpreted in the same way as the Directive, Council Regulation (EC) No. 40/94 of 20 December 1993 on the Community trade mark.

distinctiveness acquired through use may be registered. This chapter will conclude that, despite its inability to develop a protected 'common' of socially useful signs, the ECJ has nonetheless sought to reconcile the diverse public interests in keeping certain signs free for others to use and rewarding distinctiveness acquired through use with registration.

A. The Development and Nature of the Trade Mark Common in English Law

In 1909, Sir Herbert Cozens-Hardy MR made his famous comment con- **3.06** cerning an application for the registration of the descriptive word 'perfection' for soap. In rejecting the application, he stated:

> Wealthy traders are habitually eager to enclose part of the great common of the English language and to exclude the general public of the present day and of the future from access to the enclosure.[13]

However, the case which perhaps most clearly demarcated the boundaries of **3.07** the English trade mark common is the *YORKSHIRE COPPER* trade mark application in 1953, which concerned the registration of a geographical name.[14] The applicants sought to register the word 'Yorkshire' for various copper products. Initially refused, the application reached the House of Lords.

It was accepted by all parties that the mark lacked sufficient distinctiveness to **3.08** be registered without evidence of use.[15] There was similar concurrence that the mark had in fact acquired 100 per cent factual distinctive through use. However, the Court found that it was nonetheless incapable in law of being registered: although it was *in fact* adapted to distinguish the applicant's goods, it was not *inherently* adapted to do so.[16] Following *W. & G. du Cros*, the Court confirmed the Registrar's discretion to refuse the registration of factually distinctive marks, if to do so would be against the public interest.

---

[13] *Joseph Crosfield & Sons Ltd's Application* (1909) 26 RPC 837 at 854 (*PERFECTION*).

[14] *YORKSHIRE COPPER* (n 3).

[15] Under the Trade Marks Act 1938, s 9 allowed marks to be placed on Part A of the Register if they were *prima facie* distinctive. Other marks, including certain laudatory epithets, geographical names and ordinary surnames, could be registered on Part B of the Register if it could be shown that they were either inherently capable of distinguishing and were in fact capable of distinguishing (ie through use) (s 10, s 9(2), s 9(3)(a–b)).

[16] These words are taken from s 9(3) of the Trade Marks Act 1938.

Lord Simonds took the view that a descriptive word, in this case a geographic name 'is prima facie denied registrability'. It could only be 'inherently adapted to distinguish the goods of A when you can predicate of it that is such a name as it would never occur to B to use in respect of his similar goods'. Lord Simonds conceded that 'there will probably be border-line cases' but, in this instance, there was 'no doubt on which side of the border lies Yorkshire, a county not just of broad acres but of great manufacturing cities'.[17] He then stated:

> For, just as a manufacturer is not entitled to a monopoly of a laudatory or descriptive epithet, so he is not to claim for his own territory, whether country, county or town, which may be in the future, if it is not now, the seat of manufacture of goods similar to his own.[18]

3.09 Just as broadly descriptive words such as 'perfection' belonged in the English language common, so too did certain geographic names. In *Coca Cola*, the House of Lords confirmed that it took a similar approach towards shape marks. In rejecting an application for the shape of the Coca Cola bottle, again acknowledged to be factually distinctive, Lord Templeman stated that the application was

> another attempt to expand the boundaries of intellectual property and to convert a protective law into a source of monopoly.[19]

3.10 The idea of a common may be a particularly apt metaphor in relation to trade marks, for it is easy to envisage a public domain of symbols from which trade marks may be drawn.[20] The English courts were however drawing the boundaries of a particular type of common, which had three defining attributes. First, it was a protected domain of words (and shapes) to which the

---

[17]   *YORKSHIRE COPPER* (n 3) 154.

[18]   ibid.

[19]   *Coca Cola* (n 11) 456.

[20]   A seminal article in this regard was D Lange 'Recognising the Public Domain' [1981] 44 Law & Contemporary Problems 147. See also D Lange 'Reimagining the Public Domain' [2003] 66 Law & Contemporary Problems 463. Recently the commons metaphor has been more frequently applied by academics to the issue of copyright protection and the internet. See for example J Boyle, 'The Second Enclosure Movement and the Construction of the Public Domain' [2003] 66 Law & Contemporary Problems 33. Also L Lessig *The Future of Ideas: the Fate of the Commons in a Connected World* (Random House New York 2001). However, the idea of a trade mark commons has had some longevity in judicial thinking. See for example, the reference to Cozens-Hardy MR by Advocate General Jacobs in *Procter & Gamble v OHIM* Case C-383/99 [2001] ETMR 75 and recently by Jacob J in *Re Nichols plc* [2003] RPC 16.

public had a continuing right of access. This was the case whether or not the signs which belonged in the common were in fact acting as trade marks in the market or were at the time desired by other traders. Second, it was a common in which various groups were recognized to have equal and often conflicting interests. Thus, in PERFECTION, the Court of Appeal identified various competing interests in the common. Cozens-Hardy MR identified the division as between wealthy traders and the general public. Farwell LJ saw the application as

> a bold attempt by a wealthy firm to deprive their competitors great and small of the use of the laudatory term common to all.[21]

Such a sentiment was echoed in the *W. & G. du Cros* and YORKSHIRE cases. **3.11** Indeed, the English courts identified at least three different groups who had an interest in the common: the applicant (sometimes a 'wealthy trader'), other traders (both great and small) and the general public.[22] Finally, the need to protect the common was predicated upon the assumption that trade mark registration endowed a monopoly, but that certain important symbols must be protected *tout court* from the rights accorded by registration. The following section will examine how the ECJ developed the doctrine, embodied in the Trade Marks Directive (and the Community Trade Mark Regulation), that certain signs should be left free for others to use.

B. The ECJ Doctrine that Signs should be Kept Free for Others to Use

Articles 3(1)(b)–(d) of the Trade Marks Directive[23] define those categories of **3.12** signs which cannot be registered without acquired distinctiveness (Article 3(3)). The European case law to date has been primarily concerned with marks which are devoid of distinctive character (Article 3(1)(b)) and with descriptive marks, including geographical names (Article 3(1)(c)).[24] Through

---

[21] PERFECTION (n 13) at 863.
[22] See for example *Elvis Presley Trade Marks* [1997] RPC 543, and most recently Jacob J in *Re Nichols* (n 20) para 14 and below.
[23] Also art 5(1)(b)–(d) of the CTM Regulation.
[24] art 3(1)(d) concerns trade marks which consist exclusively of signs or indications which have become customary in the current language or in the *bona fide* and established practices of the trade. See *Merz & Krell GmbH & Co's Trade Mark Application* Case C-517/99 [2002] ETMR 21, concerning a mark which was 'customary in the current language'. In this case, the applicant sought to register the mark BRAVO for writing implements.

a number of judgments, the ECJ has made it clear that Article 3(1)(b)–(e) should be understood as reflecting a public interest in ensuring that certain signs are left free for other traders to use. Most notably these cases have involved (i) signs, such as colours, which because of their limited availability are easily monopolized and (ii) geographical or descriptive words, which other traders may, without improper motive, wish to apply to their own goods or services. This section will look first at descriptive signs and then at signs which are devoid of distinctive character.

3.13 The seminal case for this understanding of Article 3 in relation to descriptive signs is undoubtedly *Windsurfing*.[25] The applicants sought to register CHIEMSEE, the name of a Bavarian lake and a popular tourist attraction, for clothing. The pertinent question addressed to the ECJ by the German court was what requirements must be met under Article 3(3) in order for a mark to have acquired distinctive character through use. In particular, the question was raised whether the refusal to register a sign under Article 3(1)(c), without acquired distinctiveness, depends upon whether there is a real, current or serious need to leave that sign free.[26] In its judgment, the ECJ noted that the public interest behind Article 3(1)(c) is to ensure that descriptive signs or geographical indications relating to the relevant category of goods in respect of which registration is applied for may be freely used by all.[27] It then went on to hold that Article 3(1)(c) not only prohibits the registration of geographical names as trade marks where they already designate places which the public identifies with the relevant goods, but also geographical names which are liable to be so identified in the future.[28] On the question of acquired distinctiveness, however, the court ruled that no stricter test can be applied by

---

[25] *Windsurfing Chiemsee Produktions- und Vertriebe GmbH v Boots- und Segelzubehör Walter Huber and Franz Attenberger* Joined Cases C-108/97 and C-109/97 [1999] ETMR 585.

[26] The German courts have developed the principle of *Freihaltbedürfnis*, which essentially holds that geographical names should not be registered if there is a 'real, current or serious need to leave them free'. See *Windsurfing* (n 25) 549.

[27] *Windsurfing* (n 25) para 595.

[28] This goes further than the principle of *Freihaltbedürfnis* since the emphasis is not just on current use, but also future use by other traders, and coincides more closely with the reasoning in *W. & G. du Cros*. It is for the relevant authorities to assess whether it is reasonable to assume that such a sign is capable of acting in this descriptive manner in the future: *Windsurfing* (n 25) para 37. For an elaboration of the reasoning in *Windsurfing* in relation to signs which serve to designate the geographical origin of goods, see the CFI decision in *Nordmilch eG v OHIM* Case T-295/01 [2004] ETMR 70, which concerned an application to register the word OLDENBURGER as a CTM for, *inter alia*, milk and dairy products.

reference to the perceived importance of keeping the geographical name free for others to use.[29]

A number of cases, following *Windsurfing*, affirmed and refined the principle **3.14** that descriptive signs, in the absence of acquired distinctiveness, should in the public interest be left free for others to use. Decided in 2003, *Linde* concerned the registration of the actual shape of goods, themselves, as trade marks, namely a forklift truck, a torch and a wrist watch.[30] The ECJ confirmed that, in considering such trade marks *qua* descriptive marks, the public interest underlying Article 3(1)(c) implies that:

> subject to Art.3(3), any trade mark which consists exclusively of a sign or indication which may serve to designate the characteristics of goods or a service within the meaning of that provision must be freely available to all and not registrable.[31]

In the recent case of *Wrigley*,[32] the ECJ further delineated the criteria for **3.15** denying registration for descriptive marks, in this case under Article 7 of the CTM Regulation (equivalent to Article 3 of the Directive). The applicants had sought to register the word DOUBLEMINT for chewing gum as a CTM. Initially refused registration, the applicant's appeal reached the ECJ. In its judgment, the ECJ clarified the circumstances in which Article 7 would apply by revisiting *Windsurfing*. It noted, following *Windsurfing*, that a term does not have to be in current descriptive use to be precluded from registration. Instead, a reasonable apprehension that it may be so used in the future suffices. On the particular facts of the case before it, the court held that the fact that more than one term can be used to describe the characteristics of particular goods does not mean that those terms cease to be descriptive.[33]

It may be remembered that *W. & G. du Cros* and subsequent English cases[34] **3.16** addressed not descriptive marks, but rather marks that were not inherently distinctive and which were in limited supply. *W. & G. du Cros* held that, in relation to such marks, there was a public interest in leaving them free for

---

[29] *Windsurfing* (n 25) para 54.
[30] *Linde AG v Deutsches Patent- und Markenamt* Joined Cases C-53/01 to C-55/01 [2003] RPC 45.
[31] *Linde* (n 30) para 74.
[32] *OHIM v Wm Wrigley Jr Company* (DOUBLEMINT) [2004] RPC 18.
[33] ibid para 25.
[34] For instance, *Coca Cola* (n 11).

other traders to use. In *Linde*, the ECJ observed that each of the grounds for refusal listed in Article 3(1) is independent of the others and calls for separate examination.[35] In addition, each must be interpreted in light of the particular public interest which underlies it.[36] When considering signs that are deemed to be devoid of distinctive character, the ECJ has in a number of cases sought to define the public interest which lies behind refusing registration to such marks without proof of acquired distinctiveness. In the recent case of *Henkel* which concerned the registration of a CTM,[37] the ECJ observed that there was 'no public interest' in conferring the benefit of trade mark protection on a sign which

> does not fulfil its essential function, namely that of ensuring that the consumer or the end user can identify the origin of the product or service concerned by allowing him to distinguish that product or service from those emanating from a different origin without any risk of confusion.[38]

But the ECJ has also identified a more positive public interest in leaving certain signs, such as colours and shape of goods marks which are not inherently distinctive and which are in limited supply, free for others to use without proof of acquired distinctiveness.

3.17   Another question asked in *Linde* was whether it was legitimate to apply a higher test of distinctiveness to shape-of-goods marks under Article 3(1)(b) because there may be an interest in not allowing one undertaking to monopolize such shapes to the detriment of competitors or of consumers. The court answered that, in assessing distinctiveness under Article 3(1)(b), no stricter test could be applied than that used for other types of trade marks. But it also noted that since the public was unlikely to identify shape-of-goods marks as trade marks, this constituted grounds for denying such marks registration *ab initio*.[39] In later cases, most notably *Libertel*, the ECJ moved much

---

[35] *Linde* (n 30) para 67. For a discussion of the approach taken by the CFI to a mark which may be both descriptive and non-distinctive, see I Simon, 'What's Cooking at the CFI? More Guidance on Descriptive and Non-Distinctive Trade Marks' [2003] EIPR 322–326.

[36] *Linde* (n 30) para 73; see also *Koninklijke Philips Electronics NV v Remington Consumer Products Ltd* Case C-299/99 [2002] ETMR 955 para 77.

[37] *Henkel KGaA v OHIM* Joined Cases C-456/01P and C-457/01P [2004] ETMR 87.

[38] ibid para 48.

[39] *Linde* (n 30) para 48. In this case, the ECJ claimed to be following *Windsurfing*, but in fact the earlier case had been concerned only with descriptive marks and had held that they should not registered *ab initio* but, in assessing whether they had acquired distinctiveness following use, no higher criteria could be used than as applied to other non-distinctive marks.

closer to applying the same principles enunciated in *W. & G. du Cros* to its interpretation of Article 3(1)(b). There it held that it was precisely the limited supply of colour marks which meant that they should only be registered without acquired distinctiveness in exceptional circumstances. To allow otherwise would be to accord a monopoly which would be incompatible with a system of undistorted competition and give an unjustified advantage to a single trader.[40]

C. The ECJ and 'Need to Keep Free': Why has the Court not Developed a Commons Theory?

The trade mark common, as demarcated by the English courts, was a pro- **3.18** tected commons. Its development had been predicated upon the assumption, made by the courts, that a number of different and competing groups had an interest in the common. It was called into existence in large measure because the English courts believed that trade mark registration endowed a monopoly which might not only be anti-competitive but might also deprive the public more generally of access to a limited supply of socially useful signs.[41] In interpreting the Trade Marks Directive, the ECJ recognized that there are certain categories of signs which, in the public interest, should be left free for others to use both now and in the future. What it has not recognized is a core of protected signs which cannot under any circumstances be registered.[42] The reasons why the European trade mark regime does not (indeed, cannot)

---

[40] *Libertel* (n 4) para 54. The reasoning was followed both in *Henkel* which concerned an application to register a shape and colour mark for washing machine tablets as a CTM and in *Heidelberger Bauchemie GmbH* Case C-49/02 [2004] ETMR 99 which concerned an application to register a two-colour mark at the German Patent Office.

[41] Davis (n 3) 354–356.

[42] There is a limited category of signs which are not registrable on public interest grounds. These are set out in art 3 of the Directive. Most notably, they include certain shape marks and marks which are contrary to public policy or accepted principles of morality. In relation to the shape marks, it has been noted by the ECJ that the public interest behind this exclusion is that trade mark registration would be used to prevent shapes whose essential characteristics perform a technical function from being used by competitors, and hence to undermine competition: *Philips* (n 36) paras 78–79. It is possible, indeed likely, that these same shapes might be protected by other intellectual property rights, such as patents, at least initially. This was the case in *Philips*: see U Suthersanen 'The European Court of Justice in *Philips v Remington*— Trade Marks and Market Freedom' [2003] IPQ 257–283.

encompass a protected trade mark 'common' are to be found both in the substantive law and in the social and economic principles which shaped that law and the ways in which it has been interpreted.

3.19 Most obviously, Article 3(3) of the Directive has been interpreted in successive cases to mean that any marks identified in Articles 3(1)(b)–(d), whatever the apparent public interest in leaving them free for other traders, may be registered if they have acquired distinctiveness through use. This interpretation of the Directive was confirmed by the ECJ in *Philips v Remington*. In *Philips*, the English courts specifically asked the ECJ whether there remained, following the implementation of the Directive, a special class of signs which even though distinctive in fact, were nonetheless incapable of distinguishing as a matter of law. The ECJ held that there was not.[43] Since Article 3(1)(a) was intended to exclude from registration only those signs that are not capable of distinguishing, it followed, according to the ECJ, that there is no class of marks which have distinctive character either inherently or which have acquired distinctiveness through use, but which cannot be registered. The ECJ concluded:

> Article 3(3) therefore constitutes a major exception to the rule laid down in Art.3(1)(b),(c) and (d), whereby registration is to be refused in relation to trade marks which are devoid of any distinctive character, descriptive marks, and marks which consist exclusively of indications which have become customary in the current language or in the bona fide and established practices of the trade.[44]

3.20 The ECJ has emphasized the public interest concerns which underlie the absolute grounds for refusal of registration set out in Article 3(1)(b)–(d). It is, therefore, not surprising that the question has also been raised as to whether, in assessing acquired distinctiveness under Article 3(3), account should be taken of the extent of the need to keep certain marks free for others to use. In other words, should the degree of trade acceptance (or distinctiveness) necessary to satisfy Article 3(3) depend upon how important it is for the sign to be left free?[45] In fact, the ECJ has affirmed in a number of cases that it is not possible to apply stricter criteria in assessing whether descriptive signs or

---

[43] *Philips* (n 36) para 39.
[44] ibid para 45.
[45] *Windsurfing* (n 25) para 41.

other non-distinctive signs in limited supply have acquired sufficient distinct-iveness to be registered.[46] The Court has, however, acknowledged that as a practical matter it may be more difficult to demonstrate acquired distinctive-ness in relation to such signs, since, by definition, they are unlikely to be perceived by the public, in the first instance, as a badge of origin. As we have seen, such was the ECJ's reasoning in relation to shape marks in *Linde*.[47]

The substantive law of the Trade Marks Directive, in particular the effects of **3.21** Article 3(3) of the Directive, has not allowed the courts to recognize a core of protected signs. Furthermore, that law was adopted at a time when the idea that strong intellectual property rights enhanced rather than inhibited com-petition, particularly international competition, had become common cur-rency, at least among governments in the developed world.[48] However, it is submitted that the ECJ has not necessarily been consistent in its approach to whether trade marks should be given a wide or narrow penumbra of protec-tion. This inconsistency is most apparent if one looks not at the application of Article 3(3), but rather at those cases which have concerned the registrabil-ity of descriptive or non-distinctive signs without evidence of use. In BABY-DRY the ECJ seemed to accept that signs could be registered even if they had only a minimal level of distinctiveness.[49] In this case, it allowed the registra-tion as a Community trade mark of BABY-DRY for nappies, on the basis that Article 7(1)(c) was designed to exclude from registration only those signs which were purely descriptive. If, on the other hand, the descriptive com-ponents of a sign were presented in such as a way that the resultant whole could be distinguished from the usual way of designating the goods at issue, as was the case with BABY-DRY, it could be registered. In retrospect, it is clear that *BABY-DRY* represents, at least for the present, the high water mark of the protection afforded to minimally distinctive signs. In later cases, the ECJ has

---

[46] For example, *Windsurfing* (n 25) and *Linde* (n 30).

[47] *Linde* (n 30) para 48; see also *Libertel* (n 4) para 66. In *Windsurfing* (n 25) para 50, the ECJ concluded that in the case of a 'well-known geographical name' use would need to be both 'long-standing and intensive'.

[48] The recent move towards seeing strong intellectual property rights as an powerful asset in international trade has been convincingly documented in SK Sell *Private Power, Public Law: The Globalization of Intellectual Property Rights* (CUP Cambridge 2003). See also DM McClure 'Trade Marks and Competition: The Recent History' [1996] 95 Law and Con-temporary Problems 13–43.

[49] *Procter & Gamble v OHIM* Case C-299/99 [2002] ETMR 3 (*BABY-DRY*).

sought to hold back the tide, by returning to the reasoning in *Windsurfing*, explicitly so in the case of *Wrigley*.[50]

3.22   The question remains as to what extent the ECJ has been willing to recognize and hence to balance the different and conflicting interests which may be affected by a trade mark registration, something which we have argued was fundamental to the delineation of the English trade mark common. Clearly, the ECJ's freedom of action in this regard has been constrained by the market-led approach to trade mark registration embodied in Article 3(3) of the Directive, which determines that any sign which is acting as a trade mark, that is as a badge of origin in the market, can be registered. Furthermore, there has been some argument, put most forcefully by Advocate General Jacobs in his *BABY-DRY* opinion[51] and followed by the ECJ in its ruling, that allowing proprietors to appropriate even minimally distinctive signs did not unduly impede access to the public domain, since it is a defence to trade mark infringement if a third party uses the mark descriptively.[52] Not surprisingly it was an English judge, Jacob J, who presented what was perhaps the most cogent criticism of this view. He pointed out that such an approach inevitably favoured 'powerful traders', who will 'naturally assert their rights even in marginal cases'. Indeed, in such cases, he believed that:

> defendants, SMEs particularly, are likely to back off when they receive a letter before action. It is cheaper and more certain to do that than stand and fight, even if in principle they have a defence.[53]

3.23   It is submitted that, since *BABY-DRY*, the ECJ has backed away from the robust view of registration embodied in the judgment. Without the option of creating a protected trade mark common to protect the interest of 'the public in general and weaker and less organised companies',[54] the ECJ has

---

[50] After referring to the *Windsurfing* judgment as authority for the principle that the registration of such signs would run 'counter to the public interest', the ECJ went on: 'The Court ought therefore to make it clear, in so far as it is not evident from the judgment in *BABY-DRY*, firstly that a term does not have to be in current descriptive use to be precluded from registration . . . and second, that the fact that more than one term can be used to describe the characteristics of particular goods does not mean that those terms cease to be descriptive.' *Wrigley* (n 32) para 26.

[51] *BABY-DRY* (n 49) para A77.

[52] Trade Marks Directive art 6(1)(b).

[53] *Re Nichols* (n 20) para 14. Jacob J was 'surprised when the Court took into account the defence of descriptiveness. Traditionally that has not been the approach of the law, both in the UK, and as I understand it, in many other European jurisdictions' (ibid para 13).

[54] ibid para 15.

instead emphasized that the relevant authorities should be more rigorous in their examination of an applicant's sign before allowing a mark to be removed from the public domain in the first place. In other words, it is the 'competent authorities' who should be the gatekeepers as to which marks are removed from the public domain, rather than transferring such responsibility, *ex post facto*, to the courts.[55] In *Libertel* the ECJ noted that:

> the large number of and detailed nature of the obstacles to registration set out in Articles 2 and 3 of the Directive, and the wide range of remedies available in the event of refusal, indicate that the examination carried out at the time of the application for registration must not be a minimal one. It must be a stringent and full examination, in order to prevent trade marks from being improperly registered.[56]

In fact, by advocating this approach, the ECJ was once again reaching a **3.24** destination which had been signposted 90 years earlier by Lord Parker in *W. & G. du Cros*. He stated:

> In my opinion, in order to determine whether a mark is distinctive it must be considered quite apart from the effects of registration. The question, therefore, is whether the mark itself, if used as a Trade Mark, is likely to become actually distinctive of the goods of the persons so using it. The applicant for registration in effect says, 'I intend to use this mark as a Trade Mark, i.e., for the purpose of distinguishing my goods from the goods of other persons,' and the Registrar or the Court has to determine, before the mark be admitted to registration, whether it is of such a kind that the applicant, quite apart from the effects of registration, is likely or unlikely to attain the object he has in view. The applicant's chance of success, in this respect, must, I think, largely depend upon whether other traders are likely, in the ordinary course of their business and without any improper motive, to desire to use the same mark, or some mark nearly resembling it, upon or in connection with, their own goods.[57]

D. Conclusion: The Balance Between Leaving Marks Free for Others to Use and Recognizing Distinctiveness Acquired through Use

In its White Paper preceding the implementation of the Directive, the British **3.25** Government noted:

---

[55] *Libertel* (n 4) para 58.
[56] ibid para 59.
[57] *W. & G. du Cros* (n 1) 672.

At present it is possible for it to be established beyond doubt that a particular trade mark is distinctive in fact and yet for it to held in law to be not capable of distinguishing. Examples are geographical names and laudatory epithets. This position has been described as unattractive,[58] but the Registry and the courts have considered themselves bound by a long history of case law, much of it dating from a period in which trading conditions were very different from today. The government intends to take the opportunity offered by a new law to clarify the position so that any trade mark which is demonstrated to be distinctive in fact will in future be regarded as distinctive in law and therefore be registrable.[59]

3.26   As we have seen, the effect of Article 3(3) of the Directive has been precisely to ensure that any mark which has acquired distinctiveness through use may indeed be capable of registration. As a corollary, it is also no longer possible for certain marks to be reserved for the 'English language common', so they may be left free for others to use despite acquired distinctiveness.

3.27   It can be argued that such an approach to trade mark registration has the virtue of both simplicity and consistency. In a long line of trade mark cases, many of which preceded the Directive, the ECJ has held that:

> the essential function of a trade mark is to guarantee the identity of origin of the marked goods or services to the consumer or end user by enabling him, without any possibility of confusion, to distinguish the goods or services from others which have another origin.[60]

3.28   It follows that if a descriptive mark or a non-distinctive mark reaches the requisite level of distinctiveness through use, it will fulfil the essential function of a trade mark and should be capable of registration. Such was the simple logic followed by the ECJ in *Windsurfing* and *Philips*, for example.[61] Indeed, it may be further argued that to allow otherwise would be precisely to

---

[58] Despite the assertion in the White Paper that the 'commons' approach to trade mark registration had come to be seen as 'unattractive', it is noteworthy that in the first major trade mark decision in the UK following the passage of the 1994 Act, Jacob J in the High Court reiterated Sir Herbert Cozens-Hardy MR's warning of the danger of allowing 'wealthy traders' to enclose the English language common. The case, *British Sugar Plc v James Robertson & Sons Ltd* [1996] RPC 284 concerned, *inter alia*, the issue of whether the mark TREAT was validly registered for ice cream toppings.

[59] UK Government White Paper *Reform of Trade Mark Law* Cm. 1203 [1990] para 3.08.

[60] *Arsenal Football Club plc v Matthew Reed* Case C-206/01 [2003] ETMR 19 para 48. For an early restatement of the essential function of a trade mark, see *Hoffmann-La Roche v Centrafarm* Case C-102/77 [1978] 3 CMLR 217, Opinion of Advocate Capotorti at para 4.

[61] *Windsurfing* (n 25) para 47; *Philips* (n 36) para 35.

allow for the possibility of such confusion.[62] Finally, in its reference to contemporary 'trading conditions', the White Paper was surely recognizing the contemporary importance of branding. It would certainly be a hard thing to deny a trader the economic rewards for the investment he has made in ensuring that his mark, which might initially have been descriptive or lacking in distinctiveness, has indeed acquired distinctiveness through use.[63]

There is a clear public interest in allowing factually distinctive marks to be **3.29** registered which goes to the heart of the justification for trade mark registration. As we have seen, in a number of decisions, the ECJ has also identified a countervailing public interest in allowing certain signs to be left free for other traders to use. It would not be surprising if, at the margins, these two public interests might appear to conflict. This essay has sought to describe the process by which the ECJ has endeavoured to balance these two areas of trade mark law. It is no longer possible, under the Directive, to maintain a protected common of signs which other traders may wish to use; nonetheless, the ECJ has clearly recognized that it is desirable that such signs should remain available until and unless they have acquired distinctiveness through use.[64]

---

[62] For instance, if, following YORKSHIRE COPPER (n 3), another trader had begun to sell copper tubing under the sign 'Yorkshire'. It could however be argued that the applicant in the YORKSHIRE COPPER case would have had a remedy in the English tort of passing off.

[63] This point was made by J Phillips in *Trade Mark Law: A Practical Anatomy* (OUP Oxford 2003) 105.

[64] For a recent discussion of these issues, see J Antill and A James 'Registrability and the Scope of the Monopoly: Current Trends' [2004] EIPR 157–161.

Part C

REGISTRATION

4

DISTINCTIVE CHARACTER ACQUIRED THROUGH USE: THE LAW AND THE CASE LAW

Arnaud Folliard-Monguiral

A. Introduction	4.01	Distinctiveness and When to Claim it	4.34
B. The Sign for which Acquired Distinctiveness is Claimed	4.12	(1) When must distinctiveness have been acquired?	4.35
(1) The sign for which acquired distinctiveness is claimed is juxtaposed with other signs	4.15	(2) When can distinctiveness be claimed?	4.42
(2) The sign for which acquired distinctiveness is claimed is merged into a broader ensemble	4.18	D. The Geographical Extent of the Use Conferring Distinctiveness	4.45
(3) The acquisition of distinctiveness for signs having a function	4.24	E. The Persuasive Elements as to Acquired Distinctiveness	4.51
C. The Time of the Acquisition of		F. Conclusion	4.57

A. Introduction

Article 15(1) of the TRIPs Agreement provides an *option* for the Members of **4.01** TRIPs[1] to make registrability depend on distinctiveness acquired through use where signs are not inherently capable of distinguishing the relevant goods or services.[2] In contrast, the Trade Mark Directive[3] (hereafter 'Council Directive

---

The comments and the interpretation of the referred to cases have no official character and are the personal views of the author.

[1] The Members of TRIPs are most of the world's nation states, although certain Members are 'customs territories', for example the European Communities.

[2] The TRIPs Agreement is Annex 1C of the Marrakech Agreement Establishing the World Trade Organization, signed in Marrakech, Morocco on 15 April 1994.

[3] First Council Directive 89/104/EEC of 21 December 1988 to approximate the laws of the Member States relating to trade marks, OJ 1989 L 40 (11 February 1989) 1.

89/104') provides in positive terms that the absolute grounds for refusal relating to a lack of distinctiveness, to descriptiveness and to generic character may be overcome

> if, before the date of application for registration and following the use which has been made of it, [the mark applied for] has acquired a distinctive character.[4]

An option remains however for the Member States to provide that, in relation to this ground for invalidity,

> this provision shall also apply where the distinctive character was acquired after the date of application for registration or after the date of registration.[5]

4.02 The Community Trade Mark Regulation[6] (hereafter 'Council Regulation 40/94') contains a provision identical in substance, according to which the absolute grounds for refusal relating to lack of distinctiveness, to descriptiveness and to generic character may be overcome

> if the trade mark has become distinctive in relation to the goods or services for which registration is requested in consequence of the use which has been made of it.[7]

4.03 The text of Council Regulation 40/94 is more specific than Council Directive 89/104 since it expressly requires that distinctiveness be acquired in relation to the goods and services applied for, and not in relation to others. The European Court of Justice (ECJ) has however confirmed that Article 3(3) of Council Directive 89/104 must be interpreted to mean that the acquisition of distinctiveness must be in relation to the goods and services in respect of which registration is applied for.[8]

4.04 Regarding the absolute grounds for invalidity, Article 51(2) of Council Regulation 40/94 provides that:

> where the Community trade mark has been registered in breach of the provisions of Article 7 (1) (b), (c) or (d), it may nevertheless not be declared invalid

---

[4] art 3(3) of Council Directive 89/104.

[5] ibid, last sentence.

[6] Council Regulation 40/94 of 20 December 1993 on the Community trade mark, as amended by Regulation No 3288/94 of 22 December 1994, OJ EC No L 11 (14 January 1994) 1 and OJ EC No L 349 (31 December 1994) 83.

[7] art 7(3) of Council Regulation 40/94. The reference to the acquisition of distinctiveness through use is published with the application (art 40 of Council Regulation 40/94, Rule 12(i) IR) and registered (Rule 84(2)(k) IR).

[8] *Koninklijke Philips v Remington* Case C-299/99 [2002] ETMR 81 para 59.

if, in consequence of the use which has been made of it, it has after registration acquired a distinctive character in relation to the goods or services for which it is registered.

The ECJ has held that the essential function of a trade mark is to guarantee **4.05** the identity of the origin of the marked goods or services to the consumer or end user by enabling him, without any possibility of confusion, to distinguish such goods or services from others which have another origin.[9] Accordingly, signs or indications that are not capable of fulfilling the essential function of a trade mark cannot enjoy the protection conferred by registration. However if, after a long-standing and intensive use of the mark in relation to the goods or services for which registration is sought, the competent authority finds that the relevant class of persons, or at least a *significant proportion* of them, identify goods or services as originating from a particular undertaking because of the trade mark, it must hold that the requirement for registering the mark laid down in Article 3(3) of Council Directive 89/104 or in Article 7(3) of Council Regulation 40/94 is satisfied.[10]

By referring to the acquisition of a distinctive character as a means to over- **4.06** come the three absolute grounds of refusal or for invalidity under Article 3(1)(b)–(d) of Council Directive 89/104 or Article 7(1)(b)–(d) of Council Regulation 40/94, the wording of Article 3(3) of Council Directive 89/104 or Article 7(3) of Council Regulation 40/94 suggests that lack of distinctiveness, descriptiveness and generic character are not *separate* grounds for refusal but instead form subcategories of the 'umbrella' absolute ground formed by the lack of distinctiveness. ECJ case law has however confirmed that these three absolute grounds are independent of the others and call for a separate examination,[11] although there is a clear overlap between the scopes of these respective provisions.[12]

The underlying logic of the possibility offered by Council Directive 89/104 **4.07**

---

[9] See, *inter alia*, *Canon Kabushiki Kaisha v Metro-Goldwyn-Mayer Inc* Case C-39/97 [1999] ETMR 1 para 28.

[10] *Windsurfing Chiemsee Produktions- und Vertriebe GmbH v Boots- und Segelzubehör Walter Huber and Franz Attenburger* Joined Cases C-108/97 and C-109/97 [1999] ETMR 585 para 52.

[11] *Linde AG v Deutsches Patent- und Markenamt* Joined Cases C-53/01 to C-55/01 [2003] ETMR 78 para 67.

[12] *Koninklijke KPN Nederland NV v Benelux Trade Marks Office* (POSTKANTOOR) Case C-363/99 [2004] ETMR 57 para 67.

or Council Regulation 40/94 to 'cure' objections under certain of the absolute grounds for refusal or for invalidity is as follows: an unjustified advantage would be granted to a single trader if he were given rights over a sign which must be freely available for use by everyone due to its descriptive, generic or non-distinctive nature.[13] It is only in the event that such a sign, because of the use to which it has been put, is actually perceived by the relevant public as an indication of the trade origin of the goods or service that the economic effort made by the trade mark applicant justifies putting aside the public-interest considerations underlying Article 3(1)(b)–(d) of Council Directive 89/104 or Article 7(1)(b)–(d) of Council Regulation 40/94.[14]

4.08 In contrast, by the express intention of the legislature, the signs falling within the scope of the grounds for refusal or for invalidity provided under Article 3(1)(e)–(g) of Council Directive 89/104[15] and Article 7(1)(e)–(k) of Council Regulation 40/94[16] may never acquire distinctiveness. Indeed, it is the case that these grounds for refusal or for invalidity cannot be overcome. The underlying logic for such a prohibition against acquiring distinctiveness through use differs according to the absolute ground.

4.09 As regards Article 3(1)(e) of Council Directive 89/104 and Article 7(1)(e) of Council Regulation 40/94, the prohibition is justified (i) by the public interest that natural, functional or ornamental shapes may be freely used by all[17] and (ii) by the fact that trade mark protection is not meant to perpetuate a protection which could be granted for a limited period of time through a patent right, a copyright or a design right, where appropriate. The balance of

---

[13] *Windsurfing* (n 10) para 25.

[14] *SAT.1 SatellitenFernsehen GmbH v OHIM* Case T-323/00 [2003] ETMR 49 para 36.

[15] Natural, functional or ornamental shapes (art 31(e) of Council Directive 89/104), marks which are contrary to public policy (art 3(1)(f) of Council Directive 89/104), deceptive marks (art 3(1)(g) of Council Directive 89/104).

[16] Natural, functional or ornamental shapes (art 7(1)(e) of Council Regulation 40/94), marks which are contrary to public policy (art 7(1)(f) of Council Regulation 40/94), deceptive marks (art 7(1)(g) of Council Regulation 40/94), non-authorized reproduction of one of the elements set out in art 6*ter* of the Paris Convention (art 7(1)(h) of Council Regulation 40/94) or of badges, emblems, coats of arms other than those covered by art 6*ter* of the Paris Convention and having a particular public interest (art 7(1)(i) of Council Regulation 40/94), illicit reproduction of a geographical indication for wines or spirits that do not have the origin indicated in the mark (art 7(1)(j) of Council Regulation 40/94), signs which contain or consist of a designation of origin or a geographical indication registered in accordance with Regulation 2081/92.

[17] *Philips* (n 8) paras 78–80.

interests between the public interest protected by the absolute grounds under Article 3(1)(e) and the interest of the proprietor in protecting its investment in making its mark distinctive differs from the position taken under Articles 3(1)(b)–(d). Under those Articles, the economic effort of the trade mark applicant in making his mark *de facto* distinctive outweighs the interests protected by those articles. However, under Article 3(1)(e), the applicant's investment has already been potentially protected by the award of patent, copyright or design protection: to provide trade mark protection as a result of acquired distinctiveness would involve rewarding that investment twice.

As regards Article 3(1)(f)–(h) of Council Directive 89/104 and Article **4.10** 7(1)(f)–(k) of Council Regulation 40/94, the justification is not that the signs falling within these absolute grounds should remain free for all, but on the contrary that the use of such signs should be prohibited to all, either without exception,[18] or to all those who are not entitled to use them.[19]

The acquisition of distinctive character through use raises a number of issues **4.11** regarding in particular: (i) the sign for which acquired distinctiveness is claimed, (ii) the time of the acquisition of distinctiveness and the time to claim it, (iii) the geographical extent of the use and (iv) the persuasive (and non-persuasive) elements as to acquired distinctiveness. It is these issues that the rest of this chapter will address.

B. The Sign for which Acquired Distinctiveness is Claimed

Article 10(2)(a) of Council Directive 89/104 and Article 15(2)(a) of Council **4.12** Regulation 40/94 provide that genuine use of the mark may concern use of a sign that differs 'in elements which do not alter the distinctive character of the mark in the form' in which for the application was made for its registration. Article 3(3) of Council Directive 89/104 and Article 7(3) of Council Regulation 40/94 are silent on whether such use of a sign differing from the form in which it was applied for may or may not result in the acquisition of distinctiveness.

The case law of the Office for Harmonisation in the Internal Market **4.13**

---

[18] art 3(1)(e) and (f) of Council Directive 89/104 and art 7(1)(e)–(g) of Council Regulation 40/94.
[19] art 3(1)(h) of Council Directive 89/104 and art 7(h)–(k) of Council Regulation 40/94.

(OHIM) Boards of Appeal shows that minor variations between the manner in which the mark has been used and the form in which it is applied for will most often lead to the claim of acquired distinctiveness under Article 7(3) of Council Regulation 40/94 being rejected.[20]

4.14 In this context, regard should be had to the use of the signs the acquired distinctiveness of which is claimed, in association with other signs. This may cover three situations. In the first, a non-distinctive sign is used in conjunction with another (registered) mark, each sign being perceived by consumers as a separate or at least a separable entity. In the second, a non-distinctive sign

---

[20] See decision of the Third Board of Appeal of 21 March 2001, Case R 428/2000–3 *WORLD MASTERS GAMES* para 41: 'The goods shown in the exhibit do not only use the sign applied for. On the contrary the mark is always combined with a figurative element or another mark, namely NIKE'; decision of the Second Board of Appeal of 1 February 2000, Case R 131/ 1999–2 *QS/QUALITY STANDARD* para 17: 'As regards the suggestion of the applicant that Article 7(3) of Council Regulation 40/94 should be considered applicable by virtue of the use made of the sign in Germany, the Board observes that the examiner correctly took the position that the use, as shown in the submitted documents, concerns the use of QS/QUALITY STAN-DARD as a figurative mark and not of the mark as filed. The figurative mark shown in the documents is not the same as the word mark QS/QUALITY STANDARD, and cannot therefore constitute a basis for acquired distinctiveness'; decision of the Third Board of Appeal of 12 March 2001, Case R 865/1999–3 *MEMBER OF THE SOCIETY OF FINANCIAL ADVISERS* para 26: 'Moreover, as the examiner pointed out, the exhibits consisting of the program of the December 1995 "Update of Financial Advisers Conference", the copies of the autumn 1995 and winter 1995/96 Technical Adviser Magazine and the copies of "Sofa News", concern another mark which is figurative as depicted below'; decision of the Third Board of Appeal of 22 June 1999, Case R 63/1999–3 *Caterham Car Sales & Coachworks Ltd's Application* (7 [2000] ETMR 14), paras 23 and 24: 'where a claimed mark appears together with the name of the supplier for specific products, there is a prima facie presumption that that mark functions as a mere identifier sign. In the present case, the appellant has not provided sufficient proof that the digit "7" per se is not a mere identifier sign, but has come to function as a trade mark which indicates the origin of the automobiles or services with which it is used. In addition, it has not proven conclusively that the trade mark which has been used over the years does not differ from the trade mark applied for. Indeed, in some cases, the digit "7" is contained within a triangular shape, headed by the word "super" which is embodied into a figurative circular logo, where the name "Lotus" or "Caterham" appears (see the brochure, the List of Overseas Agents, the Newsletter and the advertising leaflet). In other cases, the digit "7" is incorporated in a styled design in the front grille of the car (see the book entitled "Caterham Seven: the Official Story of a Unique British Sportscar"). Next, in various parts of the documentation, the trade mark is not easily distinguishable from other numbers appearing on a race car (see the above book). Also, the number "7" repeatedly appears as the word "seven" throughout the material. Finally, even in those infrequent instances where the digit "7" appears on its own in certain specialised magazines (see the pages in the above book referred to by the appellant in the seventh paragraph of the letter of 4 December 1998), it is always within the context of the history of the Lotus 7 (or "Lotus Seven" or "Lotus Super Seven/7")—in that context, further, the journalistic practice of abbreviating terms cannot be discounted.'

is merged into a broader ensemble from which it is not separable. In the third, the issue at stake is the acquisition of distinctiveness for signs having a function.

(1) The sign for which acquired distinctiveness is claimed is juxtaposed with other signs

None of the provisions of Council Directive 89/104 or of Council Regula- **4.15** tion 40/94 prevent several marks, of any nature, from coexisting on the same product or even on the same label, so there is no legal obstacle to finding that consumers perceive each mark separately and do not see them as a mark as a whole. For consumers to recognize each and every element as an independent indicator of commercial origin, each of these elements must however be used *in an autonomous way*. Where the sign for which acquired distinctiveness is claimed is perceived as an ancillary element overshadowed by a prominent word and/or figurative element, it no longer performs on its own, or even on equal footing with the other elements, the function of identification of the product's or service's origin. In other words, if consumers detect the existence of several marks affixed on the same product or label, they may perceive each of them individually as a badge of origin.

The limit of this principle is reached when the sign claimed to have acquired **4.16** distinctiveness is surpassed in importance and attractiveness by the impact of the other word and/or figurative elements on the product or label in question. In such a case, it will generally be considered that the evidence does not support the claim that the sign in question has acquired distinctiveness.[21]

---

[21] See decision of the Third Board of Appeal of 4 June 2003, Case R 413/2002–3 THE WORLD BUSINESS ORGANIZATION paras 13 and 14: 'In general, the documentary evidence provided by the appellant before the examiner or the Board do not support the claim that as a result of the use of the expression THE WORLD BUSINESS ORGANIZATION, the latter has acquired distinctiveness within the Community and in particular in the United Kingdom and Ireland. This expression is ancillary to the sign ICC and is used with a mere informative purpose. The latter is written in bold, the font is remarkable due its size and the thickness of the letters, two stylised globes are depicted inside each letter C. Underneath, the expression "The International Chamber of Commerce" is written in bold in a standard font. Underneath, the expression THE WORLD BUSINESS ORGANIZATION is written in a much smaller type font, in italics. As a matter of fact, the consumers will have their attention attracted by the figurative sign ICC, because of its larger size and specific depiction'; decision of the Third Board of Appeal of 14 February 2000, Case R 229/1999–3 FLAGSHIP para 25: 'It is apparent that the designation "American Airlines" and other figurative elements predominate.'

Conversely, if each of the components of the mark as used can be separated without losing their individual ability to indicate an origin, then the trade mark applied for will acquire a distinctive character through use.[22]

4.17 This reasoning is of particular importance as regards three-dimensional marks consisting of a shape alone without labelling, where proof of acquisition of distinctiveness is adduced for a labelled product.[23] In any event, the use the shape of the product in conjunction with a word mark renders it more difficult to deduce from the sales figures or other documentary evidence submitted whether the consumers recognize the shape of the product or the word mark.[24] This was confirmed by the Court of First Instance in Case T-399/02, in relation to a trade mark application for the shape of a 'long neck bottle'.[25] The Court held, in paragraph 51 of its judgment, that the documentary evidence submitted by the applicant did not refer to the shape in the

---

[22] Decision of the Second Board of Appeal of 28 November 2003, Case R 947/2001–2 *Shape of a golden ring* para 17: 'The fact that in a lot of the material submitted to prove acquired distinctiveness, the mark has not been used on its own but in conjunction with the appellant's own name or word mark "GOLDEN RING", does not per se exclude the probative value of the evidence'; decision of the Second Board of Appeal of 17 December 2002, Case R 751/2001–2 *PLASMALAB* para 11: 'The Board does not endorse the examiner's finding that the mark has not been used as a trade mark simply because it is frequently displayed in italics and in connection with other verbal elements such as "System 90 Plus". Printing the word in italics does not significantly alter the way the mark is perceived by the relevant public. Elements such as "System 90 Plus" do not add substantially to the mark's capacity to function as a trade mark because they are endowed with a very low level of distinctiveness. The consumer will consider these elements as references to specific models of "Plasmalab" equipment and their function will therefore not be to distinguish between goods of one undertaking from those of other undertakings but rather to distinguish between various goods from the same undertaking'; decision of the Second Board of Appeal of 23 May 2001, Case R 111/2000–2 *THE GREATEST SHOW ON EARTH*. The mark was used as part of different graphic representations and always in combination with the applicant's name: P.T. Barnum's GREATEST SHOW ON EARTH, BARNUM & BAILEY'S GREATEST SHOW ON EARTH, THE BARNUM AND BAILEY LTD GREATEST SHOW ON EARTH. 'The contention of the examiner that because the words "THE GREATEST SHOW ON EARTH" have always appeared alongside the appellant's registered trade mark, the sign is not likely to be considered as evidence of trade mark use is not in the Board's view a valid one. The Board can well understand that a slogan-like phrase associated with a trade mark, like in this case, might by repetition over time, create a separate and independent impression.'
[23] See A Folliard-Monguiral and D Rogers 'The Protection of Shapes by the Community Trade Mark' [2003] 4 EIPR 169.
[24] See decision of the Second Board of Appeal, *Animal Foodstuffs Device* Case R 927/2001–2 (12 December 2002) para 22.
[25] *Eurocermex SA v OHIM* (Long neck bottle) Case T-399/02 [2004] ETMR 95 paras 50–51.

form for which registration was sought, that is, as a bare shape. Indeed, the bare shape was covered with word marks and labels. This documentary evidence was considered by the Court as non-persuasive given that it did not properly support the claim that the public perceived the bare shape, *without any additional element*, as a badge of origin.

(2) The sign for which acquired distinctiveness is claimed is merged into a broader ensemble

Where the sign for which acquired distinctiveness is claimed is merged into a **4.18** broader ensemble in which it loses its individuality, the consumer will normally not be able to perceive this ensemble as the addition of separate entities but rather as a *unitary whole* composed of various interdependent elements. This may be the case for slogans. Where the slogan has a secondary meaning resulting from the bringing together of these words or, more generally, where there is a perceptible difference between the slogan overall and the mere sum of its parts, it is unlikely that a claim regarding the acquisition of a distinctive character for a part of that slogan will be successful.[26]

A preliminary ruling currently pending before the ECJ is in this respect of **4.19** particular question.[27] The slogan 'HAVE A BREAK—HAVE A KIT KAT' and the name KIT KAT are, and for many years have been, registered trade marks in the UK in respect of goods in Class 30. In March 1995, La Société des Produits Nestlé S.A. ('Nestlé') applied to the UK Patent Office to register the mark HAVE A BREAK in respect of goods in Class 30. The application was duly published and opposed by Mars UK Ltd as being unregistrable.

In May 2002, the Hearing Officer upheld the opposition on the ground **4.20** specified in section 3(1)(b) of the UK Trade Marks Act 1994 (trade marks which are devoid of any distinctive character). Nestlé appealed to the High Court of Justice, Chancery Division, but its appeal was dismissed in December 2002. Finally, Nestlé appealed to the Court of Appeal. The Court concluded that the provisions of section 3(1)(b) preclude registration as a trade mark of the phrase applied for and decided to stay the proceedings and refer a question relating to the interpretation of Article 3(3) Council

---

[26] *Sykes Enterprises Inc v OHIM* (REAL PEOPLE, REAL SOLUTIONS) Case T-130/01 [2003] ETMR 57 para 26.
[27] *Société des Produits Nestlé SA v Mars UK Ltd* Case C-353/03.

Directive 89/104 and Article 7(3) Council Regulation 40/94 for a preliminary ruling in accordance with Article 234 of the EC Treaty.[28]

4.21 The Court of Appeal asks a question on the interpretation of the concept of 'distinctiveness acquired by use' in Article 3(3) of the Trade Mark Directive and in Article 7(3) Community Trade Mark Regulation, namely:

> Whether the distinctive character of a mark referred to in Article 3(3) of Council Directive 89/104/EEC and Article 7(3) of Council Regulation 40/94 may be acquired following or in consequence of the use of that mark as part of or in conjunction with another mark?

4.22 The application of the principles set out above in this chapter may lead the ECJ to consider that the distinctive character of a mark may be acquired through use where use was made in conjunction with another mark only where the sign sought to be protected has acquired a separate identity, i.e. when it is perceived by the consumer as a trade mark in its own right. Conversely, the distinctive character of a mark is unlikely to be acquired where the sign in question is perceived as an element of a single mark, even though consumers may associate a part of that mark with that mark overall.

4.23 The fact that a consumer might be able to complete the phrase 'HAVE A BREAK' by adding 'HAVE A KIT KAT' may not be an indication of its acquired distinctiveness. It could rather show that the slogan *as a whole* has become so distinctive that it cannot be separated into independent parts. It could furthermore mean that the part 'HAVE A BREAK' is not perceived as an independent entity by the consumer and therefore does not by itself indicate the origin of the goods.

(3) The acquisition of distinctiveness for signs having a function

4.24 The ECJ made it clear that Article 3(1)(e), second indent, of Council Directive 89/104 (or Article 7(1)(e), second indent, of Council Regulation 40/94) must be interpreted to mean that a sign consisting exclusively of the shape of a product is unregistrable if it is established that the *essential functional features* of that shape are attributable only to the technical result, whether or

---

[28] J Mutimear 'At Appeal Have a Break' [2003] 160 Trademark World 14; C McLeod 'Unlucky Break?' [2003] 154 Trademark World 23.

not the same technical result may be obtained by alternative shapes.[29] According to the Opinion of Advocate General Ruiz-Jarabo Colomer,

> use of the phrase 'essential features' means that a shape containing an arbitrary element which, from a functional point of view, is minor, such as its colour, does not escape the prohibition.[30]

In light of this guidance, can a sign having a function acquire distinctiveness through use?

The *Philips* ruling suggests that a distinction should be made between (i) **4.25** signs whose functional features are essential and (ii) those whose functional features are only ancillary. In the latter case, a sign whose functional features are ancillary could acquire distinctiveness if the use which has been made of it results in endowing the dominant non-functional features with a distinguishing capacity which they originally lacked.

Conversely, it should not be possible for a shape whose essential features are **4.26** functional to have been used *also* as an indication of origin and to have consequently acquired distinctiveness through use. Even if minor non-functional elements of the overall functional shapes are perceived as indicators of origin, this should be irrelevant.[31]

The approach of the Court of First Instance (CFI) seems however not fully in **4.27** line with this approach. In the *Daimler Grille* case, although the absolute ground of functionality was not examined, the CFI observed that

> a grille may also serve to ventilate the vehicle engine and to provide a certain degree of stability to the front part

(that is clearly a technical result), and further stated that:

---

[29] *Philips* (n 8) para 84.

[30] Opinion delivered on 23 January 2001.

[31] The Community judges' approach regarding functional signs is substantially stricter than that relating to distinctive signs. See for instance *BioID v OHIM (BioID)* Case T-91/01 [2002] ECR II-5159, [2003] ETMR 60 para 36 where the CFI did not exclude that distinctiveness may be found in minor elements: 'in that regard, it should be noted that the absence of distinctive character of a compound mark cannot be determined solely by reference to the relative importance of certain elements of which it is composed as compared with that of other elements of the mark, in respect of which an absence of distinctive character has been established. A compound mark cannot fall under Article 7(1)(b) of Regulation No 40/94 if one of its composite elements is distinctive in respect of the goods and services concerned. That is true even if the sole distinctive element of the compound mark is not dominant in relation to the other composite elements of the mark.'

the fact that a sign serves several purposes at once has no bearing on its distinct-iveness . . ., particularly if the distinguishing function outweighs the other functions.[32]

4.28 The CFI probably considered that the technical result was eclipsed by the distinctive capacity of the grille, with the result that the functional features of the grille were not deemed *essential*. The test suggested by the CFI is likely to be incorrect, however. The correct test is not whether a feature has *essentially* a technical function or has *essentially* a distinguishing one by means of a comparison between these two overlapping functions. This would go against the clear wording of Article 3(3) of Council Directive 89/104 and Article 7(3) of Council Regulation 40/94, following which a functional feature may never coincide with a distinctive one, nor may it ever acquire distinctiveness. Instead, regard should be had to the relative weight of the functional features when compared to the non-functional ones. Accordingly, a functional feature would not be considered essential where it is dominated by non-functional ones. Only where the dominant non-functional elements originally lacked distinctiveness would it then be necessary to consider the question of whether the sign overall has acquired distinctiveness through use.

4.29 The ECJ will have another opportunity to clarify its guidance on this subject in a currently pending preliminary ruling case.[33] In 1993 Dyson Ltd began the commercial manufacture of the Dual Cyclone vacuum cleaner. This is a bagless vacuum cleaner in which the dirt and dust are collected in a chamber forming part of the machine. Aside from the cyclonic technology itself, the most obvious feature of this type of vacuum cleaner, as sold in the UK, is that the collection bin is made from transparent plastic, which enables the user to see the dirt and other waste material as it is vacuumed up.

4.30 Two three-dimensional trade mark applications were filed in the UK in Class 9, consisting of 'a transparent bin or collection chamber forming part of the external surface of a vacuum cleaner'.[34] The applications were rejected by the

---

[32] *DaimlerChrysler v OHIM* (Grille) Case T-128/01 [2003] ETMR 87 para 43.

[33] *Dyson Ltd v The Registrar of Trade Marks* Case C-321/03.

[34] Dyson Ltd also lodged an application for registration of the 'clear bin' with OHIM. The application for a single trade mark was accompanied by the graphical representations of different forms of the transparent bin. The examiner and subsequently the First Board of Appeal (R 655/01–1) rejected the application for lack of a precise graphical representation. The case is presently pending before the CFI (Case T-278/02).

Registrar of Trade Marks on the absolute grounds set out in sections 3(1)(a)–(c) of the Trade Marks Act. The Hearing Officer upheld the objections and determined that the applications were not saved by the proviso of section 3(1) on grounds of acquired distinctiveness. Dyson Ltd appealed against that decision to the High Court of Justice.

By Order of 6 June 2003, the High Court of Justice referred the following **4.31** questions to the Court of Justice concerning the interpretation of Article 3(3) of Council Directive 89/104:

1. In a situation where an applicant has used a sign (which is not a shape) which consists of a feature which has a function and which forms part of the appearance of a new kind of article, and the applicant has, until the date of application, had a de facto monopoly in such articles, is it sufficient, in order for the sign to have acquired a distinctive character within the meaning of article 3(3) of the Directive 89/104/EC, that a significant proportion of the relevant public has by the date of application for registration come to associate the relevant goods bearing the sign with the applicant and no other manufacturer?
2. If that is not sufficient, what else is needed in order for the sign to have acquired a distinctive character and, in particular, is it necessary for the person who has used the sign to have promoted it as a trade mark?

One may assume that the High Court of Justice alludes to the transparency feature when referring to

> a sign (which is not a shape) which consists of a feature which has a function and which forms part of the appearance of a new kind of article.

Serious doubts may arise as to whether such a feature may be a mark in the sense of Article 2 of Council Directive 89/104 or Article 4 of Council Regulation 40/94, unless a particular shape is given thereto.[35]

The ECJ will have first to decide whether the prohibition on the registration **4.32** of functional shapes applies by analogy to signs that are not three-dimensional. Assuming that the answer is positive, it should then set guidance as how to evaluate whether the technical function is essential or not in

---

[35] See decision of the First Board of Appeal of Case R 655/01–1 (2 July 2002) para 26: 'The applicant is not entitled to apply for just the concept of any clear bin which forms part of the external surface of a vacuum cleaner. Since, in fact, this concept concerns a feature of the goods, as the applicant claimed in its letter of 28 February 1997, it needs to be represented according to Rule 3(2) IR.'

the sign applied for. Further, it should logically confirm its previous judgment in *Philips*, following which shapes or signs whose functional features are essential may never become distinctive through use. Regarding signs which escape from the 'functionality' prohibition, the Court may rely on the finding reached at paragraph 65 of its *Philips* judgment:

> where a trader has been the only supplier of particular goods to the market, extensive use of a sign which consists of the shape of those goods may be sufficient to give the sign a distinctive character for the purposes of Article 3(3) of the Directive in circumstances where, as a result of that use, a substantial proportion of the relevant class of persons associates that shape with that trader and no other undertaking or believes that goods of that shape come from that trader. However, it is for the national court to verify that the circumstances in which the requirement under that provision is satisfied are shown to exist on the basis of specific and reliable data, that the presumed expectations of an average consumer of the category of goods or services in question, who is reasonably well-informed and reasonably observant and circumspect, are taken into account and that the identification, by the relevant class of persons, of the product as originating from a given undertaking is as a result of the use of the mark as a trade mark.

4.33 Finally, whether the sign is promoted as a trade mark should be irrelevant unless it can be shown that it is perceived as a mark as a result of such a promotion. The applicant's intention to promote his sign as a trade mark should be deduced from the perception of the public rather than the contrary.

C. The Time of the Acquisition of Distinctiveness and When to Claim it

4.34 Two questions may arise, one being a substantive issue while the other is more procedural: (i) when must distinctiveness have been acquired? (ii) when may acquired distinctiveness be claimed?

(1) When must distinctiveness have been acquired?

4.35 Two cases must be distinguished, depending on whether the absolute ground under Article 3(1)(b)–(d) of Council Directive 89/104 or Article 7(1)(b)–(d) of Council Regulation 40/94 is raised as a ground for refusal (i) at the application stage, or (ii) as a ground for invalidity after registration.

(a) Application

Where one of the absolute grounds under Article 3(1)(b)–(d) of Council **4.36**
Directive 89/104 or Article 7(1)(b)–(d) of Council Regulation 40/94 is
raised against the registration of a trade mark application, documentary evidence must be adduced showing that the sign had acquired distinctiveness
through use before the application was filed, rather than before the date of
registration.[36]

According to the CFI, this is justified because such an interpretation   **4.37**

> is the only one compatible with the logic of the system of absolute and relative
> grounds for refusal in regard to the registration of Community trade marks. As
> Article 8(2)(a) and (b) of Regulation No 40/94 makes clear, the date of filing of
> the application, as defined in Article 26 of the regulation, determines the
> priority of one mark over another. In that connection, it must be pointed out
> that if a mark which became distinctive through use only after an application
> for its registration was filed were none the less registered, it could, in opposition
> or annulment proceedings, constitute a relative ground for refusal to register a
> mark whose date of filing post-dated that of the first mark. That situation
> could arise even though at the date of filing of the second mark, which had by
> that time become distinctive, the first mark had not yet acquired distinctiveness
> through use, and did not therefore satisfy the conditions for registration. Such
> an outcome cannot be accepted.[37]

This reasoning is however not entirely satisfactory. First, the underlying logic **4.38**
of this reasoning would demand that the acquisition of distinctiveness be
proved before the *date of priority*, instead of the date of filing, where a priority
is claimed. This is however doubtful. According to Article 31 of Council
Regulation 40/94, the only effect of priority is to make the date of application the priority date 'for the purposes of establishing which rights take
precedence'. Neither Article 31 of Council Regulation 40/94 nor the disposi-
tions of Article 4(A) and (B) of the Paris Convention deals with the consequence of a priority date on the examination of the registrability of a mark.

Second, the reasoning of the CFI, aimed at conciliating Article 7(3) with **4.39**
Article 8(2) of Council Regulation 40/94, is flawed on another point. The
situation considered by the CFI is that of an earlier Community trade mark,

---

[36] *eCopy v OHIM* (ᴇᴄᴏᴘʏ) Case T-247/01 [2003] ETMR 99 para 36; *Audi AG v OHIM*
(ᴛᴅɪ) Case T-16/02 [2004] ETMR 59 para 54.
[37] *eCopy* (n 36) para 37.

registered in spite of the existence of an absolute ground for refusal under Article 7(1)(b)–(d) of Council Regulation 40/94, which is used as a basis for an infringement action against a later registered mark. Assuming that a counterclaim is filed by the proprietor of the later mark and that the earlier mark has acquired distinctiveness after the later mark was filed, the CFI suggests that the Community trade mark Court should dismiss the action because the mark used as a basis for the action would be deemed an earlier mark in the sense of Article 8(2) of Council Regulation 40/94 only if it had acquired distinctiveness before the date of application of the later mark.

4.40 Within the framework of Article 51(2) of Council Regulation 40/94, it is still possible for a mark to acquire distinctiveness after registration, if the examination of that mark proves *ex post facto* to have overlooked an absolute ground for refusal under Article 7(1)(b)–(d) of Council Regulation 40/94.[38] The dramatic consequence that protection of such a mark should be deemed postdated to the effective date of the acquisition of distinctiveness would nevertheless have required a specific provision in the law, which the Community legislature deemed unnecessary. On the contrary, the logic of Article 51(2) of Council Regulation 40/94 seems to be that the acquisition of distinctiveness remedies as from the outset the substantive deficiency that formerly affected the validity of the sign.

(b) Invalidity

4.41 Where one of the absolute grounds under Article 7(1)(b)–(d) of Council Regulation 40/94[39] is raised as a ground for *invalidity* under Article 51(1)(a) of Council Regulation 40/94, the trade mark owner must show that distinctiveness has been acquired either before the date of application for his mark, or at the latest before the date of application for a declaration of invalidity.[40]

---

[38] art 51(2) of Council Regulation 40/94. This provision is optional under art 3(3), last sentence, of Council Directive 89/104.

[39] Or under art 3(1)(b)–(d) of Council Directive 89/104 as regards those of the Member States which availed themselves of the possibility left open under art 3(3), last sentence, of Council Directive 89/104.

[40] *Alcon Inc v OHIM* (ʙss) Case T-237/01 [2004] ETMR 6 (now under appeal to the ECJ) para 53.

(2) When can distinctiveness be claimed?

As regards Community trade marks, the CFI has found that there is continu-   **4.42**
ity in terms of functions between the various departments of the OHIM,
including the Boards of Appeal. Although they enjoy a wide degree of
independence in carrying out their duties, the Boards constitute a department of the Office, and they enjoy the same powers in determining an appeal
as the examiner.[41] As a result of the 'functional continuity' existing between
the examiners of OHIM and the Boards of Appeal in *ex parte* proceedings,[42] a
claim regarding the acquired distinctiveness of a mark refused to registration
may be made for the first time before the Board of Appeal, subject only to
Article 74(2) of Council Regulation 40/94 (which allows the Board to disregard facts or evidence which the parties did not submit in due time). Article
74(2) of Council Regulation 40/94 cannot apply *ex officio* to facts and evidence which have not been adduced before the first instance of OHIM,
where the applicant has indicated in the written statement setting out
its grounds of appeal that he intended to rely on Article 7(3) of Council
Regulation 40/94.[43]

Where acquired distinctiveness is claimed for the first time before the Board   **4.43**
of Appeal, the latter may either examine this claim or remit the case to the
examiner, pursuant to Article 62(1) of Council Regulation 40/94. The same
reasoning applies to *inter partes* proceedings, such as invalidity proceedings
based on Article 51(1)(a) of Council Regulation 40/94.[44] A different solution
may apply to the registration or cancellation procedures before the competent authority of each Member State, in particular where an appeal against
the decision issued by a department of that administrative authority must be
brought before a judicial court, as is the case in France, for instance.[45]

---

[41] Arts 61(1) and 62(1) of Council Regulation 40/94.
[42] *Procter & Gamble v OHIM* (BABY-DRY) Case T-163/98 [1999] ETMR 767 para 43;
Procter & Gamble v OHIM (Soap bar shape) Case T-63/01 [2003] ETMR 43 para 21.
[43] *BABY-DRY* (n 42) para 44. However, art 74(2) of Council Regulation 40/94 may justify
that facts and evidence be rejected at the appeal stage where the examiner had previously set a
time limit to bring proof of acquired distinctiveness, which the applicant failed to meet: see
decision of the Second Board of Appeal R 531/2001–2 (1 July 2003) (form of cardboard)
paras 21–23.
[44] *Henkel KGaA v OHIM* (KLEENCARE) Case T-308/01 still unreported, para 26.
[45] See Cour d'Appel de Paris *Esprit International v INPI and Chaumet International*
(14 March 2003).

4.44 In any event, the acquisition of distinctiveness can never be claimed for the first time before the CFI. This is because the sole purpose of an action before the CFI is to review the legality of the decision of the Board of Appeal and not to reopen the case. The legality of a decision of the Board of Appeal thus cannot, in principle, be called into question by submission to the CFI of facts which, although they occurred before that decision was adopted, were not relied on during the administrative procedure before OHIM. It would be otherwise only if it were shown that the Board of Appeal ought, of its own motion, to have taken account of those facts during the administrative procedure and before giving a ruling on the case.[46] The CFI confirmed that neither the examiner nor the Board of Appeal is bound to examine *ex officio* facts showing that the mark claimed has become distinctive through use unless the applicant has filed a specific claim in that sense.[47]

D. The Geographical Extent of the Use Conferring Distinctiveness

4.45 The acquisition of distinctive character through use of the mark requires that at least a *significant proportion of the relevant public* of the territory for which protection is sought identifies the goods or services as originating from a particular undertaking because of the trade mark.[48]

4.46 In the absence of any definition of Article 3(3) of Council Directive 89/104 in this respect, a national trade mark or a Benelux trade mark should not be required to have acquired distinctiveness 'throughout' the territory of the Member State(s) where protection is sought. It should be sufficient if it exists in a *substantial part* of that territory.[49] This is confirmed by the CFI case law relating to Community trade marks, where the Court held that, in order to have the registration of a trade mark accepted under Article 7(3) of Council Regulation 40/94, the distinctive character acquired through the use of that trade mark must be demonstrated in the *substantial part* of the

---

[46] *BABY-DRY* (n 42) paras 49–51; *Audi* (n 36) para 63; *Eurocermex* (n 25) para 52.

[47] *eCopy* (n 36) para 47.

[48] *Windsurfing* (n 10) para 52; *Philips* (n 8) paras 61–62.

[49] See, by analogy, *General Motors Corporation v Yplon SA* (CHEVY) Case C-375/97 [1999] ETMR 950 para 28.

Community where it was devoid of any such character under Article 7(1)(b), (c) and (d).[50]

In this respect, it should be recalled that Article 7(2) of Council Regulation **4.47** 40/94 states the following:

> Paragraph 1 shall apply notwithstanding that the grounds of non-registrability obtain in only one part of the Community.

The question of the geographical area in which the acquisition of the distinct- **4.48** ive character through use must be shown raises complex issues. Requirements vary according to the nature of the mark and each case seems to turn on its own facts. In the case of a word mark objected to due to its descriptiveness in the language of one Member State, the objection will be overcome when and if the holder proves that the mark has acquired a distinctive character through use in this particular Member State. Use in other Member States will be irrelevant.[51] In the case of colour marks, three-dimensional marks or any other mark lacking distinctiveness *per se* in all Member States, the objection extends to the whole Community.

Nevertheless, acquisition of distinctive character need not be proved in each **4.49** of the twenty-five Member States one by one, as long as it is proved for *the European Union as a whole.*

Thus, although the acquisition of a distinctive character through use in only one[52] or four[53] Member State(s) is insufficient, use in ten Member States (which might have 349 million inhabitants out of the total of 377 million), with a level of recognition amongst the public of 56 per cent, corresponds to a sufficiently broad geographical scale and thus makes superfluous the proof of recognition in each one of the twenty-five Member States.[54] In any event, it is

---

[50] *Alcon* (n 40) para 52; *Audi* (n 36) para 52; *Ford Motor Company v OHIM* (OPTIONS) Case T-91/99 [2000] ETMR 554 para 27.

[51] *Ford* (n 50) para 28. See decision of the First Board of Appeal MEDLINE Case R 230/ 2003–1 (19 December 2003) paras 32–33: 'The mark had acquired distinctiveness in the UK. Evidence of use in the UK cannot be extended to cover Ireland on the basis of a possible overspill in trade between Northern Ireland and Ireland, since it is not supported by any other evidence suggesting that, due to that overspill, the relevant Irish consumers recognize the sign as a trade mark.'

[52] See for instance decision of the Third Board of Appeal Case R 704/1999–3 para 23.

[53] See decision of the Second Board of Appeal *Shape of a Triangle* Case R 1025/2000–2 (17 December 2002).

[54] See for instance decisions of the Second Board of Appeal *Shape of a Tyre* Case R 126/ 2001–2 para 22.

expected that the enlargement of the Community in 2004 to include ten new Member States and its extension to a market of 450 million people will make it more difficult for applicants to prove the acquisition of distinctiveness in a substantial part of the Community.

4.50 Although acquisition of distinctive character need not be proved in each of the twenty-five Member States separately, the documentary evidence must paradoxically contain detailed information regarding the market share held by the mark, the amount of investment etc. (see section E below) in each of the relevant geographic markets concerned, rather than in the Community as a whole.[55]

E. The Persuasive Elements as to Acquired Distinctiveness

4.51 According to the case law of the ECJ, in assessing the distinctive character of a mark, the following may, *inter alia*, be taken into account:

- the market share held by the mark
- how intensive, geographically widespread and long-standing use of the mark has been
- the amount invested by the undertaking in promoting the mark
- the proportion of the relevant class of persons who, because of the mark, identify goods as originating from a particular undertaking
- statements from chambers of commerce and industry or other trade and professional associations.[56]

4.52 None of these factors is *per se* conclusive, but they should be assessed in an interdependent manner, each corroborating the others. Although pieces of evidence originating from the applicant himself cannot (and must not) be disregarded, more weight should be given to pieces of evidence originating from neutral sources.

4.53 As for the 'genuine use' requirement, the threshold beyond which distinctiveness will have been conferred by the use made of the mark should be directly related to the type of goods or category of service. The degree of use required of a mark sought to be protected in relation to luxury goods of

---

[55] *Eurocermex* (n 25) para 50.
[56] *Windsurfing* (n 10) paras 51–52.

limited distribution cannot be the same as for a mark employed in relation to mass-consumption goods. The volume and frequency of the transactions leading to the use of the mark must therefore be evaluated in light of the structure of the relevant market. As a result, a 5 per cent share in the market for vehicles equipped with a diesel engine would not suffice to confer distinctiveness on the acronym 'TDI'.[57] Conversely, persistent efforts and considerable investments in promoting the mark in the narrow market of riflescopes give credit to the argument that hunters perceive the three-dimensional shape of a golden ring as a mark rather than as an ornament.[58]

Similarly, use during more than twenty years in Europe and generating a very **4.54** significant turnover, supported by promotional investments higher than 100 billion Italian lire in ten years, was considered a good indication of the acquisition of the distinctiveness of the shape of bow applied to shoes. This indication was corroborated by articles attesting to the recognition of the mark, as well as by statements under oath made by competitors.[59] Even a shorter period of use can be conclusive of acquired distinctiveness, where the sale of the goods or services covered by the mark has significantly increased over a three-year period in a booming field, such as the IT-related field, and where this use was supported by important media coverage.[60]

As regards non-persuasive elements, the fact that the applicant took steps to **4.55** ensure that the distinctiveness of the mark would be maintained is not sufficient to prove that the mark has acquired distinctive character through use for the goods covered by the registration, unless those measures created an awareness among the target public that the sign in question is a trade mark.[61]

The existence of national registrations is likely to be non-persuasive, save **4.56** where registration was granted in a territory where a finding of non-distinctiveness has to be overcome. As a matter of principle, the Community trade mark is a separate industrial property right which is independent of national trade mark systems. A separate assessment must therefore be carried

---

[57] *Audi* (n 36) para 66.
[58] *Shape of a Golden Ring* (n 22) para 20.
[59] Decision of the First Board of Appeal *Salvatore Ferragamo Italia SpA's Application* Case R 254/1999–1 paras 21–24.
[60] Decision of the Fourth Board of Appeal *NETSTORE* Case R 142/2001–4 (12 May 2003) para 23.
[61] *Alcon* (n 40) para 57.

out in each case with regard to absolute grounds for refusal and the findings of national tribunals cannot simply be adopted without proper consideration.[62]

F. Conclusion

4.57 Applicants may well find that the Community judges subject the acquisition of distinctive character to overly severe criteria. There may be a number of reasons for this, one being the objective assigned by the ECJ to all trade mark offices not to register marks which cannot be successfully enforced in administrative or judicial proceedings.[63] However, there is also another reason for which Community judges cannot be held responsible. Applicants tend to confuse the justification for the grant of an exclusive right on a sign originally lacking distinctive character (ie the return on investment) with the evidence that this exclusive right is justified. Applicants should be reminded that proof of enormous investments, although a key element, is not conclusive *per se* of distinctive character acquired through use if it is not corroborated by concrete evidence that the sign originally lacking distinctiveness is perceived as a badge of origin.

---

[62] *Messe München v OHIM* (Electronica) Case T-32/00 [2000] ETMR 135 para 47.
[63] *Libertel Groep BV v Benelux-Merkenbureau* Case C-104/01 [2003] ETMR 63, [2003] ECR I-03793, paras 58–59.

5

DISTINCTIVE CHARACTER ACQUIRED THROUGH USE: ESTABLISHING THE FACTS

Anna Carboni

A. Introduction	5.01	G. Proving Acquired Distinctiveness of CTMs — 5.45
B Understanding the Objection	5.04	H. Language Issues for CTMs — 5.53
C. Remembering the Objective	5.05	I. Deciding When to Argue for Acquired Distinctiveness — 5.55
D. Legal and Regulatory Guidance	5.06	J. Making the Most of the Evidence — 5.57
E. Contents of the Evidence	5.13	K. Publication — 5.59
(1) Direct Evidence of Use	5.14	L. Concluding Remarks — 5.60
(2) Evidence of Recognition	5.29	
F. Relevant Date for Proving Acquired Distinctiveness	5.41	

A. Introduction

The reader will now be familiar with the legal concept of 'acquired distinct- **5.01** iveness'. In this chapter, we turn to the practical steps which can be taken to persuade a doubting trade mark examiner that an inherently non-distinctive, descriptive or generic trade mark has been magically transformed into one which is acceptable to be registered as a Community trade mark (CTM) or national trade mark in the EU.

In many cases, step one will be to argue with the examiner about whether he **5.02** or she is correct in rejecting a trade mark on absolute grounds, relying on such favourite authorities as *BABY-DRY*,[1] *POSTKANTOOR*[2] and *Linde*.[3] But this chapter assumes that such efforts have been to no avail. If the trade mark has not been used, then that will be the end of the road until the situation changes. However, if the applicant feels sure that the trade mark has come to distinguish his products and services from those of others as a result of being used, he should take steps to gather evidence of such 'acquired distinctiveness' under Article 7(3) of the Community Trade Mark Regulation[4] (CTMR) or the relevant national laws implementing Article 3(3) of the Trade Marks Directive[5] (the Directive).

5.03 The combined aims of this chapter are (i) to identify the most important rules, regulations and authorities about how to prove acquired distinctiveness in practice and (ii) to summarize the types of evidence that might be needed, always bearing in mind that no two cases are the same. It gives hints and tips about how to present the evidence and the common pitfalls to avoid. It also looks at the particular problem for CTMs of establishing acquired distinctiveness across the EU.

B. Understanding the Objection

5.04 Before planning evidence of acquired distinctiveness, it is crucial to understand the nature of the objection raised by the registry concerned. Although an official examination letter will normally specify the legislative provision under which the trade mark is being rejected on absolute grounds, it is not unusual for this to be expressed in such general terms that one is left uncertain as to the exact nature of the objection and how to get around it. If this is the case, do not aim at an unclear and potentially moving target; call or

---

[1] *Procter & Gamble Company v OHIM* (BABY-DRY) Case C-383/99P [2002] ETMR 3 (ECJ): authority for the proposition that syntactically unusual juxtapositions are registrable.

[2] *Koninklijke KPN Nederland NV v Benelux Merkenbureau* Case C-363/99 [2004] ETMR 57 (ECJ): a mark can be greater than the sum of its parts.

[3] *Linde AG, Winward Industries Inc and Rado Uhren AG* Joined Cases C-53/01 to C-55/01 [2003] ETMR 963 (ECJ): no stricter test for shape marks than for other signs.

[4] Council Regulation on the Community trade mark (40/94/EEC).

[5] First Council Directive 89/104/EEC of 21 December 1988 to approximate the laws of the Member States relating to trade marks.

write to the examiner to ask him or her to be more precise as to the reasons for rejecting the trade mark.[6]

C. Remembering the Objective

Remember throughout that the objective is to show that the trade mark **5.05** concerned has become distinctive in relation to the goods or services listed in the specification *in consequence of* the use which has been made of it.[7] Mere proof of use is not enough. The evidence must somehow demonstrate that the use that has been made of the trade mark has caused relevant consumers to expect that goods or services sold or supplied under the trade mark originate from a particular undertaking (even if they are unable to identify it by name). The more descriptive or non-distinctive the trade mark, the more convincing that evidence must be.

D. Legal and Regulatory Guidance

Since proof of acquired distinctiveness is a question of establishing a fact, **5.06** legal and regulatory authority is of only limited assistance. However, it is important to be aware of the guidance that is available. First, no chapter on proving acquired distinctiveness in Europe would be complete without reference to *Windsurfing Chiemsee*,[8] in which the European Court of Justice (ECJ) was asked to set out the requirements for proving acquired distinctiveness. The Court said that the competent authority (ie the Office for Harmonisation in the Internal Market (OHIM) or the national registry) 'must make an overall assessment of the evidence that the mark has come to identify the product concerned as originating from a particular undertaking, and thus to distinguish that product from goods of other undertakings'. It went on to

---

[6] For CTMs, rule 11(2) of the Commission Regulation implementing the CTMR (2868/95/EC, 'the IR') requires OHIM to notify the applicant of the grounds for refusing registration on absolute grounds.

[7] CTMR art 7(3) (emphasis added).

[8] *Windsurfing Chiemsee Produktions- und Vertriebs GmbH (WSC) v Boots- und Segelzubehör Walter Huber and Franz Attenberger* Joined Cases C-108/97 and C-109/97 [1999] ETMR 585 (ECJ).

give guidance as to the types of evidence that might be relevant in assessing the distinctive character of a mark:[9]

- the market share held by the mark
- how intensive, geographically widespread and long-standing the use of the mark has been
- the amount invested by the applicant in promoting the mark
- statements from chambers of commerce and industry or other trade and professional associations
- opinion polls (often referred to as survey evidence).

5.07   The applicant needs to establish that 'a significant proportion' of consumers that are relevant to the goods to be sold under the trade mark identify them as originating from a particular undertaking because of the mark.[10] The Court expressly stated that this could not be done by reference to 'general, abstract data such as predetermined percentages'.

5.08   As a further backdrop for the evidence preparation, applicants or their representatives should also familiarize themselves with the relevant registry rules and guidance as to the types of evidence that will be taken into account in proving acquired distinctiveness, and how this should be presented.

5.09   Article 76(1) CTMR ('Taking of evidence') provides that the means of giving or obtaining evidence in proceedings before OHIM shall include:

(a) hearing the parties;
(b) requests for information;
(c) the production of documents and items of evidence;
(d) hearing witnesses;
(e) opinions by experts;
(f) statements in writing sworn or affirmed or having a similar effect under the law of the member state in which the statement is drawn up.

5.10   In practice oral hearings are extremely rare in OHIM, both at examination level and in the Boards of Appeal. Furthermore, examiners do not tend to request information to prove distinctiveness; they rely on applicants to make their own choice of evidence to submit. However, they are open to discussing with applicants the types of evidence that might be of assistance in any

---

[9] ibid paras 51–53.
[10] Although *Windsurfing* (n 8) was about a trade mark for goods, the guidance given is equally applicable in the case of a trade mark for services.

particular case. The same is generally true in national trade mark registries which examine trade marks on absolute grounds.

The final source of guidance for CTMs is the Examination Guidelines found **5.11** on the OHIM website.[11] As they state in the introduction, 'the guidelines are not intended to, and cannot, add to or subtract from the legal contents of the Regulations' and 'cannot be expected to cover all possible situations'. However, they do give the user a general guide on the process involved in receiving and overcoming objections on absolute grounds. In particular:

8.12 Use as a means of overcoming objections

8.12.1. Objections under [CTMR 7(1)(b)] to [CTMR 7(1)(d)] may be overcome if the applicant can demonstrate that the trade mark has become distinctive in relation to the goods or services as a result of the use made of it. The onus is on the applicant to make this claim and provide evidence in support of it. The evidence should show the place, time, extent and nature of the use. The evidence may be in the form of documents and items such as packaging, labels, price lists, catalogues, invoices, photographs and advertisements. Statements in writing sworn or affirmed or having similar effect under the law of the State in which the statement is drawn up are another form of evidence. These may come from experts in the trade or trade associations. The results of opinion polls may also be submitted. There should be no need for the personal appearance of witnesses before the examiner.

8.12.2. The test is that the trade mark has become distinctive within the Community in consequence of use. If the absence of distinctiveness relates to a part of the Community only the evidence must be assessed in that context. A demonstration of distinctiveness outside the Community is not sufficient. While it is not a legal requirement that the goods or services have already been provided under the trade mark in the Community this is likely to be the case. It is possible that there would be sufficient use of the trade mark in advertising within the Community for it to have become distinctive.

The examiner must assess the evidence by reference to the nature of the goods or services, taking into account the means by which they reach customers and whether, for example, the customers are specialised or general. The extent to which the trade mark is, on the face of it, lacking distinctive characteristics must be weighed against the evidence provided.

The Examination Division of OHIM has also issued a Practice Note **5.12** which gives further detailed guidance on the preparation of evidence of

---

[11] Examination Guidelines 26 March 1996, OJ OHIM 1996, p. 1324, also available at http://oami.eu.int/en/mark/marque/directives/exam.htm.

use.[12] Similar guidance is published by some of the national trade mark registries.[13]

E. Contents of the Evidence

5.13 Once all the potential sources of guidance have been consulted, it is necessary to get on with pulling together evidence tailored to the individual case. This falls broadly into two categories: direct evidence of use (including licensed use); and indirect evidence of recognition. Superimposed on this, there is sometimes—particularly for CTMs—a species of mixed evidence and argument which may be best described as 'reasonable inference'.

(1) Direct evidence of use

5.14 The uninitiated might expect that the easiest evidence for an applicant to collate is the direct evidence of actual use of the trade mark concerned. After all, such evidence will surely be in the files, archives and accounts of the applicant. In practice, however, most companies' files, archives and accounts are not created and preserved with the primary object of supporting trade mark applications, so a significant amount of work has to be done to turn the documents and materials that are available into useful evidence. The end result needs to be a series of exhibits depicting the trade mark as it has actually been used by the applicant or his licensees, under cover of a witness statement (or equivalent under national procedure) given by the applicant (if an individual) or a senior representative of the applicant (if a company or other entity), explaining the extent of the use in detail.

5.15 Conventional practice in the UK Registry, which is also often adopted before OHIM, is to give details of use of the trade mark during each of the five years leading up to the filing date. Where a mark has been used for longer than this, the date of first use should be explained and any available additional detail in relation to the earlier period may be helpful. On the other hand, it

---

[12] Examination Division Practice Note, 'Evidence of Use', version 1—March 1999 available at http://oami.eu.int/en/mark/marque/practice_note.htm.

[13] For example, see the UK Trade Marks Registry *Work Manual* ch 6 ('Examination and Practice'—July 2004).

may not be fatal that the trade mark has been used for less than five years. The shorter the period of use, though, the more convincing the evidence may have to be to persuade the examiner that the trade mark has acquired distinctiveness in that time.

(a) Evidence of sales and supplies

If goods have been sold under the trade mark concerned, the exhibits should **5.16** include sample packaging or photographs of packaging, depicting the trade mark in use. If possible, the packaging should relate to examples of all the goods in the specification. They should also be dated in some way. If copyright notices appear on the packaging, this will convince the examiner as to the relevant dates. Otherwise, the witness statement should explain the dates when the packaging was used and how this is known. For example: 'I produce as exhibit X a sample of the packaging, depicting use of the trade mark in relation to [specify goods]. We retain samples of our packaging in our company archives, from which I am able to state that this packaging design has been used since [date] and is still in use today.'

The figures given for sales of goods or supplies of services under the trade **5.17** mark should explain which goods and services they relate to. It is no good stating that 'my company's turnover is €X million per year' if the company sells many different types of goods, only some of which are relevant to the trade mark. Again, the more focused the evidence, the more likely the examiner will find it helpful in establishing acquired distinctiveness. So the evidence should specify turnover of goods or services sold or supplied under the trade mark. If a precise breakdown is not possible, then estimates should be given, with an explanation of how they are reached. A description of the numbers of actual goods sold—or of customers supplied in the case of services—is often helpful in giving the examiner a real understanding of what the financial turnover figures mean.

If the relevant turnover data is in published accounts, these should be **5.18** exhibited to lend credibility to the figures. Even figures formerly collated for internal viewing only may be taken more seriously than figures put together purely for the purpose of the trade mark application, since it will be evident that they have not been overstated in order to secure registration of the mark.

(b) Advertising and promotion

5.19 Along with the evidence of actual sales and supplies, evidence relating to the advertising and promotion of the applicant's products by reference to the trade mark is generally of critical importance. In the case of a young mark which has been heavily promoted but has not yet generated substantial sales, it may even be the most important evidence of use. Evidence of the nature and extent of advertising has been said to be particularly relevant for trade marks comprising slogans.[14]

5.20 Again, samples should be exhibited, showing the trade mark as used in the advertisements and promotional material. These may include television, radio, newspaper or magazine advertisements, posters, billboards and web advertising. There may be evidence of specific customer promotions, perhaps by direct mailings or in-store events. And maybe there has been some sponsorship activity that has been conducted by reference to the trade mark. Where possible, details should be included which give the examiner an idea of the exposure of relevant members of the public to the advertising and promotional material, such as viewing and listening figures for television and radio; newspaper and magazine distribution figures; website hits and the size of any direct mailings.[15] Dates should be explained by the witness, and figures for expenditure on advertising and promotion should be given in a way which will satisfy the examiner that all or a substantial part of it has been relevant to the use of the trade mark on the goods and/or services in the specification.

5.21 In relation to non-conventional trade marks, such as shapes and colours, there is a current trend in the UK Registry of requiring the applicant to show that it has set out to educate the public to look upon the shape or colour as a trade mark. This can be a frustrating requirement where a sign has become distinctive of the applicant or his goods or services more by luck than

---

[14] This was stated by the UK Registry hearing officer when considering the registrability of HAVE A BREAK, as cited by Rimer J (and not disapproved) in *Nestlé SA's Trade Mark Application* [2003] FSR 37; [2002] EWHC 2533 (Ch).

[15] See for example *M & R Marking Systems Inc's Application* (IDEAL) Case R1163/2000–1 [2002] ETMR 28 in which the first Board of Appeal found evidence of advertisements in a well-known specialist trade magazine to be particularly persuasive.

judgment. It is submitted that it is also a misplaced requirement. Acquired distinctiveness is a question of fact, not of subjective intention.[16]

Having said that, it is certainly worth explaining in evidence any steps which **5.22** have been taken to educate the public that a sign is in fact a trade mark. One example was the Levi's jeans advertising campaign in the 1980s which focused attention on the (usually red) tab that is sewn into the seam of jeans back pockets and which featured statements such as 'a coloured Tab on the back pocket is a registered trade mark identifying garments made only by Levi Strauss & Co.'[17] The campaign to emphasize the triangularity of Toblerone served a similar purpose, though without expressly telling people that the shape should be treated as a trade mark.[18] A recent, more subtle, example is adidas' campaign to promote its three-stripe trade mark (already well known to trade mark lawyers for its exposure in the ECJ and other courts around Europe) by advertising via billboards bearing the three-stripe trade mark and the adidas name, but without any depiction of the goods themselves.

Efforts by an applicant to ensure that its employees treat the sign as a trade **5.23** mark may also be explained. For example, internal branding guidelines and instructions to employees to keep a look-out for unauthorized use by third parties should be exhibited. In the case of a very descriptive or non-distinctive mark, however, such evidence would have to be backed up by evidence demonstrating that the behaviour encouraged had actually produced the desired results. Efforts to educate consumers that do not in fact create the necessary awareness that a sign is a trade mark are insufficient.[19]

(c) Market size and share

Where market size and/or share data is available, this can be very helpful to **5.24** the examiner in putting the financial data into context. Many markets are

---

[16] Positive promotion of a sign as being a trade mark may be more crucial in the case of a mark used for a product that has a monopoly, such as in *Dyson Ltd v Registrar of Trade Marks* EWHC 1062 (Ch); [2003] ETMR 77, where without such evidence it is difficult to work out whether evidence of recognition relates to the trade mark or merely to the product itself.

[17] Discussed in *Levi Strauss and Co. and Levi Strauss (New Zealand) Ltd v Kimbyr Investments Ltd* [1994] FSR 335 HC (NZ).

[18] The campaign featured a delightful ditty which referred to Toblerone as being 'made with triangular almonds from triangular trees and triangular honey from triangular bees' and ending 'so, oh Mr Confectioner please give me Toblerone'.

[19] *Alcon Inc v OHIM* Case T-237/01 [2004] ETMR 6 (CFI), para 55.

analysed by independent organizations which publish this sort of data. As with all the other evidence, the person presenting figures relating to the market share of the applicant's goods or services should be able to explain that they reflect figures for goods/services supplied *under the trade mark.*

(d) Confidentiality

5.25 Trade mark applicants are sometimes concerned about releasing sales, advertising and market share figures where these have not been published previously. These are commercially sensitive data which may be valuable to a competitor. The concern is that the trade mark file at some stage (usually after publication of the trade mark) will be open for inspection. This is certainly true in the case of CTMs[20] and UK trade marks.[21]

5.26 For most registries which permit inspection of trade mark files, provision has been made to preserve the confidentiality of commercially sensitive evidence where this is legitimately claimed. For example, Article 1, Rule 88(c) IR provides that the following will be excluded from inspection:

> 'parts of the file which the party concerned showed a special interest in keeping confidential before the application for inspection of the files was made, unless inspection of such part of the file is justified by overriding legitimate interests of the party seeking inspection'.

5.27 An applicant wishing to take advantage of such a provision should assert confidentiality in specified material at the time of submitting it and, preferably, ringfence the confidential material, for example by putting it in a separate annex. Any document containing material to be withheld from inspection should be marked clearly as 'Confidential' and 'To be withheld from inspection' and a full explanation of the reasons for confidentiality should be given in a cover letter to the Registry.

5.28 Where turnover and advertising/promotion figures are very large, another way of avoiding publication of detailed data is to state that turnover or expenditure has been 'over' or 'in excess of' €X in each relevant year, and to explain why the figures are expressed in these terms.

---

[20] CTMR art 84.
[21] TMA 1994 s 67.

(2) Evidence of recognition

In cases where a trade mark only just falls short of the test of inherent **5.29**
distinctiveness, good evidence of use may be sufficient to overcome the objection to registration, with the examiner being willing to conclude that the
mark has been used in a way, and to such an extent, that a significant
proportion of the relevant public is likely to have learnt that the trade mark
denotes a particular product or undertaking.

However, in other cases, evidence of use will not be enough on its own to **5.30**
overcome the examiner's objection. For example, as Jacob J said in the TREAT
case:

> 'Mere evidence of use of a highly descriptive or laudatory word will not suffice,
> without more, to prove that it is distinctive of one particular trader—is taken
> by the public as a badge of origin.' [22]

In such cases, distinctive character can only be proved by submitting addi- **5.31**
tional, generally independent, evidence that the relevant public has been
educated as to the trade mark significance of the mark. The evidence that is
suitable to fulfil this task varies from case to case, but may include trade
evidence and survey evidence, as well as evidence from relevant consumers
themselves. Some other miscellaneous categories of evidence are also
discussed in this section.

(a) Trade evidence

Potential witnesses who are in a position to provide independent evidence as **5.32**
to distinctiveness, based on an expert knowledge of the relevant trade or
profession, might include the following: competitors, members of a relevant
trade association, and journalists or editors for trade journals. In practice, it
may be easier to persuade the applicant's suppliers or trade customers to
spend the time involved in giving evidence but, if they do so, their relationship with the applicant must be spelt out and the evidence will generally be
given less weight than that of truly independent witnesses.

Trade witnesses should give details of their current job and set out their **5.33**

---

[22] *British Sugar plc v James Robertson & Sons Ltd* [1996] RPC 281 (Ch) 286.

background in the relevant trade or service industry. They should make it clear whether they limit their comments on distinctiveness to their own views, or whether they are expressing them as generally held views in the trade or as evidence of how they would expect consumers to react to the trade mark. If the latter, they must explain why they are in a position to give what is in effect expert opinion evidence. In either event, the witnesses must explain, in their own words, that they regard the trade mark as indicating goods or services of the applicant, and why this is the case. It can be helpful to add, if true, that they consider that use of the same or a similar sign by other traders would be likely to cause confusion with the applicant or his goods/services.

(b) Survey evidence

5.34 Surveys can be of assistance for two purposes: first to produce statistically significant data as to the degree of recognition of the trade mark by relevant members of the public and second to assist the applicant in identifying individuals who recognize the trade mark and who might be prepared to give a witness statement to that effect.

5.35 Practice in relation to trade mark surveys varies around the world. Within Europe, the UK stands out as a jurisdiction where courts have been particularly critical of surveys and reluctant to accept the propositions they are said to support unless stringent criteria are met. These were set out in the early 1980s in *Imperial v Philip Morris* and are still referred to in the courts today.[23] Although surveys that do not meet these criteria will still be accepted and considered by UK and other national registries and OHIM for the purpose of assessing acquired distinctiveness, they will be given less weight than those which comply with best practice, which is summarized below.

(1) Any interviewee selection process must be explained and should result in a relevant cross-section of the public taking part in the survey. It must not have an in-built bias. For example, in a survey to establish the distinctiveness of a new Gucci logo, the interviewers should not stand outside the door of the Gucci shop and interview only those who have just been in there. Similarly, limiting interviewees in a survey about a

---

[23] *Imperial v Philip Morris* [1984] RPC 293 (Ch) per Whitford J 302–303.

trade mark comprising the shape of goods to people who say that design
of goods is important to them, will skew the results in an artificial way.[24]

(2) The questions asked must be both relevant and non-leading. They must
not cause the interviewee to speculate about something which he or she
would not even have thought about, had the question not been put.
Since the applicant is aiming to persuade the registry concerned that his
trade mark is recognized as a trade mark by the public, the questions
should not be framed so as to put that idea into the interviewee's head.
Thus, for example, when trying to establish the distinctiveness of a
product shape, the question 'Do you recognize this design of toaster?'
followed by 'Who do you think makes it?' is unacceptable; whereas
'What can you tell me about this toaster?' is a totally neutral question
which ought to elicit references to the shape and the fact that it emanates
from the applicant or relates to a named product.[25]

(3) Any instructions given to the interviewers should be disclosed, for
example as to where to conduct the interviews, how to record the
answers and how to categorize the results.

(4) The numbers of people interviewed should be stated and should match
the number of the results delivered, with any discrepancies explained.
Ideally, the survey size should be sufficient to produce a statistically
significant result. This may be fairly small in the case of a specialist
product targeted at a small and specialist market. For an everyday consumer product or service, a sample of 1000 interviewees is commonly
used.

In general, examiners will pay most attention to surveys that are conducted **5.36**
by independent organizations with experience of conducting surveys. Where
such organizations are used, a senior representative should present the results
in a report and explain the overall findings as well as the survey instructions
and other matters referred to above.

In the event that the trade mark comes under attack at a later stage, whether **5.37**
by way of opposition or in a litigation context, a robust survey conducted at
the application stage can be of considerable assistance in deflecting the attack.
It is worth adding that, in a jurisdiction where discovery or disclosure of

---

[24] *Dualit Ltd's (Toaster Shapes) Trade Mark Applications* [1999] RPC 890 (Ch).
[25] ibid para 45.

documents takes place in litigation, any surveys other than the one relied on in the registry may have to be revealed to the other side. This position is accepted in the UK following the *Philip Morris* case.[26] Indeed, as soon as it is known that a party intends to rely on survey evidence, it is common practice to write to them to ask whether a pilot survey was carried out and, if it was, to ask for full details and documents relating to it. For example, a survey which failed to elicit the desired results, or a 'pilot' survey which was adapted for the purpose of the full survey, may become subject to scrutiny. Therefore great care should be taken at all stages during the survey process to try to conduct tests in a fair and unbiased way and to be able to justify any changes made. To avoid creating discoverable documents, early pre-survey tests can be carried out on a very informal basis, without keeping written records, purely for checking the suitability of interview questions and stimuli.

5.38   Assuming that a survey complies with all these rules as to procedure and content, what results will suffice to persuade the examiner to accept the proposition that the trade mark has become distinctive? Some countries, such as Germany, have traditionally set specific percentages to be reached in order for a survey to be accepted as establishing distinctiveness.[27] However, for the purpose of CTMs, the ECJ has rejected this approach, emphasizing that the necessary degree of recognition will vary from case to case.[28]

(c) Individual consumers

5.39   As mentioned above, surveys can be used to identify individuals who may be willing to give a witness statement in support of the trade mark application. While the views of individual consumers, who will inevitably have been chosen because they say supportive things, are of no statistical significance, the way in which they express why it is that they associate the word, shape or colour comprising the trade mark with the applicant's goods or services can help to support the statistical findings of a survey.

---

[26] *Imperial v Philip Morris* (n 23).

[27] For example, a minimum of 50% recognition is required by the German Federal Supreme Court (BGH), the German Federal Patent Court and the internal examination guidelines of the German PTO. See s 9 para (a) of the internal guidelines of the German PTO, confirmed by BGH, GRUR 1990, p. 360–1 – 'Apropos Film II' and GRUR 2001, p. 1042–3 – 'Reich und Schön'.

[28] *Lloyd Schuhfabrik Meyer & Co GmbH v Klijsen Handel BV* Case C-342/97 [1999] ETMR 690 (ECJ) para 24, citing *Windsurfing Chiemsee*.

(d) National registrations

Applicants for CTMs frequently list trade mark registrations obtained in **5.40**
individual Member States as 'evidence' of acquired distinctiveness. These are
only relevant if the trade marks were accepted on the basis of acquired distinctiveness in that jurisdiction. The Examination Division Practice Note on
evidence of use[29] states that, unless there are good grounds for discounting
such a registration, the examiner should accept this as indirect evidence.[30]
However, a Benelux registration, for example, which was accepted pursuant
to a deposit system, is of no assistance.[31]

F. Relevant Date for Proving Acquired Distinctiveness

By the time evidence of acquired distinctiveness is being put together, it is **5.41**
usually several months after the application was filed and it can sometimes be
years later in a long-drawn-out case where an applicant has made incremental
attempts to persuade the registry of the merits of his trade mark. At this point
the applicant should be reminded that the crucial date for proving acquired
distinctiveness of a CTM is the filing date. This is the logical interpretation
of Article 7(3) CTMR and was confirmed by the CFI in *eCopy Inc v OHIM*,[32]
which observed that allowing for a mark's distinctiveness to be acquired post-
filing would mean that the chances of proving distinctiveness would increase
the longer the registration process takes.

In the case of national trade marks in EU Member States, there is some **5.42**
flexibility to permit distinctive character to be acquired after filing.[33] Taking
the UK as an example, it has not taken up the opportunity to allow later

---

[29] Examination Division Practice Note (n 12).

[30] Although not expressly stated in the Practice Note, it is assumed that a national registration for a word mark that has been accepted on the basis of acquired distinctiveness will only
be of assistance in relation to the Member State concerned.

[31] Despite the encouragement given by the Practice Note, while OHIM examiners and the
Boards of Appeal do take account of national registrations and the circumstances in which
they were acquired, they will not substitute the views of a national registry for their own. The
same is true in relation to establishing inherent distinctiveness by reference to the existence of
national registrations. See, for example, *Leupold & Stevens, Inc* Case R 947/2001–2 para 15.

[32] *eCopy, Inc v OHIM* Case T-247/01 [2003] ETMR 99.

[33] art 3(3) of the Directive provides that any Member State may allow registration of a trade
mark which has acquired distinctive character after the application date.

evidence of acquired distinctiveness to be shown in relation to trade mark applications, but it has done so in relation to invalidity proceedings where a UK trade mark is challenged on absolute grounds.[34]

5.43 The rule that distinctiveness must be acquired before the application date does not necessarily preclude the relevance of evidence that relates to a later date. For example, if pre-filing market share data is unavailable, a market share figure of 50 per cent a year later may be of help (in conjunction with the applicant's turnover figures) in inferring a sizeable market share at the date of filing. Similarly, a survey conducted after the application date can be relied on and argued to reflect a similar position to that before the application was filed, on the basis that the market has not changed substantially in the interim and nor have consumers' habits. This would not be a good argument in the case of a trade mark filed before the relevant product or service was launched.

5.44 So, the key thing to remember when you are in a jurisdiction where the filing date is your cut-off, is to explain why any of your evidence which relates to a later date should be taken into account. For example recent sample packaging should be explained by someone who worked for the applicant at the filing date to be the same as the pre-filing packaging. Similarly, trade witnesses giving expert evidence of consumer recognition of the trade mark should prove that they had relevant expertise at the filing date and explain that their evidence would have been the same at that time. These are examples of the 'reasonable inference' evidence discussed in the introduction to this section.

G. Proving Acquired Distinctiveness of CTMs

5.45 A CTM will be refused on examination even if any absolute grounds of non-registrability exist in only part of the Community.[35] This may be the case, for example, for a word mark which is descriptive in a particular language, but which is not understood as having any particular meaning in countries where that language is not spoken. OHIM should make clear to the applicant the geographical scope of any objection, so that the applicant can limit his efforts in preparing evidence of acquired distinctiveness to the countries where the

---

[34] TMA 1994 s 47(1).
[35] CTMR art 7(2).

objection arises. If the examiner is unclear about this, the applicant should check the position, to avoid wasting time preparing unnecessary evidence.

Absolute objections to non-verbal signs such as shapes, colours and sounds **5.46** tend to apply across the whole Community. This leaves the applicant with the unenviable task of establishing acquired distinctiveness in an ever-growing number of Member States (currently twenty-five). In the *Ty Nant* (blue bottle) case,[36] the Third Board of Appeal of OHIM stated that the trade mark must be used in the Community as a whole or at least in a substantial part thereof, so that a 'sufficiently large class of persons' recognizes the sign as distinctive.[37] The Court of First Instance went even further the following year in *OPTIONS*,[38] stating that, to be eligible as a CTM, a sign must possess distinctive character 'throughout the Community'.

In a perfect world, an applicant would be able to present evidence under each **5.47** relevant head discussed above, covering all twenty-five countries of the Community. In practice, even if a trade mark really has been used in all twenty-five countries and evidence of sales, advertising and market share can be given across the entire Community, it would be a hugely expensive task to gather trade, survey and individual consumer evidence for every country. Therefore an exercise in common sense and reasonable inference has to be carried out.

By way of example, if goods under the relevant trade mark have achieved **5.48** market shares ranging from 5 per cent to 25 per cent across the Community, one could conduct market surveys in, say, six or seven Member States having a range of market shares. Results showing recognition of the mark as a trade mark of, say, 80 per cent in the countries with 25 per cent market share and 60 per cent in the countries with 5 per cent market share could then be extrapolated and applied to other countries where the market shares are similar and where there is no particular market reason why the recognition rates cannot be assumed to be similar.

---

[36] *Ty Nant Spring Water Limited's Application* Case R5/1999–3 Third Board of Appeal [1999] ETMR 974.

[37] In *Ty Nant* (n 36) evidence of sales in the UK, Italy, France, Belgium, Spain and Germany combined with some independent trade evidence in relation to the UK only was held insufficient to overcome an objection under art 7(1)(b) CTMR.

[38] *Ford Motor Company v OHIM* Case T-91/99 [2000] ETMR 554 (CFI) para 24. This result followed from the principle set down in CTMR art 1(2) that a CTM has a 'unitary character'.

5.49   Using extrapolation and inference in this way is essentially a practical exercise aimed at satisfying the two tests of 'use in the Community as a whole or a substantial part thereof' and 'distinctive character throughout the Community'. But further legal authority would be useful to practitioners. To date, the ECJ has not issued a decision clearly telling us whether and how many countries missing from the list of those in which a mark can be proved distinctive (even by inference) will prevent the grant of a CTM, though the CFI has indicated in *OPTIONS* that one sizeable country (France) may be enough.

5.50   What if there has been no use at all in, say, Malta? One is tempted to jump to the conclusion that this would not be fatal. Further, a mark that is used everywhere else in the Community is likely to have come to the attention of people from Malta, perhaps through their travels abroad or around the internet, and evidence can be given of that fact.

5.51   Taking another example, what if a trade mark has not been used in any of the formerly Communist Eastern European countries (Czech Republic, Estonia, Hungary, Latvia, Lithuania, Poland, Slovenia or Slovakia) but has been well used throughout the pre-accession Member States plus Cyprus and Malta? In this case, the likelihood is that, even if some spillover recognition can be proved in these countries, the mark would be refused registration as a CTM. Since pre-accession CTMs were automatically extended to the ten new Member States on 1 May 2004,[39] even if they were only granted following proof of acquired distinctiveness through use in the pre-accession States, one can see that anyone with such a mark who waited until after accession made the task of proving distinctiveness considerably more difficult for themselves overnight.

5.52   Of course, all is not lost if the examiner or Board of Appeal cannot be persuaded that the trade mark has acquired distinctive character across the Community. By this time, the applicant will have pulled together good evidence of use in a number of countries and can apply to convert the CTM application into national applications in those countries where there is no examination process or where the evidence was particularly good.[40]

---

[39] By CTMR art 142a as inserted under the Accession Treaty.
[40] Under the rules set out in CTMR arts 108–110, as amended by Council Regulation (EC) No 422/2004.

H. Language Issues for CTMs

A CTM application filed in one of the five official languages of OHIM will **5.53** be dealt with in that language during the examination process.[41] If the application is made in another language, designating one of the official languages as the second language, then the norm is for the examination to proceed in the first language. This could be a problem for the US applicant who chose to file in Dutch and designate English as the second language (in order to maximize the chances of any opposition being conducted in English). In practice, however, OHIM is happy to proceed and take evidence under the second language.[42]

Translation issues can still often arise, however, when trying to prove **5.54** acquired distinctiveness across Europe, because the evidence of use and recognition is likely to be in the local language for each country. Under Article 1 Rule 96(1) IR this evidence should all be translated into the language used for filing the application or into the chosen second language. However, it may not be necessary to translate everything in order for the examiner to assess the evidence.[43] In a case involving voluminous material in a variety of languages, it is worth raising the issue of languages with the examiner at an early stage with a view to reaching a compromise that will save translation costs.

I. Deciding When to Argue for Acquired Distinctiveness

As can be seen from the details set out above, it can be very costly to do a **5.55** really good job of proving acquired distinctiveness. In a case where the applicant is convinced that the examiner is being too cautious in finding that a trade mark is non-distinctive, it can be tempting to stick with the argument on inherent distinctiveness to a final rejection and then appeal to the Boards of Appeal, rather than to change course and start gathering evidence of use. Indeed the applicant may be concerned that his evidence of use is even less

---

[41] CTMR art 115(4).

[42] Communication no. 4/04 of the President of the Office of 30 April 2004 concerning the use of the language of filing formalized this approach.

[43] art 1, r 96(2) IR provides that OHIM 'may require that a translation be supplied'.

persuasive than his arguments about the inherent distinctiveness of the trade mark.

5.56   The question that arises is whether an escalation to the Boards of Appeal of the argument on inherent distinctiveness precludes the possibility of introducing evidence of use if they agree with the examiners' rejection of the mark. Apparently not. The Court of First Instance ruled in *BABY-DRY*[44] that, where an applicant raises arguments based on Article 7(3) CTMR for the first time before the Board of Appeal, the Board must either rule on the substance of the issue or remit it to the examiner. The general approach now is to remit cases to the examiner where this occurs before OHIM.[45] Of course, in the *BABY-DRY* case, we know that the applicant went on up the judicial tree to the ECJ and got what it wanted on the inherent distinctiveness argument.[46]

J. Making the Most of the Evidence

5.57   Trade marks have often been refused not because there was insufficient evidence of acquired distinctiveness but because the evidence was inadequately presented. This normally happens behind the scenes at the application stage, but there have certainly been some public humiliations when poor evidence of use has been presented in non-use cases.[47] While some tips have been given under the separate headings in this chapter, these are some additional general points that can be made to maximize the persuasiveness of the evidence.

(1)   Explain who the witness is and why his or her evidence is relevant.
(2)   Frame witness statements in the witness's own words, using clear, non-legal language.

---

[44]   *Procter & Gamble Company v OHIM* Case T-163/98 [1999] ETMR 767 (CFI) para 28.
[45]   See, for example *The Black & Decker Corporation* Case R350/1991–2 (Second Board of Appeal) covering a figurative mark comprising a colour picture of a hand-held drill; and *Harcourt Brace & Co's Application* Case R130/1999–1 [2000] ETMR 382 (First Board of Appeal).
[46]   *BABY-DRY* (n 1). Another example of a case where persistence was rewarded is *Daimler-Chrysler Corporation v OHIM* Case T-128/01 [2003] ETMR 87 (CFI) where the applicant succeeded in establishing that a mark comprising the shape of a car grille was inherently distinctive.
[47]   See, for example, *KK Fernandes v OHIM* (HIWATT) [2003] ETMR 98 (CFI) and the English case of *Laboratoire de la Mer Trade Marks* [2002] FSR 51; [2002] ETMR 34 (Ch).

(3) State the source of any facts, if they are not within the witness's own knowledge.

(4) Use the witness statement to explain what the exhibits are. Don't just attach them and leave it for the examiner to work out what they tell him.

If evidence is being collated for a national trade mark, it is worth taking local **5.58** advice on what will 'fly' in that jurisdiction. Despite best efforts at harmonization by the legislators, there remain significant differences in national approaches to evidence. For example, the 'Continental' assumption that evidence from an officer or employee of the applicant will be untruthful or at least overenthusiastic has filtered through to OHIM,[48] whereas the German reliance on fixed percentages to show distinctiveness via a survey has not.

K. Publication

If, after any or all of the efforts described in this chapter, a sign is successfully **5.59** registered as a CTM, a note will be published on the OHIM record for the mark to the effect that it has been granted having been found distinctive in consequence of the use made of it.[49] Anyone looking at the record will thereby be notified that there is more to the trade mark than meets the eye and that they should dig a little deeper before assuming that they can knock it out on the basis that it is non-distinctive.

L. Concluding Remarks

One might ask whether the efforts described above are all worthwhile. The **5.60** answer is that the value of the exercise in proving acquired distinctiveness lies in the value to the applicant of preserving exclusivity in his trade mark. If he fails to obtain protection by registration, he will be left to pursue third parties by passing off or other unfair competition actions—possibly in many different countries. The evidence required to support such actions would be

---

[48] For example, in *Payless Car Rental System Inc's Application; Opposition of Canary Islands Car SA* [2000] ETMR 1136, the Opposition Division held that 'the perception of the party [a company director] involved in the dispute may be more or less affected by his personal interests in the matter'.

[49] art 1, r 12(i) IR.

evidence of use and acquired distinctiveness similar to that discussed above. Far better to prepare this at an early stage, and under a relatively relaxed timetable, than when people have left the company, samples cannot be found and there is time pressure to act.

5.61   That leads to the final tip. Do not throw things away! People may move on, but a well-maintained archive of materials relating to use of a developing trade mark will be of great assistance in proving its right to be registered and to be asserted against people who try to make off with it.

6

DISTINGUISHING USE VERSUS FUNCTIONAL USE: THREE-DIMENSIONAL MARKS

Thomas Hays

A. The Nature of the Problem   6.01
B. Distinguishing Trade Marks from Functional Features   6.07
C. *Philips Electronics v Remington Consumer Products*   6.12

D. Marks with Less than Complete Technical Functions   6.22
E. Peculiarities of Use of Three-Dimensional Marks   6.31

A. The Nature of the Problem

Distinctiveness is the essence of a valid trade mark, allowing it to fulfil the **6.01** purpose of identifying the goods and services of one provider from those of another.[1] So long as the definition of a mark is limited to two-dimensional words and symbols, trade mark law stays within a complicated but manageable realm of more or less superfluous adornments placed on products, their packaging and advertisements for products and services. The complications increase dramatically when the definition of a mark is expanded to include three-dimensional features and, in particular, features integral to the

---

[1] For a discussion of distinctiveness in shape marks, see D Kitchin *et al* (eds) *Kerly's Law of Trade Marks and Trade Names* (14th edn) (Sweet & Maxwell London 2004) 7–86; for distinctiveness in US and EU law, as well as in the UK, see J Phillips *Trade Mark Law: A Practical Anatomy* (OUP Oxford 2003) chs 4–5.

functioning of the products which those features, as marks, are intended to designate.[2]

6.02 The problem is one of identification. A consumer may identify a product by its distinctive shape, but does that identification result from some trademark-related connection with the undertaking ultimately responsible for putting the product on the market, or does the identification result from some technical feature inherent in the way the product is used, such that other products operating in the same way and originating from other manufactures would also have that same shape, but for the exclusivity created by a trade mark monopoly?[3]

6.03 The supersonic Concorde aeroplane provides a good example of this dual use of shapes. It was the only commercial aircraft flying with a delta-wing configuration. Even a small child would instantly recognize the delta-wing silhouette as belonging to the Concorde. But use of the delta-shaped wing structure, as with the Concorde's smaller predecessors, the French Mirage military aircraft of the 1960s, was a technical feature that aided the aircraft in flying at supersonic speeds. Was the delta-wing shape a trade mark, with the consequence that the Concorde's developers might claim a monopoly over its use as a means of identifying a particular brand of aircraft, or was it a

---

[2] See First Council Directive 89/104/EEC of 21 December 1988 to approximate the laws of the Member States relating to trade marks [1989] OJ L 40 11 February 1989 (Council Directive 89/104). Art 2 defines a mark as including 'Any sign capable of being represented graphically, particularly . . . the shape of goods or their packaging . . .'. This definition is repeated in the Trade Marks Act 1994 (1994, c. 26) (TMA) s 1; the Community Trade Mark Regulation, Council Regulation (EC 40/94) of 20 December 1993, on the Community trade mark [1994] OJ L 11 14 January 1994 (Council Regulation 40/94), art 4. Compare Agreement on Trade-Related Aspects of Intellectual Property Rights, 15 April 1994, Marrakech Agreement Establishing the World Trade Organization, Annex 1C, *Legal Instruments—Results of the Uruguay Round* vol 31; 33 ILM 1994, 1144 (the TRIPs Agreement) art 15(1), which defines the 'protectable subject matter' of marks without expressly mentioning the physical shape of goods.

[3] The widening of trade mark registration to include shapes—'anything which can convey information', in the words of Jacob J in *Philips Electronics NV v Remington Consumer Products* [1998] RPC 283, 298 in response to Philips' assertion that a shape is not a sign, though shapes can convey the vital and necessary information (from the point of view of trade mark law) concerning the origin of products; stating: 'I can see no reason to limit the meaning of the word' in reference to the inclusion of shapes under the general legal definition of signs—has been criticized by some commentators: see eg A Firth, E Gredley and S Maniatis 'Shapes as Trade Marks: Public Policy, Functional Considerations and Consumer Perception' [2001] 23 EIPR 86, and praised by others: see eg G Dinwoodie 'Reconceptualising the Inherent Distinctiveness of Product Design Trade Dress' [1997] 75 NCL Rev 471.

technical feature, which if not otherwise protected by any other exclusive right, could be used by other aircraft manufacturers, or was it a combination of the two?

An important underlying policy complication comes from the possibility **6.04** that technical features of products may be protected by other forms of intellectual property. If a feature is novel and represents an inventive step, it may qualify for patent protection. If the feature is novel but more superficial, it may be subject to the protection of one of the varieties of industrial design rights. In other instances, copyright protection may apply, a possibility shared by two- and three-dimensional marks. The shape of a product may thus receive legal protection independently of its ability to represent the origin of the product.[4]

These other forms of protection eventually come to an end. Trade marks, **6.05** however, may theoretically last forever provided they are continuously used. A technical feature protected by a patent, for example, would become available for use by other manufacturers after the expiration of a maximum of twenty years from the date of the application for a patent monopoly over that use. The policy concern is that the possibility of overlapping trade mark protection in the same physical features as that protected by a patent, where it is grounded in the same technical distinctiveness that supported the patent's novelty and then grows over time through use and through the association by consumers of the product with the patent proprietor or his licensees, may be used to extend monopolistic control indefinitely.[5]

---

[4] A significant limitation on what is a mark is contained at the end of the definition given in Council Directive 89/104 art 2: 'provided that such signs are capable of distinguishing the goods or services of one undertaking from those of other undertakings'. See also TMA s 1(1); Council Regulation 40/94 art 4.

[5] UK Government White Paper *Reform of Trade Mark Law* Cm. 1203 [1990] para 2.20, p 9, expressing the concern and explaining the exclusions listed in Council Directive 89/104 art 3(1)(e) as being to prevent the 'automatic and indefinite extension' of monopolistic control originally based on another intellectual property right. However, there is no formal prohibition of trade mark protection coinciding with other forms of protection, either in Community law or UK law. In *Philips* (n 3) the progenitor of the reference to the ECJ discussed below, Jacob J rejected the argument, based on public policy considerations, that one-time patent protection for a technical feature excluded the registration of that feature as a shape mark. However, the Court of Appeal [1999] RPC 809 (CA) at 816, accepted the argument, holding a trade-mark-based extension of the terms of patents and registered designs would be against public policy, as did Advocate General Ruiz Jarabo Colomer, *Philips v Remington*, Opinion of the Advocate General, 23 January 2001 [2001] ETMR 38, [2001] RPC 48, [2002] 2 CMLR 1329. The ECJ remained silent on the matter.

6.06 In an attempt to prevent this extension of protection when registration was broadened to included three-dimensional marks, Council Directive 89/104 imposed limitations on the registration as a trade mark of the technical features of products:

> Article 3 Grounds for refusal or invalidity
>
> 1. The following shall not be registered or if registered shall be liable to be declared invalid:
>   a. signs which cannot constitute a trade mark; [. . .]
>   c. trade marks which consist exclusively of signs or indications which may serve, in trade, to designate the kind, quality, intended purpose, value, geographical origin, or the time of production of the goods or of rendering of the service, or other characteristics of the goods or service; [. . .]
>   e. signs which consist exclusively of:
>   — the shape which results from the nature of the goods themselves, or
>   — the shape of goods which is necessary to obtain a technical result, or
>   — the shape which gives substantial value to the goods;. . .[6]

B. Distinguishing Trade Marks from Functional Features

6.07 As it has done on other issues, where its simplicity and brevity have generated varying interpretations and given rise to extensive litigation, Council Directive 89/104 leaves many questions unanswered in respect of what Article 3 actually excludes. For example, if the shape of a product was not distinctive at the time a product was first marketed, and thus unregistrable under Article 3(1)(b), can it subsequently become registrable if distinctiveness is acquired through use where the public, over time, begins to associate products of that shape with just one manufacturer?[7] If it can, how does acquired

---

[6] Council Directive 89/104 art 3(1)(a),(e). The equivalent in Council Regulation 40/94 is art 7(1), with a difference in the wording of 7(1)(a), 'signs which do not conform to the requirements of Article 4'. Since art 4 gives the definition of what is a mark, Council Regulation 40/94 art 7(1)(a) and Council Directive 89/104 art 3(1)(a) can be considered to be approximately the same. The TMA ss 3(1)(a) and 3(2) follow the Council Regulation 40/94 construction.

[7] This question is answered in Ch 4 of this volume. Firth *et al* (n 3) 91 argue shape-related grounds for a refusal of registration, as absolute bars, should be considered first in respect of three-dimensional marks, before other considerations, such as distinctiveness. This seems the more efficient approach.

distinctiveness relate to the exclusions in Article 3(1)(e), where technical features are unregistrable because of their potential use by others, not as trade marks but as technological applications? Can the repeated use of a non-distinctive technical feature give the user some exclusive claim to that feature if, through that use, it eventually becomes identified with the user?[8] Alternatively, is Article 3(1)(e) to be interpreted as meaning that *all* features of products that serve some technical function are *always* excluded from registration, no matter how distinctive those features might be at the time a product incorporating them is launched on to the market or after the repeated use of those features over time with the result that the public comes to associate those features with a certain manufacturer?

There are two approaches to answering the second of these questions. The **6.08** first is that of appliance-directed preclusion.[9] This approach looks to a product itself and to its manner of operation, denying trade mark registration for a shape if—and to the extent that—it is dictated by the technicalities of how the product is used. This approach to the problem is loosely analogous to the must-fit exclusion in design-right protection. There is no design freedom if a shape is dictated by the external need of fitting in with another part. Similarly, appliance-directed preclusion operates on the presumption that a technology-dictated shape does not leave room for any choice in a feature such that a putative trade mark owner could choose the shape as an indicator of origin.[10] Through this approach, the registrability of a shape may be saved from the bar on registrability if there is some superfluous aspect, some trivial flourish added to it, that does not have a functional role in how one uses the product.

---

[8] This would amount to something akin to trade-mark-imposed squatters' rights on public domain technology. Unprotectable technology—meaning those products and processes for which patent, design or some other, non-trade mark protection is unavailable—could be perpetually protected through use as a trade mark. Unprotected technology, originating from the putative trade mark owner and for which some other form of protection might be available, might gain a longer, potentially infinite term of protection through use as a mark.

[9] This term and the alternative, result-directed preclusion, are described by C Gielen at [2003] EIPR N28. They have not yet been used by the Community courts but are appropriate for the concepts they describe.

[10] See the design case of *Amp Inv. v Utilux Pty Ltd* [1972] RPC 103, where Lord Reid interpreted the exclusion of designs dictated by function to operate in the sense of appliance-directed exclusion: the existence of alternatives did not matter under the Registered Designs Act 1949. For a discussion see J Ellis 'Industrial Design Protection after *Philips Electronics NV v Remington Consumer Products*—The Shape of Things to Come' [1999] JBL 167.

6.09 The second approach is that of result-directed preclusion, which considers the shape of a product, rather than the product itself, as the basis for determining the technical necessity of that shape. If the product can be used in the same way even if it were shaped differently (in other words, if alternative shapes are functionally possible), then the shape feature chosen for the product may not be precluded from gaining registration as a mark. While registration would monopolize one variety of the technology involved in a type of product, competitors still would be able to carry out the same technological function through the use of one of the remaining options. Under this approach, additions of trivial details to the shape of a product would be irrelevant when the registrability of the shape as a mark is considered.

6.10 The first approach greatly restricts the registration of three-dimensional marks. The second approach is more liberal, allowing some trade-mark-based control over technology. The position of the UK courts after the implementation of Council Directive 89/104 was inconclusive. Those courts appeared to prefer to apply appliance-directed preclusion, combined with a willingness to consider trivial aspects of a shape as being separately registrable from functional aspects.[11] The Court of First Instance adopted result-directed preclusion in *Procter & Gamble v OHIM*,[12] holding that the nature-of-the-goods exclusion[13] did not apply when alternative shapes, which would allow competing products to be used in the same way, were available to competitors. As usual, it fell to the European Court of Justice (ECJ) to determine the Community's approach to the problem.[14]

6.11 The importance of the choice of approach comes from how distinctiveness can be established through use. Under appliance-directed preclusion, the use

---

[11] *Massland NV's Application* [2000] RPC 893; *Dualit Ltd's Application* [1999] RPC 304. See the discussion in D Bainbridge 'Smell, Sound, Colour and Shape Trade Marks: An Unhappy Flirtation' [2004] JBL 219.

[12] *Procter & Gamble Company v OHIM* (shaped soap) Case T-122/99 [1999] 2 CMLR 1142; [2000] ETMR 580.

[13] Council Regulation 40/94 art 7(1)(e) and Council Directive 89/104 art 3(1)(e). Because these exclusions are the same under the different pieces of legislation, for the sake of brevity, future references will be to the Council Directive 89/104.

[14] Bently and Sherman note a more fundamental issue in art 3(1)(e), that raised by the use of the phrase 'the nature of the goods'. Council Directive 89/104 does not define the qualities or perimeters of the 'nature' of goods, and Bently and Sherman point out the implicit reference to some 'platonic' notion of an abstract, presumably functional, character underlying a type of goods. See L Bently and B Sherman *Intellectual Property Law* (OUP Oxford 2001) 763 n 17.

of a necessary shape would be ineffective in establishing the distinctiveness necessary for trade mark protection as the choice of that shape was forced on the manufacturer, without the addition of some non-technical, superfluous aspect to the shape. Under result-directed preclusion, the availability of alternative shapes and the use of the particular shape for which protection is sought, to the exclusion of alternatives, reinforces distinctiveness. Under the former approach, a competitor's lack of choice as to the shape to use for a similar product diminishes the distinctiveness of the shape mark in question. Under the latter, a competitor's use of one of the available alternative shapes enhances the distinctiveness of a protected shape mark.

C. *Philips Electronics v Remington Consumer Products*

In 1985 Philips applied to register in the UK the shape and configuration of **6.12** the head of an electric shaver it had developed in 1966.[15] This shape was made up of three rotary shaving heads set in an equilateral triangle on the shaving surface of the product. Philips' application was successful. In 1995 Remington manufactured and sold a similar electric razor in the UK. Philips sued Remington for trade mark infringement and Remington counterclaimed, seeking revocation of Philips' registration.[16]

The High Court, Jacob J, allowed the counterclaim,[17] ordering the three- **6.13** dimensional mark revoked because:

• the mark was incapable of distinguishing the goods of one undertaking from those of another, as required by the Directive, Article 2

---

[15] *Koninklijke Philips Electronics NV v Remington Consumer Products Ltd* Case C-299/99 [2002] ECR I-5475, [2002] 2 CMLR 52, [2002] ETMR 81 para 11. Philips' application was made under the Trade Marks Act 1938. That Act did not allow for three-dimensional marks and Philips' application was for a device-only mark. Council Directive 89/104, which expressly allows for shape marks, also provides, in art 3(1), for a declaration of invalidity in respect of marks previously registered, which are excluded by the terms of that article. The TMA 1994 incorporates these provisions of Council Directive 89/104 and in sch 3 para 2(2), states that marks registered under the 1938 Act are treated as having been registered under the TMA. All of this is to say Philips' shape mark was subject to Council Directive 89/104 art 3(1). Somehow, in the transference of registration from under the 1938 Act to the TMA, Philips two-dimensional mark was converted into a three-dimensional mark which could be attacked under art 3(1)(e).

[16] *Philips v Remington* (n 15) paras 12–13.

[17] ibid para 14; *Philips Electronics NV v Remington Consumer Products* [1998] RPC 283.

- the mark was devoid of distinctive character, under the Directive, Article 3(1)(b)
- the mark consisted exclusively of a sign which served to designate the intended purpose of the goods, under the Directive, Article 3(1)(c)
- the sign consisted exclusively of a shape that was necessary to obtain a technical result, under the Directive, Artcle 3(1)(e)[18]
- the shape gave substantial value to the goods, also under the Directive, Article 3(1)(e).

6.14 Philips appealed. The Court of Appeal rejected result-directed preclusion stating Philips could not have saved their registration by showing other shapes could have been used which would have allowed the shaver to function in the same way and achieve the same technical result. The Court of Appeal accordingly stayed the proceedings and referred seven questions to the ECJ.[19]

6.15 The ECJ answered four of the referred questions. Two of these, which address distinguishing the use of a shape as a trade mark from the functional use or utility of that shape, concern us here.[20] Those two may be phrased as follows:

- Whether a shape can fulfil the essential function of a mark in distinguishing the goods of one undertaking from those of another if the shape contains some trivial, capricious or non-functional embellishment?[21]
- Whether the availability of alternative shapes for achieving the same technological function is the determinant of the registrability of a three-dimensional mark (result-directed preclusion), or whether the predominance of a technological purpose for a shape, irrespective of the availability of alternatives, should be the basis for a finding of invalidity (appliance-directed preclusion)?[22]

---

[18] Jacob J equated the legislative construction 'necessary to obtain' in Council Directive 89/104 art 3(1)(e) with 'dictated by function' as used in designs law, referring to Reid LJ's opinion in *Amp v Utilux* (n 10) above. In doing so, Jacob J implicitly adopted the appliance-directed preclusion discussed in the text to nn 9 and 10 above.

[19] *Philips Electronics NV v Remington Consumer Products* [1999] RPC 809 (CA).

[20] The seven referred questions, their interrelationships, the ECJ's treatment of the four questions it answered, and its reasons for not answering the remaining three are discussed in U Suthersanen 'The European Court of Justice in *Philips v Remington*—Trade Marks and Market Freedom' [2003] 3 IPQ 257.

[21] This corresponds to referred question 2. See *Philips v Remington* (n 15) para 16.

[22] This corresponds to referred question 4 (ibid). In his opinion, Advocate General Ruiz-Jarabo Colomer considered this the primary question of reference. He said: 'Any shape the

The court answered the first question by holding the shape of a product can **6.16** serve as a registered mark, in compliance with Article 2 of Council Directive 89/104,[23] without including any capricious addition, such as an embellishment which has no functional purpose.[24]

Thus a minimalist design for a product would not exclude the registration of **6.17** its shape as a three-dimensional mark, provided the shape is distinctive enough to fulfil the requirements of Article 2.[25] This makes sense, particularly in light of the alternative of requiring non-functional embellishments for registration. A rococo appearance is not necessarily more distinctive than one inspired by art deco or postmodernist art. A registration requirement of including superfluous or non-functional elements in a shape mark would establish an implicit stylistic preference without necessarily enhancing the distinctiveness of marks.

The second question goes directly to considerations of how a shape is used. **6.18** Philips argued for the adoption of result-directed preclusion, asserting that an entirely functional mark was still registrable if there were other shapes that could fulfil the same function and thus achieve the same technical result.[26] Remington argued for appliance-directed preclusion, contending that the meaning of Article 3(1)(e) was that a shape, even if it were one of several possible shapes, which is necessary to achieve a technical result, must be excluded from registration.[27] Remington pointed out that Philips'

---

essential features of which serve the achievement of a technical result must be regarded as a sign which consists exclusively of the shape of goods which is necessary to obtain such a result, irrespective of whether it is possible to achieve that result using other shapes.' *Philips v Remington*, Opinion of the Advocate General, 23 January 2001 [2001] ETMR 38, [2001] RPC 48, [2002] 2 CMLR 1329, para A.45.

[23] Council Directive 89/104 art 2.

[24] *Philips v Remington* (n 15) para 50.

[25] This requirement, designating the origin of branded products, corresponds to the 'essential function' of trade marks, described in *Centrafarm v American Home Products* Case 3/78, [1978] ECR 1823, [1979] 1 CMLR 326. The use of the term 'essential features' in the present case, see the Advocate General's opinion (n 23) and, worse, the use of 'essential functional features' in the ECJ's decision (para 66) is bound to create a confusion of terms. The rule derived from the first question could be phrased as: so long as the essential functional features fulfil the essential function, the features might be registrable as a three-dimensional mark.

[26] *Philips v Remington* (n 15) para 67.

[27] ibid para 68.

construction would require a technical evaluation of alternative designs in advance of registration, adding a substantive examination step to trade mark registration procedure.[28] The UK and French Governments agreed with Remington, although for slightly different reasons.[29] The Commission sided with Philips, arguing that the Article 3(1)(e) exception should be construed narrowly and the availability of alternative shapes for achieving a desired technical result should be the criterion for evaluating the registrability of three-dimensional marks.[30]

6.19 The Court of Justice began its analysis of the question by making four observations about the legal nature of shape marks:[31]

- Under Article 2 of the Directive, a shape mark is registrable if it is distinctive;
- All the function-related grounds for refusing registration to a shape mark are expressed in Article 3(1)(e);
- Unlike marks refused registration for a lack of distinctiveness under Article 3(1)(b), (c), or (d), which can be rehabilitated through use,[32] shapes excluded under Article 3(1)(e) are absolutely barred from registration;
- Article 3 of the Directive must be interpreted in light of the public interest, including the policy of preventing an extension of technological monopolies through trade marks.[33]

6.20 On this foundation, the court held that the function of Article 3(1)(e) is to exclude from registration three-dimensional shapes 'whose essential characteristics perform a technical function and were chosen to fulfil that

---

[28] *Philips v Remington* (n 15) para 68.

[29] ibid paras 69–71. The UK's argument followed the holding of the Court of Appeals. France argued the policy considerations underlying Council Directive 89/104 art 3(1)(e) 'is to prevent the protection of technical creations . . . from being circumvented by recourse to the rules on trade marks . . .'.

[30] ibid para 72.

[31] ibid paras 73–77.

[32] The initial lack of distinctiveness can be overcome through the use of the shape, acquiring a distinctive character under Council Directive 89/104 art 3(3).

[33] The Court referred to its decision in *Windsurfing Chiemsee Produktions- und Vertriebs GmbH v Boots- und Segelzubehör Walter Huber and Franz Attenberger* Joined Cases C-108 and 109/97 [1999] ETMR 585 (ECJ) paras 25–27, cases involving Council Directive 89/104 art 3(1)(c). The court extends these policy considerations to Council Directive 89/104 art 3(1)(e) in *Philips v Remington* (n 15), paras 80–82. These policies were discussed by the High Court in *British Sugar plc v James Robertson & Sons Ltd* [1996] RPC 281.

function'.[34] The availability of alternative shapes is irrelevant.[35] Thus the answer to the second question listed above[36] is

> a sign consisting exclusively of the shape of a product is unregistrable by virtue thereof if it is established that the essential functional features of that shape are attributable only to the technical result.[37]

The ECJ applied appliance-directed preclusion for functional shapes.[38] If **6.21** form follows function too closely, then the shape of a product is unregistrable as a mark. Such a defect cannot be overcome. For a three-dimensional mark to be validly registered, there must be an element of freedom in how the shape of the mark is determined, independent of functional concerns. Use cannot give distinctiveness to a shape mark where there was no technologically relevant choice as to that shape. Whether such freedom exists and to what degree relative to some, as yet undetermined, minimum necessary for registration is a question of fact.

D. Marks with Less than Complete Technical Functions

The *Philips v Remington* case was an extreme one: the entire mark served a **6.22** technical function because the shape gave a better shave. The court in *Philips* did not consider less technology-dependent marks, where only some of the features are attributable to a technical result, where it is necessary to determine which of the features are the essential ones. The case gives no guidance and there may be more referrals to the Court of Justice for answers to these questions.[39]

---

[34] *Philips v Remington* (n 15) paras 80, 83.
[35] ibid para 83.
[36] The fourth of the original referred questions.
[37] *Philips v Remington* (n 15) para 84.
[38] Philips' arguments were no more successful elsewhere: *Remington Rand Corp. and Remington Products (Canada) Inc v Philips Electronics NV* [1996] 2 CF 15 (Fed Ct App (Canada)); *Koninklijke Philips Electronics NV v Remington Products Australia Pty Ltd* [1999] FCA 816 (Fed Ct (Aus)), discussed in M Richardson 'Australian Intellectual Property Law: The Form/ Function Dilemma—A Case Study at the Boundaries of Trade Mark and Design Law' [2000] EIPR 314.
[39] Essentiality seems to be in the eye of the beholder. What seems an essential feature to one person, the brand-owner for instance, may be less than essential to another, such as a consumer. It would have been helpful had the ECJ at least specified from whose viewpoint essentiality is to be judged.

6.23 The range of possibilities is narrowed somewhat by the ECJ decisions in *Linde*.[40] There, three applicants appealed against decisions by the German Patent and Trade Mark Office to refuse registrations of shape marks for lack of distinctive character.[41] On appeal, the German Patents Court referred two questions to the Court of Justice.

6.24 The first question was whether, when assessing the distinctiveness of three-dimensional marks, a stricter test than that used for two-dimensional marks should be applied. The answer to this was no: a stricter test should not be used.[42] In determining objective distinctiveness, shape marks were to be treated like any other mark.[43]

6.25 It is the second question that asked about limits on how shapes should be deployed. The German court asked:

> In the case of three-dimensional trade marks which depict the shape of the product, does Art.3(1)(c) of the Directive have any significance independent of Art.3(1)(e)? If so, when considering Art.3(1)(c) . . . must regard be had to the interest of the trade in having the shape of the product available for use, so that registration is, at least in principle, ruled out, and is possible as a rule only in the case of trade marks which meet the requirements of the first sentence of Art.3(3) of the Directive?[44]

6.26 The answer to the first part of this question is that Article 3(1)(c) does have an independent significance for shape marks.[45] Having survived the absolute functional exclusions of Article 3(1)(e), a proposed shape mark must also survive being measured against the exclusions of Article 3(1)(c).

6.27 In *Linde*, the appellants sought to register relatively common shapes as marks: a fork-lift truck, a torch and a wristwatch.[46] The objection to their registration was that the shapes in each case were common within various industries, hence their lack of distinctiveness. The concern expressed by the German Court was to guard against the monopolization of common shapes used in

---

[40] *Linde AG, Winward Industries Inc and Radio Uhren AG Trade Mark Applications* Joined Cases C-53/01 to C-55/01 [2003] ETMR 78, [2003] RPC 45.

[41] Within the meaning of Council Directive 89/104 art 3 (1)(d).

[42] *Linde* (n 40) para 49.

[43] But see the ECJ's later decision in *Henkel KGaA v OHIM* Joined Cases C-456/01 and C457/01 ECJ 29 April 2004 discussed below.

[44] *Linde* (n 40) para 28.

[45] ibid para 70.

[46] ibid paras H3–H5.

trade, perhaps not entirely functional ones, which would be excluded under Article 3(1)(e), but shapes that were indicative of the type of goods they represented. In answering the second part of the second question, the ECJ invoked the public interest in limiting the monopolization of shapes that are common within an industry. It said

> Any trade mark which consists exclusively of a sign or indication which may serve to designate the characteristics of goods or a service within the meaning of [TM Dir. Art.3(1)(c)] must be freely available to all and not be registrable.[47]

One cannot register as a mark a shape that is common in the relevant trade.

For applying this last exclusion, the ECJ gave the following guidance:　　　**6.28**

> The competent authority called upon to apply Art.3(1)(c) of the Directive to such trade marks must determine, by reference to the goods or services for which registration is sought, in the light of a concrete consideration of all the relevant aspects of the application, and in particular the public interest . . . whether the ground for refusing registration in that provision applies to the case at hand.[48]

It is, therefore, not only entirely functional shapes that are ineligible for **6.29** registration as trade marks. Less functional, more generic symbols related to the identification of goods and services—indications of type, quality and the like—are likewise unregistrable as three-dimensional marks.

While these exclusions allow many shape marks to be registered, the Court's **6.30** decisions so far leave many questions to be answered.[49] The overriding policy—that of protecting the freedom to use shapes, both functional and indicative, from monopolization through trade mark registration—will provide the basis for arguments against registration, for defendants in infringement proceedings and for trade mark granting authorities. On the other hand, the general registrability of three-dimensional marks is unquestionable.

---

[47] ibid para 74.
[48] ibid para 75.
[49] For example, what is a 'concrete consideration', as used in the last quotation? See *Kerly* (n 1) para 7–140: 'The authoritative interpretation of these provisions will depend upon what the European Court decides is the purpose of each of them, as and when the Court has the opportunity to consider them.'

E. Peculiarities of Use of Three-Dimensional Marks

6.31 While shape marks are, for the most part, treated in the same way as two-dimensional marks for registration purposes, there are significant differences. A shape, lacking distinctiveness within the meaning of Article 3(1)(b), can gain distinctiveness through being used, but use cannot overcome the exclusions of Article 3(1)(e) when there is no technological freedom of choice of the shape used as the mark. The Court of Justice partially explained this difference in *Henkel v OHIM*.[50]

6.32 Distinctiveness is determined through two assessments:

- by reference to the products or services in respect of which registration is sought
- by a consideration of how the relevant portion of the public perceives the mark.[51]

6.33 Shape marks function differently from two-dimensional marks under the latter assessment. The *Henkel* court said:

> The relevant public's perception is not necessarily the same in relation to a three-dimensional mark consisting of the shape and colours of the product itself as it is in relation to a word or figurative mark consisting of a sign which is independent from the appearance of the products it denotes. Average consumers are not in the habit of making assumptions about the origin of products on the basis of their shape or the shape of their packaging in the absence of any graphic or word element and it could therefore prove more difficult to establish distinctiveness in relation to such a three-dimensional mark than in relation to a word or figurative mark.[52]

6.34 Although this statement was made with regard to inherent distinctiveness, the same logic applies, by analogy, to acquired distinctiveness. The distinctiveness of a shape mark is harder to establish through use than it is in the case of a two-dimensional mark.[53] In this regard, a lack of freedom in choosing a

---

[50] *Henkel* (n 43).
[51] ibid para 35 citing *Linde* (n 40) para 41 and *Philips v Remington* (n 15) para 34.
[52] ibid para 38.
[53] Compare *Nestle Waters France v OHIM* Case T-305/02 [2004] ETMR 41 para 35: 'It must be observed that Article 7(1)(b) of regulation No 40/94 makes no distinction between different categories of mark. Accordingly, it is not appropriate to apply more stringent criteria when assessing the distinctiveness of three-dimensional marks comprising the shape of the goods themselves or, as in the present case, the shape of the packaging of those goods than in the case of other categories of mark.'

shape, such as would justify an exclusion from registration under Article 3(1)(e), argues against distinctiveness. The court held further that 'The more closely the shape for which registration is sought resembles the shape most likely to be taken by the product in question, the greater the likelihood the shape being devoid of any distinctive character for the purposes of Article [3](1)(b).'[54]

This conceptual relationship between the exclusions of subsections 3(1)(b) **6.35** and (e) should be seen as a confluence of considerations, rather than as a continuum. They are distinct, being based on different primary policy considerations,[55] but there is a cross-application of those considerations. Article 3(1)(b) is concerned with whether a mark fulfils its essential function of identifying origin,[56] but there is also a competition aspect to it.

The ECJ held in the context of a colour mark, a situation analogous to that of **6.36** a shape mark:

> The public interest underlying Article 3(1)(b) of First Directive 89/104 . . . is directed at the need not to restrict unduly the availability of colours for the other traders who offer for sale goods or services of the same type as those in respect of which registration is sought.[57]

This is the same competition-preserving consideration that underlies Article 3(1)(e).

There are competing legal influences in this area of trade mark law. There is a **6.37** desire to treat shape marks like figurative marks, but a tendency to treat them differently, at least as far as establishing distinctiveness through use is concerned. This may pass in time as consumers and the courts become more

---

[54] ibid para 39, citing *Henkel* (n 43) para 52.

[55] 'The public interest taken into account in the examination of each of those grounds for refusal may, or even must, reflect different considerations, depending upon which ground for refusal is at issue.' Ibid para 46, referring to the various subcomponents of art 3(1)(b) but applicable as well to the rest of s 3(1) generally.

[56] ibid para 48: 'It should also be stated that there is no public interest in conferring the benefit of the full protection envisaged by Regulation No 40/94 on a trade mark which does not fulfil its essential function, namely that of ensuring that the consumer or the end user can identify the origin of the product or service concerned by allowing him to distinguish that product or service from those emanating from a different origin, without any risk of confusion.'

[57] ibid para 47. See also *Philips Electronics NV v Remington Consumer Products* [1998] RPC 283, 299, where Jacob J addresses the competition implications of extending trade mark protection to a shape in the context of art 3(1)(b).

familiar with non-figurative marks. There is a desire to view the policy considerations underlying each of the Article 3 exclusions from registration separately, but there is a considerable overlap in those considerations. In other areas of trade mark law, such as right exhaustion, the order of priority has been established with free-movement-of-goods considerations predominant—such as might act to enhance Article 3(1)(e) exclusions in the future—supported by competition considerations, and with the essential-function considerations acting as a limited exception. Whether the ECJ will follow this pattern in the case of the use of three-dimensional marks is an open question.

Part D

EXPLOITATION

7

THIRD PARTY USE OF TRADE MARKS

Neil J Wilkof

A. Introduction   7.01
B. Is Authorized Use by a Third Party
   Legally Possible?   7.06
   (1) The classic position of trade mark
       use by a licensee   7.06
   (2) The present situation   7.17

C. Use by Licensees and Revocation   7.27
   (1) Attribution of use   7.27
   (2) Use by a distributor or contract
       manufacturer   7.33
D. Conclusion   7.45

A. Introduction

Trade marks are unique among intellectual property rights with respect to the **7.01** treatment of use. In some jurisdictions, use may be a prerequisite for registration.[1] Non-use of a registered mark is a ground for cancellation of the registration. A particularly vexing aspect of trade mark use by a person other than the proprietor of the mark. Unauthorized use of the mark by a third party is a ground for infringement. As such, it poses no special problems. However the matter becomes more complicated when the use is authorized, where two major issues are encountered.

The first issue derives from the principle that a trade mark serves as an **7.02** indication of the source of the goods. This gave rise to the further principle that there can be no authorized use of a trade mark by a third party, because

The author wishes to extend his thanks to Dr Jeffrey Belson, regulatory and intellectual property manager for the Indigo Division of Hewlett-Packard, for his helpful comments and suggestions.

[1] The most notable example is the USA, where use is a prerequisite for registration except where the application is based upon a foreign registration.

at law only the owner of the mark can be the source of the goods, and that use by the third party therefore works a deception. The development of the law of trade mark licensing over the previous century can be seen as a succession of attempts to resolve this apparent legal conundrum against the background of ever-expanding forms of third party use of marks.

7.03 The second issue is grounded in the vulnerability of a trade mark registration to revocation or cancellation for non-use, the claim being that the mark is not being used by the proprietor but only by the licensee. Here the problem is one of utility. Even if a trade mark licence passes muster under the principle that a trade mark is an indication of source, a licence (especially an exclusive licence) will be of only limited value if use by the licensee will not inure to the licensor's benefit or cannot be attributed to him. If such be the case, the commercial advantages of a trade mark licence would in effect be swept away, since the grant and exercise of the licence by the licensee may well put the continuing validity of the mark in jeopardy. Alternatively, it may put the licensor's ownership in jeopardy—he could be dispossessed of the mark in favour of the licensee.

7.04 One further point merits mention. Licensing is one form of distribution of goods or services, but it is not the sole form. For example, in a decision of the European Commission, it was noted that a manufacturer of shoes used 'owned shops, franchisees, franchise-corner retailers, and traditional retailers' to distribute its goods. In each of these modes of distribution, there was some type of use trade marks.[2]

7.05 While the focus of this chapter is on authorized use of the mark by a licensee, there are other instances where a third party uses the mark of another without risk of infringement. In other words, while a licence is a form of authorized third party use of a mark, not all authorized uses of a mark by a third party (eg use pursuant to consent of the owner, or use by a distributor) are, technically speaking, licensed use. As appropriate, our discussion will also consider these other forms of third party use to the extent that such other forms of use may contribute to our understanding.

---

[2] *Charles Jourdan* [1989] EC 94.

B. Is Authorized Use by a Third Party Legally Possible?

(1) The classic position of trade mark use by a licensee

Trade mark use is characterized by a triangular relationship between the **7.06** mark, the owner of the mark and the goods to which the mark is affixed.[3] In its purest form, a mark that is affixed to the goods serves to identify the source of the goods to the purchasing public. When the public encounters the mark on the product, it can rely on the mark to indicate that the product comes from a particular source and to distinguish the goods so marked from those of its competitors.[4]

In its earliest manifestation, the identity of the source of the goods was **7.07** presumably actually known to the public, since the scope of distribution of a product was limited to a narrow geographical region. As commerce expanded, it was realized that such a limitation was not feasible. Accordingly, the purchaser in London no longer had to know the actual identity of the manufacturer in Manchester; the source could be anonymous. As long as the mark served to identify a single source for the goods, the triangular relationship was preserved between and among the mark, its owner and the goods.

Under such a view, there was no room for trade mark licensing. This is **7.08** because, whether or not the actual identity of the source of the goods could be specified, the source of the goods had to be the party that actually affixed the mark on to the goods. If a licensee were to use the mark, the connection between the mark, the physical source and the goods would be destroyed; either the owner of the mark would no longer be the physical source of the goods or the licensee would be erroneously viewed as their physical source.[5]

However, increased opportunities for commercial exploitation created situ- **7.09** ations in which the authorized use of the mark by a person other than the

---

[3] The discussion that follows is based on NJ Wilkof *Trade Mark Licensing* (Sweet & Maxwell London 1995) esp ch 2.

[4] This has been identified as the 'essential function' of a trade mark under EU jurisprudence: I Simon 'How Does "Essential Function" Doctrine Drive European Trade Mark Law' [2005] IIC.

[5] The position was given judicial expression in England: *Bowden Wire v Bowden Brake* (1913) 30 RPC 45 CA; (1914) 31 RPC 385 (HL). A similar approach was taken in the USA: *Macmahan Pharmacol Co v Denver Chemical Mfg Co* 113 F 468 (8th Cir 1908).

owner, for the manufacture and sale of a product, became desirable. Historic-ally speaking, perhaps the first industry to take advantage of licensing was the soft drink industry in the USA, where the business model provided for the grant of rights to independent bottlers in order to enable the bottlers to manufacture and market the products under the mark in discrete territories.[6] Licensing also was used on occasion when both the owner of the mark and the licensee were both part of a single corporate or commercial group.[7]

7.10   This development of variegated forms of use of the mark by a party other than the trade mark owner was coupled with a changing perception of the source function of a trade mark. It increasingly came to be realized that the mark identified a product with a certain consistent quality. Under such a view, the identity of the owner of the mark became less important for the purchaser than the fact that the mark identified a product of a certain con-sistent quality and that the owner of the mark could be seen as standing behind this form of quality assurance.[8]

7.11   Use of a trade mark by a licensee was not seen as inconsistent with the quality function, so long as the proprietor exercised some form of control over the goods sold under the trade mark. The exercise of such control was seen as ensuring that the purchaser's imputed expectation about the mark indicating consistent quality would be satisfied. It mattered not whether the goods bearing the mark emanated from the trade mark owner or from the licensee under his control. In each situation the notion that the trade mark indicates a single source is deemed to have been satisfied. In other words, consistent quality is treated as consistent with a single source.

7.12   Provided that there is satisfactory quality control, use of the mark by the licensee will inure to the benefit of the licensor,[9] thereby shielding the licen-sor from a non-use cancellation action. As a corollary, in the absence of quality control, the resulting licence might be deemed a 'naked' or 'bare' licence. Such a licence was deemed to be ineffective because it worked a deception on the public. In the absence of quality control, there could not be

---

[6] See eg *Coca Cola Bottling Co v Coca-Cola Co* 269 F 796 (D Del 1920).
[7] See eg *Re Radiation* (1930) 47 RPC 37.
[8] This may be compared with the quality function of a certification mark on which see Ch 4 of this volume.
[9] See below for further discussion of use of the mark by the licensee inuring to the benefit of the licensor.

an identity between the trade mark owner and the licensee using the mark. When a licence was 'bare', use by the licensee did not inure to the benefit of the licensor and the registration of the mark itself could be vulnerable to revocation on the grounds of non-use.

By the 1940s, the developments described above had taken root in most of **7.13** the common law jurisdictions. Two basic varieties emerged. In the UK, as part of the legislative trade mark overhaul in the Trade Marks Act 1938, 'registered user' provisions were enacted whereby the fact of the licence and representations about the terms of quality control, otherwise unexamined by the Registry, were recorded with the Registry. This arrangement could be seen as a compromise between (i) public scrutiny so as to ensure adequate quality control and (ii) the private business of the parties involved in monitoring the use of the mark by the licensee.[10] The approach adopted in the UK was also taken in most common law jurisdictions.

In the USA, no recordal requirements of the licence were imposed in the **7.14** enactment of the Lanham Act in 1946. Instead, the Lanham Act provided that controlled use of the mark by a licensee would inure to the benefit of the licensor:

> Where a registered mark or a mark sought to be registered is or may be used legitimately by related companies, such use shall inure to the benefit of the registrant or applicant for registration, and such use shall not affect the validity of such mark or of its registration, provided such mark is not used in such manner as to deceive the public. If first use of a mark is controlled by the registrant or applicant for registration of the mark with respect to the nature and quality of the goods or services, such first use shall inure to the benefit of the registrant or applicant, as the case may be.[11]

Such use was termed 'use by a related company'.[12]

At the risk of generalization, the UK's registered user requirements tended to **7.15** deflect judicial scrutiny from the extent to which quality control was in effect being carried out. By contrast, the absence of a recordal arrangement

---

[10] These provisions were ruled to be permissive rather than mandatory: BOSTITCH *Trade Mark* [1963] RPC 183.

[11] Lanham Act s 5 (15 USCA 1005).

[12] s 45 (15 USCA 1127) defines a 'related company' as 'any person whose use of a mark is controlled by the owner of the mark with respect to the nature and quality of the goods or services on or in connection with which the mark is used'.

in the US resulted in closer judicial attention to the exercise of quality control.[13]

7.16 The foregoing analysis can be seen as continuing to describe the legal position in the USA. The situation in the UK, however, appears to have dramatically changed. Two stages can be identified.

(2) *The present situation*

7.17 First, the UK Trade Marks Act 1994 was enacted as a measure to implement the Trade Mark Directive.[14] The 1994 Act does away with the recordal of the licensee as a registered user and replaces it with a registration system for licences. Registration of the licence provides the licensee with a right of action for infringement[15] and constitutes notice to third parties about the licence. It does not, however, address the existence or absence of quality control.

7.18 The second stage was more dramatic. In 2001 the House of Lords ruled in *Scandecor*.[16] The facts of this case are devilishly complicated and each of the legal instances addressing this matter took a different approach to the issues raised.[17] The principal matter at issue is whether a bare trade mark licence constitutes a ground for revocation.

7.19 Behind this question lay another question of whether quality control is required under the 1994 Act, it being agreed by the parties that no quality control had been exercised with respect to the licence at issue. Reviewing statutory developments since the first legislative enactment in the nineteenth century against the backdrop of the changing commercial role of licensing in modern trade, the Court concluded that the 1994 Act had done away with the quality control requirements. Provided that consent has been given to the

---

[13] Wilkof (n 3) ch 6.

[14] First Council Directive 89/104/EEC of 21 December 1988 to approximate the laws of the Member States relating to trade marks.

[15] Trade Marks Act 1994 ss 30 and 31.

[16] *Scandecor Developments AB v Scandecor Marketing AB et al* [2001] ETMR 74. The factual background is set out in the opinion of Lloyd J at [1998] FSR 500.

[17] Regarding the opinion of the High Court and the Court of Appeal, see NJ Wilkof 'Wake-Up Call for UK Law on Trade Mark Licensing' [1998] EIPR 386ff. Having regard to the diversity of judicial views expressed, the legal adage 'hard cases make bad law' seems particularly appropriate with respect to the *Scandecor* (n 16) case.

licensee, the mark is not susceptible to revocation on the ground that no quality control has been exercised.

The Court agreed that the function of a trade mark is to serve as an indicator **7.20** of the source of the goods. However, the statutory meaning of source can be seen as attempting to catch up with commercial developments. Under the 1938 Act, a trade mark had to indicate 'a connection in the course of trade' between the owner of the mark and the goods made and sold by the licensee. Because of this requirement, there could be only one source—the owner of the mark. The requirement of quality control was essential to satisfy this relationship between the mark and the goods.

The 1994 Act continued to recognize a trade mark as indicating the source of **7.21** the goods. However, it did away with the requirement that there be a connection in the course of trade. As such, in the view of the Court, the source need not be confined to the owner of the mark. The words of Lord Nicholls, who gave the leading opinion, set out the new position:

> But what does the mark denote about source? Must the source be the proprietor of the trade mark? On this the Act is silent. But so to read the Act would accord ill with the statutory power to grant licences. . . . [I]s the business source the person who is for the time being entitled to use the mark, whether as proprietor or exclusive licensee. I prefer this view.[18]

The result is, in the words of Lord Nicholls, that **7.22**

> [d]uring the licence period the goods come from only source, namely, the licensee, and the mark is distinctive of that source.[19]

Stated otherwise, the source can be either the trade mark owner or the **7.23** licensee, depending upon whether the licence is still in effect. So 'source' is a legally flexible concept and source status is attributable to the party having the better legal claim to such status.

As for quality control, it appears that it is no longer required. Provided that **7.24** the licensee has the consent of the trade mark owner, the licence will be deemed valid. It is wholly up to the trade mark owner to impose, or not impose, quality control. The marketplace, and not the trade mark law, will ultimately determine the wisdom of the trade mark owner's decision in this

---

[18] *Scandecor* (n 16) paras 36–37.
[19] ibid para 42.

regard. Lord Nicholls devotes extensive attention to the changing conditions with respect to the use of trade marks in the marketplace.[20] The 1994 Act, as construed by the Court, has enabled the current law to 'catch up' with current commercial practice.[21]

7.25 The *Scandecor* court acknowledged, but without providing a satisfactory solution, that the decision poses difficult issues upon termination. Lord Nicholls somewhat opaquely suggests that, if the former licensee continues to engage in the same business with the same customers, albeit under a different mark, while the licensor uses the mark on the licensed goods, confusion as to source might arise because of the goodwill that the licensee accrued in its favour during the term of the licence. If there is confusion as to source, it will result in the mark being susceptible to cancellation or reassignment under prescription to the erstwhile 'licensee'.[22]

7.26 It is unclear from the Court's decision how the decision will apply to non-exclusive or sole licences,[23] the judgment having been given in respect of an exclusive bare licence. Furthermore the fact that the matter at issue was referred to the European Court of Justice (ECJ), the dispute being settled before a ruling was given by that court, also leaves a degree of uncertainty about the precise scope and reach of the ruling.[24] Be that as it may, *Scandecor*, by uncoupling ownership from the source identification function, can be seen as proposing a new understanding of the triangular relationship between and among the mark, its owner and the goods for which it is registered.

---

[20] 'Whatever may have been the position in 1938, the public is now accustomed to goods or services being supplied under license from the trade mark owner': *Scandecor* (n 16) para 37, quoting UK Government White Paper *Reform of Trade Marks Law* Cm. 1203 [1990] para 4.36.

[21] *Scandecor* (n 16) para 40.

[22] ibid para 44. Lord Scott described this as 'easily the most difficult point in the case' (at para 14).

[23] A 'sole licence' refers to a licence where there is only a single licensee, but the proprietor is also permitted to use the mark with respect to the relevant goods and jurisdiction.

[24] For further discussion of these issues, see NJ Wilkof and D Burkitt *Trade Mark Licensing* (2nd edn Sweet & Maxwell London 2005).

C. Use by Licensees and Revocation

(1) Attribution of use

A central feature of a valid trade mark licence is that use of the mark by the **7.27**
licensee in accordance with the licence is deemed to be use by the licensor.[25]
The use by the licensee must be for the licensed mark and for some or all of
the goods that are covered by the mark. If the licensee uses the mark for
goods covered by the registration but which lie outside the terms of the
licence grant, the licensee will be liable for infringement and breach of
contract. If the licensee uses the mark for goods outside the scope of the
registration, the issue is less clear-cut. There will presumably not be any
infringement of the registered mark. Whether there is a breach of the licence
agreement will depend upon its terms. It is uncertain whether it is possible
for the licensee to claim rights on an unregistered basis in the mark with
respect to these goods.

In such a case, the registration will not be vulnerable to revocation or cancel- **7.28**
lation because of non-use. However, following the *Scandecor* decision, there
appears to be a clear difference in approach between US and English law on
what is required for the use of the mark by the licensee to inure to the benefit
of the licensor.

Thus, as noted, under the US approach, there must be quality control over **7.29**
the use of the mark by the licensee for such use to be unassailable and to inure
to the benefit of the licensor. In contrast, the *Scandecor* decision teaches that
consent to the licensee is sufficient. Control, if any, over the use of the mark
by the licensee is a commercial matter for the licensor.

This difference in approach is mirrored in the legislative language. Section **7.30**
46(1)(a) of the Trade Marks Act 1994 provides that a registration may be
revoked if, for a period of five years following registration, the mark

> has not been put to genuine use in the United Kingdom by the proprietor or
> with his consent. . . .

---

[25] See discussion at para 7.4. No specific reference to this point is contained in the Trade
Marks Act 1994.

All that is required is consent. A more formal licensor–licensee agreement between the parties serves other legal and commercial purposes.

7.31 By comparison, Article 19.2 of the TRIPs Agreement provides for the attribution of use by a third party in favour of the trade mark owner as follows:

> When subject to the control of its owner, use of a trademark by another person shall be recognized as use of the trademark for the purpose of maintaining the registration.[26]

7.32 Here the emphasis is on 'control' and not merely 'consent', although the meaning of 'control' in this context, and the relationship of this term to the notion of 'quality control' is not clear from the text or the commentators.[27] Indeed, following *Scandecor*, the relevance of this provision to English law practice is uncertain.

(2) Use by a distributor or contract manufacturer

7.33 Perhaps the most common form of third party use of a mark, other than by a licensee, is use of the mark in connection with the distribution of the goods by a person such as a distributor or wholesaler (who will be referred to collectively as 'distributor'), and the goods bear the trade mark of the manufacturer.[28] Two principal issues are raised here: First, if the distributor is not a licensee, what is the nature of the distributor's right of 'use' of the mark? Second, can a distributor ever claim ownership in the manufacturer's trade mark?

(a) Nature of distributor's use

7.34 It is generally held that a distributor who merely distributes goods that bear the mark of the manufacturer is not a licensee with respect to that mark. The

---

[26] Agreement on Trade-Related Aspects of Intellectual Property Rights, Including Trade in Counterfeit Goods.

[27] An earlier draft of the TRIPs Agreement (23 July 1990) refers to 'consent' rather than 'control'. As for commentators, see eg, D Gervais *The TRIPs Agreement: Drafting History and Analysis* (Sweet & Maxwell London 1998) and M Blakeney *Trade-Related Aspects of Intellectual Property Rights: A Concise Guide to the TRIPs Agreement* (2nd edn Sweet & Maxwell London 2003), neither of whom points to textual support from the drafting history of the TRIPs Agreement in clarification of the difference among and between 'control', 'quality control' and 'consent'.

[28] For a fuller discussion of these issues, see Wilkof (n 3) ch 7.

distributor does not apply the mark, nor does he cause the mark to be applied, to the goods. At the most, the distributor may 'use' the manufacturer's mark in the advertising or marketing of the goods. Such use, without more, is not licensed use. The distributor may under appropriate circumstances apply its own service mark, indicating that it provides a distribution function with respect to the goods. But in so doing, it does nothing to detract from the position that the distributor is not making licensed use of the manufacturer's mark with respect to the goods.

Perhaps the most accurate way to characterize the distributor's relationship to **7.35** the manufacturer's mark under such circumstances is that the mark is being used directly by the manufacturer. It is the manufacturer who is the unmediated source of the goods by virtue of having organized the manufacture of the goods and having affixed his mark to it.[29]

(b) Distributor's claim of ownership

It has long been accepted that the corollary for the fact that use by the licensee inures to the benefit of the licensor is that the licensee acquires no rights of proprietorship in the mark.[30] This position has been contrasted with that applying to a distributor, especially where the manufacturer is a foreign person. While the manufacturer is presumed to be the rightful owner of the mark that is affixed to its goods, this presumption is rebuttable: the distributor may under appropriate (albeit infrequent) circumstances be deemed the rightful owner of the mark in its jurisdiction where the parties have not entered into an undertaking setting out the issue of ownership.

In the absence of any agreement between the parties, the English courts have **7.36** identified the following considerations in determining whether a distributor may be deemed the owner of the mark affixed to the manufacturer's goods:

(1) To what extent is the manufacturer or the distributor associated with the goods?
(2) Is the distributor exclusive?

---

[29] It is held on occasion that the manufacturer has consented to the distributor's use of the manufacturer's mark: see eg *All Canada Vac Ltd v Lindsay Manufacturing Inc* [1990] 2 CPR (3d) 385, 396.

[30] But see above for the apparent erosion of the principle under English law following the *Scandecor* decision.

(3) How prompt is the manufacturer in filing the application for registration in the domestic jurisdiction?

(4) To what extent has the manufacturer consented to steps taken by the distributor to build local goodwill in favour of the distributor?[31]

7.37 In the USA, a leading case pointed to the following factors:

(1) Which party invented and first affixed the trade mark on the product?

(2) Which party designed the label and packaging?

(3) Which party's name is placed in proximity to the trade mark?

(4) Which party is responsible for the quality and uniformity of the product?

(5) To whom does the public turn for warranty work?

(6) Whom does the public identify with the goods?[32]

7.38 The common denominator between these lists is that the ultimate test for ownership is whether the consumer has come to identify the distributor as the source of the goods even though the manufacturer's mark appears on the goods and that the manufacturer is *prima facie* its owner. No court seems however to have offered any theoretical justification. A possible explanation is that, by analogy with use of a mark by a bare licensee, the mark no longer serves to identify the trade mark owner. Here, it is the manufacturer that has failed to take the necessary steps to protect its interest in the mark. If so, depending upon the circumstances, the distributor may be said to have acquired the goodwill in the mark through his use of it.[33]

(c) Contract manufacturer

7.39 The contract manufacturer stands at the opposite pole from the distributor in the chain of distribution, with the distributor standing at the front, and the contract manufacturer at the back end, of the chain. Thus the distributor sells and markets the goods but neither manufactures those goods nor affixes the manufacturer's mark to them. The contract manufacturer, by contrast,

---

[31] See further Wilkof (n 3) 146–149.

[32] *Wrist-Rocket Mfg Co Inc v Saunders Archery Co* 183 USPQ 117 (CD Neb 1974). The factor bears a similarity to the rationale provided by the *Scandecor* decision in ruling that a bare licensee can be viewed as the source of the goods during the duration of the licence.

[33] It is unclear how this explanation may be squared with the decision in *Scandecor*, where the traditional understanding of the implications of a bare licence has seemingly been rejected.

will be engaged in both the manufacture of the goods and in affixing the mark to them. However, it neither markets nor sells goods bearing the mark. Accordingly, unlike a licensee that stands in the shoes of the licensor, the contract manufacturer cannot be identified as the source of the goods by the purchasing public.

It is in precisely the situation in which a contract manufacturer seeks to sell **7.40** the goods bearing the trade mark that thorny legal issues may arise. For example when the trade mark owner, in accordance with the contract, rejects delivery of goods made and marked by the contract manufacturer would the contract manufacturer, in selling off the inventory, infringe the rights of the trade mark owner?

The resolution of this question, at least under US law, turns on whether the **7.41** court views the inventory as genuine goods. In the leading US case, *El Greco Leather Products*,[34] both the trial court and the appellate court adopted contrasting views. The majority of the court of appeal, overruling the lower court, held that because the rejected inventory of shoes had not been given explicit approval, no inspection having taken place, the goods sold by the contract manufacturer were not genuine and therefore were infringing.[35]

The dissent took a contrary view. It concluded that: **7.42**

> [a]s long as the goods are manufactured under the direction of the trademark owner, bear the mark registered and issued by the trademark owner, and are not of an inferior quality, the products are considered genuine. It is not necessary to a finding of genuineness that the goods be distributed with the trademark holder's express authorization.[36]

The position of the dissent has been echoed by other courts.[37] **7.43**

The upshot of the foregoing is that, at the most, the contract manufacturer **7.44** may, under certain circumstances, be able to take steps to sell excess inventory bearing the trade mark, but no claim that the contract manufacturer is the owner of the trade mark can be made.

---

[34] *El Greco Leather Products Company Inc v Show World Inc* 1 USPQ 2d 1016 (2d Cir 1986) reversing 224 USPQ 921 (ED NY 1984).
[35] J Belson *Certification Marks* (Sweet & Maxwell London 2002) ss 7–01 to 7–03 discusses the nexus between authenticity of goods and their authorization or approval.
[36] *El Greco* (n 34) 1020.
[37] See eg *Monte Carlo Shirt Co Inc v Daewoo International (America) Corp* 707 F2d 1054 (9th Cir 1982).

D. Conclusion

7.45 The legal regulation of trade mark use by licensees and other third parties continues to develop and evolve against the backdrop of the changing commercial landscape. Legal systems continue to pay homage, at least at the rhetorical level, to the centrality of the principle that a trade mark is an indication of the source of the goods. However, there seems to be an ever-widening gap regarding what is meant by the principle.

7.46 While it can be argued that the *Scandecor* decision has effected a tectonic shift in paradigm under English law from the existing conception regarding the quality control requirement, the decision leaves in its wake many unanswered questions. Thus the ultimate reach of the ruling remains to be seen. In the USA, by contrast, the courts continue to fill the interstices of the law, without bringing about any fundamental change regarding the quality control requirement. There, quality control remains a requirement for valid trade mark licensing and it has not been replaced by mere consent. We must watch closely to see whether international developments will force a greater convergence of these two approaches.

8

TRADE MARK USE AND DENOMINATIVE TRADE MARKS

Massimo Sterpi

A. Introduction	8.01	(1) The *TARZAN* case	8.32
		(2) The *BIANCANEVE* case	8.36
B. Unauthorized Use of Trade Marks Referring to Fictional Characters in the Music Industry	8.04	E. Unauthorized Reference to Real and Fictional Names in Business Names	8.38
(1) The *Barbie Girl* case	8.07	(1) The *Daily Planet* case	8.40
(2) The *NELLIE THE ELEPHANT* cases	8.17	(2) The *CACAO MERAVIGLIAO* case	8.42
		(3) The *Lane Capital Management* case	8.46
C. Unauthorized Use of Trade Marks Referring to Fictional Characters in a Website	8.21	(4) The *Nichols* case	8.48
(1) *Paramount Pictures* and *Time Warner*: the policy adopted by media companies	8.23	F. Unauthorized Use of a Trade Mark in Press Products and Merchandising	8.53
(2) *Elvis Presley Enterprises*: the protection of a real character's name and places referring to him	8.27	(1) The *Swatchissimo* case	8.55
		(2) The *Super Inter* case	8.57
		(3) The *Juventissima* case	8.59
D. Unauthorized Reference to Fictional Characters in Retailing	8.30	(4) The *Arsenal* case	8.62
		G. Conclusion	8.68

A. Introduction

Post-industrial market economies are increasingly conscious of what we can **8.01** call 'identity products', ie products that, apart having a functional purpose (such as shoes, which protect feet), permit their owner to show and bear witness as to his taste and to the fact that he belongs to a given social group

The author would like to acknowledge the valuable contribution of Dr Daniele Beneventi to the background research and editing of this chapter.

(rock music fan, 'radical chic' political person, member of a given profession and so forth). Also increasingly, the communication of symbolic elements that are related to the product is delegated to the trade mark, which acts as a 'semiotic summary' of the lifestyle to which the consumer aspires when deciding to buy new products. This consciousness of identity products creates a very strong market for 'background charged' or 'lifestyle charged' symbols of any sort which may be used as brands.

8.02 However, as brands—through their use—may themselves become 'cultural icons' or avatars (ie fictional characters with their own identity, personality and lifestyle), they become highly attractive for the entertainment industry, which may seek to exploit such brands/avatars by including them in new stories or events. There is, therefore, a continuous and increasing interface between real and fictional characters (who themselves tend to become brands) and brands (that tend to become fictional characters or avatars). This same interface also implies that the traditional rules of trade mark law (for brands) and copyright law (for fictional characters) may become inadequate; it may be more appropriate now to consider issues such as appropriation of third party's works (or 'free riding') and identity protection in the form of right of privacy, right of publicity and protection against defamation and libel.

8.03 This chapter will consider some examples of this interface by reference to particular types of denominative use, together with the legal remedies applied in each of the situations described. Two issues pertaining to trade mark use in the area of denominative use will be considered in particular: (i) Does denominative use by a claimant count as trade mark use? If not, is denominative use by the proprietor of a mark sufficient to keep his rights in his trade mark alive or is trade mark use (ie use to denote the origin of the defendant's goods) needed? (ii) Is mere denominative use by a defendant that is not trade mark use sufficient for infringement? Should it be? Additionally, the role of copyright in protecting the owners of such marks will also be considered.

B. Unauthorized Use of Trade Marks Referring to Fictional Characters in the Music Industry

8.04 In this chapter, the term 'denominative use' refers to the use of a trade mark in the form of a name or character, whether real or fictional, regardless of the commercial sector in which it is exploited. The first industry we are going to consider is the music business.

Within the music industry, the unauthorized use of trade marks has come to **8.05** light in two examples. First, unauthorized use of trade marks may occur in song titles. An example of this was 'Barbie Girl', a 1997 song by a group of Danish musicians who were not authorized to use the famous doll's name. Second, in a mirror image of the 'Barbie Girl' fact pattern, the title of a song that was still in copyright may be used as the name of a character and registered and used as a trade mark by third parties. An example of this is the NELLIE THE ELEPHANT case, where a company registered a song's part in order to identify a series of cartoons.

We shall now examine the two cases individually. **8.06**

(1) The Barbie Girl case

The controversy began in 1997 in the United States when MCA produced **8.07** 'Barbie Girl'. The song contained certain sexually oriented lyrics, such as 'undress me everywhere . . . I'm a blonde bimbo girl . . .'. Mattel Inc., who created the world famous Barbie doll in 1957, developing it into a product sold in more than 140 countries, moved for a preliminary injunction in its claims for trade mark infringement and dilution, asking the US District Court for the Central District of California to order the destruction of every product or packaging using the Mattel's BARBIE trade mark. The Court denied the injunction, finding that:

> the claimant failed either to show that it was likely to succeed on its infringement and dilution claims, or to demonstrate that the balance of hardships tipped sharply in its favor.

Later the same District Court granted the defendants' motion for a summary **8.08** judgment to dismiss the case, affirming that the use of Barbie fell within the non-commercial use exception to the Federal Trademark Dilution Act 1995 (FTDA). The Court held that the song constituted a parody, deserving the protection granted by the First Amendment. The judges found that the aim of the singers was mainly to ridicule the artificiality of the doll. The Court stated that:

> the fact that a parody makes a profit does not strip it of the protection under the First Amendment.[1]

---

[1] See eg *Mattel Inc v MCA Records Inc* DC No 97–06791.

8.09 The Court then observed that it would have been impossible to parody Barbie successfully without mentioning her name; moreover, singers did not use the doll's likeness on their CD or their videos. On the contrary, a disclaimer on the defendants' CD specified that the song constituted 'a social comment, and was not created or approved by the makers of the doll'.

8.10 The Court then explained that, as a result of fame, many marks become the 'natural target of parodists', rejecting Mattel's claim that the song tarnished Barbie's wholesome image through 'sexual and denigrating lyrics'. Because the song constituted a parody, the Court ruled that MCA's use was not actionable as a trade mark dilution under the FTDA. Some elements of the decisional criterion followed by the US Federal judges (specifically the impossibility of avoiding making mention of the name of other firms' products) can also be found in European case law on similar topics, especially concerning the descriptive use of a trade mark.[2]

8.11 The Ninth Circuit Court drew on the District Court's findings, saying that 'with fame often comes unwanted attention'.[3] As a result of the huge impact of the product on society as a whole, the doll must be seen not only as a toy but also as 'an American cultural icon'.

8.12 In rejecting Mattel's infringement argument, the Ninth Circuit relied on a Second Circuit opinion in a suit involving Federico Fellini's movie *Ginger and Fred*. In that action the dancer and actress Ginger Rogers sued the makers of the film, claiming that the title gave the false impression that she was somehow involved with the movie. In *Barbie* the Court observed that, just as in *Rogers*, where the defendant's alleged danger of misleading was outweighed by the danger of 'suppressing an artistically relevant' work, MCA's interest in free expression clearly outweighed the claimant's complained customer confusion.

8.13 In the core part of its decision, the Ninth Circuit stressed the importance of the non-commercial use of the trade mark, which fell within the exception provided under the First Amendment in favour of the protection of even dilutive speech: even though speech may dilute a mark, it may still be protected,

---

[2] See eg *Toshiba Europe GmbH v Katun Germany GmbH* Case C-112/99 [2002] ETMR 26.
[3] See eg *Mattel Inc v MCA Records Inc* 296 F3d 894 (9th Cir 2002).

especially where the mark has assumed an expressive function beyond mere identification of a product or a service.

The Court noted that there are three exceptions to the dilution's prohibition: **8.14** (i) comparative advertising, (ii) news reporting and commentary and (iii) non-commercial use. 'Barbie Girl' was found to fall in the last one.

The Ninth Circuit added that, by using Mattel's trade mark, MCA's primary **8.15** objective was to parody the doll and the values associated with her. As in the *Rogers* case, the Court noted that the overwhelming part of the consumers 'expect a title to describe the underlying work, not to identify the producer'.

From the trade mark use point of view, the interesting thing here is that the **8.16** defendants were not using the BARBIE trade mark to indicate the origin of their goods, so it is questionable whether they were making 'trade mark use' of the mark. It could however be argued that the parody relied on the defendants using the BARBIE mark as a trade mark for the *claimant's* goods, that is to identify the goods which were the object of the parody. It is questionable whether such 'referential' use, which does not confer the sort of benefit on the defendant that is envisaged by the essential function of a trade mark, should be classed as trade mark use of the sort that constitutes infringement.

(2) The NELLIE THE ELEPHANT cases

'Nellie the Elephant' is a children's song, well known in the UK. Dash **8.17** acquired the copyright in the song in 1956. In 1987 Dash licensed 101 Film Production Ltd. 101 Film Production's successor in title, Animated Music Ltd, intended to use the song in a television series it was preparing. Animated registered the trade mark NELLIE THE ELEPHANT in 1989. Dash applied for this registration to be revoked on the basis of non-use for a continuous period of five years.[4] Dash also applied to have the same registration declared invalid.[5]

The issues were decided by a Hearing Officer who sought to identify the **8.18** correct meaning of 'use' and 'non-use'. Referring to a case ruled by the

---

[4] *Animated Music Limited's Trade Mark; Application for Revocation by Dash Music Co Ltd* Case O-392–03, Trade Marks Registry (M Reynolds) 15 December 2003.
[5] *Animated Music Limited's Trade Mark; Application for a Declaration of Invalidity by Dash Music Co Ltd* Case O-391–03, Trade Marks Registry (M Reynolds) 15 December 2003.

European Court of Justice (ECJ), *Ansul BV v Ajax Brandbeveiliging BV*,[6] the Court stated that genuine use must be understood to denote

> use that is not merely token, serving solely to preserve the rights conferred by the mark.

8.19 The use must be consistent with the essential function of the trade mark, ie it must identify specific goods or services to the end user. The consumer should be able to distinguish the products or services from others without any possibility of confusion. In order to be considered 'genuine', the use of the mark must be referred to the goods or services protected by that mark, goods or services that are already marketed or about to be marketed. In this particular case, however, the Court found that the NELLIE THE ELEPHANT mark was used to *describe the content* of Animated's cartoons, as it did not denote the trade origin of the class of goods for which it was registered. The Hearing Officer stated that the evidence showed use of the name

> to indicate the subject matter of the films. What they do not show is use of that name as an indication of the trade source of the Class 41 services.

8.20 The consequence was that the application for revocation succeeded. This goes to show that, to avoid revocation, trade mark use is needed. Use as the title of a work or as the name of a character alone will not count as trade mark use for this purpose.[7]

---

[6] *Ansul BV v Ajax Brandbeveiliging BV* (MINIMAX) Case C-40/01 [2003] ECR I-2439, [2003] ETMR 85.

[7] A similar approach was taken by the UK Trade Mark Registry in *Application of R Delamore to Register* CHARLIE'S ANGELS; *Opposition of Columbia Pictures Industries Incorporated* (8 April 2004, unreported) paras 32–34, where the Hearing Officer found that the use of the words 'Charlie's Angels' as a film title indicated the content of the film and that it was the company that brought the opposition that would be perceived as the source of the CDs, videos and DVDs on which the film was recorded. Accordingly the 'Charlie's Angels' title had not been used in a 'trade mark sense' and it could not be shown that the opponent had sufficient reputation in the trade mark to found a claimed under the Trade Marks Act 1994 s 5(3), the provision that bars registration where an applied-for sign is detrimental to or takes advantage of the distinctive character or repute of an earlier mark. See also *Disney Enterprises Inc v Francis Fitzpatrick* (WINNIE THE POOH/PIGGLEY POOH) OHIM Opposition Division Decision 951/2001 (11 April 2001), particularly p 14, for a similar approach by OHIM. This decision was cited in both the NELLIE THE ELEPHANT and the CHARLIE'S ANGELS decisions.

C. Unauthorized Use of Trade Marks Referring to Fictional Characters in a Website

In recent years, many businesses have had to protect their trade marks against **8.21** their unauthorized use on third party websites. The problem obviously concerns, most of all, world-famous brands, which are often used in domain names. Most such businesses have often displayed, in the past, a rather aggressive legal attitude, adopting the so-called 'cease and desist' strategy: law firms working for those companies often send letters to sites' webmasters, asking either for the immediate removal of any infringing material, or for direct control over the website.

This approach, however, has certain economic consequences, particularly the **8.22** danger of damaging the company's image when the unauthorized user is a fan site. Fan sites are developed by people who are enthusiastic about a particular product or company. When that company attempts to protect its trade mark through traditional legal means, the results can seriously damage the corporate image perceived by customers. What is more, the formerly enthusiastic customer may respond by including in his pages a description of the 'corporate tyranny' that causes the fan site's demise, easily switching from a fan to a hate site. In this section we shall then take a look at the strategy adopted by some large companies in the USA as to fan sites.

(1) Paramount Pictures *and* Time Warner: *the policy adopted by media companies*

Entertainment companies appear to have tried different legal approaches **8.23** through the years. At least two different policies have been adopted since the internet explosion, in the second part of the 1990s, until today, particularly by Warner Bros.

In a letter sent in June 1996 to the registrant of a Star Trek fan site, **8.24** Paramount demanded the confirmation, within ten days, of both the complete removal of all infringing material from the fan site, and of there being no further 'posting any similar infringing material on the Internet or any other on-line service in the future'. Although letters of this kind did not 'object to all materials posted on the Internet relating to Star Trek properties', fans feared that Paramount's trade mark protection of the Trek characters' names and the words STAR TREK raised the risk that any posting of plot summaries or reviews would constitute the unauthorized use of copyrighted material.

8.25 In a letter sent in November 1995 to the webmaster of the so-called 'ACME Page', Warner Bros demanded the immediate cessation of 'any copying, transmission or other utilization of any of its protected intellectual property'. It further demanded the complete removal of such intellectual property from the site, seeking that the webmaster engage 'in no further uploading of any such infringing material to any other site'.

8.26 After having experienced many cases similar to these,[8] in most recent years Warner Bros has substantially changed its strategy. Monitoring the use of the fictional name Harry Potter, Warner Bros no longer demands the removal of copyright material, or the shutting down of fan sites on account of copyright or trade mark infringement. Webmasters who owned a domain name containing the words 'Harry Potter' were asked to turn their domain over to Warner Bros. The company gave the webmasters the opportunity to maintain the site, merely asking to be allowed to retain control of the site so that any eventual future infringements could be easily dealt with. This is a sensible approach where the owners of fan sites are not seeking to use the trade marks of the objects of their affection as a trade mark for their websites in order to fool the public into thinking that their sites are connected with the entertainment companies. Without using the trade marks, they have no other means of identifying the cultural phenomena that they so admire. Eliminating websites where the webmasters are not seeking to use the marks as trade marks for their own goods or services will not only diminish the free circulation of ideas, but will also make entertainment companies unpopular among their most devoted fans.

(2) Elvis Presley Enterprises: *the protection of a real character's name and places referring to him*

8.27 Many cases concern the unauthorized reproduction of the name and the likeness of Elvis Presley, given his worldwide popularity. The approach pursued by Elvis Presley Enterprises (EPE) varies according to the interest pro-

---

[8] per A Sackler, Time Warner Vice-President, 1999.

tected. Two cases provide a useful example of the different policies followed by the company.

In 1998, a nightclub called 'The Velvet Elvis' was opened in Houston. The **8.28** owner applied for a service mark, which was granted. EPE sued for both federal and common law unfair competition and trade mark infringement, federal trade mark dilution and violation of its right of publicity in Elvis Presley's name and likeness. The defendant's claim that it had a defence of parody was rejected by the Court, because the judges noted that the defence of parody does not apply in the case of trade mark infringement. The approach to this issue in this case is clearly different to that taken in the *Barbie Girl* case in that, in this case, the status of parody was not granted to the defendant's work. This case, and others like it, also beg the question: will people perceive every use of ELVIS as authorized by the Elvis estate, ie as a badge of origin or authenticity, or will they acknowledge that many people want to pay tribute to Elvis? It is also possible that, perhaps because of the zealousness with which EPE protects its intellectual property rights, that the ELVIS trade mark is a special case and that every use of the ELVIS trade mark will be perceived by the public as denoting that the use has been endorsed by EPE.

The trade mark approach can be contrasted with an example of EPE's **8.29** enforcement of its copyright. In 1994, EPE met the opening of a so-called 'Cyber Graceland Tour' by adopting the usual cease-and-desist strategy. In the letter sent to the creator of the tour, the company warned him that its site was infringing both EPE's exclusive right to copy, distribute and create derivatives of its copyright-protected images of Graceland and EPE's copyrights in the music used in the tour. Its final demand was for the immediate withdrawal of the cyber tour from the defendant's website. This case shows that trade mark law is not the end of the story. Different and sometimes more expansive ways of preventing the type of activity that the proprietor of the intellectual property rights finds objectionable may be available under copyright law.

D. Unauthorized Reference to Fictional Characters in Retailing

With a large number of businesses being engaged in direct or indirect market- **8.30** ing initiatives, use of real and fictional characters is becoming nowadays increasingly common.

8.31 In this section we deal with two different cases, both decided by Italian courts in the 1970s and early 1980s. These courts' opinions have been extremely significant in the development of Italian case law and European awareness on the matter.

(1) The TARZAN case

8.32 Edgar Rice Burroughs Inc. (ERB) was the owner of the copyrights concerning the fictional character Tarzan, the protagonist of several novels written by Edgar Rice Burroughs between 1911 and 1950. Candygum S.r.l., an Italian confectioner, registered the trade mark TARZAN for chewing gum. ERB sued Candygum, alleging violation of its alleged exclusive right to use the name 'Tarzan' for economic purposes and requesting the suppression of the use of the word 'Tarzan' as a trade mark in any form. ERB also claimed ownership of the TARZAN trade mark, having registered it in France in 1966. Following a French–Italian agreement of 1955, that mark would have been extended to Italy.

8.33 In 1974 the court rejected the claimant's applications, noting that ERB did not provide any evidence about the alleged exclusive right to use the name for economic purposes. ERB appealed against this decision and claimed that, under Italian law, the owner of copyright was entitled to use its creation 'in any way and form', one of the ways being the utilization of the character's name. ERB's contention was that, if copyright owners have the right to prevent third parties from using any part of a literary work, they can also prevent the unauthorized use of the names of characters.

8.34 The Court of Appeals observed that a preliminary question had to be solved: was the name of a character capable of being protected under copyright law? In other words, was a name by itself a separate part of the literary work which deserved, in this case, the protection accorded by Italian law to 'any manner and form' of economic use of artists' creations?[9] The Court stated that, even though the exclusive rights granted by Italian law refer to the whole literary work and its parts, the name of a character alone could not represent a 'part' of the work in the sense indicated by the law, since a mere name does not present the 'expressive creativity' required by the law itself. Unauthorized use

---

[9] *Edgar Rice Burroughs Inc v Candygum SpA* Court of Appeals of Milan (12 November 1976).

of several elements, each of which lack expressive creativity, may itself be considered unlawful but that is only the case where the use of all of those elements is aimed at reproducing the work's original core. The Court however found that the name had the distinctive function of identifying both the character and the novel, distinguishing them from other names and characters.

This decision would seem to indicate that there is a lacuna in the law: the **8.35** protection conferred by trade mark registration in respect of books may not confer protection against the use of the same mark for chewing gum, while the protection conferred on the book as a literary work will not be effective to prevent the commercial exploitation of so insubstantial a part of that work as a mere character name.

(2) *The* BIANCANEVE *case*

Mr Brecciaroli was the owner of the Italian trade mark BIANCANEVE (the **8.36** Italian equivalent of Snow White), registered in 1969 for ice creams and sweets. Astoria 73, an Italian cafeteria in Rome, used the word 'Biancaneve' together with its business name in order to indicate a specific kind of homemade ice cream. Mr Brecciaroli sued Astoria 73 for trade mark infringement, claiming that the defendant's use of the word was unlawful.

Astoria 73 retorted that the word 'Biancaneve' was put beside the word **8.37** 'Astoria' in the phrase 'l'Astoria di Biancaneve' in order to indicate its products and that the expression could not therefore be confused with the claimant's trade mark. The Court noted that the method of presenting products to customers focused exclusively on the fictitious character's name.[10] The word 'Astoria', used by several companies in different industries, was not an appropriate means of identifying products. In this particular case, the same word was preceded by the Italian article 'l'. The pronunciation of the whole expression, 'l'Astoria di Biancaneve', sounded in Italian like 'The story of Snow White' (ie 'La storia di Biancaneve'). For this reason, the Court stated that the word 'Biancaneve' was used as a trade mark and infringed the claimant's rights. The defendant did not argue that the ownership of the trade mark BIANCANEVE for ice creams and sweets could belong to Walt Disney

---

[10] *Giovanni Brecciaroli v Astoria 73 Srl* Court of Rome (29 December 1981).

Productions or to other persons. Finally, the Court awarded the claimant compensation in the form of damages, thus inhibiting the defendant from using the word 'Biancaneve' further to name its products. BIANCANEVE is a unique case in which the claimant was making trade mark use of the name of a character that originated with someone who was not a party to the case. This case provides a vivid example of the principle that, while use of a name as the name of a fictional character may not be considered to be trade mark use, use of the name of a fictional character for merchandising purposes (ie for goods other than the book or film in which the character appears) often will be classed as trade mark use.

E. Unauthorized Reference to Real and Fictional Names in Business Names

8.38 With the constant development of economic globalization and the ongoing lowering of trade barriers, businesses increasingly need to find a tool which makes their products stand out in the eyes of consumers. Making reference to well-known names often appears to be a good way of achieving this end.

8.39 The first and the second cases that we shall examine under this heading involve this kind of strategy as adopted by companies. The third and the fourth cases involve the use of a popular surname as a company name in the USA and in the European Union.

(1) The Daily Planet case

8.40 DC Comics' predecessors were the creators of the world-famous fictional character named Superman. The 'Daily Planet' is the name of the fictitious newspaper around which many of the Superman stories are set. Jerry Powers was the publisher of an underground news publication called the *Daily Planet* between 1969 and 1973. After its demise, Mr Powers engaged in several business ventures which, occasionally, were conducted under the name 'Daily Planet, Inc.'. The claimant, DC Comics, started its action in 1978, claiming that the defendants, the Daily Planet Inc. and its president Jerry Powers, had infringed its common law trade mark rights in the name 'The Daily Planet'. The injunction was initially denied but, after nine months, the defendants sought re-argument on their motion for a preliminary injunction.

The Court confirmed its earlier decision, observing that the defendants may **8.41** have used the name 'Daily Planet' after permitting his federal registration to lapse. But this use evidences 'a lack of commitment to the mark'.[11] In fact, only with the release of the claimant's *Superman* movie did the defendants show interest in using the name 'Daily Planet'. The Court stated that the adoption of the name 'Daily Planet' in 1969 was 'merely an attempt to cash in on the Superman story and its notoriety'. In this case, then, the Court based its decision on factual findings, specifically the time relation between the defendants' use of the trade mark and the release of a work which could significantly benefit Mr Powers. In this case the Court protected a mark that the claimant had never used as a trade mark on the market in the real world. The justification for such protection cannot be that the defendant has interfered with the source-signalling function of the 'Daily Planet' mark because it never indicated the source of any goods or services in the real world. This tends to suggest that the justification for providing protection in this case was to prevent the defendant from obtaining an unearned advantage in a term that had become famous through the claimant's efforts.

(2) *The* CACAO MERAVIGLIAO *case*

On 14 December 1987 the first episode of a satirical television programme **8.42** was broadcast in Italy. The programme featured some of the best-known Italian television artists, creating significant expectations and interest among the national television audience. Both before the programme and throughout its duration, many advertisements for a fictitious product called 'Cacao Meravigliao'[12] were broadcast. The advertisements were fictitious and parodied the way real products were promoted during ordinary television programmes. On 15 December 1987 Mr Shlomo Blanga registered the expression CACAO MERAVIGLIAO as a trade mark in Italy.

In the following months, the programme became one of the most successful **8.43** broadcasts in the history of Italian television, leading to the widespread national popularity of the expression 'Cacao Meravigliao'. The RAI-Radio Televisione Italiana broadcasting station, together with the authors of the

---

[11] *DC Comics Inc v Powers* 482 F Supp 494 (SD NY 1979).
[12] The Italian for 'Amazing Cocoa'.

programme, sued Mr Blanga, claming that the words 'Cacao Meravigliao' were protected under copyright law and that therefore they could not be the object of a trade mark registration.

8.44   The Court observed that, in general, advertising expressions cannot be protected under copyright law. In this particular case, however, the words in question might not be considered as a mere advertising expression, since they could be seen as a synthesis of the whole idea of the television programme.[13] The defendant replied that it was the entire representation which deserved protection under copyright law. Italian judges found that the fictitious advertisement represented the real central core of the programme and that it was identified with the expression 'Cacao Meravigliao'. This element alone, stated the Court, 'grants protection to the (artistic) invention'. According to Italian law, however, trade marks must not infringe exclusive rights of third parties, such as copyright. Accordingly the Court granted the claimants' applications.

8.45   This is another example of a case where, like the *Daily Planet* case, the mark had not been used as a trade mark in the real world. In this case, though, copyright rather than trade mark rights were used by the proprietor. In fact, copyright could potentially protect a wider range of works than trade marks since there is no use requirement for copyright protection. However, it is not always easy to show copyright in a name. For example, the conclusions of the Italian judges in this case differ from the decision adopted by the UK Trade Mark Registry in the *NELLIE THE ELEPHANT* case: there, the Court found that the phrase 'Nellie the Elephant' alone was not protected by copyright and the taking of a single expression (the title of a song) did not constitute the taking of a substantial part of the whole, copyright protected, literary work.

(3) The Lane Capital Management *case*

8.46   Lane Capital Management, Inc. was incorporated in Delaware in 1993, as a company providing investment advice. The founder of the company, Mr Fulenwider, said he chose the name 'Lane Capital Management' because 'Lane' was his father's and his son's middle name. Douglas C. Lane was the president of the defendant/appellant, also named 'Lane Capital

---

[13] *RAI-Radio Televisione Italiana v Old Colonial Sas and Regina Srl* Court of Rome (10 January 1990).

Management, Inc.', which was incorporated in New York in 1994. Mr Lane allegedly chose that name because Lane was his surname. In 1997 the claimant–respondent commenced its action, claiming service mark infringement under the US law. Having been granted an application for a service mark for the principal register in respect of financial services, Mr Fulenwider's company moved for summary judgment. The appellant argued that the purchasing public perceived the respondent's mark to be primarily a mere surname, underlying the fact that Lane is the 170th most common surname in the USA. The District Court found that the respondent's registered mark was 'inherently distinctive' and that the appellant's use of the mark 'would cause confusion in the marketplace'. Following the appellant's motion for re-argument, the Second Circuit Court of Appeals noted that:

> a mark is primarily merely a surname if the primary significance of the mark to the purchasing public is that of a surname.[14]

8.47 Only if a word does not have any impact upon the purchasing public will that word be considered as a mere surname and not as a real trade mark. The Court found that the evidence provided by the appellants was insufficient to show that 'Lane' was used only as a surname; it then affirmed Mr Fulenwider's company had a 'readily recognisable dictionary meaning that other surnamed financial institutions lack'. Words that are perceived only as surnames will not be perceived as indicating the origin of the goods or services that bear them: they will not be used as trade marks and will not be protected as such. However this case suggests that alternative meanings, even if they are not associated with use as a badge of origin, will save surnames from not being recognized as trade marks.

(4) *The* Nichols *case*

8.48 In 2000 Nichols plc, a company incorporated in the UK, applied to register the word NICHOLS for vending machines and products sold by them. The Trade Mark Registry granted the application for vending machines only, refusing it for other indications, on the grounds that, first, Nichols was a common surname in the UK and that, second, since the food and drinks market is made up of a large number of operators, it is difficult for consumers

---

[14] *Lane Capital Management Inc v Lane Capital Management Inc* Docket no 98–9173 (2nd Cir 1999).

to identify the commercial origin of the products denoted by a common surname. Nichols appealed against this decision to the High Court, which decided to stay the proceedings and seek a preliminary ruling from the ECJ. The High Court asked:

> in what circumstances, if any, must a trade mark consisting of a single surname be refused registration as being in itself devoid of any distinctive character within the meaning of Article 3(1)(b) of the directive?

8.49 In January 2004 the Advocate General gave his opinion before the ECJ.[15] He observed that it must be borne in mind that:

> surnames are not included in the list of marks given in Article 3(1)(c) [marks which are barred from registration on grounds of descriptiveness] of the Directive. They are not, at first sight, generic or descriptive signs for specific products or services.

8.50 He also noted that the evaluation method employed by the UK Registry differed from the approach used by the ECJ:

> However, no sufficient reasons have been put forward in favour of choosing another interpretative method.

8.51 In order to judge upon the distinctiveness of a surname, the same guidelines applicable to other types of word marks must be observed. For a trade mark, in other words, it is sufficient to enable consumers to distinguish the product or the service it designates. The Directive, stated the Advocate General, makes no distinction between different categories of marks. It would be useful to consider that, in some industries, common surnames are often employed to indicate commercial origin: this, however, needs to be assessed on a case-by-case basis, with no *a priori* abstract rules.

8.52 Eventually, on 16 September 2004, the ECJ rendered its decision stating that, in the context of Article 3(1)(b) of the First Council Directive 89/104/ EEC of 21 December 1988 to approximate the laws of the Member States relating to trade marks, the assessment of the existence or otherwise of the distinctive character of a trade mark constituted by a surname, even a common one, must be carried out specifically, in accordance with the criteria applicable to any sign covered by Article 2 of that directive, in relation, first, to the products or services in respect of which registration is applied for and, second, to the perception of the relevant consumers. Moreover, the Court

---

[15] Case C-404/02 [2004] ETMR 48.

affirmed that the fact that the effects of registration of the trade mark are limited by virtue of Article 6(1)(a) of that directive has no impact on that assessment.

F. Unauthorized Use of a Trade Mark in Press Products and Merchandising

Three of the cases we examine here refer to the use of a trade mark in printed **8.53** products, such as books, newspapers and calendars. Although all cases were discussed before Italian courts, the solutions proposed by judges are not identical. However, the evaluating method mentioned in the last case seems also to have been implicitly adopted in the two previous ones: disputes must be assessed by taking into consideration the aims and purposes of every product, on a case-by-case basis.

The fourth case discussed here is the well-known *Arsenal* case,[16] which laid **8.54** down in Europe guidelines concerning the unauthorized exploitation of a famous trade mark by way of merchandising. The trade marks in this case constituted typical examples of a sign that allows the customer to show that he belongs to a particular social group (ie the fans of a football team), as mentioned in the introduction.

(1) The Swatchissimo case

Antiquorum Italia s.r.l., an Italian publisher, published a book called *Swatch-* **8.55** *issimo*. The topic of that book concerned different watch models created by the world famous Swiss company Swatch S.A. In 1992 Swatch S.A. sued Antiquorum Italia for trade mark and copyright infringement under Italian law. Swatch claimed that the book published and distributed by the defendant contained not only representations of several Swatch models but also many advertising images whose copyrights were held by Swatch.

The Court observed that, since the term Swatchissimo was not aimed at **8.56** distinguishing the defendant's product or services, it could not be considered as a mark. It was chosen with the sole purpose of describing the *content* of the

---

[16] *Arsenal Football Club plc v Matthew Reed* Case C-206/01 [2002] ETMR 82.

book itself.[17] The Court denied that the discipline of trade mark law could be applied to this specific case, since the book could be classified as a literary work rather than a catalogue or a brochure illustrating the defendant's products. Antiquorum Italia, in fact, had never produced products similar to those of Swatch. In other words, there was no infringement because Antiquorum Italia had not been using the SWATCH mark as a trade mark for its own goods. Further, the Court found that there had been no infringement of copyright because the 'Swatch' word alone could not be considered as a literary work. Even the claimant, the Court stated, presented it as a trade mark. The concept of descriptive, rather than trade mark, use of a trade mark, protected both under Italian and European law, has therefore been employed in this case to exclude trade mark infringement for titles of books which refer to well-known trade marks.

(2) *The* Super Inter *case*

8.57 Forte Editore s.r.l., an Italian publisher, brought out a magazine named *Super Inter*. The magazine concerned news and comments on the Italian football team Internazionale Milano s.p.a. (usually known as 'Inter'). Inter sued Forte Editore s.r.l. for unfair competition, observing that Inter already ran a magazine called *Inter Football Club* and claiming actual and potential customers could be confused by the heading of the defendant's magazine.

8.58 The Court observed that only the denominative mark 'Inter' was protected by the trade mark registration, but that the title *Inter Football Club* was not. It assessed that the two headings could not be confused with each other.[18] The Court considered the mark 'Inter' to be descriptive not *per se* but 'in relation to the use made by the defendant'. The magazine's title was found to be undoubtedly descriptive of the topics covered by the magazine itself: in other words it was being used to describe the claimant, rather than as a trade mark for the defendant's goods. The issue, stated the Court, was not about the strength or weakness of the mark but whether a trade mark infringement occurred, considering its use made by the defendant.

---

[17] *Swatch S A v Antiquorum Italia Srl and Grimoldi Srl* Court of Milan (30 March 1998).
[18] *F C Internazionale Milano Spa, Nerazzurra Srl and A Paleari Srl v Forte Editore Srl* Court of Milan (29 May 1995).

(3) The Juventissima case

Forservice s.r.l., an Italian publisher, issued for the year 1996 a calendar called **8.59**
'Juventissima', including pictures of Juventus football players. Juventus F.C.
s.p.a. sued Forservice s.r.l for trade mark infringement and unfair competition, applying for both compensatory damages and destruction of produced
goods. The claimant observed it had been producing for many years another
calendar, called 'Juventus F.C. s.p.a. official calendar', adding that the
defendant's product harmed its exclusive rights. The defendant maintained
there was no possibility of confusing the Juventus mark with the layout of its
product, pointing to the weakness of the claimant's mark.

The Court found that the claimant's trade mark was strong, since there was **8.60**
no 'logical connection between the products and the employed mark'.[19]
Otherwise, a mark could be considered weak when 'its distinctive capacity
focuses on characteristics of the goods'. Being strong, a trade mark can be
protected in a broader way:

> infringement occurs even if there are relevant modifications, but the mark's
> identity is still recognisable.

The Court noted that everyone was allowed to use the word 'Juventus' and its **8.61**
logo for descriptive purposes, in order to provide pieces of information concerning the famous football team. In this particular case, however, the
defendant's product was not aimed at giving any kind of information about
the team's performances. Forservice used the mark with the objective of
'inducing customers, attracted by the mark's evocative capacity, to buy its
products'. The Court stated that, without reference to Juventus' trade mark,
the defendant's revenues would have been smaller. The Court also found that
the diffusion without consent of celebrities' images is forbidden, when
'reproduction is the effect of a mere advertising activity'. The judges noted
this was the case with the defendant's reproduction of Juventus players'
pictures because of the main goal of the calendar, which could be defined as
the making of profit. The evaluation method adopted by the Court concen-
trated on the aim pursued by the user of the trade mark, settling a distinction
between information and profit-generating purposes. The approach taken is
that use by the defendant of the mark as a trade mark to indicate the origin of

---

[19] *Juventus F C Spa v Forservice Srl* Court of Turin (5 November 1999).

his own products is *not* necessary for infringement. However, there is a limit to the bounds of infringement because descriptive use will not be classed as infringement.

(4) The Arsenal *case*

8.62 Arsenal Football Club plc ran the world-famous Arsenal football team, also known as 'the Gunners'. Their business included the sale of products bearing the marks owned by Arsenal. Mr Reed was a self-employed proprietor of a football merchandise business. Among other items, he sold articles bearing signs very similar to Arsenal's registered trade marks. Arsenal sued Mr Reed for trade mark infringement. He in turn claimed that the use of those signs did not constitute a trade mark use, since it was use as a badge of loyalty, not as a badge of origin. In fact, the High Court found that there had been no trade mark infringement, because most consumers would perceive the Arsenal signs on defendant's products as a badge of affiliation, not as indicating their trade origin.[20] However, the same judges referred to the ECJ the question whether or not the use of a sign other than in a trade mark sense could be considered a trade mark infringement.

8.63 The ECJ stated that use as a trade mark was not the relevant requirement for infringement under Article 5(1)(a). Instead, what is decisive is whether

> [T]he use of a sign which is identical to the trade mark at issue in the main proceedings is liable to jeopardize the guarantee of origin which constitutes the essential function of the mark.[21]

The ECJ found it immaterial that, in the context of that use, the sign used by Mr Reed was perceived as a badge of support or loyalty.

8.64 In its supplementary judgment,[22] the High Court considered that the ECJ had exceeded its jurisdiction: the ECJ was neither expected nor entitled to rule on the facts underlying the dispute, its task being to provide interpretation of European law. For this reason, the High Court found itself not bound by the ECJ's final conclusions: it decided to apply the guidelines coming from the European Court of Justice to the facts the same High Court had previously found.

---

[20] [2001] ETMR 77.
[21] *Arsenal v Reed* (n 16) para 60.
[22] [2003] ETMR 19.

The claimant appealed against this decision to the Court of Appeal. **8.65**

The Court of Appeal confirmed that, as to the articles sold by Mr Reed, the **8.66** trade marks, when applied to the goods, were purchased and worn as badges of support.[23] However, it also observed that goods not coming from Arsenal but bearing its trade marks were in circulation: 'that affected the ability of the trade marks to guarantee the origin of the goods'. Since this guarantee of origin was identified by the ECJ as the essential function of a trade mark which the defendant must not jeopardize, there had been infringement, even though the defendant has not used the mark to guarantee the origin of his *own* goods (ie he had not made use of the mark as a trade mark for his own goods). The test has been shifted from whether the defendant is making trade mark use of the mark for his own goods to whether the defendant is harming the claimant's ability to make trade mark use of the mark in the future. The Court of Appeal noted that the result reached by the ECJ was inevitable, deciding the case in Arsenal's favour, on the grounds that a significant proportion of customers would consider the defendant's marks as designating the origin of the goods.

This decision makes it easier for brand owners to challenge the practice of **8.67** selling unofficial merchandise in particular, and unauthorized use of a trade mark in general, although it remains to be seen what types of activity courts will perceive as jeopardizing the essential function of an earlier mark. And, in any event, don't we all as consumers purchase and proudly use our favourite branded goods with a feeling of allegiance to the brand name?

G. Conclusion

Trade mark use is often a 'make or break' factor concerning the ability of a **8.68** proprietor to enforce his trade mark rights in the field of denominative use. From the discussion above it is apparent that it is particularly important with regard to two issues: (i) whether trade mark use by a defendant is needed for a successful infringement action and (ii) how a trade mark owner may show that he has used his mark as a trade mark to avoid its revocation. Denominative use holds particular problems in these areas because it is often doubted

---

[23] [2003] ETMR 36.

whether the use of the name of a character, book, film or even organization is a use which denotes the origin, either of the mark owner's goods or services or of those who want to make a reference to the mark owner's goods or services. Where trade mark use is deemed to not be a crucial factor in any particular case, this can be an indication that interests other than the origin functions of trade marks, such as the desire to prevent free riding on another's trade mark may be at stake. However, following the ECJ's *Arsenal* ruling, it cannot be said that this will always be the case because it has been recognized that non-trade mark use can impair the origin function of a mark and that such impairment must be prevented.

8.69 It is also apparent from the cases described that in cases where there is no trade mark use, which may therefore not result in a likelihood of success in a trade mark action, copyright has been used to protect names instead. It is questionable whether this is a desirable phenomenon. The protection of names is not the core interest of copyright law. Underlying cases where a lack of trade mark use has led to the claimant being unable to enforce his rights is a careful balance made by trade mark law that seeks to protect multifarious interests, such as free speech for those who wish to criticize or adulate the mark and the ability for other traders to be able to use the mark descriptively. It would be unfortunate if copyright upset this balance in a field which is not essentially its concern.

9

USE, CERTIFICATION AND COLLECTIVE MARKS

Jeffrey Belson

A. Introduction	9.01	(1) Who can use a certification mark?	9.12
B. What are Certification and Collective Marks Used for?	9.02	(2) Authorized use of a certification mark versus trade mark use by a licensee	9.17
C. Registration of Certification Marks	9.07	(3) Licensee estoppel	9.22
(1) Is there a use requirement for a certification mark to be registered?	9.08	E. Registration of Collective Marks	9.24
D. Ownership and Use of Certification Marks	9.11	F. Ownership and Use of Collective Marks	9.28
		G. Summary	9.34

A. Introduction

The right to register certification and collective marks is a statutory right that **9.01** treats such marks as special types of marks. Regimes for the registration, ownership and use of certification marks and collective marks are strongly influenced by the need to protect the public interest in free and open competition among traders in the marked products.[1] National perceptions of the public interest and how it is to be protected vary according to prevailing commercial, social and political conditions. The variations in these perceptions result in differences across the Anglo-American and European

---

The author wishes to thank Dr Neil J Wilkof, Mark Tooke and Myles C Wolfson for helpful suggestions. The views expressed in this chapter are those of the author and should not be taken as representing the views of Hewlett-Packard Company, or any of its affiliates.

[1] For the law and practice of certification marks and collective marks generally see J Belson *Certification Marks* (Sweet & Maxwell London 2002).

jurisdictions as to the scope of rights accorded to owners and users of certification and collective marks. Among other things, there may be required a certain legal and commercial status of the registrant, exclusion of the owner from use, stipulated open access for all qualified traders, a need for official approval of the owner's regulations and official approval for the alienation of such marks.

B. What are Certification and Collective Marks Used for?

9.02 In the many countries where they are recognized, certification and collective marks are used for something other than identification of an individual source of goods or services, which is the statutory object of an ordinary trade mark. A certification mark indicates *certification*, by the proprietor, of the goods or services in connection with which it is used, in respect of one or more attributes, such as origin, material, mode of manufacture or quality. Certification marks are also used to indicate conformity to particular safety or environmental requirements. Such requirements may be voluntary standards promulgated by standard-setting institutions or industry associations, or they may be mandatory measures pursuant to government regulations. Thus certification marks are effective, convenient and widely used means of messaging conformity to regulatory enforcement bodies as well as purchasers.

9.03 Since certification marks convey a standardization message, they are available for authorized use by any number of traders so long as the proprietor's requirements are met. The normal practice is to bind the certification mark proprietor, under the statute, official rules or registry practice, to permit use to all traders whose products meet its requirements, without discrimination. In this regard a certification mark is antithetical to an ordinary trade mark, which each trader uses as his own distinctive mark.

9.04 The fact that all goods bearing a certification mark meet the standard implies a minimum quality level for a product. But there is no upper limit; the mark does not differentiate between goods or services of different quality levels above the minimum. Thus it might be argued that the certification mark is perceived as implying a message that one trader's goods are no better than any other's. However, such a perception is addressed in whatever message is conveyed by the trader's own mark, which is normally affixed to the product as well.

The statutory object of a collective mark, the second type of special trade **9.05** mark considered in this chapter, is to indicate *membership* of the individual source of the goods or services in a trading association. Use of a collective mark is reserved to individual members of the association, cooperative or other collective group or organization who are sources of the goods or services. A collective mark helps protect the reputations of the members so long as the association maintains adequate standards for membership, preferably including references to product quality. Otherwise the mark may become emblematic of inferior quality, thereby damaging the industry it aims to protect or members whose products are of superior quality.

A variant of the collective mark, known as the collective membership mark, is **9.06** registrable in the USA. Typically displayed on pins, rings or lapel badges, the mark simply enables the user to indicate membership of an association and the use requirement is consistent with this objective. Such marks are not used in business or trade and do not indicate commercial origin. Instead, the purpose of their registration is for organizations to prevent their use by others.[2]

C. **Registration of Certification Marks**

Registration of certification marks is normally integrated into the statutory **9.07** framework for registration of ordinary trade marks, subject to special provisions. These special provisions include the signs of which a certification mark may consist, the nature of the proprietor's business, the filing and approval of regulations governing use of the mark, regulation of alienation and grounds for cancellation. An applicant for registration of a certification mark is required to file with the registry proposed regulations governing use of the mark, the standard to be met for certification.

(1) Is there a use requirement for a certification mark to be registered?

In the UK, the USA, Australia and most other countries, but not Canada, an **9.08** application to register a certification mark may be made on an intent-to-use basis. Acceptance of intent-to-use applications for registration of a trade

---

[2] Trademark Manual of Examination Procedure (TMEP) 1304.01ff.

mark is required under TRIPs.[3] It is noteworthy therefore that the policy of the Canadian Intellectual Property Office is to require use before an application is filed to register a certification mark.[4]

9.09 In the USA, a certification mark is defined as a mark that certifies regional or other origin, material, mode of manufacture, quality, accuracy, or other characteristics, or that the work or labour on the goods or services was performed by members of a union or other organization.[5] 'Use in commerce' in the US statute means bona fide use of a mark in relation to goods and/or services in the ordinary course of trade. For goods this means placement on them, their containers, displays, tags, labels or associated documents. For services this means use or display in their sale or advertising and their being rendered in commerce or, if the person rendering the services is engaged in commerce, they are rendered in more than one state or the USA and a foreign country.[6]

9.10 The United Kingdom Trade Marks Act 1994 ('TMA 1994') definition of a certification mark is similar to the US definition, except that it does not provide for certification of labour on goods or services performed by members of a union or other organization. The UK Registry requires that the proprietor, among other things, has a well-known status in the trade concerned and has access to the skills and resources needed to ensure certification is authoritative. In other words, the proprietor must be competent to certify the goods or services of others.[7]

---

[3] Agreement on Trade-Related Aspects of Intellectual Property Rights, Including Trade in Counterfeit Goods, 1994. Art 15(3) of TRIPs permits making registrability depend on use, but prohibits refusal of an application for registration solely on the ground that intended use has not taken place before three years have expired from the date of application.

[4] This may however be circumvented by filing a certification mark application claiming priority from a foreign filing pursuant to s 34(1) of the Canadian Trade-marks Act.

[5] Lanham Act 15 USC §1127.

[6] ibid.

[7] In the UK well-known status is required in partial fulfilment of the sch 2, para 7(1)(b) requirement for the applicant to be competent to certify. The competence test involves (i) showing the intention to control; (ii) having well-known status; and (iii) having access to the skills and resources to ensure certification is authoritative (see n 15).

D. Ownership and Use of Certification Marks

A certification mark is supported by standards or regulations, compliance **9.11**
with which is an indispensable condition for legitimate use and legal protection of the mark. Standard-setting bodies include government agencies,
independent inspection, testing and certification laboratories, trade associations and professional institutions. Both governmental and non-
governmental bodies may adopt certification marks or 'seals of approval'
which are affixed on products or used in connection with services that are
deemed to comply with the relevant standards. Voluntary or consensus
industry standards acquire mandatory status when government stipulates
compliance with them as a regulatory requirement. The use of certification
marks on products is well established, for example, as a means of attesting to
their compliance with particular health, safety or environmental regulations.

(1) Who can use a certification mark?

In most jurisdictions, the owner of a registered certification mark is excluded **9.12**
from using it. Indeed the owner may not even carry on a business in goods or
services of the kind certified. Disregard of these prohibitions renders the
mark subject to cancellation. The prohibitions are safeguards against certifier
distortion, in its favour, of free competition in the market for products that
he certifies. An owner's role is focused on controlling use of the mark by
others, ensuring that their products meet his requirements for certification.

The major exception to owner exclusion from use is Australia. The goods or **9.13**
services certified may be those of any person, including the owner of the
mark or any person approved by the owner for the purpose of certifying
goods or services.[8] This non-exclusion of the owner derives from the
unorthodox notion, apparently accepted by the legislature, that certification
marks serve a dual purpose by

> distinguishing a trade source in the traditional sense but also identify that the
> goods or services have a certification as to some characteristic or quality.[9]

---

[8] Trade Marks Act 1995 note to s 169.
[9] Trade Marks Bill 1995 Bill Digest vol. 112 [1995].

9.14 In Australia, use of a certification mark by its owner or an approved certifier is subject to the same rules that govern its use by authorized users. The Australian Competition and Consumer Commission (ACCC) is charged by Parliament with safeguarding the public interest where certification mark registration is concerned. Before the mark can be registered, ACCC must consider the application and certify that the applicant or the approved certifiers are competent to certify and that the rules of use of the mark would not be to the detriment of the public.[10] ACCC considers rules not to the detriment of the public as rules that are not 'in themselves anti-competitive or misleading or deceptive'. However, ACCC notes that:

> [it] is a matter for the Registrar to determine if any use of a trade mark is misleading or deceptive.[11]

9.15 An additional notable feature of a certification mark is that permission to use the mark must not be refused to anybody whose products meet the requirements. A certification mark is subject to cancellation if, in the language of the US law, the registrant discriminately refuses to certify or to continue to certify the goods or services of any person who maintains the standards or conditions which such mark certifies.

9.16 A US registered certification mark receives the same protection as a trade mark.[12] A registrant may obtain an injunction to preserve the value of its mark and to prevent future infringement.[13]

(2) Authorized use of a certification mark versus trade mark use by a licensee

9.17 The term 'license' to denote authorized use is being adopted increasingly by certification mark proprietors, users, the statutes,[14] registry manuals[15] and the

---

[10] Trade Marks Act 1995 s 175 and reg 16.3.

[11] *Summary of the Trade Practices Act 1974 and Additional Responsibilities of the Australian Competition and Consumer Commission under Other Legislation* (ACCC Canberra 2003) 77.

[12] Lanham Act 15 USC §1054.

[13] ibid §§1114, 1116.

[14] s 23(2) of the Canadian Trade-marks Act provides: 'The owner of a certification mark may *license* others to use the mark . . . and the use of the mark accordingly shall be deemed to be use thereof by the owner.' [Emphasis added.]

[15] 'Competence to certify is usually a question of the applicant's ability to monitor and control its licensees, or "authorised users".' *Work Manual* (UK Trade Marks Registry London 2001) ch 12: Certification Marks.

courts.[16] This is unfortunate, because authorized use of a certification mark is different from licensed use of an ordinary trade mark. Schedule 2 of the TMA 1994 likens an authorized user to a licensee in specified matters, relating to an authorized user's rights when there is unauthorized use by others.[17] In the interest of clarity, it is recommended that the terms 'license' and 'licensee' be relinquished in favour of 'authorized use' and 'authorized user'.

Classical trade mark licensing theory,[18] which is based on the source-designating role of an ordinary trade mark, adopted quality control as the instrumentality for connecting the licensed user to the trade mark owner, thereby preserving the source-designating role of the trade mark. In the USA, complete failure to address quality control can lead to the loss of trade mark rights. However, as Douglass[19] observes, courts generally seek to construe sufficient quality control if the license agreement has no quality control provision or if no such control is exercised, in order not to force surrender of rights. In some cases, mere agreement between the parties that the licensor has the right to exercise quality control has been deemed sufficient. **9.18**

In the UK the general rule has been that the licensed use of a trade mark without any quality control is inherently deceptive ('bare licence'). This meant that the mark could be held to be invalid because it ceased to be distinctive as it failed to designate a single source.[20] Recently however, in *Scandecor*, there has been judicial acknowledgement of changed conditions of trade and the opinion could be read as implying that quality control is no longer a legal requirement for a valid trade mark licence in the UK. In *Scandecor*, the view expressed by the court suggests that the requirement is for consent not quality control: **9.19**

> When they [customers] see goods to which a mark has been affixed, they understand that the goods have been produced either by the owner of the mark or by someone else acting with his consent.[21]

---

[16] The court in *Idaho Potato Commission v M&M Produce Farms and Sales* 335 F 3d 130 (2d Cir 2003) used the term 'license' throughout its opinion.

[17] TMA 1994 sch 2 para 13.

[18] NJ Wilkof *Trade Mark Licensing* (Sweet & Maxwell London 1995) s 2–03.

[19] S Douglass 'Basic Elements of Trademark Licenses' [2000] Licensing Journal 6–8.

[20] See David Young QC's 'golden thread' description in the *Scandecor* opinion: *Scandecor Development AB v Scandecor Marketing AB and others* [2001] United Kingdom HL 21; [2001] 2 CMLR 30 para 10.

[21] ibid 38.

9.20 For their quality assurance, customers are now deemed to rely on the self-interest of the owner in maintaining the value of its brand name, rather than protection supposedly afforded by a legal requirement for control over the licensee's activities.[22]

9.21 The underlying purpose of quality control in a certification mark scheme is different from a licensed ordinary trade mark. The proprietor of a certification mark is responsible for controlling use of the mark so that it performs its quintessential statutorily defined function of indicating attainment of the required quality standard. The proprietor must demonstrate, to the satisfaction of the registry, the legal and practical ability to certify, and is required to exercise sufficient supervision and control over the affixing of the mark upon the goods. The function of the certification mark is not a source-identifying function and authorized use implies no relationship between the certifier and the user based on a common trading interest in the certified products. Normally, such a relationship is not even possible, in view of the ban on the mark's proprietor having any business interest at all in goods or services of the kind certified. The ban is one measure for protecting the public interest in maintaining a free market for the product because it eliminates possible competing economic interests of the proprietor.

(3) Licensee estoppel

9.22 Generally, a licensee of an ordinary trade mark is estopped from challenging the validity of the licensed mark. The doctrine of licensee estoppel embodies the judicial position that it is inconsistent and inequitable for a licensee of an ordinary trade mark to accept a licence and then deny the validity of the registration.[23]

9.23 In the case of a certification mark, the US perception at least is that authorized use of a certification mark is not a licensing arrangement and licensee estoppel does not apply.[24] The principle of no licensee estoppel for a certification mark has been upheld recently on public policy grounds in *Idaho Potato*, a US appeal case.[25] Relying on *Lear, Inc. v Adkins*,[26] a US Supreme Court case

---

[22] ibid 39.
[23] J Phillips *Trade Mark Law: A Practical Anatomy* (OUP Oxford 2003) 524–525.
[24] Wilkof (n 18) 162.
[25] *Idaho Potato* (n 16).
[26] 395 US 653, 23 L Ed 2d 610, 89 S Ct 1902 (1969).

that invalidated licensee estoppel in the patent licensing context, the court concluded that the public interest in certification marks closely resembles the public interest in the 'full and free use of ideas in the public domain', stated in *Lear* to be central to the patent laws. It was considered in the public interest that certification mark licensees should be free to challenge the licensing scheme.

E. Registration of Collective Marks

The examination of applications to register marks used or intended to be **9.24** used by collective organizations is normally conducted in the same manner as for other trade marks and service marks, using the same criteria of registrability. In the UK, registration of collective marks is provided for under section 49 of TMA 1994, subject to Schedule 1. A collective mark is defined in section 49 as a mark distinguishing the goods or services of members of the association which is the proprietor of the mark from those of other undertakings.[27] An applicant for registration must submit regulations governing the use of the mark and the regulations must specify the persons authorized to use the mark, the conditions of membership of the association and any conditions of use of the mark, including any sanctions against misuse.[28] Failure to observe, or secure the observance of, the regulations governing use of the mark is a ground for revocation of the registration.[29]

The UK Registry will not register the same mark as a collective mark and an **9.25** ordinary trade mark or service mark for identical goods or services.[30] The thinking behind this is that the mark is owned by an association on behalf of its members. Its use must be such that it indicates origin in the members of the association rather than origin in an individual 'source'. The Registry views registration of the same mark as different types of mark, ie both collective mark and ordinary trade mark, as *prima facie* evidence that the mark cannot serve the function specified under the Act. It is also contrary to TMA 1994

---

[27] TMA 1994 s 49.
[28] TMA 1994 sch 1 para 5.
[29] ibid para 13.
[30] The Registry states that it will not register identical marks of different 'statuses' for identical goods/services in any circumstances. Whether there is consent or they are in the same name is considered irrelevant.

Schedule 1, paragraph (2). A collective mark is not for use by the owner association on an equal footing with, and in the same manner as, the individual members. However the association *qua* association may use the collective mark to identify its role as representative of its members on business papers, publications and the like.[31]

9.26 Where the marks are only similar, or the goods/services are only similar, there is no absolute bar to the registration of the later mark in the same ownership or, where there is consent, in different ownerships. However, depending on the degree of similarity between the marks/goods or services, the registry may object. Even where a later application is allowed, if the use of marks with different 'statuses' (eg collective mark and ordinary trade mark) causes confusion, this is a ground for revoking a certification or collective mark.

9.27 Collective marks may also be registered in the USA. Provisions similar to the UK provisions for regulations governing the use of the mark and control of its use apply. However, the Lanham Act extends registration to collective membership marks as well, suggesting a broader concept of a collective mark than in the UK and elsewhere. Collective membership marks merely indicate membership in an organization and may be registered in addition to the identical mark registered as a collective trade or service mark to the same proprietor.[32]

F. Ownership and Use of Collective Marks

9.28 Under the UK definition, collective marks are meant to be owned by associations.[33] As owner, such associations cannot use the mark in the way in which the proprietor of an 'ordinary' trade mark would use his mark (ie to indicate the origin of his goods or services). Instead, it must use it to exercise control over the members' use of the mark. The result of this is that there is a different concept of 'use' for such marks compared to the standard idea of 'trade mark use'. However, TMA 1994 does not define what is meant by an 'association'. The definition should not hinge on whether the applicant has a

---

[31] See further Belson (n 1) para 3–30.
[32] For example, SEBASTIAN COLLECTIVE SALON MEMBER and logo is registered as both a collective membership mark and a collective service mark.
[33] TMA 1994 s 49.

trading or commercial establishment, since Article 7*bis*(1) of the Paris Convention requires acceptance for filing and protection of collective marks belonging to associations even if such associations do not possess such an establishment.

Furthermore the term undertaking ('distinguishing the goods or services . . .   **9.29** from those of other undertakings') is used without elaboration in TMA 1994 and the Trade Mark Directive,[34] for which the Act makes provision. The term 'undertaking' is used in TRIPs, which incorporates Article 7*bis* of the Paris Convention, to cover individuals and companies in whatever form they are carrying on business.[35] In the competition law context, undertaking is taken to mean an economic unit, which may consist of several persons natural or legal.

Regarding the corporate status required of the applicant for a collective mark, **9.30** current UK practice appears to be ambiguous. The Registry accepts applications from unincorporated as well as incorporated associations. However, an unincorporated association has no legal personality apart from the members of which it is composed and cannot normally own property,[36] which is problematic in light of the wording of section 49 of TMA ('the association which is the proprietor of the mark'). Furthermore, registration of a collective mark in the name of a member or members of an unincorporated association raises concerns because the registrant would not then be the 'association which is the proprietor of the mark' and the mark could not perform its function. Additionally, the Community Trade Mark (CTM) Regulation makes it clear that the applicant for a Community collective mark must have legal personality.[37] From the point of view of use, the fact of legal personality will enable the proprietor of the mark to sue to stop others using the collective mark,

---

[34] First Council Directive 89/104/EEC of 21 December 1988 to approximate the laws of the Member States relating to trade marks, art 2.

[35] CM Correa and AA Yusuf *Intellectual Property and International Trade: The TRIPs Agreement* (Kluwer London 1998) p 169 n 8.

[36] See generally J Warburton *Unincorporated Associations: Law and Practice* (2nd edn Sweet & Maxwell London 1992).

[37] Council Regulation 40/94 of 20 December 1993. Art 64 of the Regulation provides that associations which have the capacity in their own name to have rights and obligations of all kinds, to make contracts, or accomplish other legal acts and sue or be sued, as well as legal persons governed by public law, may apply for Community collective marks. The CTM's collective mark requirement that the owner have legal personality is thus in contrast with practice in the UK, where the Registry accepts applications from unincorporated associations.

though it should be noted that members of an unincorporated association must carry any liability incurred by the association both as an association and as individuals if they are the subject of legal action.

9.31   It is submitted that the ambiguity could be resolved by a strict requirement that applications be in the name of an association that has legal personality, an entity that can sue or be sued under the law.[38] This requirement is met by incorporated associations registered with the Registrar of Companies or, if the association has a benevolent purpose, the Registrar of Friendly Societies. Also, industrial and provident societies, such as producers' cooperatives, and non-profit organizations established for the benefit of the community carrying out a business can acquire corporate status by registering with the Registrar of Friendly Societies. In this way, the association assumes limited liability, and a capacity to own property and to sue in its own name.

9.32   Section 162 of the Australian Trade Mark Act 1995 defines a collective trade mark as a sign used or intended to be used, in relation to goods or services dealt with or provided in the course of trade by members of an association to distinguish those goods or services from goods or services so dealt with or provided by persons who are not members of the association. Thus there is no explicit requirement for the association to be the proprietor of the mark. The applicant must *not* be a body corporate[39] and the application must be made in the name of the association and not in the name of an individual or individuals. Any member or members, duly authorized by the association, can be signatories to the application. Unlike UK and US practice, the use of collective trade marks is not required to be subject to rules. An Australian collective trade mark may not be assigned or transmitted.

9.33   Regarding US practice, the definition of a collective mark limits ownership of such a mark to a 'cooperative, an association or other collective group or organisation and includes marks used to indicate membership in a union, an association or other organisation'.[40] The persons that compose a collective group may be either natural or juristic persons.[41] Goods sold or services

---

[38]   *Trade Marks Registry Work Manual* (n 15) ch 13 §3.2.
[39]   The Corporations Law defines a body corporate as a corporation or body of persons or even an individual, with a legal existence distinct from the individual person(s) making up the corporate entity.
[40]   Lanham Act 15 USC §1127.
[41]   37 CFR §2.56(b)(3); TMEP 1303.02(b).

provided under the collective mark of a cooperative must be the goods of the individual members of the cooperative. A specimen of use of a collective trade mark or service mark must show use of the mark by a member on the member's goods or in the sale or advertising of the member's services. For example, where an agricultural cooperative is composed of produce sellers and the collective organization merely promotes the sellers' produce and does not sell its own goods or render services under the mark, the cooperative may qualify for ownership of a collective mark. In *B.F. Goodrich Company v National Cooperatives, Inc.*[42] it was held that where a mark was used to identify tyres made for a cooperative and sold by its distributors, the mark was an ordinary mark, not a collective mark that identifies goods of the applicant's associated organizations; the applicant alone provided specifications and other instructions and the applicant alone was responsible for faulty tyres.

G. Summary

Certification and collective marks are special types of marks, different from ordinary trade marks, for which a universally valid legal definition exists under TRIPs. Article 7 *bis* of the Paris Convention (which is incorporated by reference into TRIPs[43]) provides for registration and protection of collective marks. However, the Convention leaves each country to be the judge of the particular conditions under which a collective mark is to be protected.[44] The law and practice governing their registration and use therefore varies considerably among the Anglo-American and European countries. **9.34**

Since there is no multilateral treaty requiring countries to make provisions specifically for ownership and registration of certification marks it is surprising that there is not more variation in their conditions of registration, ownership and use. Like ordinary trade marks and collective marks, it is through their use that certification marks acquire meaning in the market. However, the audience for certification marks extends beyond purchasers to include regulatory enforcement bodies. Use of certification marks, often on non-consumer products, to indicate regulatory compliance with health, safety and **9.35**

---

[42] 114 USPQ 406 (1957).
[43] TRIPs art 2.
[44] Paris Convention art 7 *bis*(3).

environmental requirements is perhaps more common than is generally realized.

9.36 Whether certification marks are privately or non-privately owned, use by authorized others is considered the same as use by the owner. Compared to ordinary trade marks, the rights legally accorded the owner are, in the public interest, more restricted, carefully regulated and controlled. As a matter of public policy all qualified products from any number of traders must be allowed to use the mark. Furthermore, use in most countries is reserved to parties other than the owner. Exclusion of the owner from use is a feature of exclusive licensing of an ordinary trade mark, agreed between licensor and licensee. However, owner exclusion from use of a certification mark, or a collective mark, is not a matter of choice on the part of the owner; it is an incident of ownership. Where the owner-exclusion rule is not adopted, measures and procedures in the examination of the application must be sufficiently robust to safeguard the public interest against rules of use that could result in anti-competitive or deceptive practices. In such instances, statutorily mandated involvement of a separate public 'watchdog' body, such as the national consumer affairs agency, in addition to the Registry, is vital for securing the public interest in open and free competition.

Part E

INFRINGEMENT

10

INFRINGING 'USE IN THE COURSE OF TRADE': TRADE MARK USE AND THE ESSENTIAL FUNCTION OF A TRADE MARK

Rob Sumroy and Carina Badger

A. Introduction	10.01	(2) *Reed Executive v Reed Business Information* 10.29
B. Merchandising and the Importance of Brands	10.04	E. Reasons for the Inertia 10.31
		(1) The 1938 Act 10.32
		(2) Broadening of the monopoly 10.35
C. The *Arsenal* Litigation	10.12	F. Infringing Use Under the 1994
(1) The First High Court decision	10.14	Act 10.37
(2) The ECJ ruling	10.16	(1) Implementation of the Trade
(3) The Second High Court decision	10.20	Mark Directive 10.37
(4) The Court of Appeal decision	10.22	(2) The Defences to Trade Mark
		Infringement 10.40
D. Infringing Use in the English Courts after *Arsenal*	10.23	(3) Anti-competitive practices 10.45
(1) *R v Johnstone*	10.24	G. Concluding Thoughts 10.47

A. Introduction

The recent *Arsenal* litigation discloses divergent views between the European **10.01**
Court of Justice (ECJ) and certain of the English courts as to what protection
a registered trade mark should confer on its owner under the Trade Mark
Directive.[1] In a brave new world of brands, where the exploitation of intellectual property is key, the legal uncertainty arising from such division is
acutely unsatisfactory for rights owners in general and, in particular, for those

---

[1] First Council Directive 89/104/EEC of 21 December 1988.

who derive significant revenue from licensing and merchandising opportunities.

10.02 This chapter briefly considers the changing role of trade marks in increasingly brand-driven sectors and asks why clarification of what constitutes infringing use is important for brand owners in enforcing their rights. This chapter also surveys the lie of the land following the *Arsenal* litigation and examines the central question: does infringing use of a registered trade mark necessarily require use of that mark as an indicator of trade origin (ie 'trade mark use'), or do other unauthorized uses of the mark also count as infringing acts? The associated commercial issue is the extent of brand protection: does the Trade Mark Directive merely protect trade mark owners against unauthorized use that diverts custom by 'brand hijacking' (ie by copying or similar reproduction of the trade mark as a trade mark) or is the scope of the protection wider so as to allow trade mark owners to take action against other forms of appropriation of the mark?

10.03 The ECJ's position seems clear: since trade mark use is not a necessary element of infringing use, the protection is therefore broad. However, this thinking is somewhat lost in translation under English law by virtue of the apparent reluctance on the part of the English judiciary to depart from the traditional, narrower view of infringing use. It is submitted that such reluctance is out of step with European jurisprudence and is contrary to the objectives of the Trade Mark Directive.[2]

B. Merchandising and the Importance of Brands

10.04 The value of trade marks to their owners, and more particularly the manner of their exploitation, has been evolving for some time. Nowadays, the race is on to develop bare trade mark registrations into brands. Building on the trade mark, a brand is a wider concept intended to attract consumer loyalty by virtue of values, including lifestyle messages, associated with that brand. The concept of a brand therefore goes much further than the technical notion of a trade mark as a mere indicator of trade origin.

---

[2] This paper does not distinguish between the different heads of infringement under art 5 of the Trade Mark Directive, since each head requires that the defendant use 'in the course of trade any sign'.

For the consumer, brands play an important role as signage in a world of **10.05**
increasingly abundant choice, providing the consumer with the means to
shop with confidence. It is very often the consumer's appreciation of and
identification with the values underpinning the brand that will ultimately
influence a purchase decision. For businesses and their investors, the value of
the brand is correspondingly the effectiveness of the brand to drive those
decisions. As an indication of the importance of brands in the modern marketplace, the success of the COCA COLA brand alone in terms of consumer
affiliation in the competitive soft drinks market was in 2004 reported to
represent a value of roughly US$67.39 billion.[3]

In sectors where revenues from traditional sources are waning or costs are **10.06**
escalating, organizations increasingly turn to their intangible assets as sources
of further revenue. Non-profit organizations, for example, have accordingly
begun to embrace the concept of the brand as a key asset in obtaining
donations and sponsorships, as well as for licensing purposes. For example,
on the 'Corporate Partnerships' page of the Save the Children (UK) website,
the charity states that the

> right fit with Save the Children can lend caring values and a human face to
> your product or service while raising essential funds.[4]

The charity invites retailers to engage in licensing arrangements such as SAVE
THE CHILDREN branded Christmas cards and shopping bags.

In relation to the film industry, box office sales currently account for only a **10.07**
marginal element of overall income from a production. Escalating costs of
film production and promotion, as well as increased competition between
production companies, have rendered the film industry progressively more
dependent on other forms of revenue.[5] Filmed entertainment today is as
much about selling games, toys, yoghurt pots, bed covers and other para-
phernalia, as it is about the film itself. *The Economist* reports that, in this

---

[3] Interbrand (compiler) 'The 100 Top Brands' [2004] Business Week August.
[4] http://www.savethechildren.org.uk/scuk/jsp/getinvolved/corporategiving.jsp?subsection=
promotions.
[5] 'The Spider's Bite' [2002] The Economist 9 May. The latest *Spider-Man* film, for
example, reportedly cost Sony an estimated US$150 million to produce and a further US$50
million to promote.

sector, the market for licensed products for children alone was in 2002 worth roughly US$132 billion.[6]

10.08 Similarly football clubs are feeling the pinch despite soaring revenues, predominantly due to high salaries of players. *The Economist* reports that in Italy, Lazio and Fiorentina (which are amongst the richest clubs in the world) have struggled in paying their players' salaries.[7] British football clubs in particular have been wise to the potential of merchandising. In 2003, Manchester United reported a commercial turnover from merchandising and sponsorship of £46.2 million representing 27 per cent of total turnover. In its 2003 Annual Report, Manchester United FC's Chief Executive stated that:

> I intend to continue to pursue the central objective that has guided our progress in the recent past: to grow Manchester United not just as a football club, but also as a global brand.[8]

10.09 Organizations have been increasingly willing to enter into licensing and merchandising arrangements with third parties to associate their name with a variety of goods and services. Hence we may stumble across UNICEF credit cards, HARRY POTTER duvet covers, WESTLIFE T-shirts and ARSENAL football scarves. The extent of protection conferred by a registered trade mark is therefore crucial for brand owners, particularly those who derive core income in this way.

10.10 In sectors where licensing and merchandising is crucial, the ability to maximize revenue from a brand depends on the ability of the rights holder to license third parties to manufacture or provide goods or services in which the brand owner itself is not active. However, a licensing deal will only be attractive to potential licensees if the rights holder has sufficient control over its brand to be able to prevent unauthorized third parties from undertaking the activities that are the subject of the licence. The licence will otherwise lack sufficient value for a potential licensee. Indeed, the potential licensee may well be in a position to provide the branded goods or services in question without requiring the trade mark owner's authorization.[9]

---

[6] ibid.

[7] 'For Love or Money' [2002] The Economist 30 May.

[8] David Gill (30 September 2003).

[9] Note in this regard *Rugby Football Union and Nike European Operations Netherlands BV v Cotton Traders Ltd* [2002] EWHC 467.

Further, the principal attraction for a licensee is the brand itself and the **10.11** ability of that brand to influence consumer decisions by virtue of the values underpinning the brand. For licensing to be an appealing prospect (and for the rights owner to maximize return), the trade mark owner must demonstrate control over the quality of the brand and, in particular, control over the values associated with the brand which serve to maintain or draw consumer affiliation. The trade mark owner must therefore be able to take action against unauthorized third party use of the mark that damages the brand's pulling power.

C. The *Arsenal* Litigation

The ECJ decision in *Arsenal* is an important statement of what constitutes **10.12** infringing use for the purposes of the Trade Mark Directive. However, the decisions of various courts in *Arsenal* before and after the ECJ ruling have highlighted both a divergence of views on this issue and a reluctance within the English judiciary to bow to the ECJ's broader interpretation of infringing use under the Trade Mark Directive.

Arsenal owned various trade marks including the ARSENAL and ARSENAL **10.13** GUNNERS word marks in respect of articles of clothing and sports footwear (Class 25). Reed sold items of clothing, particularly scarves, bearing those signs without a licence from the club, albeit with a point-of-sale disclaimer that not all products were official merchandise. Arsenal sued Reed for, *inter alia*, trade mark infringement under sections 10(1) and 10(2)(b) of the Trade Mark Act 1994.[10]

(1) The First High Court decision

In the first High Court decision,[11] Laddie J held that the signs used by Reed **10.14** were perceived as badges of 'support, loyalty or affiliation'. They were not perceived as indicating Arsenal as the trade origin of the merchandise, and hence were not used by Reed as trade marks. He considered that, if infringing use included non-trade mark use of those signs, a wide construction of

---

[10] Corresponding to arts 5(1)(a) and 5(1)(b) of the Trade Mark Directive.
[11] *Arsenal Football Club plc v Matthew Reed* [2001] ETMR 77.

section 10 of the 1994 Act would have to apply and that Act would thereby confer 'a new and very wide monopoly'. Noting en passant that use of a sign that is a registered trade mark in a non-trade mark sense might infringe the rights in a registered trade mark,[12] Laddie J concluded that the law on this point was not settled and would require a reference to the ECJ.

10.15 Although he did not expressly state as much, Laddie J appears to take issue with the nature of the ARSENAL mark, in that he perceives a difference between the name as a brand and the name as used by supporters. Why the position should be different for the ARSENAL mark in contrast with the NIKE mark, for example, is not clear. Without an express statement of the reasons for the differentiation, one presumes that this is a policy-driven prejudice against entities with a fan/consumer base whose affiliation and loyalty is not easily moved to competing organizations; ie an Arsenal fan would be highly unlikely to transfer their support to another Premier League club such as Spurs.[13] However, similar affiliations can be found among well-known brands in retailing industries. For example, a consumer may be highly loyal to the APPLE brand while highly adverse to the MICROSOFT brand, or to the PEPSI brand over the COCA COLA brand. Moreover, it is submitted that concerns regarding a trade mark proprietor's position in respect of its ownership of, and activities in relation to, a mark should properly be addressed in the context of the competition provisions of the EC Treaty and should not be brought into considerations on the nature of infringing use.[14]

(2) The ECJ ruling

10.16 The ECJ began by stating that a trade mark owner can only exercise his trade mark rights to protect his specific interests as a proprietor of the mark, that is, in a situation where the functions of his mark are put at risk.[15] The court then emphasized that trade marks constitute an essential element in a system of undistorted competition and that the essential function of a trade mark in such a system is to guarantee the identity of the origin of the goods or services

---

[12] *Philips Electronics Limited v Remington Consumer Products* [1998] RPC 283.
[13] For further consideration of issues concerning denominative use, see Ch 8 of this volume.
[14] arts 81 and 82 of the EC Treaty; see paras 10.45–10.46.
[15] *Arsenal Football Club plc v Matthew Reed* Case C-206/01 [2002] ECR I-10273.

to the consumer or end user.[16] A trade mark must therefore guarantee that all the goods or services bearing it have been manufactured or supplied under the control of a single undertaking which is responsible for their quality. The trade mark owner must be able to take action when that guarantee is jeopardized.

The ECJ considered that the use of Arsenal's registered marks by Reed was **10.17** such as to create the impression that there was a material link in the course of trade between the goods concerned and the trade mark proprietor. The Court drew this conclusion despite the indications on Reed's stall that the goods were not official Arsenal merchandise. It was sufficient that there was a 'clear possibility' that some consumers might interpret the use of the logos as designating Arsenal as the origin of the goods. The ECJ may have been persuaded in this regard by the EFTA Surveillance Authority's submission that a third party who affixes the trade mark to goods but indicates that they do not come from the trade mark proprietor does not exclude the risk of confusion among a wider circle of consumers (for example those who first encounter those goods as presents or buy them second-hand). If the proprietor were not entitled to prevent third parties from acting in that way, a generalized use of the sign would result. In the end, this would deprive the mark of its distinctive character, thus jeopardizing its essential function.

Once it is found that the use of the sign by a third party is liable to affect the **10.18** guarantee of origin of the goods, and that the trade mark proprietor must be able to prevent this, it is immaterial that the sign is perceived as a badge of support for, or loyalty or affiliation to, the proprietor of the mark.

This statement of the essential function of a trade mark is set out in the tenth **10.19** recital to the Trade Mark Directive and is emphasized early on in European trade mark law in *Hoffmann-La Roche v Centrafarm*.[17] Moreover, a number of ECJ cases have reiterated the broader functions of a trade mark.[18]

---

[16] ibid paras 48, 50.
[17] *Hoffmann-La Roche & Co. AG v Centrafarm Vertriebsgesellschaft Pharmazeutischer Erzeugnisse mbH* Case 102/77 [1978] ECR 1139.
[18] See for example *Parfums Christian Dior SA v Evora BV* Case C-337/95 [1998] ETMR 26, where the ECJ recognized that marks have an advertising function in addition to their essential function. See also *Bayerische Motorenwerke AG (BMW) and BMW Nederland BV v Deenik* Case C-63/97 [1999] ECR I-905, where the ECJ ruled that a trader may not take unfair advantage of the earlier mark, but only within the context of exhaustion and not within the context of traditional infringement. See also *SA CNL-Sucal NV v HAG GF* Case C-10/89 [1990] ECR I-3711.

(3) The Second High Court decision

10.20 On return from the ECJ, Arsenal applied for a final disposition of the action.[19] Having reviewed some unfortunate phrasing in the reply from the ECJ, Laddie J held that the ECJ had made findings of fact when making its ruling and such findings were inconsistent with the High Court's view of the facts in the original hearing. The ECJ had therefore exceeded its jurisdiction and the High Court was not bound to its final conclusion.

10.21 Laddie J proceeded to apply his interpretation of the ECJ's guidance on the law to the High Court's original findings of fact. As to the interpretation of the law, Laddie J identified and emphasized *dicta* of the ECJ that certain uses of a registered trade mark, for example purely descriptive use, are excluded from the scope of the infringement provisions of the Trade Mark Directive, since they do not affect any of the interests which trade mark law aims to protect. Laddie J found that as 'a badge of support, loyalty or affiliation', Reed's use of signs identical to Arsenal's registered trade marks was not intended by him, or understood by the public, to be a designation of trade origin. Therefore, Laddie J, apparently making trade mark use a requirement for infringing use, concluded that there was no infringement on the basis that the defendant's use did not prejudice the essential function of the registered mark.

(4) The Court of Appeal decision

10.22 Finding in favour of Arsenal,[20] the Court of Appeal held that Laddie J's two judgments were based on the erroneous premise that trade mark infringement requires use as a trade mark on the part of the alleged infringer; ie use indicating trade origin. The Court of Appeal's interpretation of the ECJ judgment was that the registration of a trade mark gave the proprietor a property right. Accordingly, the relevant consideration was whether the allegedly infringing use was likely to damage that property right because it was likely to affect or jeopardize the guarantee of origin that constitutes the essential function of the mark. The answer to that question did not depend on whether the use complained of was a 'trade mark use'. Instead, the Court of Appeal took a very wide view of the types of use that might jeopardize the

---

[19] *Arsenal Football Club plc v Matthew Reed* [2002] EWHC 2695 (Ch).
[20] *Arsenal Football Club plc v Matthew Reed* [2003] EWCA Civ 696.

essential function. This appears to include all uses bar descriptive use, saying

> Unchecked use of the mark by a third party, which is not descriptive use, is likely to damage the function of the trade mark right because the registered trade mark can no longer guarantee origin, that being an essential function of a trade mark.[21]

That the mark may also perform a different function (eg decorative or as a badge of allegiance[22]) is immaterial.

D. Infringing Use in the English Courts after *Arsenal*

The broad scope of the protection conferred on trade mark owners by the **10.23** Trade Mark Directive appears clear following the ECJ and Court of Appeal judgments in *Arsenal*. However, it cannot be said with any certainty that the final Court of Appeal determination in *Arsenal* saw an end to the application of the narrower, traditional view in the English courts. Two subsequent judgments of the English appellate courts continue to cast a shadow of uncertainty over what is required for infringing use.

(1) R v Johnstone

The day after the Court of Appeal delivered its decision in *Arsenal* (although **10.24** the case was argued prior to the *Arsenal* hearing), the House of Lords handed down its judgment in *Johnstone*.[23] The case related to copies of bootleg recordings made of performances by world-renowned performers including Bon Jovi and to the criminal sanctions under section 92 of the 1994 Act (the words BON JOVI having been registered as a trade mark). The House of Lords considered that there could be no liability under the criminal provisions of section 92 without a finding of infringement under section 10 of the 1994 Act. The defendants argued that the use of the name Bon Jovi was not trade mark use but descriptive use, and there was therefore no section 10 infringement.

Allowing the appeal, the basis of the House of Lords' reasoning was that a **10.25**

---

[21] ibid para 45.
[22] Or presumably also as a badge expressing non-allegiance.
[23] *R v Johnstone* [2004] ETMR 2.

trade mark is in essence a 'badge of origin'; ie an indicator of trade source. Since use of a mark in a manner not indicative of trade origin does not encroach upon the proprietor's monopoly rights, it does not amount to infringement. The Court cited in this regard *Mothercare*[24] (which, notably, was decided under the Trade Marks Act 1938, repealed by the 1994 Act), adding:

> It stands to reason that a Trade Marks Act would only be concerned to restrict the use of a mark as a trade mark or in a trade mark sense, and should be construed accordingly.

10.26 While, under the 1994 Act, there is no express statement that the offending use must be use as a trade mark (as found under the 1938 Act), the Court did not consider this a sufficient reason to assume that Parliament had intended to depart from that principle. Moreover, looking behind the 1994 Act to the Trade Mark Directive, the House of Lords considered that the ECJ in *Arsenal* had reaffirmed such characterization by its emphasis on the essential function of a trade mark as a guarantee of trade origin. The House of Lords' conclusion was that non-trade mark use does not fall within section 10 of the 1994 Act, thereby perpetuating the narrower, traditional view of infringing use.

10.27 Given that *Johnstone* was concerned with the criminal sanctions under the 1994 Act[25] which are not found in the Trade Mark Directive, it is arguable that the raising of the barrier for a finding of infringement applies *only* to the sanctions under section 92. The more recent Court of Appeal decision in *Isaac*[26] supports the view for this narrow application of the requirements for infringing use in *Johnstone*. Concerned with an appeal on the direction to the jury in respect of those criminal sanctions, Pill LJ's language is careful to restrict his application of *Johnstone* to the criminal offence and hence held that the jury

> must be directed that a *criminal offence* is committed only when as a first element the offending sign is used as an indication of trade origin, as explained in *Johnstone*. [emphasis added]

10.28 Nevertheless, the reasoning as set out in the House of Lords' judgment in *Johnstone* does not make this distinction. Indeed, its acknowledgement and

---

[24] *Mothercare (UK) Limited v Penguin Books Ltd* [1988] RPC 113.
[25] On which see Ch 12 of this volume.
[26] *R v Isaac* [2004] EWCA Crim 1082.

interpretation of the ECJ's decision in *Arsenal* would seem to run contrary to the view that *Johnstone* leaves the interpretation of infringing use for the purposes of civil proceedings unaffected. In any case, it would be strange to have separate understandings of 'use' for criminal and civil proceedings.

(2) Reed Executive v Reed Business Information

Reed concerned, among other things, invisible metatag[27] use by a publisher, **10.29** Reed Business Information of the REED mark registered as a trade mark by Reed Executive, an employment bureau.[28] Jacob LJ was not convinced that invisible use of a mark as a metatag could constitute 'trade mark use' for the purposes of trade mark infringement. The main basis for this position is that if metatag use is the sole use made of a mark, it would be 'strange' if such use were sufficient to enable that mark to withstand a revocation challenge on the basis of non-use. This begs the question whether use for the purpose of revocation is the same as use for the purposes of infringement.

Strictly, Jacob LJ's comments in relation to metatag use are *obiter* since he **10.30** had already found that there was no trade mark infringement. Nevertheless, the reasoning is significant in its failure to mention *Arsenal*. Moreover, Jacob LJ had at one point been credited as being more amenable to the broader view of infringing use.[29] If Jacob LJ had applied the Court of Appeal's formulation in *Arsenal* that non-trade mark use can be infringing use if it jeopardizes the essential function of the mark (ie to guarantee trade origin), it seems likely that the metatag infringement claim would have had a higher prospect of success, provided confusion could be made out.

---

[27] A word that appears in the source code of a web page but not in the visual appearance of that page, generally used to optimize the website on search engines.

[28] *Reed Executive plc and another v Reed Business Information Ltd and others* [2004] EWCA Civ 159.

[29] *British Sugar plc v James Robertson & Sons Ltd* [1996] RPC 281 in which Jacob J (as was) considered that there is nothing in ss 9 or 10 of the 1994 Act that requires infringing use to be trade mark use (note that Jacob J cast doubt on that formulation in *Philips v Remington* Case C-299/99 [2002] ECR I-5475, although Aldous LJ's opinion was that such approach was correct).

E. Reasons for the Inertia

10.31 With the notable exception of the Court of Appeal in *Arsenal*,[30] the English judiciary seems to be operating in the jurisprudence of the 1938 Act. The main reason for the English judiciary's reluctance to depart from the traditional position appears to be a political response to the broadening of the monopolistic nature of the intellectual property right.

(1) The 1938 Act

10.32 As mentioned, trade mark use was a necessary condition to a finding of infringing use under section 4(1)(a) of the 1938 Act. The 1994 Act was enacted to implement the Trade Mark Directive. However, the provisions of Article 5 are not replicated exactly in section 10. Rather than a registered trade mark conferring on the proprietor 'exclusive rights therein' (Article 5), the 1994 Act confers

> exclusive rights in the trade mark *which are infringed by the use of the trade mark* in the United Kingdom without his consent. [emphasis added.]

The rewording is a source of speculation that the spirit of section 4 of the 1938 Act continues to apply, with the consequence that infringing use must be trade mark use.[31]

10.33 Under the 1938 Act, unauthorized third party use of a registered trade mark was generally viewed either as trade mark use (and therefore as infringing) or as falling under descriptive use (and therefore as not infringing). The effect of this thinking was that decorative and promotional use of a sign would not infringe a registered mark. For example, in *Unidoor*,[32] the claimant complained of Marks & Spencer's use of its registered mark COAST TO COAST as a decoration on T-shirts. The Court doubted that the use of the

---

[30] See also *dicta* of Jacob J in *British Sugar* (n 29) and the judgment of Aldous LJ in *Philips v Remington* [1999] ETMR 816.

[31] Even if the Trade Mark Directive were misadopted into English law, national provisions must be interpreted in such a way as to comply with the wording and purpose of the Trade Mark Directive (*Marleasing SA v La Comercial Internacional de Alimentacion SA* Case C-106/89 [1990] ECR I-4135).

[32] *Unidoor Ltd v Marks & Spencer plc* [1988] RPC 275.

sign in that case was a use that indicated a trade origin.[33] In the words of Whitford J:

> There is nothing to indicate that the words are being used to identify the origin of goods and I am bound for my own part to say that, just looking at them, I do not think I would have thought that the words as they appear on either of these items were being used as a trade mark.

The reluctance to permit licensing activities in areas in which the licensor was **10.34** not active is evident from the recordal provisions of section 28(6) of the 1938 Act, which permitted the registrar to refuse to register a user of a mark if a grant would 'tend to facilitate trafficking in a trade mark'. In *HOLLY HOBBIE*,[34] the applicant sought to register a mark in respect of classes of goods to be made exclusively by their licensees, subject to quality control requirements of the applicant under a registered user agreement. The applicants themselves neither used nor intended to use the marks in those classes. The applicant also sought to register the licensees as registered users of the mark. Registration was refused on the ground that it was prohibited by section 28(6) of the 1938 Act, ie it would tend to facilitate trafficking in the mark. Upholding the decision, the House of Lords considered that, if there was no real trade connection between the proprietor and licensee or his goods, there was room for the conclusion that the grant of a licence was a trafficking in the mark. This was a question of fact and degree in each case. Licensing in classes that were not primary business activities of the owner was not prohibited *per se*.[35] However the recordal provisions under the 1938 Act did disclose an unwillingness to permit what is today a core activity of merchandising sectors.

---

[33] In a similar vein see *KODAK Trade Mark* [1990] FSR 49 in which the High Court held that promotional use of the KODAK mark on T-shirts for promotional purposes did not amount to trade mark use since it did not indicate the source of the trade marks. The High Court found that there could not be trade in goods which are merely ancillary to the primary trade; that is, the T-shirts could not be considered as 'an essential article' for the purposes of Kodak's primary (photographic) trade.

[34] *American Greeting Corp's Application* [1984] FSR 199.

[35] Lord Brightman noted that a number of famous trade marks had been registered for goods in which the proprietor was not primarily interested, such as COCA COLA for T-shirts.

(2) Broadening of the monopoly

10.35 On its face, if infringing use under the 1994 Act does not require 'trade mark use', the protection conferred on an owner of a registered trade mark appears significantly broader than that under the 1938 Act.

A clear concern of the English judiciary is the use of intellectual property law to create an unwarranted monopoly. For example, in *Wagamama*,[36] Laddie J is clear that the narrower construction of infringing use (ie requiring trade mark use) is to be preferred:

> If the broader scope were to be adopted, the Directive and our Act would be creating a new type of monopoly not related to the proprietor's trade but in the trade mark itself. Such a monopoly could be likened to a quasi-copyright in the mark.

A key issue is that, unlike copyright, there would be no fixed duration for such a right and it would be a 'true monopoly effective against copyist and non-copyist alike'.

10.36 This concern is also evident in *Johnstone*. Having cited *Mothercare*,[37] a case decided under the 1938 Act, Lord Nicholls discussed the 'fundamental principle' of limiting the scope of the rights of the proprietor of a registered trade mark. Lord Nicholls noted that, in relation to the infringement provisions of sections 10(1)–(3) of the 1994 Act, there was no express statement that the offending use must be use as a trade mark. He continued:

> I would not regard this as sufficient reason to suppose that Parliament intended to depart from such a basic principle.

F. Infringing Use Under the 1994 Act

(1) Implementation of the Trade Mark Directive

10.37 As a matter of Community law, Articles 5 to 7 of the Trade Mark Directive constitute a comprehensive code of the rights of the trade mark owner. The English courts are bound to follow rulings of the ECJ as to the interpretation

---

[36] *Wagamama v City Centre Restaurants* [1995] FSR 713.
[37] *Mothercare* (n 24).

of the Trade Mark Directive. The English courts therefore do not have an unfettered discretion as to what use should be treated as infringing use.[38]

The object of the Trade Mark Directive is to promote harmonization of the **10.38** national laws of the Community. The peculiarities of English law prior to the Trade Mark Directive have no place in the modern European system of trade mark law. This is particularly so in relation to the nature of infringing use, since it must not be the case that a trade mark in England confers less protection than the same trade mark in another Member State.[39] This point is evident from the recitals to the Trade Mark Directive which state that:

> it is fundamental, in order to facilitate the free circulation of goods and services, to ensure henceforth registered trade marks enjoy the same protection under the legal systems of all the Member States.

The attempt by the English courts to introduce into English trade mark law a **10.39** hurdle for a finding of infringing use that is not there, on its face in the name of curbing the monopoly afforded by registration of the mark, is contrary to the pro-competitive principles underpinning the common market.

(2) The Defences to Trade Mark Infringement

As a matter of European Community law, the Trade Mark Directive *does* **10.40** confer broader protection as compared with that under the 1938 Act. However, while section 10 of the 1994 Act no longer has a necessary criterion in respect of the nature of the use in question, section 11 (Article 6 of the Trade Mark Directive) contains a number of defences to trade mark infringement. Certain types of unauthorized use of a mark, for example wholly descriptive use, will not amount to trade mark infringement because there is a defence in respect of such use. Arguments based on the apparent increase in the monopoly afforded by a registered trade mark on enactment of the 1994 Act tend to ignore the corresponding widening of the defences under section 11 as compared with those under the 1938 Act.

It is regrettable that a number of cases relating to the interpretation of **10.41** infringing use have failed to address satisfactorily the defences under Article

---

[38] *Zino Davidoff SA v A&G Imports Ltd and Levi Strauss & Co v Tesco Stores and Costco Wholesale UK Ltd* Joined Cases C-414/99, C-415/99 and C-416/99 [2002] ETMR 9.
[39] At least, for the purposes of article 5(1).

6. In *Hölterhoff*,[40] the defendant used the registered marks SPIRIT SUN and CONTEXT CUT to refer to a particular cut of diamonds and other precious stones. The German court accepted that the defendant had used the marks solely to describe the type of cut of the precious stones offered for sale. The ECJ considered that, in such circumstances, Article 5(1) does not entitle the registered proprietor of a trade mark to rely on his exclusive right where a third party uses the registered trade mark only to denote the particular characteristics of the goods being offered for sale. In such circumstances there was considered to be 'no question of the trade mark being used to indicate the origin of the goods'.

10.42   That the ECJ decision in *Hölterhoff*, in reaching its conclusion, fails to mention the defences under Article 6 of the Trade Mark Directive is both surprising and unfortunate. Article 6(1)(b) states that a trade mark shall not entitle the proprietor to prohibit a third party from using, in the course of trade, indications concerning characteristics of goods or services, provided he uses them in accordance with honest practices. This seems to be a case clearly deserving of consideration of the Article 6 defences, and nothing in the referral from the German court would appear to preclude such consideration.

10.43   The ECJ's failure in *Hölterhoff* to approach the issues before it in this way has given rise to unnecessary confusion in relation to the ECJ's decision in *Arsenal*, where the ECJ stressed that a proprietor may not prohibit the use of a sign if that use cannot affect his interest as proprietor of the mark. Thus, citing *Hölterhoff*,

> certain uses for purely descriptive purposes are excluded from the scope of Art.5(1) of the Directive because they do not affect any of the interests which that provision aims to protect, and do not therefore fall within the concept of use within the meaning of that provision.

10.44   It is submitted that a better formulation would be that certain uses for purely descriptive purposes *do* fall within the scope of the wording of Article 5 but that such use is not infringing use because there is a *defence* in respect of such use under Article 6.[41] Those defences curb the proprietor's ability to take action against 'innocent' uses of the mark that do not affect any of the interests which Article 5 aims to protect, such as purely descriptive use. The

---

[40] *Hölterhoff v Freiesleben* Case C-2/00 [2002] ECR I-4187.
[41] For a contrasting approach, see Ch 11 of this volume.

ECJ's formulation in *Arsenal* otherwise imports into the wording of Article 5 a consideration in relation to infringing use already provided under Article 6.

(3) Anti-competitive practices

As stated, the English courts have been vocal in highlighting competition **10.45** concerns in respect of the protection afforded by the registration of a trade mark. It is submitted that such fears misplace policy concerns regarding the monopolistic nature of trade marks, which are properly the terrain of competition law.

A trade mark is anti-competitive to a certain extent due to its monopolistic **10.46** nature. However, the grant of that monopoly has to be earned. The proprietor is required to pay fees and go to the time and expense of prosecuting the mark. Moreover, on the basis of a protectable name, the proprietor is encouraged to invest and thereby stimulate the market in the goods or services covered by the mark. The grant of a monopoly in a trade mark is integral to a pro-competitive economic system. However, such grant does not release the proprietor from the body of competition law governing the exercise of that monopoly. In particular, Article 82 of the EC Treaty[42] prohibits the abuse of a dominant position.[43] There is little case law on this point in relation to trade marks, although it is clear that the courts will consider the competition implications of practices of proprietors in relation to their marks, such as licensing practices (including the refusal to license).[44]

G. Concluding Thoughts

Laddie J, in *Arsenal,* spoke of Reed's use of Arsenal's registered marks as use as **10.47** a badge of 'support, loyalty or affiliation', and not therefore as being trade mark use. This phrasing is curious, since a brand manager of non-legal persuasion might well view the phrase as describing a core goal of any brand. Investing in trade marks and building brands is about creating a relationship

---

[42] See also s 18 of the Competition Act 1998.

[43] Although in practice, the proprietor's exercise of its rights in a registered trade mark generally will be unlikely to constitute abuse of a dominant position because a competitor could in theory supply the same goods or services under a different mark.

[44] For an unsuccessful attempt to argue that the trade mark owner's refusal to licence was an abuse of its dominant position, see *Claritas (UK) Ltd v The Post Office and Post Preference Service Ltd* [2001] ETMR 63.

between consumers and the brand[45] and encouraging consumers to support, be loyal to and feel affiliation with the values, including the lifestyle concept, that surrounds the trade mark. This applies equally to washing powder as to a football club. Football clubs are as much about profit and loss as about successes or otherwise on the pitch.[46]

10.48 The ECJ's position seems clear: trade mark use is not a necessary element of infringing use. This chapter has argued that there is an apparent reluctance on the part of certain of the English judiciary to depart from the traditional, narrower view of infringing use. It is submitted that such reluctance

- is out of step with European jurisprudence, despite the requirement upon the English courts to following rulings of the ECJ as to the interpretation of the Trade Mark Directive
- introduces into English trade mark law a requirement for infringement not found in the Trade Mark Directive, thereby defeating the purpose of the Trade Mark Directive to harmonize the laws of Member States
- ignores the purpose of and value in the structure built into the Trade Mark Directive to protect unauthorized users of registered marks against their descriptive use (and other 'innocent' uses) of such signs
- misplaces policy arguments regarding the monopolistic nature of trade marks, which are properly the terrain of competition law.

10.49 It is hoped that the English courts will follow the Court of Appeal's decision in *Arsenal* and embrace the ECJ's broader view of infringing use of a registered trade mark. In the interim, trade mark owners and practitioners are left with unsettling uncertainty as to the extent of protection enjoyed in a registered mark. This is contrary to the aims of the Trade Mark Directive and serves to hamper the pro-competitive objectives of the common market. The Trade Mark Directive was implemented in December 1988 pursuant to such objectives, and it is undoubtedly time to acknowledge changes to trade mark law within the European Community that such harmonization demands.

---

[45] The relationship created is not always between the brand owner and the consumer since the brand owner may be 'invisible' to the purchasing public; for example, it seems highly unlikely that most consumers associate PRINGLES or TAMPAX with the same trade origin, Procter & Gamble. Awareness of the identity of the trade origin may prompt a re-evaluation by the consumer of its perception of the visible brand.

[46] See eg the recent misfortunes of Leeds United Football Club: 'Fall of Leeds from Distinction to Near-Extinction' [2004] *Independent on Sunday* (9 May).

11

PERMITTED INFRINGING USE: THE SCOPE OF DEFENCES TO AN INFRINGEMENT ACTION

Ashley Roughton

A. **Infringement and Defences in Context** 11.01
    (1) Infringing use 11.01
    (2) The 'owner' and the 'user', the 'mark' and the 'sign' 11.02
    (3) Three kinds of infringement 11.03
    (4) Types of defence 11.04

B. **The Scope of This Chapter** 11.05

C. **Defences: The Legislation** 11.06

D. **Honesty** 11.11
    (1) The *Gerolsteiner* case: of fairness and plodding horses 11.12
    (2) A use-related definition of honesty? 11.13
    (3) Non-use related definitions of honesty 11.20
    (4) Does honesty equate to a duty not to cause prejudice to another's trade mark? 11.23
    (5) The concept of honesty in UK criminal law 11.26
    (6) Does *Gerolsteiner* import an objective or subjective definition of honesty? 11.33
    (7) Pure objective sense 11.36

E. **Objective and Subjective** 11.39

F. **Article 6(1)(a): Own Name and Address** 11.41

G. **Article 6(1)(b): Other Indications** 11.42

H. **Comparative Advertising** 11.49

I. **Article 6(1)(c): Other Indications** 11.50

K. **Article 6(2): Prior Marks** 11.52

L. **Conclusion** 11.58

A. Infringement and Defences in Context

(1) Infringing use

11.01 Infringing use is now pretty well defined, at first glance at least,[1] though there may be more surprises in store. Most of the current domestic case law on

---

[1] Or so some would say. This proposition has its detractors though, including the author of this chapter.

infringement is a result of factual disputes; this comment is driven by experience rather than being based upon any real authority.

(2) The 'owner' and the 'user', the 'mark' and the 'sign'

11.02 In this chapter references to the 'owner' are to the proprietor of the registered trade mark in the UK or the European Community and references to the 'user' refer to the putative defendant. References to the 'mark' are to the corresponding registered trade mark and references to the 'sign' are to what it is that the user is using.

(3) Three kinds of infringement

11.03 There are generally accepted to be three kinds of infringement. These are:

(a) Identical use

Identical use, ie the use of an identical sign for identical goods or services in respect of which the mark is registered.[2]

(b) Similar or confusing use

Similar or confusing use, ie the use of an identical sign for similar goods or services, similar sign for identical goods or services and similar sign for similar goods or services in respect of which the mark is registered which results in confusion between the marks of the two parties.[3]

(c) Doing down the mark

Doing down the mark, ie where the use of the sign *might* not fall into the preceding categories but instead affects the distinctive character or repute of the mark.[4] The current (incorrect in this author's opinion) status of the law is that such infringement can occur whether the use in question is in relation

---

[2] art 5(1)(a) of the First Council Directive 89/104/EEC of 21 December 1988 to approximate the laws of the Member States relating to trade marks (the Directive); art 9(1)(a) of Council Regulation 40/94 of 20 December 1993 on the Community trade mark (CTMR); s 10(1) of the Trade Marks Act 1994 (the Act).

[3] art 5(1)(b) of the Directive; art 9(1)(b) CTMR; s 10(2) of the Act.

[4] art 5(2) of the Directive; art 9(1)(c) CTMR; s 10(3) of the Act.

to goods or services in respect of which the mark is registered.[5] This is so notwithstanding the clear wording of Article 5(3) of the Directive. This form of infringement is often, though perhaps inaccurately, labelled 'dilution'.

(4) Types of defence

Defences fall into five distinct types which are: **11.04**

(a) Legal requirements not made out

The legal requirements for infringement have not been made out, ie no identical or similar use or no doing down the mark.

(b) Factual requirements not made out

The factual requirements for infringement have not been made out, i.e. didn't do it, wasn't there, wasn't me.

(c) Permitted exception

The use falls within one of the permitted exceptions listed in the Directive, the CTM Regulation or the Act.

(d) Owner not entitled to sue

The owner is not entitled to sue because the mark should not have been registered in the first place or should be revoked, if the revocation is deemed to have taken effect prior to the infringement complained of.[6]

(e) Licensed use

In fact we were licensed.

---

[5] *Davidoff & Cie Société Anonyme v Gofkid Ltd* Case C-292/00 [2003] 1 WLR 1714; [2003] All ER (EC) 1029; [2003] I ECR 389; [2003] 1 CMLR 1039; [2003] CEC 208; [2003] ETMR 534; [2003] FSR 490; *The Times* (22 January 2003); ECJ confirmed in *Adidas-Salomon AG and Adidas Benelux BV v Fitnessworld Trading Ltd* Case C-408/01 [2004] ETMR 10. The UK has subsequently amended s 10(3) of its Trade Marks Act, removing the requirement for the later use to be on a dissimilar good for such infringement to be shown.

[6] This will be the case if the relevant authority is satisfied that the grounds for revocation existed prior to the date that revocation is applied for (TMA s 46(6)(b)).

B. The Scope of This Chapter

11.05 This chapter concentrates upon unauthorized uses of another's trade mark which constitute permitted exceptions to the trade mark right, ie the exceptions to be found in Article 6 of the Directive, Article 12 CTMR and section 11 of the Act. In doing so, particular attention will be paid to the role of use. This chapter will not, however, cover use which is governed by the comparative advertising exclusions to be found in section 10(6) of the Act, though it is necessary to consider the position of comparative advertising in certain other contexts.

C. Defences: The Legislation

11.06 The exclusions are set out in Article 6(1) of the Directive and are couched in identical terms to Article 12 CTMR. Likewise section 11(2) of the Act is in similar terms. Given that most, if not all, of the important jurisprudence in this area of law (such as it is) is governed by interpretations of the Directive or the CTMR (which themselves are identical in the relevant respect) references below will be to the Directive alone. Further, when an unqualified reference to an article is made, that should be taken to mean the corresponding Article of the Directive.

11.07 Article 6(1) reads:

Limitation of the effects of a trade mark

1. The trade mark shall not entitle the proprietor to prohibit a third party from using, in the course of trade,

   (*a*) his own name or address;

   (*b*) indications concerning the kind, quality, quantity, intended purpose, value, geographical origin, the time of production of goods or of rendering of the service, or other characteristics of goods or services;

   (*c*) the trade mark where it is necessary to indicate the intended purpose of a product or service, in particular as accessories or spare parts;

   provided he uses them in accordance with honest practices in industrial or commercial matters.

11.08 At first glance the provisions of Article 6 seem to make sense. The net result is, or should be, that there is no infringement where the use is either descriptive of the user or of the product or service in question. The necessary proviso at the end (the proviso), which states that the use has to be in accordance with honest practices in industrial or commercial matters stops, or is intended to stop, those who use Article 6 improperly. One major question is what is to be understood by 'proper'? Further, there can be no doubt that the list is exhaustive, although it might be the case that trade mark use or, more properly, non-trade mark use, which does not fall within Article 6 is also an exception which takes a trader outside Article 5.

There is no recital in the Directive which deals with this aspect of Article 6. **11.09**

Although there are a number of factual scenarios covered in Article 6(1)(a), **11.10** (b) and (c) it is important to have the proviso at the forefront of one's mind since the proviso applies to all situations arising under Article 6 and also is pervasive in the cases. This is dealt with separately at the end of this chapter.

D. Honesty

The proviso certainly uses the word 'honest'. Many courts have taken the **11.11** proviso to mean just that—that to gain an exception from infringement one has to fall within the operative provisions of Article 6 *and* one has to be honest in so doing. This seems odd if the qualifying words of the proviso are considered, as they must be. Honesty in, say, religious matters, is potentially different from honesty in gambling, honesty amongst thieves or honesty in industry or commerce. Further, the proviso tends to imply that there is one code of honesty which applies to all 'industrial or commercial matters' whereas there may be different codes of honesty in different sectors. This chapter is not the place to embark upon a philosophical discussion of what is meant by honesty or honest behaviour and a defence has yet to be raised on the basis of such distinctions, if any, as may exist between sectors of industry or commerce. That said, a practical appreciation of the philosophical questions is important.

(1) The Gerolsteiner *case: of fairness and plodding horses*

Gerolsteiner[7] concerned a dispute between GERRI, the mark and 'Kerry **11.12**

---

[7] *Gerolsteiner Brunnen GmbH v Putsch GmbH* Case C-100/02 [2004] ETMR 559.

Spring', the sign, both for, *inter alia* mineral water. The European Court of Justice (ECJ) said:

> 25. The mere fact that there exists a likelihood of aural confusion between a word mark registered in one Member State and an indication of geographical origin from another Member State is therefore insufficient to conclude that the use of that indication in the course of trade is not in accordance with honest practices. In a Community of 15 Member States, with great linguistic diversity, the chance that there exists some phonetic similarity between a trade mark registered in one Member State and an indication of geographical origin from another Member State is already substantial and will be even greater after the impending enlargement.

> 26. It follows that, in a case such as that in the main proceedings, it is for the national court to carry out an overall assessment of all the relevant circumstances. Since the case concerns bottled drinks, the circumstances to be taken into account by that court would include in particular the shape and labelling of the bottle in order to assess, more particularly, whether the producer of the drink bearing the indication of geographical origin might be regarded as unfairly competing with the proprietor of the trade mark.[8]

(2) A use-related definition of honesty?

11.13 The ECJ said in *Gerolsteiner* that the proviso to Article 6 means 'a duty to act fairly in relation to the legitimate interests of the trade mark owner'[9] and that what is required is the tired plodding horse of an 'overall assessment'.[10] It is hard to know what these legitimate interests are. One view of the law of trade marks is that its purpose is to help consumers buy things by providing information as to the attributes of a certain product. Traders will not provide such information unless they are given incentives to do so and some would say that the continued enjoyment of such incentives constitutes a legitimate interest of the trade mark owner. So, accordingly, the legitimate interest of the trade mark owner must be to see that the trade mark system works fairly and properly in accordance with its social objectives.

11.14 From this spring two further arguments. First, if the trade mark owner is

---

[8] [2004] ETMR 559, 564, paras 25 and 26.

[9] ibid, para 24.

[10] *System 3R International Aktiebolag v Erowa Aktiengesellschaft and Erowa Nordic Aktiebolag* Case T 14711–01 [2003] ETMR 916 shows how the Tingsratt, Stockholm, approached this, perhaps incorrectly, where this was done. Since the defendant's use was trade mark use, that use could not be said to be honest.

deprived of incentives, he will not work in accordance with the system. Second, the system does not work anyway: the operation of the trade mark system leads to an overall reduction of social welfare. The consequences of the first argument may be shortly stated: if you do not play by the rules, you do not benefit from them. The consequence (or perhaps more properly the corollary) of the second argument is that, if the commercial interests of the brand owner are not to be allowed to dominate or overcome social interests, the system has to be worked in a way that provides marginal positive incentives to traders. Accordingly the 'legitimate' interest of a trade mark owner cannot be pure profit (though there is nothing wrong with that) but rather an interest to ensure that such incentives to operate the trade marks system and benefit from it as there are provide overall social benefits.

There is, however, a bigger picture in that producer prosperity is a good **11.15** thing. This is the other view of trade marks. If, so the argument goes, a business can make a lot of money by operating the trade marks system to its advantage but without causing customer confusion, the right of the producer to do that must be protected. Accordingly, anything which interferes with this right must be prohibited under the banner of honest practices (or such other things in the Directive as might provide a basis for such producer protection). This latter argument might better be described as the right to make money and was an argument which occupied the mind of the Advocate General in *Arsenal v Reed.*[11]

From this broad social commentary can be distilled the notion of trade mark **11.16** use. If use can be such that it causes no producer detriment, in the sense of interfering with the informational bond between producer and consumer, there can be nothing wrong with it. Thus it is not dishonest or an interference with the legitimate interests of the trade mark owner to behave in a way which does not interfere with this bond. If, on the other hand, the test is the right to be rich then, as seemed to be the case in the Advocate General's mind in *Arsenal v Reed,* then almost anything short of pure non-brand competition will be within the legitimate interest of the trade mark owner to prevent.

Given the ECJ's response in *Arsenal v Reed* (where the Advocate General's **11.17** opinion had very little persuasive effect) it is hard to know what the

---

[11] *Arsenal Football Club plc v Matthew Reed* Case 206/01 [2002] ETMR 82; [2002] I ECR 10273 A–G.

philosophical answer to these questions is. However as a matter of practice, since the ECJ in *Arsenal v Reed* took a hard line against the trade mark user whose use, it was submitted, was not a trade mark use, it would appear that the legitimate interests of the trade mark owner (and thus the definition of what constitutes honest use) is the right to make money or at least something approaching that and retreating from the social welfare argument.[12]

11.18 There was no dispute in *Gerolsteiner* that the use of the sign, if honest within the meaning of the proviso, was use as a geographical indication.[13]

11.19 More startling, if a plodding horse can be described as startling, is the fact that the ECJ in *Gerolsteiner* has once again rewritten the Directive. There is no mention in the Directive of unfair competition or prejudice to the owner. The proviso does not say that and cannot mean that on any rational reading of it. Teleologically it might be a justifiable means of construction to say that honesty and fairness are to be equated. Although *relevant* dishonest trading is a necessary and probably sufficient condition for unfair trading on the one hand, unfair trading, on the other, does not imply dishonesty. The difficulty with the approach of the ECJ is that it has substituted one word—fairness— for another—honesty.

(3) Non-use related definitions of honesty

11.20 An example of where dishonest use was encountered was in relation to section 10(6) of the Act, where the same proviso applies, as in *Emaco*,[14] where Jonathan Parker J concluded, in relation to the two competitors who both produced misleading advertising documents:

> each was a thoroughly misleading document, containing a number of false representations. Given that the test of an 'honest practice' for the purposes of the proviso to section 10(6) of the . . . Act . . . is agreed to be an objective one, the conclusion is . . . inescapable that in each case the use made of the competitor's trade mark was 'otherwise than in accordance with honest practices in industrial or commercial matters' within the meaning of the proviso. To hold the publication of documents such as these to be an 'honest practice' for this

---

[12] Editor's note: A different view of the ECJ's judgment in *Arsenal v Reed* can be found in Ch 10 of this volume.

[13] *Gerolsteiner* (n 7) para 13.

[14] *Emaco Ltd and Aktiebolaget Electrolux v Dyson Appliances Ltd* [1999] ETMR 903; (1999) 96(7) LSG 36; *The Times* (8 February 1999).

purpose would in my view be to render the proviso of negligible practical use or effect.

Similarly in *Scandecor*[15] Lloyd J said: **11.21**

> There is however a separate issue that is raised by way of defence . . . as [to] the use by a person of his own name . . . [U]se must [also] be in accordance with honest practices in industrial or commercial matters.
>
> . . . [T]he defence applies to the use of the word as a trade mark . . . In *The European Limited v The Economist Newspaper Limited* [1996] FSR 431, Rattee J. said that the test under section 11(2) must be objective; I agree. In *NAD Electronics Incorporated v NAD Computer Systems Limited* [1997] FSR 380, Ferris J. held that neither section afforded a defence in that case since the full corporate name (but for Limited) had not been used and he questioned whether the defence applied to the use of the corporate name of an artificial person such as a company. In my judgment it does. A company name adopted for the purpose of trading on someone else's goodwill would not satisfy the honest use test. A name adopted years before the question arises and used consistently in ordinary commercial ways can be a proper subject of the defence just as can the proper name of a natural person.

It seems beyond doubt that, where there is deceptive behaviour, this will take **11.22** the behaviour of the putative defendant outside the proviso.[16]

(4) Does honesty equate to a duty not to cause prejudice to another's trade mark?

Gerolsteiner follows on from *BMW v Deenik*.[17] These are the only two cases, **11.23** so far, which deal with Article 6 defences. In *BMW v Deenik*, the ECJ was asked to rule on the use of the terms 'the BMW specialist' or suchlike to indicate selling or repairing of the genuine article (cars). When considering what the proviso meant the ECJ said that:

> it must be regarded as constituting in substance the expression of a duty to act *fairly* in relation to the legitimate interests of the trade mark owner. [Emphasis added.]

The ECJ held that the trade mark owner could not object unless there was a **11.24** commercial connection between the owner and the person using the sign.

---

[15] *Scandecor Development Aktiebolaget v Scandecor Marketing Aktiebolaget and another* [1998] FSR 500, 521, 522; (1998) 95(12) LSG 28; *The Times* (9 March 1998).

[16] See also *Cable & Wireless Plc v British Telecommunications Plc* [1998] FSR 383 Jacob J.

[17] *Bayerische Motorenwerke Aktiengesellschaft and BMW Nederland Besloten Vennootschap v Ronald Karel Deenik* Case C-63/97 [1999] All ER (EC) 235; [1999] I ECR 905; [1999] 1 CMLR 1099; [1999] CEC 159; [1999] ETMR 339.

11.25 In *Gerolsteiner* and *BMW v Deenik*, the ECJ seems to be saying that the test is one where the rights of the owner are prejudiced in some way. If that were correct, then Article 6 could be drafted in much simpler terms, stating that any use that falls within one of the situations envisaged in Articles 6(1)(a)–(b) that does not prejudice the rights of the owner will provide an exception. However, Article 6 does not say that. Equating honesty with prejudice seems to be wrong. If a person behaves honestly, no matter what prejudice he causes by his actions, then it cannot be said that he had been dishonest. If, of course, that person deliberately closes his eyes to that which he ought to know then, arguably, he has not been honest. Difficulties may arise in practice, however. Usually a person proposing to use a mark may instruct trade mark agents or other professional advisors. It may be that advice is sought and negligently given that there is no infringement. In those circumstances the user of the sign cannot on any view be said to be dishonest. Yet if the ECJ is right, because any resultant use prejudices the rights of the owner, he is still deemed to have been dishonest. While this may be correct once the true position is known by the user, it cannot be correct up to that point and yet the ECJ says that it is.

(5) The concept of honesty in UK criminal law

11.26 Close analysis reveals that understanding what is fair, as the ECJ would have us do, is just as difficult as understanding what is honest. It is for this reason that the UK adopts the approach that it does in its domestic criminal law which is, in the view of the author, very practical and valuable. Though Article 6 and the domestic criminal law of the UK are not to be equated, some discussion of the domestic criminal law of the UK is warranted in order to provide an example of how the problem of understanding the meaning of honesty can be solved.

11.27 Traditionally honesty contains two elements to it: (i) subjective honesty ('Did you know you were doing wrong?') and (ii) objective honesty ('Ought you to have known that you were doing wrong?'). No defendant can escape from the clutches of the proviso by simply asserting that he genuinely believed that what he was doing was honest if, by contemporary standards, what he was doing was regarded as manifestly dishonest. However the civil law or, at least, the domestic civil law in the UK has never sought to impugn those who, though they attempt to do wrong, have not in fact managed to do so.

This assessment of dishonesty should be distinguished from the notion that, **11.28** where a defendant is brought to court and a claim of fraud of some sort is made against him, it is no answer for him to say that his fraud was unsuccessful, though this argument must be tempered by degree. Either a defendant is dishonest or he is not. There is no trade mark tort of attempted dishonesty, though a person attempting to do so has a harder task (and in some cases an impossible one) in persuading the court that the fraud was unsuccessful. Put another way, if you do not cause damage then you do not cause damage whatever your intentions might have been. Where there is a grey area and it is not clear whether the activity in question is honest, courts tend to find that the activity was dishonest, having regard to the fact that sincere or honest businessmen do not engage in practices that come close to being dishonest.

In *R v Deb Baran Ghosh*,[18] Lord Lane said: **11.29**

> [One] must first of all decide whether according to the ordinary standards of reasonable and honest people what was done was dishonest. If it was not dishonest by those standards, that is the end of the matter . . .

> If it was dishonest by those standards, then . . . [one must ask] whether the defendant himself must have realised that what he was doing was by those standards dishonest. In most cases, where the actions are obviously dishonest by ordinary standards, there will be no doubt about it. It will be obvious that the defendant himself knew that he was acting dishonestly. It is dishonest for a defendant to act in a way which he knows ordinary people consider to be dishonest, even if he asserts or genuinely believes that he is morally justified in acting as he did. For example, Robin Hood . . . [is] acting dishonestly, even though . . . [he] may consider . . . [himself] to be morally justified in doing what . . . [he did], because . . . [he knew] that ordinary people would consider these actions to be dishonest.

Defendants in criminal trials who are accused of dishonesty are entitled, in **11.30** the main, to have their behaviour judged by their peers. It is for this reason that juries were previously simply asked 'Do you think that the defendant has been dishonest?' with no further explanation of the word 'dishonest' being deemed necessary. However, following the case of *R v Deb Baran Ghosh*, where the issue arises, juries are also directed that in appreciating that question they ought to bear in mind that a defendant who genuinely believed that he was doing right (a matter of fact to be decided by the jury) cannot be said

---

[18] *R v Deb Baran Ghosh* [1982] QB 1053, 1064; [1982] 3 WLR 110; [1982] 2 All ER 689; [1982] 75 Crim App Rep 154; [1982] 126 SJ 429 CA.

to be dishonest unless what he thought so offends what right-thinking people would regard as honest (those 'right-thinking' people being the jurors) and, if there is a doubt or, more properly, a reasonable doubt, then the defendant is entitled to the benefit of it. This last proposition holds even if the acts (as opposed to intentions) of the defendant, measured objectively, might be regarded as dishonest.

11.31 Further, under UK domestic civil law, honesty is also important and warrants consideration. In *Royal Brunei Airlines v Tan*[19] the defendant, an individual who took part in the illegal siphoning off of trust monies belonging to another, was held jointly liable as a matter of law if it could be shown that his participation was dishonest. An honest employee who was simply obeying orders could clearly not be impugned, at least not in equity, which founded the claim for joint tortfeasorship, since equity requires unconscionable behaviour. In *Royal Brunei Airlines Sendirian Berhad v Philip Tan Kok Ming*[20] Lord Nicholls of Birkenhead in giving the opinion of the Privy Council said:

> Before considering this issue further it will be helpful to define the terms being used by looking more closely at what dishonesty means in this context. Whatever may be the position in some criminal or other contexts (see, for instance, *Regina* v *Ghosh* [1982] QB 1053, CA), in the context of the accessory liability principle acting dishonestly, or with a lack of probity, which is synonymous, means simply not acting as an honest person would in the circumstances. This is an objective standard. At first sight this may seem surprising. Honesty has a connotation of subjectivity, as distinct from the objectivity of negligence. Honesty, indeed, does have a strong subjective element in that it is a description of a type of conduct assessed in the light of what a person actually knew at the time, as distinct from what a reasonable person would have known or appreciated. Further, honesty and its counterpart dishonesty are mostly concerned with advertent conduct, not inadvertent conduct. Carelessness is not dishonesty. Thus for the most part dishonesty is to be equated with conscious impropriety. However, these subjective characteristics of honesty do not mean that individuals are free to set their own standards of honesty in particular circumstances. The standard of what constitutes honest conduct is not subjective. Honesty is not an optional scale, with higher or lower values according to the moral standards of each individual. If a person knowingly appropriates

---

[19] *Royal Brunei Airlines Sendirian Berhad v Philip Tan Kok Ming* [1995] 2 AC 378; [1995] 3 WLR 64; [1995] 3 All ER 97; [1995] BCC 899; (1995) 92(27) LSG 33; (1995) 145 NLJ 888; (1995) 139 SJLB 146; *The Times* (29 May 1995); *The Independent* (22 June 1995) PC.
[20] [1995] 2 AC 378, 389.

another's property, he will not escape a finding of dishonesty simply because he sees nothing wrong in such behaviour.

Thus under the criminal and civil standards there is room and even a neces- **11.32** sity for consideration of both objective and subjective notions of honesty— what the defendant thinks matters.

(6) Does Gerolsteiner *import an objective or subjective definition of honesty?*

It is submitted that the qualifying words of the proviso, along with *some* of **11.33** the statements of the ECJ, raise a strong implication that the nature of honesty must be measured *solely* objectively. Although the proviso is to be read and understood autonomously and not in the light of any Member State's domestic law, it seems that the proviso forms part of an exception to the definitional scope of an infringing act (and is not an exception to an exception[21]) but there has as yet been no indication from the ECJ that these exceptions should be construed narrowly. However, given the strength of the judgments of the ECJ, the best view is that honesty is to be measured objectively.

Against this argument is the fact that the ECJ in *Gerolsteiner* said that the **11.34** question must be considered by means of an overall assessment of all the relevant circumstances. If it is assumed that honesty involves a state of mind, the state of mind of the defendant must be a relevant circumstance. This reasoning tends to imply that subjective elements of honesty are relevant.

It is impossible, given the current state of the law or, more properly, the **11.35** current understanding of the law as has been explained by the ECJ, to con- clude with concrete certainty whether honesty is to be understood in a purely objective sense or in the combined objective and subjective sense. Thus until further guidance is forthcoming from the ECJ each case must be considered separately, if briefly.

(7) Pure objective sense

If honesty be measured in a pure objective sense, this implies that honesty **11.36** is not what the defendant knows or thinks but rather what it is that the

---

[21] This is so because the language of art 6 makes it clear that the exceptions to infringement and the proviso live together.

defendant *ought* to have known or thought, measured by some clearly definable criteria. If that is so, then assessment of honesty must be carried out by reference to objective facts: that assessment will be carried out by the tribunal of fact applying its own code or its educated code as to what constitutes honesty in industrial or commercial matters. This seems to have been the approach in the UK. In *Reed v Reed*,[22] Jacob LJ said:

> 129. I conclude from . . . [Case C-100/02 *Gerolsteiner Brunnen Gesellschaft mit beschränkter Haftung & Co v Putsch Gesellschaft mit beschränkter Haftung*] that a man may use his own name even if there is some actual confusion with a registered trade mark. The amount of confusion which can be tolerated is a question of degree—only if objectively what he does, in all the circumstances, amounts to unfair competition, will there also be infringement. In practice there would have to be significant actual deception—mere possibilities of confusion, especially where ameliorated by other surrounding circumstances (mere aural confusion but clearly different bottles) can be within honest practices. No doubt in some cases where a man has set out to cause confusion by using his name he will be outside the defence (*cf.* the English passing off cases cited above)—in others he may be within it if he has taken reasonable precautions to reduce confusion. All will turn on the overall circumstances of the case.

11.37 Helpfully, for the purposes of the current debate Jacob LJ went on:

> 131. The ECJ has not yet ruled on more subtle questions concerning 'honest practices.' Suppose the defendant at the time believes that what he is doing will not cause substantial deception or confusion and will not amount to unfair competition but is shown to have been wrong. There is no doubt that he must stop once he knows that. But is he liable to compensate the trade mark owner for his past use? . . .

> 132. . . . I am inclined to favour [a] solution . . . [based upon the principle] that the defendant must compensate the trade mark owner if he has even unwittingly caused damage by significant, but unintended deception. I think that is what an honest man would do. Moreover the language of the provision rather suggests that the actual defendant's state of mind is irrelevant—referring as it does to 'honest practices' rather than 'honest use.'

11.38 A reading of those passages of the judgment of Jacob LJ highlights the difficulty involved. The ECJ has yet to rule but, until such times as it does—which may be some time away—the UK may adopt the pure objective

---

[22] *Reed Executive Plc and Reed Solutions Plc v Reed Business Information Limited and others* [2004] EWCA Civ 159; (2004) 148 SJLB 298; *The Times* (9 March 2004) CA, as applied by Lewison J in *International Business Machines Corporation and another v Web-Sphere Limited and others* [2004] EWHC 529 (Ch); [2004] All ER (D) 328 (Mar).

approach, employing a strict test that, if the activity complained of causes damage to the owner's rights, it is enough to found liability.

E. Objective and Subjective

What matters here is what the defendant thought of his actions. The object- **11.39** ive element is whether the defendant was dishonest and, if he was, whether he realized it. There may be cases where it is obvious that the action in question is dishonest but there will also be a grey area. This view has not apparently found favour with the Court of Appeal.

In future editions of this book, further comment may be made under this **11.40** head once the ECJ has ruled on more subtle questions concerning 'honest practices'.

F. Article 6(1)(a): Own Name and Address

Reed v Reed was, in part, a case concerning the defendant's use of its own **11.41** name. Jacob LJ said:

> 116. . . . It would be very strange if no company could avail itself of the defence. Think, for instance, of a company formed to take over a business established under an individual's name and having his name. It would be outrageous if the defence were lost upon incorporation.
> . . .
> Any fear that dishonest people might form companies with misleading names so as to take advantage of the defence is easily removed by the use of the pro- iso—such a deliberate attempt to avail oneself of another's mark would not be an honest practice.

Hence the use of an own name, as Article 6(1)(a) makes clear, is permissible and is subject to little or no qualification.[23]

---

[23] See also the citations from *Scandecor* (n 15) and *Electrolux v Dyson* (n 14).

G. Article 6(1)(b): Other Indications

11.42 Article 6(1)(b), subject to the proviso that has been discussed above, excepts 'indications' concerning:

(a) the kind of goods or services,
(b) quality of goods or services,
(c) quantity of goods or services,
(d) intended purpose of goods or services,
(e) value of goods or services,
(f) geographical origin of goods or services,
(g) the time of production of goods or of rendering of the service, or
(h) other characteristics of goods or services.

11.43 What the word 'indication' means has not been the subject of judicial interpretation but must mean anything which indicates: making something known, pointing something out, a hint, a suggestion or, perhaps, a piece of information from which more may be inferred. It seems fairly clear that the word is to be given an unrestricted meaning since the purpose of Article 6 is to enable honest traders to describe their goods, at least in relation to the things set out in the above list.

11.44 One case on the subject of Article 6(1)(b) is *Hölterhoff*[24] which, unfortunately, was decided by the ECJ on the basis of trade mark use and the proper interpretation of Article 5. Advocate General Jacobs did, however, provide some guidance.[25] He started by saying that any indication would do, any characteristic, and that it was not necessary for the indication used to be a descriptive term:

> 50. .... [Article 6(1)(*b*)] might be thought to be intended primarily to cover a different situation [from the notion of non-trade mark use], namely where a trade mark proprietor seeks to prevent competitors from relying on a descriptive term or terms forming part of his trademark to indicate characteristics of their goods. (. . . see, for example, Joined Cases C-108/97 and C-109/97 *Windsurfing Chiemsee* [1999] I ECR 2779, in particular at paragraph 28 of the judgment.) However, its wording is in no way specific to such a situation and on a normal reading also covers use of the kind in issue in the present case, where a trade mark having no directly descriptive element is used by a

---

[24] *Michael Hölterhoff v Ulrich Freiesleben* Case C-2/00 [2002] ETMR 917 ECJ.
[25] [2002] ETMR 66; [2002] FSR 362 A–G.

competitor to indicate characteristics shared by the competitor's goods and those sold under the trade mark by the proprietor, where the characteristics are commonly associated with the trade mark.[26]

Similarly in *Windsurfing* itself (at paragraph 28) the ECJ makes it clear that **11.45** one position is that Article 6(1)(b) does not confer the right to use the mark as a trade mark. Rather, it is a derogation from the proprietor's right, such derogation being confined to descriptive use. However, *Windsurfing* is not authority for the proposition that there is no right to use another's trade mark as a trade mark since the ruling is confined to the factual situation with which the ECJ was faced. *Windsurfing* itself is limited in its effect to geographical indications. This is not surprising, it is a geographical indications case. The ECJ has to move slowly through uncharted waters, though *Gerolsteiner* is slightly stronger where the ECJ said that all one needed to do was to interpret Article 6(1)(b) in accordance with its terms.[27] If this is right (as surely it must be) then it matters not whether the use made by the putative defendant is trade mark use or not, the only test is whether one of the exceptions in Article 6(1)(b) is satisfied. Thus the position in *Gerolsteiner* is that Article 6(1)(b) is *not* a set of narrow exclusions. If the facts fit, the putative defendant walks free. If any paragraph of this chapter is important, this is the one.

However what both the judgment of the ECJ and the opinion of the Advo- **11.46** cate General say is that the classes of activity set out in Article 6(1) which form exceptions are not the only exceptions. This latter aspect is dealt with elsewhere in this book.[28]

Examples are all that can, in the current state of law, be given. The most **11.47** striking way that traders might want to do this is by way of comparison: 'this chocolate is like CADBURY'S DAIRY MILK'. It is a taxing question as to whether this is something which falls within Article 6(1), though, in cases of comparison, the European legislators took the view that comparative indications were not within Article 5[29] provided, *inter alia*, that there was no possibility of confusion, discredit to the trade mark or taking of an unfair advantage of

---

[26] [2002] ETMR 66, 79.
[27] *Gerolsteiner* (n 7) para 19.
[28] See Ch 10 of this volume.
[29] See recital 15 of Directive 97/55/EC of European Parliament and of the Council of 6 October 1997 amending Directive 84/450/EEC concerning misleading advertising so as to include comparative advertising: OJ 1997 L 290 p 18.

the trade mark.[30] A list of examples of use which is not within the scope of infringement is given below:

(a) the kind of goods or services: 'We provide IMRO approved financial advice' where IMRO is a registered trade mark for financial advice
(b) quality of goods or services: 'Our software complies with the ADA standard' where ADA is registered for computer software
(c) quantity of goods or services: 'We will provide you with share information on a once a day basis' where ONCE A DAY is a registered trade mark for the provision of financial information
(d) intended purpose of goods or services: 'This petrol will run in all Ford engines' where FORD is registered for cars
(e) value of goods or services: 'These bananas are a bargain' where BARGAIN is registered for bananas
(f) geographical origin of goods or services: 'These cakes are made in our Bakewell factory' where BAKEWELL is registered for cakes
(g) the time of production of goods or of rendering of the service: see the ONCE A DAY example above. Another example might be 'Our sausages are made in the early morning' where EARLY MORNING is registered for sausages
(h) other characteristics of goods or services: that's anybody's guess, but it is arguable that it might include something like a name of a football team on a scarf.[31]

11.48 The CTM Office cites the following as being examples of descriptive marks (though without endorsement by the author), which may by analogy be classed as descriptive uses for the purpose of Article 6(1)(b):

> kind, for example 'light', for low tar cigarettes
> quality, for example 'premium'
> quantity, for example numbers, whether in words or digits, will often describe quantity
> intended purpose, for example 'kitchen' or 'bathroom' for cleaning agents
> value, for example 'cheapest'

---

[30] See, generally, art 3a as appearing in art 1(4) of Directive 97/55/EC of European Parliament and of the Council of 6 October 1997 amending Directive 84/450/EEC concerning misleading advertising so as to include comparative advertising.
[31] The author of this chapter admits that he has a personal interest in this aspect of Article 6(1)(b) and, therefore, this suggestion is not to be taken as authoritative.

geographical origin, namely the place, whether locality, region or country where the goods are produced or the service is provided or where the relevant public would expect that this would be the case

or the time of production of the goods, for example a particular year for wine or 'fresh each day' for vegetables

the time of rendering of the service, for example '24 hour banking'; or other characteristics of the goods or services, such as 'lead free' for petrol.

H. Comparative Advertising

In relation to comparisons, Advocate General Jacobs gave some support to **11.49** the notion that comparative advertising was not within the concept of infringement in the Directive when he said in *Hölterhoff*:

> 74. The Community legislator clearly took the view, when it amended the Advertising Directive to include comparative advertising, that the Trade Marks Directive in no way precluded such advertising.
>
> . . .
>
> 76. It may further be noted that in their joint statements entered in the minutes of the Council meeting at which the Community Trade Mark Regulation was adopted on 20 December 1993 the Council and the Commission considered that the reference to advertising in Article 9(2)(d) (Article 9(2) . . . [CTMR] is essentially identical to Article 5(3) of the . . . Directive) did not cover the use of a Community trade mark in comparative advertising. Thus, in their view the use of a competitor's trade mark in comparative advertising is not something which can be prohibited by the trade mark owner.[32]

Hence the current view is likely to be that use by way of comparison is not even covered by the Directive even though such use is likely to amount to trade mark use.

I. Article 6(1)(c): Other Indications

The key feature of Article 6(1)(c) is that the users use must be 'necessary' to **11.50** 'indicate the intended purpose of a product or service, in particular as accessories or spare parts'.

---

[32] [2002] ETMR 66, 84, 85.

11.51 What constitutes necessity is, it is submitted, that which is necessary for the purposes of providing information about purpose; the particularization of the class of goods being accessories or spare parts is nothing more than a list of specific examples and adds nothing to the overall construction of Article 6(1)(c). The key is what is meant by purpose which, it is assumed, means the function which something has to perform. An example might be something like 'this will optimize your WINDOWS operating system'.

K. Article 6(2): Prior Marks

11.52 Article 6(2) reads:

> The trade mark shall not entitle the proprietor to prohibit a third party from using, in the course of trade, an earlier right which only applies in a particular locality if that right is recognised by the laws of the Member State in question and within the limits of the territory in which it is recognised.

In other words local rights prevail, provided that they are earlier. There is no definition of 'earlier right', though Article 4(2) to (4) does define what is meant by an earlier trade mark, for the purposes of registrability. There is, as yet, no case law on this part of the Directive.

11.53 In *Compass Publishing Besloten Vennootschap v Compass Logistics Ltd*[33] the defendant claimed that the claimant's marks were invalid by reason of prior use in the UK, though the defendant did not rely upon Article 6(2). Rather the defendant claimed that the claimant's marks were invalid by reason of prior use. Laddie J found that the claimant's use was to be distinguished from that of the defendant (COMPASS, the mark as against COMPASS LOGISTICS, the sign) but that local rights were irrelevant,[34] so far as the Community trade mark was concerned; there was also a UK registered mark which was found to be invalid. Since they were confusingly similar, infringement was found. If an Article 6(2) argument were run, this might have made a difference to the defence.

11.54 There is an equivalent to Article 6(2) in the CTMR. This is Article 107(1), which reads:

---

[33] [2004] EWHC 520; (2004) 101(17) LSG 32; *The Times* (29 April 2004) Laddie J.
[34] See art 8(4) CTMR which requires prior, unregistered, rights to be of more than 'mere local significance'.

Prior rights applicable to particular localities

1. The proprietor of an earlier right which only applies to a particular locality may oppose the use of the Community trade mark in the territory where his right is protected in so far as the law of the Member State concerned so permits.
2. Paragraph 1 shall cease to apply if the proprietor of the earlier right has acquiesced in the use of the Community trade mark in the territory where his right is protected for a period of five successive years, being aware of such use, unless the Community trade mark was applied for in bad faith.
3. The proprietor of the Community trade mark shall not be entitled to oppose use of the right referred to in paragraph 1 even though that right may no longer be invoked against the Community trade mark.

A distinction must be drawn (as it was in *Compass Publishing Besloten* **11.55** *Vennootschap v Compass Logistics Limited*) between registrability ('more than mere local significance') and the right of the prior user to oppose subsequent use by the owner as envisaged by Article 107 CTMR. It appears, therefore, that Article 107 CTMR is not the same as Article 6(2). The former provides a means of attack (unless Article 107(3) CTMR were invoked, which is possible but was not done in *Compass Publishing Besloten Vennootschap v Compass Logistics Limited*, for reasons which the judge declined to speculate over[35]) whereas the latter provides a means of defence.

Article 107(3) CTMR provides something similar to Article 6(2), though the **11.56** wording is different; it is submitted that the effect is the same.

Placed side-by-side and inserting the relevant parts of Article 107(1) CTMR, **11.57** Articles 6(2) and 107(3) CTMR may be written thus:

The trade mark shall not entitle the proprietor to prohibit a third party from using, in the course of trade, an earlier right which only applies in a particular locality if that right is recognised by the laws of the Member State in question and within the limits of the territory in which it is recognised.	The proprietor of the Community trade mark shall not be entitled to oppose use of an earlier right which only applies to a particular locality in the territory where his right is protected in so far as the law of the Member State concerned so permits . . .

---

[35] *Compass Publishing Besloten Vennootschap v Compass Logistics Ltd* (n 33) para 65.

L. Conclusion

11.58 This chapter is about permitted infringing use. In it, discussion has ranged around honesty and the exceptions in the Directive. A major part of the discussion, even if expressed in terse terms, focuses upon the argument that using the expression 'trade mark use' may be the wrong way of looking at the issue of defences to legal liability, unless that expression is used as a label to explain the difference between expropriating and free riding upon the informational advantage (over and above any traditional or dictionary sense) which has been engendered by the trade mark owner, and not doing so. This was precisely the argument put forward by the brand owner in *Arsenal v Reed* (though it is unclear whether it found favour with the ECJ) and is one which, in this author's experience, is repeated often. However none of the authorities looks at the expression in this way and, perhaps, for good reason in that the only way to explain trade mark law is after lengthy periods have elapsed (ie push it out a little bit, see what happens; if it works, push it out a little more. Put less prosaically, 'slowly, slowly, catchee monkey').

12

INFRINGING USE OF A TRADE MARK AS A CRIMINAL OFFENCE

Andreas Rahmatian

A. Introduction	12.01	Proceedings as Interpreted by *R v Johnstone*	12.13
B. Criminal Offences in Relation to Trade Mark Infringement	12.02	E. Criminal Infringement of Trade Marks in Other European Jurisdictions	12.27
C. An Outline of the House of Lords' Decision in *R v Johnstone*	12.08		
D. Infringing Trade Mark Use in Criminal		F. Conclusion	12.35

A. Introduction

Intellectual property lawyers are normally far more interested in the civil **12.01**
law of trade marks rather than in the criminal offence provisions of the
Trade Marks Act 1994[1] and tend to consider trade mark use in the civil
infringement context only. The criminal liability which may result from
the infringement of a registered trade mark is usually only briefly
discussed.[2] However, the increase of prosecutions for criminal infringement
of registered trade marks, the possibility of a maximum sentence of ten years'

---

[1] Trade Marks Act 1994 c.26. In the following, section numbers refer to the Trade Marks
Act 1994 if not stated otherwise.

[2] Compare WR Cornish and D Llewelyn *Intellectual Property* (5th edn London Sweet &
Maxwell 2003) paras 2–20, 17–108 n 19; L Bently and B Sherman *Intellectual Property Law*
(OUP Oxford 2001) 1032–1034. Longer treatment of the trade mark offences in C Morcom
et al The Modern Law of Trade Marks (Butterworths London 1999) ch 20, 419–478; D
Kitchin *et al Kerly's Law of Trade Marks and Trade Names* (13th edn Sweet & Maxwell
London 2001) ch 19, 715–730; A Worsall and A Clark *Anti-Counterfeiting: A Practical Guide*
(Jordans Bristol 1998) 156–162 (paras 5.28–5.49).

imprisonment on indictment[3] and the House of Lords' decision of *R v John-stone* of 22 May 2003[4]—which contains an important interpretation of infringing trade mark use in criminal proceedings[5]—call for a significantly higher awareness of this neglected area.

B. Criminal Offences in Relation to Trade Mark Infringement

12.02 The criminal offences in relation to trade mark infringement are contained in sections 92, 94 and 95, with additional largely procedural provisions in sections 92A, 93, 96–98 and 101. The only practically relevant provision of substantive criminal law is section 92, which applies to registered trade marks only[6] (section 92(4)(a)[7]) and (arguably) not to service marks.[8] The offence of section 92 entitled 'unauthorised use of trade marks, &c. in relation to goods' is complex and contains three similar, though not identical, separate offences in subsections (1), (2), (3), and a defence provision in subsection (5). Subsection (6) sets out the criminal penalties under this offence: imprisonment for a term not exceeding six months and/or a fine (up to £5000) on summary conviction and, on indictment, a ten years' maximum sentence and/or an unlimited fine. This criminal provision does not follow the EU Trade Marks Directive,[9] which does not contain the requirement of a criminal offence[10] and its scope goes beyond the TRIPs Agreement[11] in Article

---

[3] s 92(6).

[4] *R v Johnstone* [2003] UKHL 28, [2004] ETMR 2, [2003] FSR 748, [2003] 3 All ER 884, [2003] 1 WLR 1736.

[5] Discussed below under C and D.

[6] The situation is less clear in relation to registered, but subsequently revoked, trade marks, or marks declared invalid under ss 46–47; see *Kerly* (n 2) para 19–43.

[7] s 92 also protects trade marks with a reputation in the UK, where the use of the sign takes unfair advantage of, or is detrimental to, the distinctive character or repute of the trade mark: s 92(4)(b). This (criminal) protection of the mark with a reputation extends to goods for which the mark is not registered, which mirrors the civil provision of s 10(3); *Kerly* (n 2) paras 19–27, 19–28.

[8] This can be argued on the basis of s 92(4)(a): 'A person does not commit an offence . . . unless (a) the goods are goods in respect of which the trade mark is registered . . .'. See also Morcom (n 2) para 20.1; *Kerly* (n 2) para 19–05.

[9] First Council Directive 89/104/EEC of 21 December 1988 to approximate the laws of the Member States relating to trade marks OJ 1989 L 40.

[10] Worsall and Clark (n 2) para 5.28.

[11] Agreement on Trade-Related Aspects of Intellectual Property Rights, Annex 1C to the WTO Agreement 1994.

61.[12] In the following, the offence of section 92 will be discussed, first with regard to the prohibited conduct (*actus reus*), and second as to the state of mind required (*mens rea*).

In sections 92(1), (2) and (3) the *actus reus*, ie all the elements of the crime **12.03** which refer to the prohibited behaviour or conduct,[13] includes (i) the application to goods of a sign identical to, or likely to be mistaken for,[14] a registered trade mark, or (ii) the sale, distribution etc., or (iii) the possession, control etc. in the course of a business, of goods with such a sign.[15] Similarly, the application of an identical or confusingly similar sign to material intended to be used for labelling etc. goods, or, in the course of a business, the use of material bearing such a sign for the labelling etc. of goods; or the possession or control in the course of a business for these purposes, constitute prohibited behaviour.[16] Another kind of criminal conduct is the making of an article specifically designed for making copies of a sign identical or confusingly similar to a registered trade mark.[17]

None of these variants of unauthorized trade mark use in section 92 mirrors **12.04** the infringing acts in the civil infringement provision of section 10. In fact, section 92 does not expressly refer to the civil infringement rules (sections 9–11) at all.[18] This omission leads to problems regarding the interpretation of the relationship between the civil and criminal infringement provisions, as highlighted in *R v Johnstone*.[19] Two examples may illustrate this point:

---

[12] The EU Council Regulation against counterfeit and pirated goods (Council Regulation (EC) no 1383/2003 of 22 July 2003 concerning customs action against goods suspected of infringing certain intellectual property rights and the measures to be taken against goods found to have infringed such rights, OJ L 196 2 August 2003) is not directly relevant to s 92, because for the purpose of this Council Regulation the actual determination whether the goods in question are infringing is left to the laws of the Member States; see Recital (8) and art 2.

[13] A Ashworth *Principles of Criminal Law* (4th edn OUP Oxford 2003) 96.

[14] Thus the marks need not be identical, but there has to be likelihood of confusion—a vague criterion (especially within criminal law) which a defendant may find difficult to disprove: see *Kerly* (n 2) paras 19–16, 19–17.

[15] s 92(1). The enumeration above concentrates on the main elements of the crime.

[16] s 92(2), which contains more features of criminal behaviour not mentioned in the main text.

[17] s 92(3).

[18] *Kerly* (n 2) para 19–06. The reason why s 92 does not reflect the civil infringement provisions is not clear: see Morcom (n 2) paras 20.10–20.11.

[19] Compare discussion in Morcom (n 2) paras 20.97–20.98, which must now be read in the light of *R v Johnstone* (n 4) especially paras 33–34, 70, 73–74; see also below. In the following, references within *R v Johnstone* are made to the paragraph numbers provided in the judgment.

(i)   The prerequisite of criminal liability under all offences within section 92 is the use of the trade mark 'without the consent of the *proprietor*'.[20] If section 92 is considered independent from the civil law of trade marks, as its way of drafting suggests, then the meaning of 'proprietor' would not include the exclusive licensee, because a clarifying definition within criminal trade mark law is lacking, and a construction according to civil law (sections 29–31), may not be acceptable in the criminal law context. Thus, curiously, the consent of the licensee—in civil law, potentially the only person entitled to give such consent as a consequence of his/her exclusive licence (section 29 (1))—would theoretically not remove criminal liability.[21] Or does the grant of the licence imply the proprietor's consent for the purpose of section 92?[22]

(ii)   The defence provision in section 92(5) against criminal prosecution exculpates the defendant who can show that he believed on reasonable grounds that the use of the sign in the manner in which it was (to be) used was not an *infringement* of the trade mark. The burden is on the defendant to prove the relevant facts.[23] Is 'infringement' to be understood in the sense of the civil law of sections 9–11,[24] or is it to be interpreted on the basis of the section 92 offence only? As will be shown,[25] *R v Johnstone* deals with the problem the second example poses.

12.05   Structurally more complicated than the *actus reus* is the *mens rea* of section 92, ie that part of the offence which refers to the defendant's state of mind.[26] The *mens rea* of all offences in section 92 contains the element that the defendant must have acted either 'with a view to gain for himself or another' or 'with intent to cause loss to another'.[27] Only in section 92(3) the defendant must have the basic *mens rea* of 'knowing or having reason to believe' that

---

[20]   Identical wording in s 92(1), (2), (3).

[21]   However, the prosecution would have to prove lack of consent: *Kerly* (n 2) para 19–18.

[22]   The licence may have provisions dealing with this issue (compare s 31(1)), and the proprietor may also be compelled contractually on the basis of the exclusive licence to give consent (see also s 30(2) and (3) in relation to civil infringement actions).

[23]   Compare the wording in s 92(5): 'It is a defence for a person charged . . . to show that he believed on reasonable grounds that the use of the sign . . . was not an infringement . . .'. See also *R v Johnstone* (n 4) para 46; *Kerly* (n 2) para 19–31.

[24]   That is maintained by Morcom (n 2) para 20.98.

[25]   See below under D.

[26]   AP Simester and GR Sullivan *Criminal Law: Theory and Doctrine* (Hart Publishing Oxford 2001) 113.

[27]   ss 92(1), (2) and (3).

the article specifically designed or adapted for making copies of an infringing sign is, or will be, used to produce goods or material for labelling, advertising goods etc. However, neither in section 92(1) nor in section 92(2) is intention or any other *mens rea* in respect of the infringing acts themselves required.[28] This means that, in respect of the ambit of the prohibited behaviour (ie the *actus reus*), section 92 can be regarded as an offence of near strict (absolute) liability;[29] this view was confirmed by the House of Lords in *Johnstone*.[30]

The *mens rea* preconditions in subsections (1), (2), (3), of intention to cause **12.06** loss, or of acting with a view to gain, can be described as a kind of 'ulterior (specific) *mens rea*': the crime is also committed if the use of the unauthorized sign has not actually resulted in a gain for the defendant or caused loss to another. The accurate term would normally be 'ulterior intent' which is founded on a 'basic intent'.[31] However, since 'with a view to gain for himself or another' does not denote the requirement of intention, the term 'ulterior *mens rea*' is used. From an analytical perspective, the specific *mens rea* in section 92(1) and (2) exists without a basic intent as its foundation,[32] a rather unsatisfactory legal structure. As already mentioned, the alternative *mens rea* element 'with a view to gain for himself' does not necessarily involve any intention, purpose, or the knowledge to gain, but implies only foresight to gain, which indicates the *mens rea* of recklessness.[33] The distinction between

---

[28] Compare *Kerly* (n 2) para 19–10.

[29] On the terminology regarding strict and absolute liability and its problems, see Ashworth (n 13) 165; CMV Clarkson and HM Keating *Criminal Law* (5th edn Sweet & Maxwell London 2003) 231: strict liability is probably the correct term, but absolute liability is often used by the courts, also in *R v Johnstone* (n 4).

[30] *R v Johnstone* (n 4) para 52.

[31] Compare JC Smith (Smith & Hogan) *Criminal Law* (8th edn London Butterworths 1996) 74; Simester and Sullivan (n 26) 125. On ulterior (specific) intent, see also RA Duff 'Intentions Legal and Philosophical' [1989] 9 OJLS 76, 88 and n 48; J Gardner and H Jung 'Making Sense of *Mens Rea*: Antony Duff's Account' [1991] 11 OJLS 559, 573.

[32] In s 92(3) the requirement of knowledge or of having reason to believe that the article made/in possession etc is an infringing article when performing the incriminated acts, constitutes basic intent, or more precisely, basic *mens rea*, because 'having reason to believe' indicates recklessness (awareness of a risk of a prohibited circumstance but wilful refusal to check true situation); compare Ashworth (n 13) 192. 'Having reason to believe' is to be distinguished from 'knowledge or belief', which is *not* the wording in s 92(3): in the latter case a criminal statute extends slightly the ambit of intention (in its version as 'knowledge'): see Ashworth (n 13) 188.

[33] Simester and Sullivan (n 26) 118–120. See also discussion of *R v Zaman* [2003] FSR 230 CA. The problem is more complex than outlined here: see generally AP Simester 'Moral Certainty and the Boundaries of Intention' [1995] 16 OJLS 445.

'*view* to gain' and '*intent* to cause loss' in section 92 indicates that the law seeks to extend the scope of liability beyond intention,[34] and one gains support for this interpretation in *R v Zaman*.[35] Thus not only the *intentional* infringement of a trade mark is an offence: criminal liability under section 92 extends to the area of recklessness, whereby the unauthorized use of the trade mark itself (the *actus reus*) need not be accompanied by a *mens rea* in all cases.

12.07 The fact that section 92 can be regarded as an offence of near strict liability, as confirmed by *Johnstone*,[36] is highly unsatisfactory in theory,[37] but has probably less relevance in practice. When committing any of the acts in section 92(1) or (2), one must realistically have the *mens rea* of at least recklessness to fulfil the necessary requirement of the ulterior *mens rea*: it is virtually impossible that one has the *mens rea* of 'intent to cause loss' or of 'acting with a view to gain for himself', but not some degree of *mens rea* in relation to the act of unauthorized use of a sign etc itself. In this way, criminal liability may be justified.[38]

C. An Outline of the House of Lords' Decision in *R v Johnstone*

12.08 The main issues of *R v Johnstone*, as far as relevant for the present discussion, are as follows: Johnstone and others sold bootleg recordings (unauthorized recordings of live performances) on compact discs. These CDs bore the names of the performer or the band name, which were registered as trade marks. Johnstone was prosecuted for unauthorized use of trade marks under section 92.[39] Johnstone's defence was based on the premise that criminal

---

[34] Compare discussion in Morcom (n 2) paras 20.17–20.19.

[35] *R v Zaman* [2003] FSR 230 paras 12, 16–18 CA.

[36] *R v Johnstone* (n 4) para 52. The HL uses the term 'absolute liability'.

[37] Ashworth (n 13) 88, 166; A Ashworth 'Is the Criminal Law a Lost Cause?' [2000] 116 LQR 225, 240.

[38] For a longer discussion of the *mens rea* in s 92, together with a second argument to improve the otherwise unsatisfactory *mens rea* system see A Rahmatian 'Trade Mark Infringement as a Criminal Offence' [2004] 67 MLR 670, 678.

[39] It is worth noting that *R v Johnstone* is really a disguised copyright case, a fact that the judges have pointed out in paras 40, 60, 86. The parallel criminal provisions of ss 107, 198 in the Copyright, Designs and Patents Act 1988 require a higher level of *mens rea* (knowledge or having reason to believe that the article in question is an infringing copy) which is arguably more difficult to prove, so 'bootlegging' can probably more easily be prosecuted on the basis of the trade mark component of a case, if there is one. See also on the issue of *Johnstone* in a copyright environment R Calleja 'Case Comment: *R v Johnstone*: Bootlegging and Legitimate use of an Artist's Trade Mark' [2003] Ent LR 14 (7), 186–188.

liability requires civil infringement (which the prosecution did not prove) and that, for civil infringement, use as a trade mark is required. He relied on section 11(2)(b) for his defence of not having infringed, ie that the use of a name (the performers' name on the CD) was a descriptive non-trade mark use.

The trial judge rejected the defendant's submission that the commission of a **12.09** section 92 offence presupposes civil infringement; in his view section 92 was a free-standing offence. The Court of Appeal reversed this decision: civil infringement law (sections 9–11) *was* a prerequisite for the operation of section 92 and that also defined the meaning of 'infringement' in the defence provision in section 92(5).

Following the Crown's appeal, the House of Lords in its ruling disagreed **12.10** with the Court of Appeal's opinion: section 92 is to be seen as an independent offence in principle. It should be considered as self-contained, because

> it would be burdensome if lay magistrates and juries regularly had to go into the intricacies of the law of civil infringement,

apart from the defence provision of section 92(5).[40] The 'ingredients of the offences created by section 92 are to be found within the section itself': section 92 focuses on unauthorized use of a sign identical to, or likely to be mistaken for, a registered trade mark.[41] It is, due to these ingredients, implicit in section 92 that the offending use of the sign requires 'use as a trade mark'[42] and is not purely descriptive use: the latter cannot attract criminal liability because this type of use is lawful.[43] The House also endorsed the view that section 92 is an offence of near absolute (strict) liability.[44]

The defendant's alternative defence was based on section 92(5), ie the **12.11** defence of reasonable belief that the use of the sign was not an infringement of the trade mark. The burden of proof is reversed: it is for the defendant to prove the relevant facts on the balance of probability. The House of Lords

---

[40] *R v Johnstone* (n 4) paras 26, 33 per Lord Nicholls, paras 73, 88 per Lord Walker. In s 92(5), the definition of 'infringement' has to be made in accordance with s 104 which refers to the civil infringement law of ss 9–10; ibid para 33.

[41] ibid para 26 per Lord Nicholls.

[42] ibid para 27 per Lord Nicholls, para 88 per Lord Walker.

[43] This point is discussed below under D.

[44] *R v Johnstone* (n 4) para 52; see also above para B.

justified this exception from the presumption of innocence principle[45] with the protection of honest traders and the public from counterfeiting and fraudulent trading, and with the protection of consumers from low-quality and potentially hazardous counterfeit goods.[46]

12.12 The House dismissed the Crown's appeal: the Court of Appeal was correct in considering the defendant's conviction as unsafe because the defendant was wrongly denied the chance to put forward the defence that his use of the performers'/bands' names was not trade mark use.[47]

D. Infringing Trade Mark Use in Criminal Proceedings as Interpreted by *R v Johnstone*

12.13 According to *Johnstone*, it is implicit in the provisions of section 92 that the offending use of a sign must be *use as a trade mark*.[48] Lord Nicholls in his judgment defines 'trade mark use' in the context of criminal law in the following way:

12.14 In civil law, the function of a trade mark is a badge of origin, indicating a trade source. The use of a mark in a manner not indicative of trade mark origin does not encroach on the proprietor's monopoly rights.[49] Lord Nicholls also obtained support for his interpretation from a passage in the decision of the European Court of Justice (ECJ) in *Arsenal v Reed*,[50] which characterizes the essential function of a trade mark as

---

[45] art 6(2) of the European Convention on Human Rights.

[46] *R v Johnstone* (n 4) paras 52–54. This justification is problematic in that the principal function of a trade mark is to guarantee the identity of the origin of the trade marked goods to the customer or end user (compare *Arsenal v Reed* (n 50)), together with its nowadays equally important advertising and communication function. Trade marks are not a consumer protection measure as such (despite the increasing tendency to emphasize this aspect), and trade marks denoting products/services of any quality are protected by trade mark law. Thus consumer protection should not form part of the justification to allow the reversal of the burden of proof in s 92(5). For a longer discussion of the reverse burden of proof in s 92(5) and the reasoning on this point in *Johnstone* see Rahmatian (n 38) 670, 679.

[47] *R v Johnstone* (n 4) para 55 per Lord Nicholls, para 89 per Lord Walker.

[48] ibid paras 27, 76, 88.

[49] ibid para 13. In this context, Lord Nicholls referred approvingly to Dillon LJ in *Mothercare UK v Penguin Books* [1988] RPC 113, 118.

[50] *Arsenal Football Club plc v Matthew Reed* Case C-206/01 [2003] 1 CMLR 345, [2003] RPC 9, 144, 171, para 48.

to guarantee the identity of origin of the marked goods or services to the consumer or end user by enabling him, without any possibility of confusion, to distinguish the goods or services from others which have another origin.

According to Lord Nicholls, the approach of the ECJ accords with that of **12.15** English law in that it follows from the statement in *Arsenal v Reed* that the exclusive right of the trade mark proprietor under Article 5(1)(a) of the Trade Mark Directive does not extend to purely descriptive use. Thus non-trade mark use is not within the civil infringement provisions of section 10(1)–(3).[51]

The House of Lords applied its interpretation of 'trade mark use' in the civil **12.16** law to the criminal law provision of section 92. The House agreed with the prosecution (and the trial judge)[52] that section 92 is in principle a provision separate from the civil infringement law (sections 9–10) and that the ingredients of the offences created by section 92 are found within the section itself, without reference to the civil infringement regime in the Trade Marks Act directly.[53] However, the civil law could apparently play a role if it was in some way contained (or could be detected) within the wording of section 92 itself. This was the case (according to the Lords' view) in relation to the interpretation of unauthorized use in section 92.

Contrary to the prosecution, the Lords construed section 92 in such a way **12.17** that 'use as a trade mark' was a prerequisite for criminal liability. This seems to appear from the words and structure of section 92 itself. Thus the meaning of 'use as a trade mark' must be interpreted by reference to its meaning in the civil law as the House of Lords construed it. The use of a trade mark protected word or sign in a (purely[54]) descriptive sense is unobjectionable and section 92 could not have been intended to criminalize such a conduct. However, in the present writer's view, an interpretation of the wording of section 92 does not give any indication in which way (and whether with or without reference to the civil law[55]) the various types of unauthorized use have to be understood.

---

[51] *R v Johnstone* (n 4) paras 16–17.
[52] ibid para 22.
[53] ibid para 26.
[54] 'and the word "purely" is important . . .', per Lord Walker, ibid para 85 interpreting a passage in the ECJ ruling *Arsenal v Reed* (n 50) para 54.
[55] Apart from s 92(5), which refers to the civil law via s 104.

12.18 According to Lord Nicholls' interpretation, the need for trade mark use could be found within section 92 by referring to the requirement of the conduct in question as being 'without the consent of the proprietor'.[56] This prerequisite indicates that section 92 only criminalizes a conduct to which the proprietor can object. As descriptive use is legally permitted, and the proprietor cannot raise any objections, there cannot be a criminal sanction where the absence of the proprietor's consent is legally irrelevant.[57]

12.19 A second argument the House gave for its interpretation is that the defence provision of section 92(5) (defence of reasonable belief that the use of the sign was not an *infringement* of the trade mark) presupposes the infringement of a registered trade mark. This defence provision would be superfluous if an infringement were irrelevant for the criminal offences.[58] Whether, in the present case, the use of the name of the group or an artist on a CD is descriptive of the content of the CD (mere identification of the performer, ie no section 92 offence), or an indication of the trade origin of the disc itself (trade mark use triggering liability under section 92), is a question of fact in each case[59] and, for that reason, Lord Nicholls was of the opinion that *Arsenal v Reed*[60] did not assist on this point.[61] Lord Walker, who agreed with Lord Nicholls in all material respects,[62] pointed out that the defendant would have difficulty in proving that he had made descriptive use of the registered trade mark when he was using it to denote the performer on the CDs, but that did not deprive him of the opportunity to run the defences on which he wished to rely, even if these defences were potentially weak.[63]

12.20 Both Lord Nicholls[64] and Lord Walker[65] stressed the compatibility of their interpretation of trade mark use with the ECJ judgment in *Arsenal v Reed*,[66] but one cannot resist doubting these assertions.[67] Although the ECJ limited

---

[56] s 92(1), (2) and (3) all contain this ingredient.
[57] *R v Johnstone* (n 4) paras 27–28 per Lord Nicholls.
[58] ibid para 29.
[59] ibid para 36 per Lord Nicholls.
[60] *Arsenal v Reed* (n 50).
[61] *R v Johnstone* (n 4) para 41.
[62] ibid paras 73, 87–88.
[63] ibid para 89.
[64] ibid paras 16–17.
[65] ibid paras 85, 87.
[66] *Arsenal v Reed* (n 50).
[67] A more detailed analysis of the ECJ case *Arsenal v Reed* can be found in Ch 10 of this volume. The present discussion is restricted to aspects relevant to s 92.

the protection of the trade mark proprietor to 'cases in which a third party's use of the sign affects or is liable to affect the functions of the trade mark, in particular its essential function of guaranteeing to consumers the origin of the goods',[68] one must have regard to the true extent of the effect of this limitation, and in this light, the harmonious coexistence of *Arsenal* and *Johnstone* is difficult to sustain. For the ECJ continues that the proprietor may not prohibit the use of an identical sign 'if that use *cannot affect his own interests* as proprietor of the mark, having regard to its functions', and concludes that '*certain uses* for *purely descriptive purposes* are excluded from the scope of Art.5(1) of the Directive[69] because they do not affect *any* of the interests which that provision aims to protect, and do not therefore fall within the concept of the use within the meaning of that provision . . .' (my italics).[70]

Thus prohibited use, that is, use which affects the trade mark proprietor's **12.21** interests, comprises use as a trade mark but goes beyond it. Whether the use was trade mark use is not relevant for infringement. Instead, the test is whether the essential function of the trade mark as the guarantor of the origin of the goods is impeded or damaged by the use. This is typically the case with the use of a sign as a trade mark. It can nevertheless occur in situations where the use does not amount to trade mark use, but is a kind of descriptive use with a damaging impact on the function of the trade mark. Only *certain* uses for *purely* descriptive purposes which do not affect *any* of the protected interests fall outside the prohibition. Descriptive uses with a component that is *not* purely descriptive (typically in the context of sales to customers[71]), and/or uses which *do* affect adversely one of the protected interests of the trade mark proprietor, are infringing use—irrespective of whether this use also qualifies as trade mark use (although this will typically be the case). This view was also taken (and arguably had to be taken) by the Court of Appeal following the ECJ decision.[72]

The ECJ decision in *Arsenal* can be reconciled with an interpretation that the **12.22** fixing of a trade mark-protected artist's or band name on a CD to indicate

---

[68] *Arsenal v Reed* (n 50) para 51.
[69] Directive 89/104 is implemented by Trade Marks Act 1994 ss 9, 10.
[70] *Arsenal v Reed* (n 50) para 54.
[71] That was the case in *Arsenal v Reed* (n 50) paras 15, 55, because Reed sold the football merchandise with signs referring to the Arsenal football club to customers. That is, according to the ECJ, obviously not intended for purely descriptive purposes.
[72] *Arsenal Football Club plc v Matthew Reed* [2003] RPC 39, 696 CA para 45 per Aldous LJ.

the performer(s) on that CD constitutes prohibited use in civil law within the meaning of *Arsenal*, whether or not it also constitutes trade mark use. Such use could therefore be regarded as criminal use for the purpose of section 92. Following from the civil law, the requirement for a criminal liability under section 92 is not whether the unauthorized use is 'use as a trade mark', as *Johnstone* claims. Instead, the crucial point is (according to *Arsenal*) whether the use damages the essential function of the trade mark (as a guarantor of origin) and therefore affects (any of) the interests of the proprietor. In *Johnstone*, the use of the performers' names took place in the context of sales to customers and can presumably not normally be intended for purely descriptive purposes,[73] even if every CD clearly indicates that the performers did not authorize the use of their trade-mark-protected name on the CDs to counteract the trade mark's function as guarantor of origin.[74] In addition, the labelling of bootleg recordings with trade-mark-protected signs is most likely to affect the proprietor's interests which trade mark law protects; it falls within the prohibition, irrespective of whether this use also qualifies as trade mark use.

12.23 The discrepancy between the interpretation of infringing use in *Arsenal* and *Johnstone* is noticeable,[75] but this is not necessarily the end of the matter. *Arsenal* discusses use which may constitute civil infringement, whereas *Johnstone* interprets 'use' in the context of a prerequisite of a criminal law provision. Thus it is *prima facie* acceptable to conclude that the meaning of unlawful 'use' in criminal law is narrower than the civil law meaning of 'use', although *Johnstone* did not reach this outcome on that basis. *Johnstone* has introduced the problem of 'trade mark use' into section 92 by assuming that

---

[73] Such a view is also reflected in the qualification of the descriptive use defence in art 6(1) of the Directive, corresponding to TMA 1994 s 11(2) in that such use is also unlikely to be in accordance with honest practices in industrial or commercial matters. Whether the use in question is purely descriptive is a matter of fact in each case. However, even if, according to the facts, the use of a performer's name on a CD is not to be understood as use as a trade mark (*R v Johnstone* (n 4) para 40), the right test is still whether there is damage to the essential function as a trade mark, rather than whether there is use as a trade mark, although in reality the scope of both tests will largely overlap.

[74] Compare *Arsenal v Reed* (n 50) paras 55 and 57. The offence of s 92 could be committed in such a case (provided the other requirements are also met), because the wording of s 92 does not require the defendant to mislead the customers into thinking that the goods offered are genuine: *Kerly* (n 2) para 19–08.

[75] See also M Lindsey and M Chacksfield 'Exhaustion of Rights and Wrongs: Section 92 of the Trade Marks Act 1994; Recent Developments and Comments' [2003] EIPR 388, 395.

this provision is in principle a separate criminal rule which is supposed to contain all necessary ingredients of the offence: thus the material used for any interpretation is to be found in section 92 only, with as little direct reference to the civil law as possible.[76]

Only certain elements of the civil law, such as the interpretation of what **12.24** is unauthorized use, seem to be contained, or are a hidden ingredient, in section 92. The wording of section 92 does not suggest this construction, because it does not refer expressly to civil infringement[77] (and is worded very differently from sections 9–10). One cannot really ascertain which parts of section 92 could be regarded as 'implicitly' referring to the civil law without making a largely arbitrary decision. Thus it would have been favourable if the House of Lords had abandoned the artificial separation of the criminal offence from the civil infringement law (even if that separation is indicated by the drafting of section 92), and had followed the Court of Appeal in *Johnstone* in requiring civil infringement as a prerequisite for the commission of the section 92 offence.[78] It is doubtful where the benefit of this separation lies when, on the one hand, one should strive to construct a comprehensive legal system of criminal infringement law which is supposed to emanate from section 92 alone,[79] while on the other hand, one effectively has to resort to civil law frequently on crucial points because of the incompleteness of the current criminal law in this area. In any event, if criminal liability arises, there is almost always civil liability too, as Lord Nicholls himself pointed out.[80] In addition, criminal offences (especially property offences) often interpret elements of the *actus reus* by reference to the civil law, so trade mark crimes are no anomaly in this respect.[81]

Despite formally maintaining a separation between the civil infringement law **12.25** and the criminal law of unauthorized use of a trade mark, the House of Lords resorted to the civil law to determine what 'unauthorized use' in the context

---

[76] *R v Johnstone* (n 4) paras 26, 73.

[77] There is an indirect reference to civil law in the defence rule of s 92(5) as regards the meaning of 'infringement' via the interpretation rule in s 104. The House of Lords held that 'infringement' was to be determined with reference to ss 9–10 of the civil law of infringement, following s 104: see *R v Johnstone* (n 4) paras 29, 70.

[78] *R v Johnstone* [2003] ETMR 1, 15 para 46 CA.

[79] Compare *R v Johnstone* (n 4) paras 26, 73.

[80] ibid para 33; see also para 73 per Lord Walker.

[81] eg Theft Act 1968 s 1: 'property belonging to another'. For a more detailed discussion of the arguments against this 'separation' approach in *Johnstone* see Rahmatian (n 38) 670, 675.

of section 92 actually meant, then construed unauthorized use in section 92 as presupposing trade mark use—a construction which was perhaps designed to apply and, at any rate, inevitably applied, to the civil and the criminal laws of trade marks alike. However, within the realm of the civil law, the House's view on what constitutes prohibited use is arguably partially in conflict with the ruling in *Arsenal*.[82] One way in which *Johnstone* can be reconciled with *Arsenal* is to restrict *Johnstone's* interpretation of unlawful use ('trade mark use') to the criminal provision of section 92 only, with no relevance to the civil infringement law at all, because *Arsenal* focuses on the civil law.[83]

12.26 The wide interpretation of trade mark protection in *Arsenal*, when imported into section 92, may lead to an extensive construction of unauthorized use in that criminal provision, and potentially to extended criminal liability. This was effectively averted in *Johnstone* by requiring 'trade mark use' as a pre-requisite of prohibited use within section 92. However, that approach is not consistent with *Arsenal* and arguably not necessary either. Despite the wording of section 92, which suggests apparent independence of the civil law of infringement,[84] section 92 should rather be interpreted in the context of the whole law of trade marks and therefore in connection with the civil infringement law. Thus section 92 should be regarded as a criminal infringement provision, based on civil infringement[85] plus any additional aggravating factors set out in the *actus reus* of section 92 and plus the requisite *mens rea*,[86] consisting of a basic *mens rea* and an ulterior *mens rea*. The offence of section 92 should therefore be interpreted as consisting of an act of civil infringement (according to the *Arsenal* test, where relevant) as one part of the *actus reus*, plus additional prohibited behaviour (as set out in section 92) to the extent that it does not constitute civil infringement anyway, which together form the whole *actus reus* of section 92; plus the requisite *mens rea* (basic and ulterior), all of which lead together to criminal infringement, punishable under section 92, provided no defence applies (eg section

---

[82] Compare H Norman 'Time to Blow the Whistle on Trade Mark Use' [2004] IPQ 1, 33.

[83] This narrow interpretation of 'trade mark use' may, however, not necessarily be applicable to the whole of s 92, because it may conflict with s 92(4)(b) and the similar s 10(3), both reflecting art 5(2) of the Directive (protection of a trade mark with a reputation in relation to dissimilar goods); see Norman (n 82) 33–34.

[84] The motive for this manner of drafting is unclear; compare Morcom (n 2) paras 20.10, 20.11.

[85] This was the view taken by the Court of Appeal in *R v Johnstone* (n 78) para 46.

[86] Preferably this would be the *mens rea* of intention, but s 92 does not require that.

92(5)).[87] Thus the factor that limits criminal liability under section 92 should not be (i) whether there is use as a trade mark (however construed), but (ii) whether a civil infringement has been accompanied by additional elements of the *actus reus* (as far as required) and (iii) the requisite *mens rea* at the time of the *actus reus*, in line with the principles of general criminal law.[88] However, that approach would presuppose a departure from the view in *Johnstone* that section 92 is in principle a free-standing offence, although the aspect of trade mark use as part of the civil infringement law seems to be contained (opaquely) in the wording of section 92.[89]

E. Criminal Infringement of Trade Marks in Other European Jurisdictions

Limited space does not permit me to give more than a very broad overview of criminal offences in the trade mark laws of a few continental European countries. The countries chosen (Germany, Austria, Switzerland and France) should not be regarded as representative of the whole of Europe. However, certain valuable comparisons with the UK can still be made. **12.27**

The civil law systems of the continental European countries have the advantage of an existing comprehensive criminal code, the background against which provisions of trade mark crimes are drafted and on which basis they have to be construed. **12.28**

In Germany, §143 of the Trade Marks Act 1994[90] prohibits, *inter alia*, the use of a sign, or the use or offering of packaging etc bearing a sign which **12.29**

---

[87] Thus the suggested components are, schematically: civil infringement + further *actus reus* (application to goods of a sign identical to, or likely to be mistaken for, a registered trade mark etc) to the extent that this act does not constitute civil infringement anyway + basic *mens rea* (effectively only in case of s 92(3)) + ulterior *mens rea* (with a view to gain / with intent to cause loss) = criminal sanction under s 92.

[88] Ashworth (n 13) 96; Simester and Sullivan (n 26) 113.

[89] Effectively, this is a decision the House of Lords chose to make. The wording of s 92 does not assist at all in this respect. Walker LJ's statement that trade mark use as a necessary ingredient in s 92 'is adequately (if not pellucidly) expressed in the language of s 92' (*R v Johnstone* (n 4) para 88) must therefore be doubted. For the purpose of legal certainty it would be better to consider the whole civil infringement law as a precondition for the operation of s 92.

[90] Gesetz über den Schutz von Marken und sonstigen Kennzeichen (Markengesetz 1994) BGBl. I 1994, 3082, as amended.

infringes according to civil law (§§14–15).[91] *Mens rea* is required for the incriminating acts and, in addition, a specific intent to damage the distinctive character or repute of the trade mark in relation to certain subsections of the crime. The offence is punishable by imprisonment of up to three years or a fine and, in the case of infringement for gain, by imprisonment of up to five years or a fine. The less serious type of the offence (three years' maximum sentence) is to be prosecuted at the request of the trade mark owner only.

12.30 In Austria, §60 of the Trade Marks Protection Act 1970[92] punishes the intentional infringement (according to civil law) of a trade mark in the course of business. The offender is liable to a fine, and in case of infringement for gain, to a maximum sentence of two years' imprisonment.[93]

12.31 The Swiss Article 61 of the Trade Marks Protection Act 1992[94] provides that the intentional infringement of a trade mark by way of, *inter alia*, using, copying or imitating someone else's trade mark, is punishable at the request of the trade mark proprietor. The sanction is up to one year imprisonment or a fine of SF100,000, and in case of infringement for gain, imprisonment and a fine. In the latter case, no request of the owner for prosecution is necessary. Article 62 prohibits the fraudulent use of someone else's trade mark (maximum imprisonment of five years, if the offender has acted for gain).

12.32 In France, the industrial production and import of goods with counterfeit trade marks with a view to their sale or hire is an offence under Article L716–9 of the Intellectual Property Code,[95] its maximum sentence being four years and a fine (€400,000). The sale of goods with counterfeit marks, as well as the reproduction, imitation, use and affixing of someone else's trade mark, etc is also a crime according to Article L716–10. This crime is punishable by three years' imprisonment and a fine (€300,000). The commission of these offences by organized gangs attracts punishment of up to five years' imprisonment.

---

[91] These provisions are modelled upon art 5 of Directive 89/104.
[92] Markenschutzgesetz 1970 BGBl. 260/1970, as amended.
[93] Prosecution is at the trade mark proprietor's request, §60a (1) Markenschutzgesetz 1970.
[94] Bundesgesetz über den Schutz von Marken und Herkunftsangaben (Markenschutzgesetz 1992), 28 August 1992 (AS 1993 274), as amended.
[95] Code de la Propriété Intellectuelle 1992 (Law No. 92–597 of 1 July 1992), as amended. arts L 716–9 and L 716–10 were last amended by the Law No. 2004–204 of 9 March 2004 art 34.

An analysis of these offences shows that the incriminating acts generally also **12.33**
amount to infringement in civil law, and sometimes the criminal provision
refers to the civil infringement law expressly.[96] The incriminating acts must
be committed with some degree of *mens rea* to attract punishment, which can
be inferred from the underlying general system of criminal law in the country
in question.[97] This required *mens rea* can be that of intention, which is either
expressly provided in the trade mark statute itself,[98] or can be concluded from
the general part of the relevant criminal code containing the core criminal
law.[99] Furthermore, the maximum penalty, the application of which tends to
presuppose the commission of the offence for gain on a professional (or
organized) basis, is five years' imprisonment, and in less severe cases, considerably below that. Generally, criminal infringement is prosecuted at the
proprietor's request.

If one compares the offences in these four continental European jurisdictions **12.34**
with the UK provision of section 92, one notices the foundation of the
European criminal provisions rest primarily on the civil infringement law,
sometimes by virtue of express reference. Therefore the question of use as a
trade mark is discussed in the context of the civil law and, in this respect, the
ruling in *Arsenal* must be considered.[100] Thus a special discussion of trade
mark use is arguably unnecessary in a criminal law context as soon as civil
infringement has been established as a prerequisite of criminal liability. The
continental European examples provide a good argument for regarding the
actus reus of section 92 as essentially constituting civil infringement[101] (and
section 92 may contain additional *actus reus* elements beyond civil infringement). This *actus reus*, plus a *mens rea* in relation to all infringing acts, should
conjunctively lead to criminal liability, as was suggested above.

---

[96] As in Germany, §143 Markengesetz 1994.
[97] Compare Germany, §15 Criminal Code 1871; France, art 121–3 Penal Code.
[98] As is in Switzerland, art 61 Markenschutzgesetz 1992: 'wer *vorsätzlich* das Markenrecht
eines anderen verletzt . . .'.
[99] As for example in Austria: §7 of the Austrian Criminal Code 1975 provides that only
intentionally committed conduct is a criminal offence, unless a criminal statute expressly
provides otherwise (as is the case with offences involving recklessness). Thus if a criminal
provision is silent as to its *mens rea*, this denotes intention. The rule is similar in Germany: see
§15 of the German Criminal Code 1871.
[100] Apart from Switzerland which, as a non-EU country, is not bound by the ECJ.
[101] Thus civil infringement according to s 10 would be a necessary precondition for a
criminal liability under s 92.

F. Conclusion

12.35 *R v Johnstone* has attempted to define criminal liability under section 92, but, although this attempt was commendable, the method used is not fully convincing and sits uneasily with the ECJ's ruling in *Arsenal v Reed. Johnstone* upholds the principle of a separation of civil infringement law from unauthorized use under section 92, but effectively introduces elements of the civil law by interpreting section 92 as containing in its wording the civil law ingredient of 'use as a trade mark' as a prerequisite for criminal unauthorized use. However, this approach is not only rather inconsistent with the ruling in *Arsenal* but is arguably unnecessary, because it is not suggested by the wording of section 92. An improvement of the current situation should perhaps be based on a different concept. Civil infringement law should not come into criminal law with regard to only those elements which a court chooses to detect in section 92 on a fairly random basis. The criminal infringement of a registered trade mark should therefore not be regarded as independent from the civil law subject to uncertain exceptions, but always as civil infringement with additional aggravating factors specified principally in a clearly defined *mens rea* which encompasses all elements of the *actus reus* (ie the acts of civil infringement plus perhaps additional acts). The drafting of section 92 does not support the suggested interpretation, but it does not stand against it either. However, consistency between civil and criminal trade mark laws, and improvement of the quality of a severely sanctioned criminal law provision towards maximum certainty and predictability,[102] could be achieved in this way.

---

[102] Ashworth (n 13) 75.

Part F

DEATH OF A TRADE MARK

13

USE FOR THE PURPOSE OF RESISTING
AN APPLICATION FOR REVOCATION
FOR NON-USE

Belinda Isaac

A. What is Meant by 'Genuine Use'? 13.06   C. The Intentions of the Proprietor 13.24
B. What Level of 'Use' is Required? 13.14   D. Conclusion   13.29

It is a fundamental principle of trade mark law, and indeed it is expressly **13.01** stated in European law,[1] that registered trade marks must actually be used if the proprietor is to continue to benefit from the exclusive rights granted by virtue of registration.[2] In Europe, if a registered trade mark is not used, it will become liable to revocation unless legitimate reasons for the non-use exist. But what is meant by 'use' in this context and just how much *use* is required to withstand an action for revocation? The aim of this chapter is to address these two questions and, in seeking to answer them, to provide an insight into the approach adopted by the European Court of Justice (ECJ). This should enable us to identify the underlying principle governing the concept of 'use' in this context. The UK has implemented specific provisions relating

---

[1] Recital 8 of the First Council Directive 89/104/EEC of 21 December 1988 to approximate the laws of the Member States relating to Trade Marks (the Directive).

[2] It is also one of the bedrock principles of US trade mark law that trade mark ownership rights flow from actual use of the mark in the market. See *Allard Enterprises v Advanced Programming Resources* 146 F 3d 350 (6th Cir 1998). Under s 45 of the Lanham Act a mark will be deemed abandoned when its use has been discontinued with intent not to resume use. Intent not to resume may be inferred from the circumstances. Non-use for three consecutive years will be regarded as *prima facie* evidence of abandonment of the mark.

to revocation for non-use in the Trade Marks Act 1994[3] based on the Directive. However, in light of the comments of Jacob LJ (as he now is) expressed in *Goemar*[4] where he described that section as an 'unnecessary re-write of the Directive' I do not propose to dwell on the wording of the UK provision here. Instead I will focus on the Directive itself.

13.02 One of the reasons for the necessity to use a registered trade mark given by the Directive is

> to reduce the total number of trade marks registered and protected in the Community and, consequently, the number of conflicts which arise between them . . .[5]

A consequence of the sheer number of trade marks being registered within the Community[6] and the number of conflicts (oppositions) encountered[7] is that there is a strong public interest in the removal from the register of marks that are not being used.[8] Indeed, some would argue[9] that there are only a finite number of useful or valuable marks and that revocation therefore helps to ensure that unused marks are recycled. If such unused marks were not removed, the register would become clogged and the number of conflicts would soon make the system unworkable. Revocation therefore restricts the protection conferred by registration to the proprietor's legitimate and actual trade requirements, avoiding the inconvenience, cost and interference with trade that would result from allowing trade marks to be registered by traders who have no intention of using them, but only wish to prevent other traders from using them.[10]

---

[3] s 46(1).

[4] *La Mer Technology Inc v Laboratoires Goemar* [2002] ETMR 34.

[5] Recital 8 of the Directive.

[6] As at 31 December 2003 there were more than 217,000 registered Community trade marks; applications for a further 57,000 were filed in 2003. See www.oami.eu.int statistics.

[7] During 2003 nearly 10,000 oppositions were filed. See www.oami.eu.int statistics.

[8] Jacob J described unused trade marks in *La Mer Technology Inc v Laboratoires Goemar* [2002] ETMR 34 as 'abandoned vessels in the shipping lanes of trade', para 19(a).

[9] S Carter 'The Trouble with Trademarks' [1989–90] 99 Yale Law Journal 759.

[10] *Imperial Group v Philip Morris* (NERIT) [1982] FSR 72 CA is the classic example in the UK of a situation involving the registration of a mark that the proprietor had no real intention to use. The registration was for the word NERIT in Class 34 for tobacco products. The mark was registered by Imperial primarily to stop Philip Morris from introducing a brand of cigarettes called MERIT although Imperial did produce about a million NERIT cigarettes. Albeit rare, such attempts at pre-emption between rival businesses do sometimes occur. It is, however, more common for brand development teams to 'reserve' names for products in

The use requirements of the Directive are set out in Articles 10 and 12. The **13.03**
former states that:

> If, within a period of five years following the date of completion of the registra-
> tion procedure, the proprietor has not put the trade mark to genuine use in the
> Member State in connection with the goods or services in respect of which it is
> registered, or if such use has been suspended during an uninterrupted period of
> five years, the trade mark shall be subject to the sanctions provided for in this
> Directive unless there are proper reasons for non-use.

Article 12 goes on to say that: **13.04**

> A trade mark shall be liable to revocation if, within a continuous period of five
> years, it has not been put to genuine use in the Member State in connection
> with the goods or services in respect of which it is registered, and there are no
> proper reasons for non-use . . .

A trade mark owner therefore has five years from the granting of its registra- **13.05**
tion to put the trade mark to 'genuine use' before he needs to be concerned
about the threat of revocation. A mark will also not be revoked for non-use if,
after the expiry of the five year period and before the filing of the application
for revocation,[11] the proprietor puts the mark to genuine use. However, what
is meant by *genuine* use, and over what period of time does it need to be
demonstrated? Will use in advertising or promotional activity alone suffice or
does the proprietor have to go further than this and demonstrate actual sales
in the Community? If so, what level of sales is required? Will a single transaction suffice or must there be a series of transactions? Does an intention to use
the mark on a commercial scale have any impact on the assessment of the
genuineness of the use?

---

development by means of registration. For various reasons those products may be abandoned
during the development process by the owner, but the owner nonetheless maintains the
registration as part of a name bank from which it can select future names for new products.
While there might have been an original bona fide intention to use the mark when the
application was originally filed the continued maintenance of the trade mark can act as a
barrier to other traders.

[11] But any such use after the expiry of the five-year period but within the three months
immediately preceding the filing of the application for revocation will be discounted unless the
proprietor can show that preparations for the commencement or resumption of use began
before the proprietor became aware of the application for revocation: art 12(1) of the Directive.

A. What is Meant by 'Genuine Use'?

13.06 At the time of writing, there have been three significant decisions on the question of 'genuine use': one from the Court of First Instance (CFI)[12] in the context of opposition proceedings, and two later decisions of the ECJ[13] on the interpretation of Article 12.

13.07 *Ansul* was the first opportunity that the ECJ had to consider the issue of genuine use. The case was referred by the Benelux Court (Hoge Raad der Nederlanden) and concerned the use of the mark MINIMAX for various goods including fire extinguishers, extinguishing substances and services relating to the installation, repair and maintenance of fire extinguishers. The lower Benelux court, the Regional Court of Appeal The Hague, had found that during a period of five years Ansul had not been putting the MINIMAX mark to 'normal use'[14] and that it had not been releasing new products on to the market under the mark. Instead, it had merely maintained, checked and repaired used equipment. The Regional Court of Appeal had held that use of stickers and strips bearing the mark was not distinctive of the origin of the fire extinguishers and could not be regarded as 'normal use' because the object of the use was not to create or preserve an outlet for the goods.[15] Ansul appealed to the Hoge Raad, which referred several questions on the matter to the ECJ.

13.08 The ECJ was first asked to consider how the concept of genuine use within the meaning of Article 12(1) of the Directive should be interpreted and whether it might be defined using the same criteria as 'normal use', a term recognized under Benelux law. The Court took the view that the meaning of

---

[12] *Kabushiki Kaisha Fernandes v OHIM* Case T-39–01 [2003] ETMR 98 (*HIWATT*). Although the context of the *HIWATT* decision is slightly different, the Court made some interesting observations that are also relevant to art 12 which are discussed in further detail below.

[13] *Ansul BV v Ajax Brandbeveiling BV* Case C-40/01 [2003] ECR I-2439; [2003] ETMR 85 (*Ansul*) and *La Mer Technology Inc v Laboratoires Goemar* [2004] ETMR 640 (*Goemar*).

[14] The equivalent term in the Dutch translation of the Directive and the word used in the Uniform Benelux Law implementing the Directive. Prior to the implementation of the Directive in the Benelux the existing legislation—the Uniform Benelux Law which entered into force in 1971—also contained provisions relating to the revocation of the mark if there had been no 'normal use' of the mark for a period.

[15] This concept is discussed further below.

'genuine use' should be given an autonomous and consistent interpretation throughout the Community so that the level of protection that trade marks enjoyed would not vary according to jurisdiction. The Court also noted that the term 'genuine use' appeared in the Regulation relating to the Community trade mark[16] and that it was therefore incumbent on the Court to give the phrase a uniform interpretation as between the Directive and the Regulation. Thus, it was inappropriate to determine its meaning by reference to the Benelux concept of 'normal use'.

In determining what was meant by 'genuine use', the Court made reference **13.09** to the various official translations of the recital and the revocation provisions in the Directive in the Member States[17] and concluded that genuine use meant actual use of the mark. The Court specifically stated that token use, that is use that is intended merely to maintain the rights conferred by registration, would not constitute genuine use. Of itself this statement is not especially helpful since it provides no guidance as to what is meant by 'token use'. Fortunately, the Court did not leave the matter there but went on to hold that the use of the mark must be consistent with the essential function of a trade mark which is to guarantee the identity of the origin of the goods or services for which the mark is registered to the consumer so that the consumer can distinguish, without the possibility of confusion, the products or services of one trade from those of another. The commercial *raison d'être* of the mark therefore is to create or preserve an outlet for those goods or services that bear the mark as distinct from those of other undertakings. It follows therefore that 'genuine use' must involve actual use of the mark on the market for the products or services in question and not just internal use within the organization. The use must therefore relate to products or services already marketed or about to be marketed and for which preparations by the undertaking to secure customers are under way, for example by advertising. Whether this requirement has been satisfied is a question of fact in each case

---

[16] arts 15 and 50 of Council Regulation (EC) no 40/94 of 20 December 1993 (the Regulation).

[17] Dutch ('normaal'), Spanish ('uso efectivo'), Italian ('uso effettivo'), English ('genuine use'). In *La Mer Technology Inc v Laboratoires Goemar* [2002] ETMR 34 Jacob J extended the list of translations to include French ('sérieux'), German ('ernsthaft'), Portuguese ('serio'), Danish ('reel') and Swedish ('verkligt'). The point here is that there is no exact correspondence between the terminologies employed by different texts of the Directive and that many of the versions suggest that the use must be 'serious' and that use that is very slight will be insufficient.

which requires an assessment of all the circumstances in order to determine whether the commercial exploitation of the mark is real. The assessment may include consideration of:

- the nature of the goods or services at issue
- the scale and frequency of the use
- the characteristics of the market concerned
- an assessment of whether the use is warranted in the economic sector concerned in order to create or maintain market share.

13.10 The ECJ conceded that the proprietor did not need to use the mark in relation to new goods if the mark had been used in the past and was now used only for component parts of or accessories for those goods, provided that the parts were integral to the make-up or structure of the goods. This should equally be the case if the proprietor of the mark makes actual use of the mark under the same conditions for products or services which, although not integral to the make-up or structure of the goods previously sold, are directly related to those goods and intended to meet the needs of customers of those goods (for example the provision of after-sales services such as repair and maintenance services, or the sale of accessories or related parts). How broadly these provisions will be interpreted remains to be seen, but on the face of it use of a mark for razors on razor blades alone should be sufficient to maintain the registration for razors and the use of a mark for lawnmowers in connection with the servicing of them or the supply of accessories for them should be sufficient to constitute genuine use of the mark for lawnmowers even if the lawnmowers are no longer sold.

13.11 The principle underlying this decision appears to be the Court's responsibility to remove marks from the register that have not actually been used for a period of five years since registration. This responsibility is derived from Recital 8 of the Directive which states that, in order to reduce the total number of trade marks registered and protected within the Community, it is essential to require that

> registered trade marks must actually be used or, if not used, be subject to revocation. . . .

13.12 Provided that the use in question cannot be said to have been undertaken solely for the purposes of defeating an action for revocation, it appears that any legitimate use of the mark on or in relation to the goods or services for which the mark is registered, for the purposes of indicating the origin of those goods, will amount to 'genuine use'. Or, as the ECJ put it

> 'Genuine use' must be understood to denote use that is not merely token, serving solely to preserve the rights conferred by the mark.[18]

This suggests that the phrase might be better understood (by English lawyers, **13.13** at least) as meaning bona fide use. This was the expression used in section 26 of the Trade Marks Act 1938 (which provided the basis for actions for revocation prior to the implementation of the Directive in the UK). Under that section, so long as a proprietor could demonstrate a genuine intention to establish a market in the goods under the mark concerned the extent of the use was only one of the factors to be considered.[19] Limited use of the mark only to maintain a registration was not considered bona fide.[20]

B. What Level of 'Use' is Required?

The second case, *Goemar*, followed six months later[21] and was a reference **13.14** from the English High Court. The case involved an appeal from a decision of the Trade Marks Registry to revoke two registrations for the mark LABORATOIRE DE LA MER covering 'perfumes and cosmetics containing marine products' (Class 3) and 'pharmaceutical, veterinary and sanitary products, dietetic products for medical use; all containing marine products' (Class 5). The appeal came before Jacob J (as he then was) and was heard by him before the ECJ's decision in *Ansul* had been handed down. As with *Ansul*, the case turned on the meaning of 'genuine use' and, in particular, whether there was any *de minimis* threshold to such use. In *Goemar* the registered proprietor, a French company, was able to demonstrate some use of the mark in the UK but the scale of the use during the relevant period was very small indeed (£600 in relation to the sale of goods in Class 5 (although this was disputed), and £800 in relation to goods in Class 3). Approximately £6000 of goods of all kinds (including those that fell outside Classes 3 and 5) had been sold within the relevant period although the sales were not shown to have been made under the mark in question.

---

[18] *Ansul* (n 13) para 36.
[19] BON MATIN *Trade Mark* [1989] RPC 537.
[20] NERIT (n 10).
[21] *Goemar* (n 13).

13.15 Although Jacob J felt that the question justified a reference to the ECJ, he nonetheless gave his own provisional views on the questions of what amounts to genuine use and whether a minimum level of use would be required to maintain the registration. Jacob J recounted the history of the revocation for non-use section of the previous UK Trade Marks Act[22] and the attempts to circumvent the requirement for bona fide use by large organizations that either registered 'ghost marks'[23] or embarked on 'trade mark protection programmes'.[24] The purpose of the latter, he said, was not to create a profitable brand but rather to establish bona fide use of the mark. Both activities had, however, been discredited by the Court of Appeal[25] which, having considered the intentions of the registered proprietor, held that the use was not bona fide.

13.16 Under the 1938 Act there was no *de minimis* rule. If the use was only slight it might raise a question as to whether the trader was genuine in his activities but all the circumstances had to be taken into account, including the scale of the use, the size of the organization, how it and similar entities usually went about marketing and so on. Provided that the use was genuine, and had not taken place merely to stop the mark from being revoked for non-use, it would be sufficient. Thus, a small amount of use coupled with a genuine intention to establish a market in the goods under the mark has in the past been held to be sufficient.[26] The Court then considered the wording of the Directive (which effectively replaced the 1938 Act in the UK) and in particular the different translations of the word 'genuine' used in other language versions of the Directive. Jacob J noted that the wording used in some languages might mean that the use must be more than very slight while others suggested that the use must be more than insubstantial. In his view there were real problems in trying to formulate a *de minimis* rule. Should it depend on the size of the organization—what might be slight for a large organization may not be for a

---

[22] Trade Marks Act 1938 s 26 (the 1938 Act).

[23] Where a mark could not be registered eg MERIT, a different, but similar word (eg NERIT) would be registered and relied upon to provide protection.

[24] To protect a mark from a non-use attack, the proprietor would arrange for the mark concerned to be specially applied to a product normally sold under some other mark. Minor sales of the specially marked goods were made. There would be no real advertising or marketing. The idea was that any sales would be sufficient to protect the mark from attack. *NERIT* (n 10) is an example of such a practice.

[25] *NERIT* (n 10).

[26] *BON MATIN* (n 19).

small organization. Does it matter whether the owner is relying on use by importation rather than local sale? Does it make a difference if the use is at the beginning, middle or end of the relevant period? All these factors, he said, made the idea of a minimum level of use an unattractive proposition. In his view,

> provided there is nothing artificial about a transaction under the mark then it will amount to genuine use.[27]

Jacob J's views are in contrast to the findings of the CFI a year later in the **13.17** *HIWATT* case, where it held that genuine use meant that the mark must be present in a substantial part of the territory[28] and should exclude minimal or insufficient use. However, the Court did not go as far as indicating what would be regarded as minimal.

HIWATT concerned the use of a trade mark relied upon as an earlier right in **13.18** opposition proceedings. The mark HIWATT was registered in Germany in the name of a Japanese company in connection with goods in Class 9 including amplifiers, among other things. Having filed its opposition, the Japanese company was requested by the applicant for a later Community trade mark (against whom HIWATT had filed the opposition) to prove genuine use of its HIWATT mark.[29] By way of evidence of use the Japanese company filed a number of documents including an extract from a catalogue showing a HIWATT amplifier and mentioning an address in Japan; various excerpts from the programme for the 1999 and 2000 trade shows in Frankfurt and some pages from an official catalogue of a trade fair naming Hiwatt Amplification International as an exhibitor at the fair; a Hiwatt catalogue in English from 1997 showing HIWATT amplifiers and mentioning an address in the USA.

The Office for Harmonisation for the Internal Market (OHIM) Opposition **13.19** Division rejected the opposition on the basis that the Japanese company had not proved genuine use of the mark. The Japanese company appealed first to the Board of Appeal of OHIM and then to the CFI. The CFI was of the view that genuine use implied real use for the purpose of trading in the

---

[27] *La Mer Technology Inc v Laboratoires Goemar* [2002] ETMR 34 at para 29.

[28] *HIWATT* (n 12); in this case the mark relied upon for the purposes of the opposition was an earlier German registration. Accordingly, references to use of the mark in the territory are to use of the mark in Germany.

[29] In accordance with art 43(2) and (3) of the Regulation and Rule 22(1) of Regulation no 2868/95.

goods. Genuine use should, it said, exclude minimal or insufficient use; the mark should, be

> objectively present on the market in a manner that is effective, consistent over time and stable in terms of configuration of the sign[30]

so that a consumer who acquires the goods is able to repeat the experience, if it proves to be positive, or avoid them if it proves to be negative. The Court went on to hold that genuine use meant that the mark must be present in a substantial part of the territory in which it is protected. The Court did not elaborate on what it meant by 'present', presumably it means visible either by advertisement or some other form of promotion or by means of the actual sale of the product or service. The CFI reviewed the evidence relied on in support of the opposition and found that it not only lacked the detail required by Rule 22 (in that it did not specify the place, time, extent and nature of the use) but it also left the reader to make assumptions or suppositions about the use. The CFI held that:

> genuine use must be demonstrated by solid and objective evidence of effective and sufficient use of the trade mark on the market concerned[31]

It cannot be based on probabilities or suppositions.

13.20 Use of a company name would not, of itself, constitute genuine use of the trade mark because the trade mark must be used in connection with the provision of goods or services and such use cannot be assumed from the use of a company name.

13.21 It is not clear from the judgment in *HIWATT* what the source of the authority for the interpretation of the term 'genuine use' was. It appears as if the Court itself initiated the proposition without reference to any specific authority other than the general principle concerning the essential function of a trade mark.

13.22 In January 2004 the ECJ handed down its decision in *Goemar* and in so doing clarified the position regarding the threshold for genuine use. It held that:

> it is not possible to determine *a priori*, and in the abstract, what quantitative threshold should be chosen in order to determine whether use is genuine or

---

[30] *HIWATT* (n 12) para 36.
[31] ibid para 47.

not. A *de minimis* rule, which would not allow the national court to appraise all the circumstances of the dipute before it, cannot therefore be laid down.[32]

The Court reiterated the comments made in *Ansul* that the use of the mark had to be consistent with the essential function of a trade mark as an indication of origin and that the use should not be token use. It accepted that in some cases this might mean that use that was not quantitatively significant might still be regarded as genuine.

> Even minimal use can . . . be sufficient to qualify as genuine, on condition that it is deemed to be justified, in the economic sector concerned for the purpose of preserving or creating market share for the goods or services protected under the mark . . .[33]

Whether the use is sufficient to preserve or create market share will depend **13.23** not only on the factors identified in *Ansul*—the characteristics of the products/services in question, the frequency or regularity of the use of the mark, whether the mark is used for marketing all the identical products/services of the proprietor or merely some of them—but also on the characteristics of the market for the goods or services in question.

> When it serves a real commercial purpose even minimal use by only a single importer in the Member State concerned can be sufficient to establish genuine use within the meaning of the Directive.[34]

C. The Intentions of the Proprietor

As a result of *Goemar*, we can say that whether use of a trade mark can be **13.24** regarded as genuine is a question of fact in each case requiring consideration of all the circumstances by the national court. There is no standard quantitative threshold. However, the use must be to indicate the trade origin of goods and must not be token use for the purposes of merely maintaining a registration or defeating an application for revocation. The assessment of the surrounding circumstances requires not only an assessment of all the external circumstances but also, I would suggest, a subjective test involving an assessment of the proprietors intentions *vis-à-vis* the use made of the mark and the

[32] *Goemar* (n 13) para 25.
[33] ibid para 21.
[34] ibid para 27.

future of the mark. Although there may be evidential difficulties in establishing the intentions of the proprietor subsequent to the events under examination, and a danger that once the mark is attacked the proprietor might alter its position, some form of subjective analysis is required in order to determine whether the use is 'merely to maintain a registration'. This pushes the European approach to 'use' closer to the US position regarding abandonment, despite the fact that in Europe proof of intent not to resume use is not required. In the USA, the Lanham Act provides[35] that a mark shall be deemed abandoned

> when its use has been discontinued with intent not to resume such use. Intent not to resume may be inferred from circumstances. Non-use for 3 consecutive years shall be prima facie abandonment. 'Use' of a mark means the bona fide use of such a mark in the ordinary course of trade, and not merely to reserve a right in a trade mark.[36]

13.25 Loss of trade mark rights through abandonment therefore requires proof of non-use as well as proof of an intention not to resume use of the mark.[37] To the extent that there is any bona fide use of the mark at all, it may be relied upon to support an argument that there is an intention to resume use of the mark[38] although an intention to use by itself may not suffice to maintain the registration.[39]

13.26 As regards the importance of the registered proprietor's intentions in Europe, the Court in *Goemar* held that

> While the Directive makes the classification of the use of the trade mark as genuine use consequential only on consideration of the circumstances which pertain in respect of the relevant period and which predate the filing of the application for revocation, it does not preclude, in assessing the genuineness of use during the relevant period, account being taken, where appropriate, of any circumstances subsequent to that filing. It is for the national court to determine whether such circumstances confirm that the use of the mark during the relevant period was genuine or whether, conversely, they reflect an intention on the part of the proprietor to defeat that claim.

---

[35] §45.

[36] 15 USC §1127.

[37] CT Micheletti 'Preventing Loss of Trademark Rights: Quantitative and Qualitative Assessments of "Use" and Their Impact on Abandonment Determinations' [2004] 94 TMR 634 at 636.

[38] ibid 683.

[39] ibid.

The relevance of the proprietor's intentions therefore appears to be limited to informing the court's assessment of whether the use of the mark relied upon was genuine. The determination of whether or not the use of the mark during the relevant period was genuine may therefore be affected by the actions of the proprietor even after the revocation action has been filed if these give any insight into the proprietor's intentions in using his mark.

The underlying principle that the ECJ seems to be applying (both in *Goemar* **13.27** and *Ansul*) is whether there has been any use of the mark that is not token use. Provided that there is some use during the relevant period, albeit limited,[40] provided the actions of the proprietor were sincere, were consistent with the manner that those types of goods/services are ordinarily marketed, and were not token, the court would regard the use as genuine. As Jacob J put it in *Goemar*,

> provided there is nothing artificial about a transaction under the mark then it will amount to 'genuine use'.[41]

That said, in the absence of any use, unless there are proper reasons for non-use, a mere intention to resume use is unlikely to save a registration in Europe from revocation[42] although the ECJ has not yet commented on this issue.[43]

In *Ashwood Grove*[44] the hearing officer noted that: **13.28**

> the primary requirement on a proprietor whose registration has been challenged in revocation proceedings is to show actual use of his mark. There is nothing to indicate that a firm intention to use can save a registration. Nevertheless the ECJ's observations in *Ansul* suggest that something short of actual sales may in certain circumstances be enough. . . . It seems to me what the ECJ had in mind are circumstances where the relevant public has . . . been alerted to

---

[40] Perhaps on price lists and promotional material while the proprietor genuinely seeks a distributor, licensee or business partner who will actively market the product/services.

[41] *La Mer Technology Inc v Laboratoires Goemar* [2002] ETMR 34 para 29.

[42] In *Re Invermont Trade Mark* [1997] RPC 125 (*Invermont*) which preceded *Goemar*, a registration was revoked in the absence of use despite a stated intent to commence use in part because no corroborative detail as to the plans for commencing use were provided.

[43] In the UK a trader that commences or resumes use of the mark, or has taken real steps towards resuming use after the expiry of the five-year period but before becoming aware of the application for revocation (or the threat to file such an application), may still be able to defeat the application in the absence of actual sales by relying upon s 46(3) Trade Marks Act 1994. There is not, however, a corresponding provision in the Directive.

[44] *Re Ashwood Grove Trade Mark* O–015–04 14 January 2004 (*Ashwood*) a decision by the UK Trade Marks Registry para 30.

the actual or imminent availability of a product and where the proprietor's plans are sufficiently far advanced that they are able to promote such availability.

In *Ashwood*, the proprietor had a genuine intention to establish a brand but its plans had not developed beyond the initial inquiry stage. Although letters had been sent to possible distributors offering the product there was no evidence to suggest that matters had progressed further or that any discussion had taken place. This and the importation of a small number of bottles to be displayed at a Wine Fair (the evidence for which was said to be 'unconvincing and unsubstantiated'[45]) fell short of genuine use.

D. Conclusion

13.29 Much will no doubt depend on whether the national court has any general discretion to allow a mark to remain on the register even in the absence of either genuine use or proper reasons for non-use[46] or whether the discretion extends only as far as evaluating the reasons given for non-use.[47] If national courts have a general discretion, then even if there are no actual sales and the reasons given for non-use are unacceptable (because they are considered too vague) the court would have the power to prevent revocation. If, however, the scope of the courts' discretion is limited to the assessment of the authenticity of the use (ie whether it is genuine) then in the same scenario the court would have no alternative but to revoke the registration.

13.30 The Directive, the Regulation, the CFI and the ECJ all stress that what will not be acceptable for the purposes of defeating an action for revocation is token use, ie use of the mark for the sole purpose of maintaining a registration without a desire to create or maintain a share in the market for the goods or services concerned. The focus of future revocation proceedings is therefore likely to be on proving to the court that the use made by the proprietor of the mark during the period in question should not be regarded as token use. In

---

[45] ibid para 27.

[46] In *Invermont* (n 42) the hearing officer found that the Registrar had a discretion; however, in *Re zippo Trade Mark* [1999] RPC 173 a different hearing officer held that the Registrar had no discretion.

[47] This is the extent of the discretion suggested by A Michaels in *A Practical Guide to Trade Mark Law* (2nd edn Sweet & Maxwell London 1996) 61–62.

this context those responsible for advising trade mark owners and drafting evidence should heed the comments of Jacob J:

> Those concerned with proof of use should read their proposed evidence with a critical eye—to ensure that use is actually proved—and for the goods or services of the mark in question. All the t's should be crossed and the i's dotted.[48]

Postscript

On 21 December 2004, Blackburne J handed down the final decision of the High Court in the *Goemar* case following its referral to the ECJ. Contrary to the view expressed by the Court prior to the referral, Blackburne J[49] held that in the light of the ECJ's decision the very limited use of the mark by the proprietor was insufficient to amount to *genuine use*. This was because the goods concerned were not put on the market, in the sense that the goods did not come to the attention of the end user, but rather because they were sold to a distributor who failed actively to market them and thus start to create a market share. Although the Court accepted that the use had not been a sham (in the sense of purely being undertaken to defeat a revocation action), that use had not gone far enough to maintain or create an outlet for the goods themselves as required by the ECJ in *Ansul*. While Blackburne J accepted that the activities of the proprietor of the mark subsequent to the filing of the revocation action could be taken into account, he said that this was only in circumstances where there was a question as to whether the use was a sham, as opposed to whether a market for the goods had been established. This decision underlines the need for proprietors of marks to show that goods or services bearing a trade mark have come to the attention of end users during the relevant period, either through actual sales or an advertising campaign for goods or services about to be marketed. Anything short of this is unlikely to be regarded as genuine.

---

[48] *Goemar* (n 13) para 9.
[49] This case was originally heard by Jacob J but, following his appointment to the Court of Appeal, was passed to Blackburne J.

14

THE REQUIREMENT FOR EVIDENCE OF USE OF EARLIER TRADE MARKS IN OPPOSITION AND INVALIDATION PROCEEDINGS

Allan James

A. The Purpose of the Provisions	14.01	J. The Applicant or Proprietor of the National Trade Mark does not have to Make a Request	14.48
B. The Community Trade Mark Regulation	14.09		
C. The Timing and Nature of the Request for the Earlier Conflicting Mark to be Shown to have been put to Genuine Use	14.12	K. The Preliminary Indication in Opposition Proceedings	14.52
		L. The Time for an Opponent to File Supporting Evidence	14.54
D. What Form must the Evidence Take at OHIM?	14.16	M. The Time for an Applicant for Invalidation to File Supporting Evidence	14.56
E. When must the Evidence of Use be Filed at OHIM?	14.23	N. What Form must the Evidence Take?	14.57
F. The Period within which Genuine Use must be Shown	14.27	O. What must be Shown	14.61
		P. The Period within which Genuine Use must be Shown	14.64
G. The Territorial Extent of the Use	14.30		
H. What must be Shown	14.38	Q. The Notional Specification	14.69
I. The UK Trade Marks Act 1994	14.45	R. Conclusion	14.74

A. The Purpose of the Provisions

The growth in the number of registered trade marks and the introduction of **14.01** supra-national systems of registration, such as the Community trade mark, have the potential to increase the number of conflicts between proprietors of similar trade marks and thus the prospect of any particular trade mark encountering a third party opposition or invalidation action.

14.02 The potential for conflicts between trade marks proprietors is further increased by the practice whereby trade marks are registered in respect of descriptions of goods and services which are rather wider than the actual trade conducted (or sometimes even envisaged) under the marks.

14.03 Recognition of this problem within the European Union can be found in the Trade Mark Directive approximating the trade mark law of Member States (Council Directive 89/104) and in the Community Trade Mark Regulation, establishing the Community trade mark (Council Regulation 40/94).

14.04 The eighth recital to the Directive states that:

> Whereas in order to reduce the total number of trade marks registered and protected in the Community and, consequently, the number of conflicts which arise between them, it is essential to require that registered trade marks must actually be used or, if not used, be subject to revocation: whereas it is necessary to provide that a trade mark cannot be invalidated on the basis of existence of a non-used earlier trade mark, while the Member States remain free to apply the same principle in respect of the registration of a trade mark or to provide that a trade mark may not be successfully invoked in infringement proceedings if it is established as a result of a plea that the trade mark could be revoked; whereas in all these cases it is up to the Member States to establish the applicable rules of procedure;

Thus Article 11(1) of the Directive states that a trade mark may not be declared invalid on the grounds that there is an earlier conflicting trade mark if the latter does not fulfil the use requirements set out in Article 10 of the Directive. Article 11(2) gives Member States the option of introducing analogous provisions in pre-registration procedures, such as opposition.

14.05 This mixture of mandatory and optional provisions covering closely analogous types of proceedings may appear at first sight to be inconsistent, but it is probably explained by the fact that invalidation of a registered trade mark on the basis of an unused conflicting earlier trade mark could have the effect of unjustly extinguishing a potentially valuable existing object of property, whereas in pre-registration procedures the worst case scenario is the unjust refusal of only a prospective object of property. Further, not all the Member States provide for objections to registration on relative grounds to be made prior to registration. It would thus have been difficult to make Article 11(2) mandatory without also requiring the harmonization of the procedures for raising relative grounds objections, which are expressly left to the Member States to determine.[1]

A number of the Member States, including Germany and Denmark, intro- **14.06** duced provisions requiring the proprietor of earlier trade marks relied upon in opposition proceedings to demonstrate that the earlier trade mark is not susceptible to revocation for non-use.

The Community Trade Mark Regulation (CTMR) takes a more uniform **14.07** approach to the matter. The ninth recital boldly states that:

> there is no justification for protecting Community trade marks, or as against them, any trade mark which has been registered before them, except where the trade marks are actually used;

The Regulation therefore contains provisions analogous with those described above, which are exercisable in respect of applications to invalidate and oppose a Community trade mark.

It is not difficult to understand why the use requirement was introduced into **14.08** opposition proceedings in the Community trade mark system. The unitary nature of the Community trade mark requires that it be free from objection on relative grounds on the basis of earlier conflicting trade marks in any Member State.[2] Without restrictions on the reliance which may be placed on unused trade marks, the vast potential for oppositions may have made the Community trade mark system unworkable.

B. The Community Trade Mark Regulation

Articles 43 and 56 of the CTMR set out the provisions governing the exam- **14.09** ination of oppositions to, and applications for invalidation of, Community trade marks. The relevant parts of Articles 43 and 56 are set out below:

> 43(2) If the applicant so requests, the proprietor of an earlier Community trade mark who has given notice of opposition shall furnish proof that, during the

---

[1] See the fifth recital to Directive 89/104.
[2] Subject to certain transitional provisions covering the Member States which joined the Community on 1 May 2004.

period of five years preceding the date of publication of the Community trade mark application, the Community earlier trade mark has been put to genuine use in the Community in connection with the goods or services in respect of which it is registered and which he cites as justification for his opposition, or that there are proper reasons, for non-use, provided the earlier Community trade mark has at that date been registered for not less than five years. In the absence of proof to this effect, the opposition shall be rejected. If the earlier Community trade mark has been used in relation to part only of the goods or services for which it is registered it shall, for the purposes of the examination of the opposition, be deemed to be registered in respect only of that part of the goods or services.

43(3) Paragraph 2 shall apply to earlier national trademarks referred to in Article 8(2)(a), by substituting use in the Member State in which the earlier national trade mark is protected for use in the community.

56(2) If the proprietor of the Community trade mark so requests, the proprietor of an earlier Community trade mark, being a party to the invalidity proceedings, shall furnish proof that, during the period of five years preceding the date of the application for declaration of invalidity, the earlier Community trade mark has been put to genuine use in the Community in connection with the goods or services in respect of which it is registered and which he cites as justification for his application, or that there are proper reasons for non-use, provided the earlier Community trade mark has at that date been registered for non-use, provided the earlier Community trade mark has at that date been registered for not less than five years. If, at the date on which the Community trade mark application was published, the earlier Community trade mark has been registered for not less than five years, the proprietor of the earlier Community trade mark shall furnish proof that, in addition, the conditions contained in Article 43(2) were satisfied at that date. In the absence of proof to this effect the application for a declaration of invalidity shall be rejected. If the earlier Community trade mark has been used in relation to part only of the goods or services for which it is registered it shall, for the purpose of the examination of the application for a declaration of invalidity, be deemed to be registered in respect only of that part of the goods or services.

56(3) Paragraph 2 shall apply to earlier national trade marks referred to in Article 8(2)(a), by substituting use in Member State in which the earlier national trade mark is protected for use in the community.

14.10 The consequence of failing to provide proof of genuine use of the earlier mark, or of proper reasons for non-use, is that the opposition, or application for invalidation, must be rejected in so far as it is based upon the trade mark in question. If the earlier trade mark is shown to have been put to genuine use in respect of some of the goods and services for which it is registered, but not for others, the earlier trade mark shall, for the purposes of the proceedings, be deemed to have been registered only for the goods or services for which it has been used.

It is not therefore surprising that requests that opponents and applicants for **14.11** invalidation show genuine use of any five-year-old-or-more trade marks relied on in the proceedings have become a regular feature of proceedings before the Office for Harmonisation in the Internal Market (OHIM).

C. The Timing and Nature of the Request for the Earlier Conflicting Mark to be Shown to have been put to Genuine Use

Neither the CTMR nor the Implementing Regulation expressly deal with the **14.12** period in which the applicant for, or proprietor of, a Community trade mark should make the request for the other party to submit proof of genuine use of the earlier conflicting trade mark, nor do they stipulate the form such a request should take.

Once OHIM has accepted the opposition or application for invalidation it is **14.13** required to communicate the opposition or application for invalidation to the applicant for, or proprietor of, the Community trade mark, and to invite him to make observations.[3] The request for the other party to provide genuine use of the earlier trade mark will normally be contained in these initial observations.

The Opposition Division at OHIM appears to have initially taken the view **14.14** that, in the absence of a formal request from the applicant under Article 43, it was obliged to assume that the earlier trade mark was entitled to protection in respect of all the goods or services for which it is registered. Thus in *Laboratorios Menarini SA v Takeda Chemical Industries Ltd*[4] the Opposition Division declined to take into account the applicant's assertions that the earlier mark had only been used in respect of a single product because no formal request under Article 43(3) had been made. On appeal, the OHIM Board of Appeal held that the opponent's failure to deny the applicant's assertions should have been taken as an admission that the earlier trade mark had only been used for

---

[3] By Regulation 2868/95 rr 19(1) and 40(1).
[4] [2002] ECR II-2879, [2002] 3 CMLR 8, [2002] ETMR 93.

that one product, and the likelihood of confusion assessed on that basis. This resulted in the rejection of the opposition.

14.15 Where the applicant for, or proprietor of, a Community trade mark is uncertain whether the earlier trade mark has been used, or has reason to believe that it has not been used, or not used for all the material goods or services, the best course of action would appear to be to invoke Article 43(2) or (3) or Article 56(2) or (3) in the observations sent to OHIM in response to the notice of opposition or application for invalidation. Additionally, where it is known that the earlier mark has only been used for particular goods or services, he should state this in the observations, which may save time if the statement is admitted.

D. What Form must the Evidence Take at OHIM?

14.16 Paragraphs 2 and 3 of Rule 22 of Commission Regulation 2868/95 (the Implementing Regulation), which are set out below, indicate what is required to be sent to OHIM as evidence of genuine use.

Rule 22(2)

> The indications and evidence for the furnishing of proof of use shall consist of indications concerning the place, time, extent and nature of use of the opposing trade mark for the goods and services in respect of which it is registered and on which the opposition is based, and evidence in support of these indications in accordance with paragraph 3

and by Rule 22(3)

> The evidence shall, in principle, be confined to the submission of supporting documents and items such as packages, labels, price lists, catalogues, invoices, photographs, newspaper advertisements, and statements in writing as referred to in Article 76(1)(f) of the Regulation.

The 'statements' referred to in Article 76(1)(f) of the CTMR are 'statements in writing sworn or affirmed or having a similar effect under the law of the State in which they were drawn up'. Although this Rule ostensibly applies only to opposition proceedings, it in fact applies also to invalidation proceedings.[5]

---

[5] By virtue of Regulation 2868/95 r 40(5).

The Rule leaves the party required to file evidence of genuine use to select the **14.17** form in which the evidence is filed. In particular, there does not appear to be a requirement to submit an affidavit or similar sworn evidence to support other documents showing sales made under the trade mark.[6]

The Opposition Division at OHIM appears to take the position that an **14.18** affidavit or declaration in lieu of an oath attesting to use of a trade mark, which is provided by a person who is not independent of the party required to submit evidence of use, is not sufficient, without further supporting evidence, to establish genuine use.[7]

On the other hand it has been held that copies of ten invoices supported by **14.19** undated labels were sufficient evidence of use to satisfy the requirement,[8] although the court noted that it would have been preferable to have had more evidence relating to the nature of the use during the relevant period.

The best course is to submit documents and items sufficient to *show* genuine **14.20** use of the trade mark, at least some of which should date the use within the relevant period, and to support these documents and items with a written statement providing a fuller picture of the place, time, extent and nature of use of the trade mark in question.

It has been held that,[9] where an opponent of a Community trade mark **14.21** application has already had to prove use of an earlier trade mark in earlier proceedings, he may refer to documents already filed with OHIM in those proceedings where he is called upon to provide evidence of use of the same trade mark on a subsequent occasion.

Where the evidence is supplied in a language which is not a language of the **14.22** proceedings, OHIM may require that a translation of the evidence be filed in one of the languages of the proceedings.[10]

---

[6] See para 37 of the judgment of the CFI in *Sunrider Corp v OHIM* Case T-203/02 8 July 2004.

[7] See, for example, decision no 601/2000 of the Opposition Division of OHIM.

[8] *Sunrider* (n 6) paras 46–54.

[9] *Institut für Lernsysteme GmbH v OHIM* Case T-388/00 [2004] ETMR 17 para 31.

[10] Regulation 2868/95 r 22(4).

E. When must the Evidence of Use be Filed at OHIM?

14.23 Rule 22(1) of the Implementing Regulation states as follows:

> Where, pursuant to Article 43(2) or (3) of the Regulation, the opposing party has to furnish proof of use or show that there are proper reasons for non-use, the Office shall invite him to provide the proof required within such period as it shall specify. If the opposing party does not provide such proof before the time limit expires, the Office shall reject the opposition.

14.24 This Rule appears very clear and, not surprisingly, the Opposition Division of OHIM and the OHIM Boards of Appeal have tended to exclude evidence of use filed after the period specified for filing it. This approach has been supported by the fourth chamber of the Court of First Instance in at least one case where, on further appeal, it held that OHIM had been right to exclude the further evidence of use submitted by the opponent in that case in response to the applicant's comments on the evidence of use which it had filed within the specified period.[11]

14.25 However, in a more recent case the second chamber of the same court appears to have taken a more relaxed approach to the matter.[12] It stated that the Rule cannot be interpreted as precluding additional evidence from being taken into account where new factors emerge, even if the additional evidence is adduced after the expiry of the time limit set by OHIM. Rather it held that the Rule gives OHIM a discretion as to whether to take account of evidence produced after the expiry of the time limit.

14.26 Notwithstanding the court's more recent view of the discretionary effect of the Rule, it would be wise for an opponent or applicant for invalidation to file within the period specified by OHIM for doing so, whatever evidence and submissions it intends to rely upon to show genuine use of an earlier trade mark.

---

[11] *Institut für Lernsysteme GmbH v OHIM* (n 9) paras 28–30.
[12] *MFE Marienfelde GmbH v OHIM* Case T-334/01 8 July 2004 paras 56 and 57.

F. The Period within which Genuine Use must be Shown

In opposition proceedings, the requirement to provide proof of genuine use, **14.27** or proper reasons for non-use, can only be invoked if the earlier trade marks had been registered for five years at the date on which the Community trade mark was published for opposition purposes.

The same applies in invalidation proceedings, although in this case the **14.28** requirement can also be invoked if the earlier trade mark had been registered for five years at the date of the application for invalidation. Where the earlier trade mark had been registered for five years at the date of publication of the Community trade mark, the applicant for invalidation may be required to show genuine use of the earlier trade mark at the date or publication of the Community trade mark *and* at the date of the application for invalidation. As the Community trade mark system becomes more mature, the former requirement could require that records of use of trade marks be retained for extended periods of time.

The CTMR does not expressly state whether the five-year period is to apply **14.29** to earlier trade marks with a date of *filing* five years prior to one of the dates specified above, or whether the five-year period instead commences from the later date on which the earlier mark was actually placed upon the relevant register. However, the corresponding provision of the Directive to the Member States is express on this point: Article 10 indicates that the five-year period commences on the date of the completion of the registration procedure. The CTMR is interpreted as having the same meaning.

G. The Territorial Extent of the Use

Where the earlier trade mark is registered in a Member State, the use shown **14.30** must be in the territory of that State. Where the earlier trade mark is a Community trade mark, the use must be in the Community.[13] It is not yet entirely clear whether the use must be of a certain territorial extent in order to satisfy this requirement. This is because it is only relatively recently that the

---

[13] CTMR arts 43(2) and 56(2).

position has been reached whereby large numbers of Community trade marks have been registered for the five-year period necessary before their continued registration or enforceability could be challenged on the ground of non-use. There is therefore a shortage of directly applicable case law on the point.

14.31   In *Kabushiki Kaisha Fernandes v OHIM*,[14] the Court of First Instance stated (in paragraph 37 of its judgment) that, in relation to a national trade mark:

> genuine use means that the mark must be present in a substantial part of the territory where it is protected . . .

It might be expected that the same would apply to trade marks registered at Community level. The court's finding was a consequence of its reasoning that the requirement for genuine use went further than simply the exclusion of artificial use for the purpose of maintaining a mark on the register. That view appears to find support in Article 108(2) of the CTMR, which sets out the circumstances in which a Community trade mark, which has been revoked for lack of genuine use, can be converted into one or more national applications. The provision stipulates that such a conversion can only be permitted where the Community trade mark has been put to use which would be considered to be genuine use under the laws of the Member State(s) for which conversion is requested.

14.32   The relevant laws of the Member States had been harmonized by the time the CTMR was made, and were, in substance, identical to the revocation provisions of the CTMR. It is therefore difficult to see how use which is found to be a sham, undertaken simply to maintain the Community trade mark registration, could subsequently be found to be genuine use by a court of a Member State. Thus the apparent recognition in the CTMR that there might be use which is not sufficient to be considered as genuine use at Community level, but which might be regarded as such at national level, appears supportive of the view that the obligation to make genuine use of the trade mark includes an obligation to make sufficient use of the mark within the territory in which it is registered in order to justify its continued registration. Determining whether such use is sufficient would naturally include as assessment of the territorial extent of the use, and the answer

---

[14]   [2003] ETMR 1200.

could then vary, depending on whether the question is posed at Community or national level.

However, in the light of the European Court of Justice's (ECJ) judgment in **14.33** *Ansul*[15] it appears that any use which is really intended to create or preserve an outlet for the goods or services in question is to be regarded as genuine.

The use required in order to maintain an enforceable Community trade mark **14.34** registration is genuine use 'in the Community'. The term 'use in the Community' appears in a number of the provisions of the Directive and the CTMR. The most relevant in this context is Article 13 of the CTMR, which covers exhaustion of rights. In that provision any 'use [of the mark] in the Community' by, or with the consent of, the proprietor would ordinarily exhaust the proprietor's trade mark rights with regard to subsequent commercialization of the products in question.

It would not therefore appear that the words 'use in the Community' of **14.35** themselves introduce any minimum requirement as to the territorial extent of the use of the mark within the Community in order to fall within this description of use.

Further, it should be noted that for the purposes of assessing whether there **14.36** has been genuine use of a Community trade mark, 'use in the Community' includes affixing the trade mark to the goods or their packaging in the territory concerned in respect of goods exported from the territory.[16]

It therefore appears clear that there is no requirement for a proprietor of a **14.37** Community trade mark to use it throughout the territories of all the Member States. Indeed the CTMR envisages situations where it would be unlawful to use a Community trade mark in certain Member States.[17] And in the light of *Ansul* it would appear that the Court of First Instance may have gone too far in suggesting that genuine use requires the trade mark to be present in even a substantial part of the territory in which it is protected. Having said that, it is easy to identify policy considerations which might (when and if the question is put to the ECJ) cause the Court to shy away from a finding that even a trivial amount of genuinely intentioned but local use is sufficient to maintain

---

[15] *Ansul BV v Ajax Brandbeveiling BV* Case C-40/01 [2003] ETMR 85.
[16] CTMR art 15(2)(b).
[17] CTMR art 106.

an exclusive right to a trade mark across the territories of the Community's twenty-five Member States. Consequently, further guidance from the ECJ may be required in order to completely clarify the law on the use required to sustain the registration of a Community trade mark.

H. What must be Shown

14.38   The requirement in Articles 43(2) and (3) and 56(2) and (3) to provide proof of genuine use of the earlier conflicting trade mark in the Community or (in the case of national trade marks) in the relevant Member State is expressed in virtually identical terms to the way in which the conditions for revocation of a trade mark for non-use are expressed in Articles 15 and 50 of the CTMR, which in turn are substantially the same as Articles 10 and 12 of the Trade Mark Directive.

14.39   What is therefore required is for the party seeking to rely upon an earlier mark to support a ground for refusal or invalidation of the Community trade mark to show that if there had been an application to revoke the earlier trade mark on the grounds of non-use in the same five-year period, it would not have succeeded, or at least would not have succeeded in relation to goods or services which are material to the outcome of the opposition or invalidation proceedings.

14.40   Consequently, the case law of the ECJ[18] with regard to the meaning of the words 'genuine use' for the purposes of the Trade Mark Directive may also serve to inform proprietors of trade marks cited in opposition and invalidation proceedings at OHIM as to what is necessary to resist a challenge under Articles 43 and 56 of the CTMR.

14.41   The Court of First Instance has stated that:

> In interpreting the concept of genuine use, account must be taken of the fact that the rationale for the requirement that the earlier mark must have been put to genuine use if it is to be capable of being used in opposition to a trade mark application is to restrict the number of conflicts between two marks, in so far as there is no sound economic reason resulting from an actual function of the mark on the market (Case T-174/01 *Goulbourn v OHIM—Redcats (Silk*

---

[18] Particularly *Ansul* (n 15) and *La Mer Technology Inc v Laboratoires Goemar* [2004] ETMR 47.

Cocoon) [2003] ECR II-789, paragraph 38). However, that provision is not concerned either with assessing the commercial success of an undertaking or monitoring its economic strategy, or designed to reserve the protection of trade marks for large-scale commercial uses of them.[19]

However, the court went on to note that: **14.42**

> However, the smaller the commercial volume of exploitation of the mark, the more necessary it is for the party opposing new registration to produce additional evidence to dispel possible doubts as to it genuineness.[20]

*Kabushiki Kaisha Fernandes v OHIM (*HIWATT*)*[21] provides an example of a **14.43** case in which an opponent failed to provide OHIM with sufficient evidence of genuine use. The proprietor filed only catalogues which did not show that the mark had been used in respect of the opponent's products on the relevant (German) market, but only that the company (which bore the same name as the trade mark) had a 'sporadic and occasional presence' on the German market. As to the opponent's claims that, having regard to its business, it was more than likely that its trade mark had been used on the German market, the court stated:

> In that regard it must be held that genuine use of a trade mark cannot be proved by means of probabilities or suppositions, but must be demonstrated by solid and objective evidence of effective and sufficient use of the trade mark on the market concerned.

Where the extent of the use is small and only commences in the period **14.44** running up to the date of publication of the opposed Community trade mark, the evidence of use is likely to be subject to particularly close scrutiny in order to determine whether the use was genuine or merely to preserve the enforceability of the trade mark.[22]

I. The UK Trade Marks Act 1994

The UK introduced similar provisions into its national law on 5 May 2004, **14.45** when The Trade Marks (Proof of Use, etc) Regulations 2004[23] came into effect.

---

[19] *MFE Marienfelde* (n 12) para 32.
[20] ibid para 37.
[21] [2003] ETMR 98.
[22] *MFE Marienfelde* (n 12) paras 47 and 48.
[23] SI 2004 No 946.

14.46 These provisions serve a broadly similar purpose to those found in the CTMR. They aim to reduce the number of conflicts between trade marks where the earlier trade mark is susceptible to full or partial revocation for non-use. The success of the Community trade mark system has increased the number of conflicts which arise between Community and national trade marks and forced Member States to look at means of limiting the scope for such conflicts. The Regulations are timely because, in the last year or so, substantial numbers of Community trade marks have passed the fifth anniversary of their registration and have therefore become susceptible to challenge on the basis of non-use.

14.47 The Trade Mark Rules 2000 have been amended by The Trade Marks (Amendment) Rules 2004. These Rules introduce a clear framework for national opposition and invalidation proceedings, including provisions for assessing whether an earlier trade mark is entitled to protection and, if so, for which goods and services. Although the national procedures are similar to those found in the CTMR, there are a number of important differences and these are explained below.

J. The Applicant or Proprietor of the National Trade Mark does not have to Make a Request

14.48 Unlike the CTMR, the national law places a general obligation on the Registrar not to refuse to register a trade mark as a result of opposition or invalidation proceedings unless any earlier trade marks cited as the basis for the proceedings satisfy the use conditions.[24] The requirement to satisfy the use conditions is not only invoked at the request of the applicant for, or proprietor of, the national trade mark, as in the Community trade mark system. Instead, Rule 13(2)(e) requires that a 'statement of use' be made in respect of every earlier trade mark cited in an opposition which has been registered for five years or more at the date of the publication of the later trade mark. The Rule indicates that what is required is 'a statement detailing whether during the period referred to in Section 6A(3)(a)(a) the (earlier) mark has been put to genuine use in relation to each of the goods and services in respect of which the opposition is based or whether there are proper reasons for non-use'.

---

[24] Trade Marks Act 1994 (as amended), ss 6A(2) and 47(2A)(c).

What is expected at this stage, as a minimum, is a list of the goods and **14.49** services in respect of which it is claimed that genuine use of the earlier trade mark occurred during the relevant five-year period. An opponent can include more detail, eg of dates, scale and territorial extent of use if he wishes, and doing so may increase the credibility of the claim and thereby make it less likely to formal challenge.

The applicant for registration is expected to address the statement of use in **14.50** his counter-statement. If he denies, or refuses to admit, the truth of the opponent's statement of use, or any part of it, the opponent is required to file evidence supporting the statement of use, or at least that part of it which is in dispute.[25] As with any other pleading, if the applicant is later shown to have denied something he knew to be true, there may be consequences when it comes to the award of costs at the conclusion of the proceedings. It is not therefore advisable to put an opponent to proof of use simply as a tactic to cause nuisance.

The statement of use is also required in applications for the invalidation of **14.51** a national trade mark. Rules 33 and 33A[26] include provisions which are analogous to those described above.

K. The Preliminary Indication in Opposition Proceedings

The Rules now include a procedure whereby, following the statement of use **14.52** and the completion of the pleadings, the Registrar issues a 'preliminary indication' of the likely outcome of an opposition insofar as it is based on a likelihood of confusion between the earlier and later trade marks. This will take, as its starting-point, only those goods or services included in the statement of use of the earlier trade mark(s).

The preliminary indication is intended to provide the Registrar's provisional **14.53** view as to whether the identity or similarity between the respective trade marks and goods and services is such as to create a likelihood of confusion on the part of the public. If the Registrar is inclined to the view that there is no likelihood of confusion, the opponent will know that, not only may he have

---

[25] r 13C(1)(b)(ii).
[26] Trade Mark Rules 2000 (as amended).

to support his statement of use with evidence, he will also have to displace the Registrar's provisional view of the likelihood of confusion through argument or evidence. The expectation is that this will result in a larger proportion of unpromising oppositions falling away early in the proceedings. It may also help to avoid the sort of situations which have arisen in the Community trade mark system whereby a protracted dispute about whether there has been genuine use of the earlier trade mark is eventually resolved only for the opponent to learn that in the Office's view that there was no likelihood of confusion anyway.

L. The Time for an Opponent to File Supporting Evidence

14.54 After the parties have received the Registrar's preliminary indication, either party has one month to file a notice of intention to proceed with the application or opposition. The date on which the Registrar notifies the parties that such a notice has been filed opens a three-month period within which the opponent may file evidence in support of the opposition, including (where the statement of use has been challenged or not admitted) evidence of genuine use of the earlier trade mark.

14.55 If the opponent fails to file such evidence his opposition is deemed withdrawn unless the Registrar directs otherwise.[27] This may be expected where there are other grounds of opposition.

M. The Time for an Applicant for Invalidation to File Supporting Evidence

14.56 The practice of issuing a preliminary indication does not apply to invalidation proceedings. The period for the applicant to file evidence in support of his application commences on the date he is sent the proprietor's counterstatement.[28] If that includes a denial (or non-admission) of the applicant's statement of use, the applicant's supporting evidence must include evidence

---

[27] r 13C(2).
[28] rr 33(7) and 33A(1).

supporting the statement of use.[29] The applicant is allowed six weeks to file his evidence, the shorter period (compared to opposition) being accounted for by the fact that the applicant controls the date on which the invalidation application is made and can therefore be expected to have taken steps to assemble the necessary documents before the proceedings are started.

N. What Form must the Evidence Take?

The documentary evidence is likely to take a similar form to that required at **14.57** OHIM, ie invoices, labels, price lists, catalogues, invoices, photographs, newspaper advertisements etc. showing use of the earlier trade mark.

Unlike in the Community system, a written statement is an essential part of **14.58** the evidence required under the national law. Rule 55 of the Trade Mark Rules 2000 (as amended) requires that evidence be submitted by way of affidavit, statutory declaration or witness statement, although the Registrar has a discretion to accept oral evidence instead. The latter would always be given under oath. The statement will normally provide details of the use that has taken place, typically with the use broken down into periods, and with an indication of where the mark has been used, what form the mark has been used in and what the scale of the use has been. It may also include details of customers who have purchased goods or services by reference to the mark, and where and how the mark has been promoted.

Although such a statement forms a necessary part of the evidence in national **14.59** proceedings, it is unlikely to be regarded as sufficiently probative without some documentary support. Thus it is usual to see the statement accompanied by a number of exhibits showing use of the mark.

Unlike the Community system, it is not possible for a party simply to refer **14.60** the Registrar to documents filed in earlier like proceedings in order to satisfy the Registrar that the trade mark in question has been put to genuine use. Rather, the party concerned must file a statement formally adopting the evidence filed in the earlier proceedings into the later proceedings.

---

[29] r 33A(1)(b)(iii).

O. What must be Shown

14.61 As in the Community trade mark system, what must be shown is that the earlier trade mark sought to be relied upon by the opponent or applicant for invalidation was not susceptible to revocation for non-use at the relevant date. The case law of the Court of Justice on the question of what constitutes genuine use can be relied on to evaluate what is required for this purpose.[30]

14.62 The onus of proving use of an earlier trade mark is on the opponent or applicant for invalidation.[31] The smaller the amount of use of the earlier trade mark, the greater the need to prove that it is genuine. Where there is doubt, the party seeking to rely upon the use would be well advised to provide a full explanation for the small amount of use. Sometimes evidence of events that occurred after the end of the relevant five-year period may help to shed light on the nature of the use which occurred within the five-year period. For example, a substantial expansion of use after the end of the five-year period may support a claim that a product was relaunched in the fifth year of the relevant five-year period and thus show that, even though there was very little use of the trade mark in the relevant period, the use that did occur was genuine.

14.63 Where the earlier trade mark is a national mark, the use shown must be within the UK. Where the earlier trade mark is a Community trade mark, the use shown must be within the Community. As in the Community system, use includes affixing the trade mark to the goods or their packaging in the territory concerned in respect of goods for export from that territory.

P. The Period within which Genuine Use must be Shown

14.64 As with opposition proceedings before OHIM, the requirement to provide proof of genuine use, or proper reasons for non-use, can only be invoked if the earlier trade marks had been registered for five years at the date on which the national trade mark was published for opposition purposes. In order to calculate this period it is necessary to start with the date on which the

---

[30] Particularly *Ansul* (n 15) and *Laboratoires Goemar* (n 18).
[31] Trade Marks Act 1994 s 100.

registration procedure was completed in respect of the earlier trade mark.[32] As in the Community system, the relevant five-year period ends on the date at which the later trade mark is published for opposition purposes.

However, the national Rules differ when it comes to the calculation of the **14.65** relevant five-year period for the purposes of invalidation proceedings. In the Community system the proprietor of the Community trade mark can request that the applicant for invalidation show genuine use of the earlier conflicting trade mark within *both* the five-year period preceding the publication of the Community trade mark for opposition purposes, *and* in the five-year period preceding the filing of the application for invalidation.

In the national system, the proprietor of the earlier trade mark only has to **14.66** make a statement of use of the earlier conflicting trade mark in the five-year period preceding the application for invalidation.[33]

This raises the question of whether a proprietor of an earlier trade mark who **14.67** is not in a position to oppose an application for registration at the date of its publication because of non-use of the earlier trade mark can later apply to invalidate the registration on the basis of resumed use of the earlier trade mark. There does not appear to be anything to prevent such an approach, but use that is commenced primarily to make the earlier trade mark enforceable rather than to create or retain a market for the goods or services is unlikely to be regarded as genuine.

Because the requirements to provide proof of use in opposition and invalida- **14.68** tion proceedings are quite new there is not yet any directly relevant case law. However, it is suggested that decisions on applications for revocation for non-use made under Section 46 of the Trade Marks Act provide a guide as to the likely result in such a case. In *Domenico Tanzarella v Stella Products Ltd*[34] it was held that a small volume of use which commenced just after a hostile exchange of correspondence between the proprietor and a potential infringer was not genuine use and could not save the registered trade mark from revocation for non-use. It is likely that use of a trade mark which commences shortly after the publication of a later conflicting trade mark will be subject to careful scrutiny in order to assess whether the use was genuine.

---

[32] Trade Marks Act 1994 (as amended) s 46(1)(a).
[33] ibid s 47(2B).
[34] BL O/104/03.

Q. The Notional Specification

14.69 As explained above, the policy behind the requirement for proof of use in opposition and invalidation proceedings is that a trade mark should not be protected to the extent that it is susceptible to revocation for non-use. Consequently, where the evidence (or the lack of it) indicates that the earlier trade mark is susceptible to partial revocation, it becomes necessary to construct a notional specification of goods and services for the earlier trade mark for the purpose of the opposition or invalidation proceedings. The notional specification will cover only those goods and services in respect of which the earlier trade mark has been put to genuine use, or in respect of which there are proper reasons for non-use.

14.70 The scope of the notional specification should therefore be identical to that which would have resulted if an actual application to revoke the earlier trade mark had been made and determined on the same evidence. Consequently, when it becomes necessary to construct a notional specification, the case law relating to partial revocation of trade marks should provide guidance as to the correct approach.[35]

14.71 The notional specification should consist of a fair description of the goods and services in respect of which the earlier trade mark is free from the conditions which would justify its revocation.[36] It should not, however, reflect other characteristics of the proprietor's trade under the earlier trade mark shown in the evidence, such as the channels of trade through which goods bearing that mark reached the market unless that is necessary to fairly characterize the goods or services in question, eg 'prescription drugs'. So, if the earlier trade mark has been shown to have been put to genuine use in respect of (say) fruit and vegetables sold to supermarkets, the notional specification should be simply 'fruit and vegetables'.

14.72 Further, if a trade mark has been shown to have been used in respect of a sufficient range of products which fall within a more general description, so that the general description fairly describes the proprietor's trade under the

---

[35] *Minerva Trade Mark* [2000] FSR 734; *Decon Laboratories Ltd v Fred Baker Scientific Ltd* [2001] RPC 17; *Thomson Holidays Ltd v Norwegian Cruise Line Ltd* [2003] RPC 32.
[36] *Animal Trade Mark* [2004] FSR 19.

mark, that description of goods or services may be retained. For example, if the evidence shows that the mark has been used in relation to a number of different types of fruit juice, the notional specification should include 'fruit juices', even though there may be some types of fruit juice which were not represented in the evidence of use of the earlier trade mark.[37]

The Registrar will substitute the notional specification of goods and services **14.73** for the one in respect of which the earlier mark is actually registered. He will then proceed to assess whether, having regard to the notional specification of the earlier trade mark, registration of the later trade mark is contrary to any of the pleaded relative grounds for refusing or invalidating the registration of the later trade mark.

R. Conclusion

The requirement to show use of earlier trade marks relied on as the basis for **14.74** opposing or invalidating a later trade mark is now a routine but important aspect of opposition and invalidation proceedings before OHIM. The recent changes to the law in the UK mean that proof of use is set to become an equally regular and important feature of opposition and invalidation proceedings before the UK Patent Office.

The relevant law is, in most respects, already well settled and should not **14.75** present too many difficulties for would-be opponents/applicants for invalidation. The practice whereby trade mark owners are required to prove use of the trade marks they invoke in such proceedings does, however, complicate such proceedings, and has limited but inescapable consequences for the cost of mounting such proceedings. However, the necessity to consider what use can be shown of the senior trade mark, which is often registered for a very long list of goods and services, is likely to reduce the number of unnecessary conflicts between trade marks, and limit the scope of those that do still occur to more closely resemble the parties' actual trading activities. This is crucial to the maintenance of an accessible and effective system of trade mark protection in Europe.

---

[37] This was the approach of the Court of First Instance in *Sunrider* (n 6); see also *Animal Trade Mark* (n 36).

PART G

BROADER PERSPECTIVES

15

TRADE MARK USE ON THE INTERNET

Spyros Maniatis

A. Introduction	15.01	D. Warehousing	15.28
B. Trade Marks and Domain Names	15.03	E. Enforcement and Territoriality Questions	15.31
C. 'New' Types of Infringement	15.12	F. Conclusion	15.35
(1) Adapting trade mark law principles	15.13		

A. Introduction

Looking at trade marks on the internet from a 'trade mark use' perspective, **15.01** this chapter will explore two issues. First, how trade mark jurisprudence confronts 'new types of infringement' that can be committed using the internet. Second, how it responds to the challenges that the omnipresence of the internet poses to the 'territoriality' principle underlying trade mark law. Selective references to English and American cases will illustrate these issues.

It is argued that, despite the technological complications, both matters can be **15.02** resolved according to established trade mark law principles. In terms of trade mark law, the technology and the vocabulary of the medium are new but the substance remains the same.[1]

---

[1] For a similar argument see S Maniatis 'New Bottles, but No Wine' in E Barendt and A Firth (eds) *Yearbook of Copyright and Media Law 2000* (OUP Oxford 2000).

B. Trade Marks and Domain Names

15.03 Trade marks are distinguishing signs; their primary function is to distinguish products according to source and enable consumer choice. They also facilitate communication between market players: they enable traders to advertise their wares and consumers to exchange information. Trade mark law aims to protect traders and consumers alike. At its core lies protection against 'the mistaken belief that the plaintiff is in some way associated with defendant's goods' and at its expanding boundaries protection against 'the accurate recognition that a mark once associated exclusively with the plaintiff is now also in use as an identifying symbol by others'.[2] Public policy considerations—like competition and freedom of speech—are limiting protection within a commercial competitive sphere. Trade mark rights conferred through registration or use are exclusive but narrow; they cover the products in relation to which the trade mark is used.

15.04 Domain names are disguising signs. They are alphanumeric combinations that make arbitrary and long combinations of distinguishing numbers, the internet protocol (IP) numbers, easier to memorize. IP numbers serve as virtual unique cyberspace addresses for computers sharing standardized communication protocol software. A packet of information travelling through the internet carries the IP number of its sender and the IP number of its destination. In order to create a stable and user friendly internet engineers have developed the Domain Name System (DNS), a database that matches and replaces each IP number with its unique domain name. Each time an internet user keys in a domain name the resolution process is initiated. It starts within 'root servers' at the top of the system (storing a list of Top Level Domain Names (TLDs), for example. int) pointing to 'name servers' (containing lists of second-level domain name registered under that name, for example eu.int), and so on down the hierarchy (for example oami.eu.int).[3] The number of top-level domains is limited; they are classified according to genre (generic top-level domain names (gTLDs) including .aero, .biz, .com,

---

[2] s 25 of the Restatement (Third) of Unfair Competition in the USA depicts clearly the distinction between the two types of protection. The latter type of harm is commonly known as 'dilution'.

[3] Soon .eu will itself become a top level domain, exemplifying how the system develops.

.coop, .info, .museum, .name, .net and .org) or geographical divisions (country code (ccTLDs) for states, federations of states, or supra-national organizations formed by two-letter combinations as adopted by the International Standards Organization). The value of the DNS has grown as a result of the commercialization of the internet since the first half of the 1990s.

This is how Mueller has described the value adding process: **15.05**

(i)   technology vests a new resource with value;
(ii) market players compete to appropriate pieces of the new resource;
(iii) the new arena is regulated through institutional innovations.[4]

One such innovation is the internet Corporation for Assigned Names and **15.06** Numbers (ICANN), a non-profit, private entity, created by the US Government in 1988 to manage the internet. In essence, this meant the privatization of the DNS. ICANN manages the registries—private, non-profit corporations—that administer gTLDs and approves the registrars that assign second-level domain names on a first come first served basis. The registrars are non-adjudicatory bodies and registration does not imply that the holder of the domain name is granted an official right to use the sign. Contrary to 'popular, non-legal, folklore' by 'reserving' a domain name a user does not get any 'official' right to use that domain name free from legal claims.[5] The concept of 'domain name registration' should be accordingly distinguished from that of 'trade mark registration' which confers exclusive rights.

Irrespective of its characterization though, registration of a domain name **15.07** results in the registrant 'having' the name. In an analogous case an English court considered that, although there is no property right in a telephone number, telephone companies cannot divest the 'owner'.[6] A telephone number could trump a subsequent trade mark application. Jacob J rejected the claim that his approach would render the Trade Mark Registry subservient to the telephone companies by using the example of a natural monopoly. Ownership of a mineral water source would render use of the name of the source for

---

[4] M Mueller 'Competing DNS Roots: Creative Destruction or Just Plain Destruction?' available at http://arxiv.org/ftp/cs/papers/0109/0109021.pdf; see also M Mueller 'Technology and Institutional Innovation: Internet Domain Names' [2000] 5 International Journal of Communications Law and Policy 1.
[5] JT McCarthy *McCarthy on Trademarks and Unfair Competition* (West Group St Paul 2004) §25:73.3.
[6] *1-800 Flowers Inc v Phonenames Ltd* [2000] ETMR 369 ChD 376.

water by a party other than the owner deceptive. If factors external to the trade mark registration make the mark deceptive in the hands of the applicant, that is a fact that has to be taken into account. A US court[7] has also strongly implied that, in essence, domain names are property satisfying the criteria that there be: (i) an interest capable of precise definition, (ii) exclusive possession or control and (iii) the establishment of a legitimate claim to exclusivity.[8]

15.08 In practice ICANN has been recognized by the global community, if by silent acceptance rather than positive acknowledgment, as the main institutional player created by an informal agreement between national governments, international organizations, commercial actors and representatives of interest groups. ICANN's nature and power[9] over an exclusive global resource have caused concerns about the private character of its monopoly, the inequalities the DNS creates and ICANN's accountability.[10] Others dread the possibility of governmental—potentially authoritarian—intervention.

15.09 One commentator has claimed that domain names

> present a case study in the possibility of global governance, with the internet authority ICANN as a world executive and the World Intellectual Property Organization as its judicial arm,[11]

supporting that the present focus on freedom of speech, creativity, privacy and autonomy issues bypasses concerns for equality and distributive justice.

---

[7] *Kremen v Cohen* 325 F3d 1035 67 USPQ 2d 1502 (9th Cir Cal 2003).

[8] R Dixon 'To Fight Domain Name Theft: Sex.com Gives Birth to a New Property Right' (6 May 2004) available at http://www.circleid.com/article/584_0_1_0_C/; *Mattel Inc v Barbie-Club.com* 310 F3d 293 64 USPQ 2d 1879 (2nd Cir NY 2002) n 7: 'Congress clearly intended to treat domain names as property for purposes of the ACPA *in rem* provisions.' The Anticybersquatting Consumer Protection Act (ACPA), signed on 29 November 1999, effective from 1 January 2000; 15 USC §1125 (d)(2)(A). See HA Forrest 'Drawing a Line in the Constitutional Sand Between Congress and the Foreign Citizen "Cybersquatter" ' [2001] 9 Wm & Mary Bill of Rts J 461.

[9] In the USA so far ICANN has successfully bypassed antitrust challenges. For a journalistic overview see C Oakes 'External Forces Chip Away at internet's Overseer' International Herald Tribune (8 March 2004) available at http://www.iht.com/cgi-bin/generic.cgi?template=articleprint.tmplh&ArticleId=509038 and J Schenker 'Debate over Auctions for Internet Addresses' International Herald Tribune (14 July 2004) available at http://www.iht.com/articles/529268.html.

[10] See for instance the open letter of Ethan Katsh to ICANN 'Where is our Ombudsman?' available at http://www.odr.info/icann expressing reservations regarding ICANN's accountability.

[11] A Chander 'The New, New Property' [2003] 81 Texas Law Review 715 at 718.

The rule of first possession on which the allocation of domain names is founded favours the technologically adept and wealthy. Alternatively domain names could be perceived as a new form of international property presenting a global commons of the Information Age.

In pre-empting or responding to criticism, ICANN has adopted a wide and **15.10** representative membership structure and bureaucratic mechanisms[12] that are constantly being reconsidered in order to confront challenges from governments and national registries for ccTLDs. Erkki Liikanen, the EC Commissioner responsible for the internet at the time of writing, has described ICANN as

> a unique experiment in self-regulation . . . the expectation among governments at the outset was that ICANN would provide a neutral platform for consensus-building . . . It was also hoped that ICANN would provide a way for the US government to withdraw from its supervisory role. In this way, we could achieve a greater internationalisation and privatisation of certain key functions . . . It has yet to fully deliver on either of these objectives.[13]

So, while supporting the integration of European national registries within **15.11** the Country Code Names Supporting Organization (ccNSO),[14] set up by ICANN and so far boycotted by major European registries, Liikanen recognizes the power struggles and warns that ICANN has to improve its performance otherwise governments might intervene.[15]

C. 'New' Types of Infringement

The World Wide Web, still a relatively new trade mark infringement arena, **15.12** has brought about the adaptation of traditional trade mark law. New doctrines have been developed and linked with existing principles in order to deal with the opportunistic stockpiling of domain names by cyber and typo

---

[12] Mueller supports the view that ICANN behaves more like a regulatory agency than a private corporation or a typical industry standards-setting forum.

[13] In a speech titled 'Internet Governance: The Way Ahead' available at http://europa.eu.int/rapid/start/cgi/guesten.ksh?p_action.gettxt=gt&doc=SPEECH/04/191/0/RAPID&lg=EN.

[14] http://ccnso.icann.org/.

[15] K McCarthy 'EC Tells ICANN and Europe to Make Peace' available at http://www.theregister.co.uk/2004/04/ec_icann_warning_shot/.

squatters, who register names, trade marks, and their most commonly misspelled variations.

(1) Adapting trade mark law principles

15.13 When the signs and the relevant products are identical or similar, established principles are applied. A domain name is an electronic address that can function as a distinctive sign that is, like any other distinctive sign, potentially in conflict with a trade mark. Accordingly its wrongful registration or use can fall within a trade mark court's jurisdiction, notwithstanding the existence of separate specific regulations dedicated to domain names.[16] Courts have accepted that domain names can signify the source of a product and be perceived as trade marks; web users often assume that the domain name of a company will consist of the company's name or recognized trade mark followed by '.com'.[17]

15.14 From the opposite perspective, it is common practice for trade mark registries worldwide to accept the registration of domain names as trade marks provided they function as such and satisfy other registrability requirements.[18] Additionally, use of a domain name may constitute use as a trade mark where the specified goods or services are offered for sale under the domain name.

15.15 The comparison between a trade mark and a domain name follows known trade mark law principles. For example, the registered trade mark WEBSPHERE was found to be identical with 'Web-Sphere' used as part of a company name (Web-Sphere Ltd) and a domain name (web-sphere.org). The existence of the hyphen was not insignificant in the global assessment of the two signs since the average consumer would be a sophisticated computer user aware of

---

[16] *Inditex SA v Compagnia Mercantile Srl* [2002] ETMR 2 Trib (Turin): in Italy, use of Zara, a cloth retailer's name, for a website selling cloths of other brands—but not Zara clothes— constituted infringement because it was used as a gateway for the sale of clothes. Similarly in the USA it is recognized that when a domain name is used only to indicate an address on the internet, it is not functioning as a trade mark. Trade mark law intervenes when the domain name identifies the source of specific goods and services: *Data Concepts Inc v Digital Consulting Inc* 150 F3d 620 47 USPQ 2d 1672 (6th Cir Mich 1998).

[17] *Sallen v Corinthians Licenciamentos LTDA* 273 F3d 14 60 USPQ 2d 1941 (1st Cir Mass 2001).

[18] Registration of the gTLD or ccTLD element of the mark is considered to be analogous to an abbreviation like 'Co.' or a telephone prefix. Top-level domains and signs like 'http://' and '@' are considered non-distinctive.

its distinguishing importance in web searching. However 'Websphere' has been also promoted in the conventional media and the two signs would not be compared side by side at the point of keying in the address.[19] The judge required Web-Sphere Ltd to change its name and to cease using the domain name or to assign it to the claimant, the most common and effective remedy in such cases.

Pre-sale confusion involves cases where confusion is resolved before the com- **15.16**
pletion of the transaction where, for example, purchasers are confused at the point of choosing, though not at the point of the actual sale or delivery,[20] but decide to stay with their original mistaken choice.[21] This led to the development of the 'initial interest confusion' doctrine[22] that has been successfully applied in cases where a trade mark is used without authorization as, or part of, a domain name in order to lure visitors into a website. Attracting visitors in this way becomes problematic from a trade mark law perspective when the site is promoting products not linked with the trade mark holder. In some cases the consumer may not be confused at the time of sale but the interruption of its journey to the trade mark owner's original website may be actionable.[23] How the domain name functions in such cases depends on the aim of the journey of the web searcher. The case will be much clearer when someone wanting to find the site of a company perceives the domain name as use of the company's name or trade mark on the internet; it will be more complicated when someone aimlessly drifting on the World Wide Web is drawn into the website by an interest triggered by the domain name alluding to the trade mark.

---

[19] *International Business Machines Corporation, IBM United Kingdom Ltd v Web-Sphere Ltd and Richard de Serville* [2004] EWHC 529 Ch.

[20] *Lindy Pen Co v Bic Pen Corp* 796 F2d 254 230 USPQ 791 (9th Cir 1986) considered an over the telephone order for pens where there was evidence of traditional confusion as to source. At the point of delivery a diligent customer would realize that the pens delivered were not the pens supposedly ordered but might, nevertheless, decide not to bother to return them at that late stage.

[21] *McNeil—PPC v Guardian Drug Co* 984 F. Supp 1066 45 USPQ 2d 1437 (ED Mich 1997).

[22] See *Mobil Oil Corp v Pegasus Petroleum Corp* 818 F. 2d 254 2 USPQ 2d 1677 (2nd Cir 1987) where it was held that cold calls to oil traders from Pegasus Petroleum could be attributed by their receivers to Mobil, the owners of a pictorial trade mark incorporating a flying horse. This constituted infringement despite the sophistication of the traders involved.

[23] For example *Brookfield Communications Inc v West Coast Entertainment Corp* 174 F3d 1036 50 USPQ 2d 1545 (9th Cir Cal 1999) and *Planned Parenthood Federation of America Inc v Bucci* 42 USPQ 2d 1430 (SDNY 1997).

15.17 Courts do not rush to make assumptions; for example the presence of a trade mark in a uniform resource locator post-domain path of a retailer's website offering for sale a competing brand has been found not likely to cause confusion regarding the source of the web page or the competing product, because post-domain paths do not typically signify source; they would not ordinarily be perceived as trade marks.[24]

15.18 'Free ride' arguments have been employed in cases where a trade mark has been used as a metatag—in a way that is invisible to the user but visible to search engines—in order to hijack customers searching the web for the proprietor of the trade mark.[25] Metatags, though, can also be used fairly as signs that convey factual information. A 'Playmate' appearing in *Playboy* magazine has been held entitled to use those two words as metatags in her personal website.[26] This is a typical example of use of a trade mark as a descriptor rather than an indication of source with courts balancing trade marks rights and freedom of speech, competition and unfair competition.[27] Freedom of speech and aggressive comparative advertising are accepted by trade mark law, provided the consumer is not deceived. Use of a trade mark on the internet in order to identify the object of criticism or the target of competition should be allowed.

15.19 A recent English decision has posed the following questions in respect of metatag use. First, does metatag use count as use of a trade mark at all?

In this context it must be remembered that use is important not only for infringement but also for saving a mark from non-use. In the latter context it

---

[24] *Interactive Products Corporation v A2Z Mobile Offices Solution* 326 F3d 687 66 USPQ 2d 1321 (6th Cir Ohio 2003).

[25] *Roadtech Computer Systems Ltd v ManData (Management and Data Services) Ltd* [2000] ETMR 870 ChD.

[26] *Playboy Enterprises Inc v Welles* 47 USPQ 2d 1186 (SD Cal 1998) aff'd 279 F3d 796 61 USPQ 2d 1508 (9th Cir Cal 2002).

[27] In *Bihari v Gross* 119 F. Supp. 2d 309 56 USPQ 2d 1489 (SDNY 2000) a US court made the point that a broad injunction can effectively foreclose all discourse and comment about the plaintiff; accordingly a website of an unhappy customer could contain a metatag with the plaintiff's business name because there was no likelihood of confusion and use was supported by freedom of speech arguments. See also *Ford Motor Co v 2600 Enterprises* 177 F. Supp 2d 661 61 USPQ 2d 1757 (ED Mich 2001) refusing a preliminary injunction against 'fuckgeneralmotors.com' which also incorporated a link to an official website. Commercial gain and the absence of a message of parody in the domain name itself can taint such arguments: *People for Ethical Treatment of Animals v Doughney* 263 F3d 359 60 USPQ 2d 1109 (4th Cir Md 2001).

would at least be odd that a wholly invisible use could defeat a non-use attack. Mr Hobbs, counsel for the trade mark owner, suggested that metatag use should be treated in the same way as uses of a trade mark which is ultimately read by people, such as uses on a DVD. But in those cases, the ultimate function of a trade mark is achieved—an indication to someone of trade origin. Uses read only by computers may not count since they never convey a message to anyone.[28]

Second, if metatag use does count as use, is there infringement if the marks **15.20** and goods or services are—as in this case—identical?

> This is important: one way of competing with another is to use his trade mark in your metatag, so that a search for him will also produce you in the search results. Some might think this unfair while others hold that this is good competition provided that no-one is misled.[29]

Finally, if metatag use falls within the infringement provisions, can defences like the own-name defence apply? Jacob LJ implied that in principle they should.

A dilution rationale underlines cases of unauthorized domain name or **15.21** metatag use of trade marks with a reputation, in particular where tarnishment of the mark for which protection is sought is combined with commercial benefit for the party tarnishing the mark.[30] Nevertheless, courts are resisting the application of a new sweeping type of dilution that covers all cases of use of a reputed trade mark as a domain name; they insist instead that the rigorous trade mark enforcement requirements must be satisfied.[31]

A defence raised in cases against search engines using adware, software that **15.22** generates advertisements unconnected with a trade mark owner, whenever its trade mark is keyed in, is that the advertisers are engaged in lawful comparative advertising. The trade marks refer to the competitor's rather than to the advertiser's goods.[32] Recently, the US Ninth Circuit has ruled that likelihood

---

[28] *Reed Executive plc, Reed Solutions plc v Reed Business Information Ltd, Reed Elsevier (UK) Ltd* [2004] ETMR 56 CA Jacob LJ at para 149.

[29] ibid.

[30] *Hasbro Inc v Internet Entertainment Group Ltd* 40 USPQ 2d 1479 (WD Wash 1996).

[31] *Hasbro Inc v Clue Computing Inc* 66 F. Supp. 2d 117 52 USPQ 2d 1402 (D Mass 1999); *Playboy Enterprises Inc v Netscape Communications Corp* 52 USPQ 2d 1162 (CD Cal 1999) followed the same line in a case involving non-Playboy-sponsored adult banner advertisements triggered by the search terms 'playboy' or 'playmate'; however see n 33 for the appeal.

[32] For a case involving unfair competition and dilution arguments see *Estee Lauder Inc v The Fragrance Counter Inc* 189 FRD 269 52 USPQ 2d 1786 (SDNY 1999).

of initial interest confusion precluded summary judgment in favour of search engines; issues of fact had to be resolved according to the classic infringement tests. Use of the trade marks constituted commercial use that was not considered functional.[33] Linking advertisements to trade marks could lead to the impression that there exists an affiliation between the search engine advertiser and the trade mark owner. This could be actionable even if the user realizes, before concluding a transaction, that no affiliation actually exists because the visit to the competing website has been triggered by its initial interest in the trade mark. One judge, however, questioned whether the initial interest confusion is no longer a useful tool to resolve such cases, now that the internet has matured. Judge Berzon believed that it would not be reasonable

> to find initial interest confusion when a consumer is never confused as to source or affiliation, but instead knows, or should know, from the outset that a product or web link is not related to that of the trademark holder because the list produced by the search engine so informs him. There is a big difference between hijacking a customer to another website by making the customer think he or she is visiting the trademark holder's website (even if only briefly), which is what may be happening in this case when the banner advertisements are not labeled, and just distracting a potential customer with another *choice*, when it is clear that it is a choice. True, when the search engine list generated by the search for the trademark ensconced in a metatag comes up, an internet user might *choose* to visit westcoastvideo.com, the defendant's website in *Brookfield*, instead of the plaintiff's moviebuff.com website, but such choices do not constitute trademark infringement off the internet, and I cannot understand why they should on the internet.[34]

15.23 English courts are sceptical, assuming that a

> web-using member of the public knows that all sorts of banners appear when he or she does a search and they are or may be triggered by something in the search. He or she also knows that searches produce fuzzy results—results with much rubbish thrown in. The idea that a search under the name Reed would make anyone think there was a trade connection between a totaljobs banner making no reference to the word 'Reed' and Reed Employment is fanciful. No likelihood of confusion was established.[35]

---

[33] *Playboy Enterprises Inc v Netscape Communications Corp* 354 F3d 1020 69 USPQ 2d 1417 (9th Cir 2004).
[34] ibid 1034–1035.
[35] *Reed v Reed* (n 28) Jacob LJ at para 140.

Pop-up advertisement cases[36] and Google's pursuit of the claim that its key- **15.24**
word-triggered advertising program does not violate trade mark law will
challenge the concept further. From the perspective of the purchaser, purchasing high placements from search engines when specific search terms are
keyed in has been found not to be unlawful *per se*: the owner of a trade mark
violates no law by purchasing high placements.[37] The court noted, by way of
analogy with a more traditional medium, that the purchase of advertising in a
periodical is not *per se* unlawful. In a different context search rankings generated by search engines have been characterized as opinions within the scope
of the First Amendment.[38]

Finally, traditional confusion deals with 'deep linking'—carrying a web user **15.25**
through a link to a page within another's website rather than its homepage.
If, however, the provider of such a link makes clear that the new destination is
not associated with the page where the link is found there is no confusion.[39]

Framing[40]—bringing a page from another website into the page the web user **15.26**
is viewing—potentially combines confusion, free ride and tarnishment trade
mark infringement arguments with copyright infringement.[41] The transferred page may contain distinguishing insignia that will lose directly advertising revenue as a result of the transfer or be linked with unsavoury content
in the new page.

It is suggested that in a consumerist society there are no straight and direct **15.27**
lines linking consumers and marketers. Marketers compete to catch the
attention of the consumer on the high street; this has been accepted by trade

---

[36] See for example *U-HAUL International Inc v WhenU.com Inc* 279 F. Supp. 2d 723 68
USPQ 2d 1038 (DC Va 2003) and *Wells Fargo & Co v WhenU.com Inc* 293 F. Supp. 2d 734
(ED Mich 2003) where pop-up advertisements have been found not to constitute use in
commerce.
[37] *Nissan Motor Co Ltd v Nissan Computer Corp* 204 FRD 460 (CD Cal 2001).
[38] *Search King Inc v Google Technology Inc* 2003 WL 21464568 (WD Okla 2003).
[39] *Ticketmaster Corp v Tickets.com Inc* 54 USPQ 2d 1344 (CD Cal 2000).
[40] So far in the USA cases have been settled out of court. See S Weinberg 'Cyberjackings:
Trademark Hijackings in Cyberspace through Hyperlinking and Meta Tags' [1997] 87 TMR
576 at 584–587. For a comparative approach see IJ Garrote 'Linking and Framing: A Comparative Law Approach' [2002] EIPR 184.
[41] For the copyright issues contrast *Shetland Times Ltd v Dr Jonathan Wills & Another*
[1997] FSR 604 OH with *Futuredontics Inc v Applied Anagramics Inc* 45 USPQ 2d 2005 (CD
Cal 1997) aff'd 152 F3d 925 (9th Cir Cal 1998) for the UK and the USA respectively.

mark law. To the extent that the World Wide Web functions as a high street there is no reason to transform the rationale behind the law.

D. Warehousing

15.28 Dealing with cybersquatters, US courts accept that the offer to sell a domain name is not in itself actionable, although this position is reversed when the offer is linked with a threat to sell the domain name to the highest bidder[42] or when there are seventy-four domain name registrations of variations of a single trade mark.[43] This introduces an element of mischief in the behaviour of the domain name registrant, which can prove crucial. It shows that, more than anything else, it aims to preclude the trade mark owner from finding an appropriate domain name. The unauthorized registration of a trade mark as a domain name in order to extort money from the owner of the mark or prevent the owner from using the mark as a domain name is not a legitimate competing use of a contested sign.

15.29 Also, the combination of a name with '.com' is not considered commercial use *per se*. The intent though to trade in domain names commercializes the nature of use.[44] Use in commerce is always required for trade mark infringement and often the courts will look at the content of the website. A fan website that contains no links to commercial sites, no advertisements and no other specifically commercial content has been found not to be commercial.[45] Similarly, where the owner of a website recounted a dispute with a homebuilder, despite the existence of a section inviting visitors to share information on good builders there was no intent to make the site commercial since the owner never accepted payment for listing in the section and charged no money for viewing it.[46]

15.30 In the UK the organized but unauthorized registration of well-known trade

---

[42] *Virtual Works Inc v Volkswagen of Am Inc* 238 F3d 264 57 USPQ 2d 1547 (4th Cir Va 2001) and *E & J Gallo Winery v Spider Webs Ltd* 286 F3d 270 (5th Cir Tex 2002).
[43] *Garden of Life Inc v B Letzer S Letzer and Garden of Life LLC* 2004 WL 1151593 (CD Cal 2004).
[44] *Panavision International LP v Toeppen* 141 F3d 1316 46 USPQ 2d 1511 (9th Cir Cal 1998).
[45] *Taubman Co v Webfeats* 319 F3d 770 (6th Cir Mich 2003).
[46] *TMI Inc v JM Maxwell* 368 F3d 433 70 USPQ 2d 1630 (5th Cir Tex 2004).

marks as domain names, combined with offers to sell and warnings of tenders to third parties, has been considered to provide the registrant with an instrument of fraud, actionable under both registered trade mark law and passing off.[47] This approach has not been followed when the meaning of the domain name is ambiguous and there is evidence that it is actually used as a web address.[48] An analogy can be drawn with the case of trade marks consisting of descriptive terms which in practice are only granted a narrow scope of protection.[49]

E. Enforcement and Territoriality Questions

A sign on the internet can potentially infringe a trade mark anywhere in the world. Yellow.com can infringe the word mark YELLOW, both where it is registered in France for flowers and where it is registered independently in the USA for books. The exclusivity required for each domain name requires global solutions in terms of both geographical and product markets. As such, 'Yellow.com' cannot be assigned one way in France and another in the USA or one way for cars and another for flowers.[50] This is why ICANN has adopted a Uniform Dispute Resolution Policy (UDRP) that allows the owner of an earlier right to file an administrative complaint against a registrant of a conflicting gTLD. The Policy was updated and rationalized in January 2000, following WIPO's recommendations.[51] The decisions on the complaints can be challenged before the courts. However, the UDRP changes the balance between the players. All gTLD holders have to accept the applicability of the **15.31**

---

[47] *Marks & Spencer plc (& Ladbrokes plc & J Sainsbury plc & Virgin Enterprises Ltd & British Telecommunications plc) v One In a Million* [1998] FSR 265, [1999] FSR 1 CA. In such cases the transfer of the domain name to the trade mark proprietor appears the most appropriate remedy: see *Easyjet Airline Co Ltd v Dainty (t/a EasyRealestate)* [2002] FSR 6 ChD.

[48] See *French Connection Ltd v Sutton* [2001] ETMR 341 ChD for the ambiguity, credibility and trade mark meaning of FCUK.

[49] *Reed v Reed* (n 28) Jacob LJ at paras 83 and 84.

[50] Some trade mark commentators have been proposing the use of link or gateway pages that will allow multiple users for each domain name. See JR Dupre 'A Solution to the Problem? Trade Mark Infringement and Dilution by Domain Names: Bring the Cyberworld in Line with the "Real World" ' [1997] 87 TMR 613 and P Singh 'Gateway Pages: A Solution to the Domain Name Conflict?' [2001] 91 TMR 1226. Some companies have already adopted this synergistic approach.

[51] Rules for Uniform Name Dispute Resolution Policy available at http://www.icann.org; for WIPO's report see http://wipo2.wipo.int.

UDRP; this means that a trade mark owner has a cheap and effective way for attacking a conflicting domain name outside the public judicial system. Since there is no provision for appeal within the UDRP it is the domain name holder who has lost that has to turn to the courts. At the same time if a trade mark owner abuses the process—'reverse domain name hijacking'—the dispute resolution panel can declare in its decision that the complaint was brought in bad faith but there is no provision for penalties. In the USA the Anticybersquatting Consumer Protection Act (ACPA) provides that the party attacking the domain name may be liable for damages.[52]

15.32 Dispute resolution providers are approved by ICANN; among them WIPO, having reinvented itself, is active not only as a service provider but also as policy setting forum. Both the substance and the application of the UDRP have been much criticized.[53] Critics argue that trade mark concepts like 'bad faith' and 'common law marks' are interpreted liberally to circumvent freedom of speech arguments and accommodate protection of personalities and geographical indications. The risk is that this mood will also prevail in court cases. There is however evidence that courts are resisting. The international administrative process that is enforced by contract has been positively acknowledged by legislative developments in Europe, by the principles governing registration according to Commission Regulation 874/2004 laying down public policy rules concerning the implementation and functions of the .eu Top Level Domain,[54] and in the USA, by the ACPA.

15.33 In terms of trade mark infringement, it is necessary to ascertain whether access equals use in the jurisdiction. Common sense dictates that courts must

---

[52] Lanham Act (amended by the ACPA) s 32(2)(D)(iv).

[53] For an overview see S Maniatis 'Trade Mark Law and Domain Names: Back to Basics' [2002] EIPR 397; see also A Goldstein 'ICANNSUCKS.BIZ (and Why You Can't Say That): How Fair Use of Trademarks in Domain Names is Being Restrained' [2002] 12 Fordham Intell. Prop. Media & Ent. LJ 1151. According to the UDRP the following constitute evidence of bad faith: (i) the name has been reserved or acquired for the purpose of being transferred to a trade mark owner or its competitors, at a price that exceeds the domain name holder's costs; (ii) the name has been reserved in order to prevent the trade mark owner from embodying its mark in a domain name, if this falls within a pattern of similar conduct; (iii) the name has been reserved in order to disrupt the business of a competitor; evidence of use as an intentional attempt to attract for commercial gain visitors to its site by creating a likelihood of confusion as to source, sponsorship, or affiliation.

[54] OJ 2004 L 162/40. It requires that the Alternative Dispute Resolution system under the .eu regime should respect a minimum of uniform procedural rules, similar to the ones set out in the UDRP.

look at all the circumstances of the case, particularly the purpose of the website owner and the nature of the message conveyed to the visitor. If a service or product is provided only at a particular geographical location we can presume, first, that any goodwill accrued will be for a business based at this location and, second, that protection should be accordingly limited. If on the other hand the site encourages commercial interactivity with its visitors it becomes easier to establish jurisdiction.[55] For ccTLDs in particular the country code should be among the factors taken into consideration.[56] The internet provides marketers with the opportunity of cheap and effective global presence; constantly worrying about infringement would cancel this benefit.

Courts should act with self-restraint and with the awareness that the facts of a **15.34** case they have to resolve may be viewed under a different light from a court in another jurisdiction dealing with a different aspect of the dispute. This means that the scope of injunctions and declarations should be thoroughly appraised without preventing the claimant from obtaining judgment to which it is entitled within the jurisdiction of the court.[57] Trade mark law

---

[55] On appeal in *1–800 Flowers Inc v Phonenames Ltd* [2002] FSR 12 CA, Buxton LJ has provided *obiter* these guidelines on whether use of a mark on the internet might be sufficient to constitute use of the mark in the UK for the purpose of trade mark law. Placing a mark on the internet from a non-UK location would not suffice. An active move, like direct encouragement to purchase the product or advertisement, would be necessary in order to establish the necessary use. In the US personal jurisdiction cases can be divided into three categories: '1. *Active Web Sites*: cases . . . where defendants actively conduct business on the internet in the forum state and personal jurisdiction is found. 2. *Intermediate Web Sites*: interactive web site cases . . . where a user exchanges data with the host computer. In such cases, jurisdiction is determined by examining the level of interactivity and commercial nature of the information exchange. 3. *Passive Web Sites*: sites that merely provide information or advertisements. Decisions . . . refuse to find personal jurisdiction in such cases.' McCarthy (n 5) §32:45.1.

[56] *Euromarket Designs Inc v Peters and Crate & Barrel Ltd* [2001] FSR 20 ChD. An advertisement in a magazine circulating in Ireland and the UK and an .ie website, both referring to a shop in Dublin, were considered under the same light: the issue is where the advertised trade is being conducted and who are the customers. The real world prevailed over the virtual world.

[57] See *Prince plc v Prince Sports Group Inc* [1998] FSR 21 ChD for such a balancing exercise. Although the circumstances of the case are different, contrast with *Barcelona.com Inc v Excelentisimo Ayuntamiento de Barcelona* 189 F. Supp. 2d 367 63 USPQ 2d 1189 (ED Va 2002) where a US court without hesitation applied and deciphered Spanish trade mark law. However the Court of Appeal 330 F. 3d 617 67 USPQ 2d 1025 (4th Cir Va 2003) held that the dispute had to be adjudicated under US trade mark law according to the incorporation of the doctrine of territoriality through s 44 of the Lanham Act setting that US courts do not entertain actions seeking to enforce trade mark rights that exist only under foreign law.

should serve as a shield against foreign uses that have significant trade mark damaging effects in the marketplace where the law is applied[58] rather than a sword with extraterritorial global effect.

F. Conclusion

15.35 It has been shown that trade mark law has adapted its tools to fit the challenges posed by the internet at its early days without departing radically from its basic concepts, particularly the notion of trade mark use and its central role within infringement. Trade mark law serves the marketplace. The World Wide Web is nothing more that a widespread and accessible marketplace for products and ideas. The message is clear: avoid sweeping changes that will end up fragmenting or suffocating the market rather than protecting consumers and marketers.

Applying the Lanham Act it found that registration and use of the name 'Barcelona' was not unlawful. Still, potentially, US courts can become global trade mark rights enforcers in conflicts with domain names despite the territorial nature of national trade mark laws; *Cable News Network LP, LLLP v CNNews.com* 162 F. Supp 2d 484 61 USPQ 2d 1323 (ED Va 2001), aff'd in part, 56 Fed Appx 599 66 USPQ 2d 1057 (4th Cir 2003), held that jurisdiction under the ACPA exists in the Eastern District of Virginia for all .com disputes because Verisign, a company incorporated in the jurisdiction, is the exclusive registry for all .com domain names. See also JP Hugot and N Dalton 'The Universal Jurisdiction of French Courts in Civil and Criminal Cases: The Road to Digital Purgatory?' [2002] Ent LR 49 for an increasingly restrained approach in France.

[58] See *Sterling Drug Inc v Bayer AG* 14 F3d 763 29 USPQ 2d 1321 (2d Cir NY 1994) for a more traditional case. In *Mecklermedia Corporation v DC Congress* [1997] FSR 627 ChD Jacob J, decided that operating a website in Germany could cause passing off in the UK according to the facts of the case; where an organization wishes to use a domain name globally it risks infringing national rights throughout the world.

16

TRIPs AND TRADE MARK USE

G E Evans

A. Trade Mark Use and the Bounds of Property	16.13	development and the public interest	16.44
B. Expansionary Pressure on Descriptive Marks: Leaving Marks Free for Others to Use Contrasted with Registrability Acquired through Use	16.23	D. Expansionary Pressure and Trade Mark Infringement	16.51
		(1) Well-known marks and anti-dilution protection: protection for unused marks and use requirements for infringement by dilution	16.55
C. Trade Mark Use and the Impact of WTO Jurisprudence	16.31		
(1) Article 20: unjustifiable encumbrances involving trade mark use	16.32	E. Towards a Holistic Approach to the Interpretation of TRIPs	16.62
		(1) Ordinary meaning: beyond the dictionary	16.65
(2) National treatment and MFN	16.40		
(3) Article 8: exceptions for economic		F. Conclusion	16.72

In an era of advanced industrialization, the perceived link between trade **16.01** marks and the origin of the goods or services to which they attach is increasingly attenuated by developments in distribution and marketing methods. In the 'global network economy'[1] of the twenty-first century, the symbolic value of the trade mark has assumed even greater significance. The modern mark tends to attract the consumer through these 'extrinsic' qualities, which go beyond their 'intrinsic' function as indicators of origin. With the help of sophisticated advertising, manufacturers are able to associate individual

---

[1] The 'global network economy' is explained by Manuel Castells as follows: 'Economies throughout the world have become globally interdependent, introducing a new form of relationship between economy, state, and society, in a system of variable geometry.' See further M Castells *The Rise of the Network Society* (Blackwell Oxford 2000) 1.

aspirations and values with their products to create a desirable 'brand'. Marks that have acquired such extrinsic qualities and have global recognition due to investment in advertising are highly valued as 'intellectual capital'.[2]

16.02 Traditionally however, the law has not viewed trade marks as valuable in themselves.[3] The core concept of use as a trade mark remains the yardstick of property in the mark. Hence as a condition for the maintenance of the owner's exclusive rights, 'use in the course of trade'[4] or 'use in commerce'[5] is required. Moreover, it is said to be the trade mark's capacity to function as a badge of origin that differentiates it from other forms of intellectual property.[6] The trade mark's value is said not to depend upon any novelty, invention or discovery; nor to require any imagination, genius or laborious thought.[7] Instead, its value is derived from its use in commerce and its ability to act as a source of information for consumers that prevents confusion, lowers search costs and provides incentives for businesses to produce goods of consistent quality.[8] The US Constitution reflects this rationale. Authority for trade mark legislation rests on the Commerce Clause rather than on the Intellectual Property Clause,[9] to the effect that 'use in commerce' is an explicit requirement for trade mark jurisdiction.

16.03 Recent European case law reveals that the two most significant pressures on the concept of trade mark use have been branding and its counterpart, licensing. These global marketing phenomena have in turn given rise to expansionary pressures on the law concerning the acquisition of trade marks

---

[2] W Anson *Trademark Law Basics, Basics of Trademark Law Forum Coursebook* (International Trademark Association 2001) 'Chapter 2: Defining and Building the Brand' and 'Chapter 9: Section 1: Business and Legal Aspects of Licensing' available at http://www.consor.com/publications/index.html.

[3] *American Steel Foundries v Robertson* 269 US 372 (Sup Ct 1926).

[4] Council Directive 89/104 art 5(1) and (2).

[5] Lanham Act §1 (15 USC §1051). Trademarks registrable on the principal register.

[6] In *SA CNL-Sucal v HAG GF AG* [1990] 3 CMLR 571, 608, paras 13 and 14, the European Court of Justice described the essential function of a trade mark as giving to the consumer or ultimate user 'a guarantee of the identity of the origin of the marked product by enabling him to distinguish, without any possible confusion, that product from others of a different provenance'.

[7] *Trade-Mark Cases* 100 US 82 93–94 (Sup Ct 1879).

[8] ibid.

[9] The US Constitution art I §8, cl 8 provides Congress with the power 'to promote the Progress of Science and useful Arts, by securing for limited Times to Authors and Inventors the exclusive Right to their respective Writings and Discoveries'.

and the breadth of personal property in the mark. Today, corporate 'brand strategy' is likely to include promotional licensing, brand extension licensing, co-branding and endorsement licensing that is built upon regionally or globally based programmes. Given the global dimensions of 'brand power' and the financial stakes involved in the multifaceted licensing of trade marks, it was inevitable that a dispute of transatlantic proportions would occur. Intense competition between the USA and the European Union for worldwide market access has erupted into a battle over property rights concerning trade marks on the one hand and geographical indications for agricultural products and foodstuffs on the other.[10] The USA claims that the EU's regulation of geographical indications prejudices the 'right to use the trademark in commerce'.[11]

This dispute may be said to epitomize the *vita nuova* of trade mark law and legal practice in so far as it highlights the unprecedented impact of the WTO–TRIPs Agreement[12] on the future shape of property rights in the mark.[13] The implementation of TRIPs in over 140 countries dramatically illustrates the influence and dimensions of the global regulation of **16.04**

---

[10] On 1 June 2003 the USA filed a complaint with the World Trade Organization Dispute Settlement Body claiming that the EU Origin Regulation discriminates against foreign geographical indications and provides insufficient protection to pre-existing trade marks similar or identical to those protected in the EU. See 'European Communities—Protection of Trademarks and Geographical Indications for Agricultural Products and Foodstuffs', 24 February 2004, WTO, Constitution of the Panel Established at the Requests of the United States and Australia WT/DS174/21, WT/DS290/19.

[11] See Council Regulation 2081/92 on the protection of geographical indications and designations for agricultural products and foodstuffs. Council Regulation 2082/92 on Certificates of Specific Character for agricultural products and foodstuffs. TRIPs art 24.5 stipulates that measures in respect of geographical indications should not prejudice the 'right to use the trademark'. The EC argues that the GI Regulation permits the continued 'use' of the trade mark in commerce and thus does not prejudice the 'right to use the trademark', satisfying the art 24.5 requirement. Further see M Blakeney 'Proposal for the International Regulations of Geographical Indications' [2001] 4 Journal of World Intellectual Property 629; J Phillips *Trade Mark Law: A Practical Anatomy* (OUP Oxford 2003) para 18.23.

[12] Final Act Embodying the Results of the Uruguay Round of Multilateral Trade Negotiations, Marrakesh Agreement Establishing the World Trade Organisation, signed at Marrakesh (Morocco) 15 April 1994 ('WTO Agreement'), Annex IC, Agreement on Trade-Related Aspects of Intellectual Property Rights ('TRIPs Agreement' or 'TRIPs'), reprinted in *The Results of the Uruguay Round of Multilateral Trade Negotiations: The Legal Texts* (GATT Secretariat Geneva 1994) 1–19, 365–403.

[13] MA Leaffer 'The New World of International Trademark Law' [1998] 2 Marquette Intellectual Property Law Review 1.

intellectual property under the 'trade constitution'.[14] In contrast to the persuasive approach to international harmonization that existed under the Paris Convention, TRIPs Article 1 binds Member States to give effect to the provisions of the Agreement in their domestic laws.[15] By virtue of Articles 3 and 4 the major categories of intellectual property are subject to the former General Agreement on Tariffs and Trade (GATT) disciplines of most favoured nation and national treatment.

16.05   Significantly, Part II sets out comprehensive substantive provisions for the acquisition, maintenance, exploitation and enforcement of trade mark rights. It does so by incorporating Articles 1 to 12 and 19 of the Paris Convention,[16] supplemented by requirements concerning the eligibility of signs for protection,[17] the term of their protection[18] and the requirements for use, licensing and assignment.[19] The critical articles on enforcement are contained in Part III which sets out the obligations of Member governments to provide procedures and remedies under their domestic law to ensure that intellectual property rights can be effectively enforced by foreign and national right holders alike.

16.06   In accordance with the Understanding on Rules and Procedures Governing the Settlement of Disputes (DSU), international trade mark law is endowed with a permanent, integrated, interpretative body with virtually compulsory jurisdiction to hear any dispute arising under the Agreement Establishing the WTO and covered agreements.[20] Attesting to the legalistic character of the

---

[14]   GE Evans *Lawmaking under the Trade Constitution* (Kluwer The Hague 2000) analyses the impact of the trade mark provision of TRIPs on domestic law.

[15]   The Paris Conferences of 1880 and 1883 adopted the theory of minimum protection, which approximates the minimum standard of behaviour expected within civilized communities known to international law. Accordingly, the substantive provisions of the Paris Convention constitute the minimum of protection secured to foreign rightholders. SP Ladas *Patents, Trademarks and Related Rights: National and International Protection* (Harvard University Press Cambridge 1975) vol II 241.

[16]   As concluded at Stockholm 1967.

[17]   art 15.

[18]   art 18.

[19]   art 21.

[20]   art 1 of the DSU mandates that its rules and procedures shall apply to the settlement of disputes brought under any agreement contained in the WTO Agreements. Art 1.1 provides that the 'rules and procedures of this Understanding shall apply to disputes brought pursuant to the consultation and dispute settlement rules and procedures' under the 'covered agreements', which include the TRIPs Agreement. Complementary provisions reinforce art 1 in the covered agreements. Thus art 64 of TRIPs mandates the application of 'the provisions of Arts

WTO,[21] the former GATT dispute settlement system was strengthened by the addition of a standing Appellate Body[22] and binding quasi-judicial decision-making. As the USA found in the first major trade mark dispute with the European Communities, the *Havana Club* case,[23] the Appellate Body has jurisdiction to rule that governments must amend or repeal domestic laws that are inconsistent with world trade norms or risk the imposition of trade sanctions.[24]

Given the universal application of TRIPs norms,[25] the approach of adjudica- **16.07** tors to questions of legal interpretation is crucial not only to the effective harmonization of trade mark law but also to the continued cooperation of less developed countries to its implementation.[26] Since TRIPs entered into force on 1 January 1995,[27] the resulting interaction between WTO dispute settlement, the European Court of Justice (ECJ) and national tribunals increasingly requires the legal profession take account of the nature and approach to its interpretation. Moreover, it is not only public international disputes that involve the interpretation of TRIPs.

XXII and XXIII of the GATT 1994 as elaborated and applied by the Dispute Settlement Understanding ... to consultations and the settlement of disputes arising under [the] Agreement'.

[21] Evans (n 14) ch 6.

[22] art 17, Understanding on Rules and Procedures Governing the Settlement of Disputes (DSU), Final Act, pt 2, Annex 2, reprinted in [1994] 33 ILM 1236–37.

[23] WTO Appellate Body, United States Section 211 Omnibus Appropriations Act of 1998, WT/DS176/AB/R, 2 January 2002 ('US—Havana Club').

[24] C-D Ehlermann and N Lockhart 'Standard of Review in WTO Law' 7(3) [2004] Oxford Journal of International Economic Law 493; and WJ Ethier 'Intellectual Property Rights and Dispute Settlement in the World Trade Organization' [2004] 7(2) JIEL 449: arguing that the incorporation of IPRs into the global trading system raises a new dimension for settling disputes.

[25] The *erga omnes* character of TRIPs norms is demonstrated by the decision in *US— Havana Club* (n 23) paras 360–363. Note: an *erga omnes* right is one that is opposable to, that is, must be respected by, all states: I Brownlie *Principles of Public International Law* (5th edn OUP Oxford 2002).

[26] JR Reichman 'The TRIPs Agreement Comes of Age: Conflict or Cooperation with Developing Countries' [2000] 32(3) Case Western Reserve Journal of International Law 441; 'Enforcing the Enforcement Procedures of the TRIPs Agreement' [1997] 37(2) Virginia J of International Law 335 at 356.

[27] Under art 65.1 of TRIPs, WTO Members were not required to apply the provisions of TRIPs until 1 January 1996, that is, after a general period of one year following the date of entry into force of the WTO Agreement (1 January 1995). Economies in transition and developing countries had additional time under arts 65.2 and 65.4.

16.08 With respect to the thorny question of private individuals being able to rely on the TRIPs provisions, in the first place an *indirect effect* already exists for TRIPs provisions[28] by virtue of the 'concurrent jurisdiction' that is exercised by Member States in their own right and the European Community.[29] Secondly, as to the *direct effect* of TRIPs, in *Parfums Dior* the ECJ ruled that:

> where the judicial authorities of the Member States are called upon to order measures for the protection of intellectual property rights falling within the scope of TRIPs and a case is brought before the Court of Justice in accordance with the provisions of the Treaty, the Court of Justice has jurisdiction to interpret the Article of TRIPs in question.[30]

16.09 In view of this elegant compromise, in so far as the relationship between TRIPs and the trade mark law of the European Community is concerned, the ECJ has stressed that Member States have a duty to cooperate with Community institutions in carrying out their obligations with respect to the implementation of TRIPs.[31] In short, to the extent that TRIPs is capable of applying to situations falling within the scope of national law and concurrently to situations within the scope of Community law, it is clearly in the Community's interest to avoid differences of interpretation.[32]

16.10 Consider therefore how you might pursue an interpretation of trade mark use

---

[28] *Nakajima All Precision Co Ltd v Council* Case C-69/89 [1991] ECR I-2069, EC held to be bound by GATT.

[29] The TRIPs Agreement was approved on behalf of the EC, as regards matters within its competence, by Council Decision 94/800/EC of 22 December 1994 (OJ 1994 L 336, 1 and 214). Although Member States are entitled to be also Members of the WTO in their own right, most matters treated in the WTO come under Community discipline according to art 113 of the EC Treaty, which gives exclusive competence in the field of commercial policy to the EC, see Opinion 1/75 [1975] ECR 1355.

[30] *Parfums Christian Dior SA v Tuk Consultancy BV*, Case C-300/98 [2001] ETMR 277 para 9; *Anklagemyndigheden v Peter Michael Poulsen and Diva Navigation Corp* Case C-286/90 [1992] ECR I-6019.

[31] Agreements establishing the WTO, approved on behalf of the Community by Council Decision 94/800/EC of 22 December 1994 concerning the conclusion on behalf of the EC, as regards matters within its competence, of the agreements reached in the Uruguay Round multilateral negotiations (1986–1994) [1994] OJ L 336/1. Generally, see P Kuijper 'The Conclusion and Implementation of the Uruguay Round Results by the European Community' [1995] 6 EJI 1–244.

[32] *Hermès International and FHT Marketing Choice BV* Case C-53/96 [1998] ECR I-3603 para 32. Further see G Bontinck 'The TRIPs Agreement and the ECJ: A New Dawn?' available at http://www.jeanmonnetprogram.org/papers/01/013901.html.

that is in conformity with TRIPs if, in a reiteration of *Arsenal v Reed*,[33] you were preparing a brief for the ECJ. Is Article 5(1)(a) coextensive with TRIPs Article 16.1 to the effect that it allows the trade mark owner to prohibit the use of a sign identical to the mark and does not make exercise of that right conditional on the sign being used as a trade mark? On the other hand, is it the case that the commercial activities in question, the third party sale of unofficial club merchandise with disclaimer, do not fall within the purview of either Article 5(1)(a) or TRIPs Article 16.1?

In the next decade, the synergies between the WTO Dispute Settlement **16.11** System and the ECJ as a unique transnational tribunal, and national courts, will be critical to an informed international consensus concerning the characterization of property rights in trade marks. This is an important subject, given the dearth of scholarship on the substantive interpretation of international instruments such as TRIPs.[34] Accordingly, the following analysis seeks to explore the role played by trade mark use in the implementation of the TRIPs Agreement. This chapter's thesis is that, in view of the expansionary pressures to which the trade mark is subject, it is in the interests of continued cooperation in the global harmonization of the law that the concept of trade mark use, the traditional instrument for calibrating the scope of property in the mark, should remain capable of performing the task.

Accordingly, Part A outlines the boundaries of property rights in trade marks **16.12** and the interests to be weighed in their enforcement before inviting the reader to consider why society might wish to draw upon the concept of trade mark use in order to restrain the undue expansion of trade marks. Part B considers the demand from multinational business for 'descriptive' marks against the provisions of the TRIPs Agreement regarding the scope of protectable subject matter in light of recent decisions of the WTO Appellate Body. It explains how, at a time when the law has indeed extended the scope of eligible subject to include colour and shape, the concept of trade mark use is critical to achieving a suitably measured response. Part C explains how the

---

[33] *Arsenal Football Club Plc v Matthew Reed* Case C-206/01 [2003] 3 ETMR 227; [2003] 10 ETMR 895.

[34] F Dessemontet 'The TRIPs Dispute Settlement Procedure' ATRIP Conference, Lausanne, September 2001, arguing that scholars should help with up-to-date, accurate and objective commentary of the substantive provisions of the main international intellectual property conventions.

incorporation of intellectual property within the trade regime has imported considerations to the concept of trade mark use, notably principles of non-discrimination that formerly attached exclusively to international trade in goods. Part D examines the expansionary pressure on the scope of trade mark infringement, particularly in view of the fact that TRIPs Article 16.3 appears to import the doctrine of dilution into domestic trade mark law worldwide. It shows how the concept of trade mark use can be instrumental once again in mediating the inherent tensions between the values of commerce and those of free expression. Part E sets out to show how international courts and tribunals might approach the interpretation of TRIPs in such as way as to facilitate the key role the concept of trade mark use plays in a balanced application of trade mark norms. Having briefly compared the merits of the 'meaning of the text' approach over the teleological approach to the inter-pretation,[35] in conclusion the author advocates a holistic approach to the interpretation of TRIPs, in order to allow the concept of trade mark use to work to maximum advantage.

A. Trade Mark Use and the Bounds of Property

16.13 Contentious theoretical and policy questions are connected with the func-tion of a trade mark and the scope of property rights in the mark. To facilitate the connection between theory and practice consider the rights and liabilities of the parties in the following situation:

> Eve runs a wholesale and retail football merchandise business and sells identical goods bearing signs identical to the registered trade marks and goods of Adam's football club. Adam's trade marks are widely advertised and the merchandise to which they are attached is labelled 'official club merchandise'. Adam brings infringement proceedings. Eve's defence is that she is not using the signs as trade marks that is, so as to indicate trade origin. She has a disclaimer clearly displayed at the point of sale. She claims that she is merely using the marks as signs of affiliation to Adam's football club. Should Adam be able to prevent the use as signs of affiliation?

16.14 Isn't the reason Adam's goods cost twice the price because he has built a

---

[35] For a description of the various approaches to treaty interpretation see G Fitzmaurice 'The Law and Procedure of the International Court of Justice: Treaty Interpretation and Certain Other Treaty Points' [1951] BYIL 1ff.

monopoly power on the 'reputation' that his products are better than his competitors? If a consumer buys Eve's goods thinking they are Adam's, how has he been injured? On the other hand, isn't Eve in fact selling nothing more than counterfeit goods which are packaged identically to Adam's? Shouldn't the law seek to enforce trade mark law only against 'counterfeiters' of lower quality? If the goods are indeed identical in kind and quality, is there any reason to protect Adam's trade mark against infringement at the expense of consumers?

If we approach the above questions from perspectives of Adam's property in **16.15** the mark and that of unfair competition, the law's failure to recognize the infringement of his rights seems undesirable. One problem is that, if imitation is permitted, there may be less reason to invest in product quality in the first place. A related problem is that Adam's brand differentiation surplus is a result of his investment in goodwill. Allowing competitors to free-ride on that goodwill would discourage companies from investing in goodwill. Even if they continue to make quality products, they may have no particular incentive to advertise their brand name, increasing the search costs of consumers.[36] Consistently with this logic, the ECJ has stressed that the essential function of the mark is to

> Guarantee the identity of the origin of the trade-marked product to the consumer or ultimate user, by enabling him without any possibility of confusion to distinguish that product from products which have another origin.[37]

The TRIPs Agreement is in fact premised upon the notion of personal prop- **16.16** erty in the mark. This is evident from its characterization of intellectual property as personal property in the Preamble to the Agreement and its substantive trade mark provisions.[38] However, the rights of the trade mark

---

[36] Further see *Arsenal Football Club Plc v Matthew Reed (no 2)* [2003] ETMR 895 CA, taking account of evidence of consumer confusion at 910–911.

[37] *Hoffmann-La Roche v Centrafarm* Case 102/77 [1978] ECR 1139 para 7. See also the Preamble to Directive 89/104, cl 8 which in describing the protection afforded by the registered trade mark, states that 'the function of which is in particular to guarantee the trade mark as an indication of origin'.

[38] The Preamble to TRIPs states 'recognising that intellectual property rights are private rights'; see also TRIPs art 21 concerning the assignment of the trade mark with or without the transfer of the business to which the trade mark belongs; see UK Trade Marks Act 1994 ss 2 and 22: 'A registered trade mark is personal property (in Scotland, incorporeal moveable property).'

owner are distinctly circumscribed by the concept of trade mark use.[39] Outside the limited grace periods TRIPs allows for 'intent to use' and 'non-use': if a trade mark is not used in the course of trade, its registration is open to attack by rival traders. Although TRIPs Article 15.3 allows applicants to apply for and be granted a registered trade mark without any use having been made of the trade mark,[40] the mark is vulnerable to revocation if no use is made of it within three years of the grant[41] and there are 'no valid reasons for its non-use'.

16.17 Unlike copyright and patent owners, trade mark owners have no rights in gross.[42] Thus the law does not *per se* prohibit the use of trade marks or service marks. When granted trade mark registration, the owner has a 'negative right' entitling him, in accordance with TRIPs Article 16, to 'prevent all third parties not having his consent from using in the course of trade identical or similar signs for goods or services which are identical or similar to those in respect of which the trade mark is registered'. If the owner consents to use of the mark, he is no longer entitled to prevent its use. This consent underlies the principle of exhaustion of rights in Article 7 of the European Trade Marks Directive,[43] which provides that a trade mark shall not entitle the owner to prohibit its use in relation to goods which have been put on the market in the Community under that trade mark by the proprietor, or with his consent. The exhaustion of those rights therefore provides a third party with a defence to an infringement action.

16.18 Traditionally trade mark owners are only granted the right to prevent other trade mark uses that are likely to cause consumer confusion. Arguably, by

---

[39] On the exclusive rights of the trade mark owner see TRIPs art 16; EC Trade Mark Directive art 5; *US—Havana Club* (n 23) paras 179–202.

[40] TRIPs art 15.3 provides that registration may not be denied during a three-year application period solely on the grounds of non-use. The USA moved to a modified use-based registration during the Uruguay Round. The US system remains grounded in 'use' as a condition of registration, but it is now acceptable to file for registration declaring 'intent to use' a mark and subsequently filing, within a prescribed period, a verification that the mark has actually been used in commerce.

[41] Compare art 10.1 of the Trade Mark Directive; implemented in s 46(1) of the UK Trade Marks Act. With respect to what constitutes non-use and 'genuine use' see *Ansul BV and Ajax Brandbeveiliging BV* (MINIMAX) Case C-40/01 [2003] ECR I-2439, [2003] ETMR 85 paras 37–39.

[42] *Anheuser-Busch Inc v Balducci Publications* 28 F3d 769, 777 (8th Cir 1994).

[43] First Council Directive 89/104/EEC of 21 December 1988 to approximate the laws of the Member States relating to trade marks, OJ 1989 L 40 p 1.

importing the doctrine of dilution, in the case of well-known trade marks, TRIPs Article 16.3 would extend the scope of the trade mark owner's rights to situations where consumers are not actually confused as to the origins of two identical or similar marks. Thus the Federal Trademark Dilution Act of 1995 (FTDA), enacted with a view to implementing Article 16.3, gives the owner of a 'famous mark' protection

> against another person's commercial use . . . of a mark or trade name, if such use begins after the mark has become famous and causes dilution of the distinctive quality of the mark.[44]

Just how far should the law go in creating property rights in public goods? **16.19** From an economic perspective, the subject-matter of trade marks is an inexhaustible, non-excludable non-rivalrous 'public good'.[45] The problem for social uses of the language is that trade mark registration places under private control certain uses of the mark which would previously have been freely available to the public domain for a potentially indefinite period. So, for example, a review of a new software application for website design that discusses the product's qualities or other characteristics and is intended to inform readers, but not to promote the product, should not be prevented by the mark owner as a use in the 'course of trade'.[46]

Whereas Article 6 of the European Trade Mark Directive provides certain **16.20**

---

[44] See Federal Trademark Dilution Act: s 43(c), codified at 15 USC § 1125(c). According to the legislative history of the Federal Trademark Dilution Act, the TRIPs Agreement includes a provision designed to provide dilution protection to famous marks: H R Rep no 104–374, at 2 (1995), US Code Cong. & Admin. News at 1029. Whether this is in fact an accurate reading of art 16(3) might ultimately need to be submitted for resolution through the WTO's international dispute settlement process. See also *Moseley v V Secret Catalogue Inc* 537 US 418 (Sup Ct 2003) regarding the need for actual proof of dilution. See further Oversight Hearing on 'Committee Print to Amend the Federal Trademark Dilution Act' (22 April 2004) available at http://www.house.gov/judiciary/courts.htm.

[45] 'Public good' in the sense that it is possible for many people to simultaneously benefit from an invention without interfering with one another: *Dictionary of Free Market Economics* (Edward Elgar London 1998). See also R Cooter and T Ulen *Law and Economics* (2nd edn Addison-Wesley Reading 1997) 40–41 (noting that public goods are both non-excludable and non-rivalrous). See further WM Landes and RA Posner 'Trademark Law: An Economic Perspective' [1987] 30 (2) Journal of Law and Economics 265 at 308–309.

[46] Some companies have included 'no review' clauses in their software licences. See *State of New York v Network Associates Inc D/B/A Mcafee Software* Supreme Court of New York (2002) where New York State sued the maker of antivirus software alleging it is restricting free speech by barring customers from publishing product reviews without its consent: available at http://news.findlaw.com/hdocs/docs/cyberlaw/nyntwrkass020702pet.pdf.

limitations on the effects of trade marks, Article 17 of the TRIPs Agreement is the first such stipulation at the multilateral level. It establishes that:

> Members may provide limited exceptions to the rights conferred by a trademark, such as fair use of descriptive terms, provided that such exceptions take account of the legitimate interests of the owner of the trademark and of third parties.

16.21 The practical effect of permitting any undue expansion of the doctrine of dilution would be to create property rights in gross in suitably well-known marks.[47] In *Anheuser-Busch, Inc. v Balducci Publications*,[48] for example, the Eighth Circuit Court of Appeals found that a parody of an advertisement in a humorous magazine violated the state of Missouri's anti-dilution statute. The bogus advertisement, which appeared on the back of *Snicker Magazine*, purported to sell MICHELOB OILY and featured Anheuser-Busch's trade marked eagle being soaked with oil from a beer can. The parody's dual purpose was to mock Anheuser-Busch's brand proliferation and to express outrage at the Shell oil spill in the Gasconade river, a source of the company's water supply.[49] The case clearly shows that trade mark owners may resort to anti-dilution law to curtail what is arguably legitimate social comment. Indeed, in *New Kids on the Block v America Publishing*,[50] the Court of Appeals recognized that trade marks have an expressive dimension. The court stated that much useful social and commercial discourse would be almost impossible if speakers were under threat of an infringement lawsuit every time they made reference to a product by using its trade mark.[51]

---

[47] Concerning the definition of 'well known' see *General Motors Corp v Yplon SA* Case C-375/97 [2000] RPC 572; see also Joint Recommendation Concerning Provisions on the Protection of Well-Known Marks, adopted by the Assembly of the Paris Union for the Protection of Industrial Property and the General Assembly of WIPO at the Thirty-Fourth Series of Meetings of the Assemblies of the Member States of WIPO 20–29 September 1999: available at http://www.wipo.int/about-ip/en/development_iplaw/. On the implications of trade marks as property see A Kur 'The Right to Use One's Own Trade Mark: A Self-Evident Issue or a New Concept in German, European, and International Trade Mark Law?' [1996] European Intellectual Property Review 198 at 200–201.

[48] 28 F3d 769 (8th Cir 1994).

[49] ibid 772.

[50] 971 F2d 302 (9th Cir 1992).

[51] See *Nike Inc v Marc Kasky* 539 US (Sup Ct 2003) per Breyer J dissenting. See further BA Jacobs 'Trademark Dilution on the Constitutional Edge' [2004] 104 Columbia Law Review 161; K Aoki 'How the World Dreams Itself to be American: Reflections on the Relationship Between the Expanding Scope of Trademark Protection and Free Speech Norms' [1997] 17 Loy L A Ent L J 523 available at http://www.law.uoregon.edu/faculty/kaokisite/articles/dreamamerican.pdf; RJ Coombe 'The Cultural Life of Things' [1995] 10 Am U J Int L and Policy 791.

It is therefore critical that the concept of trade mark use should be well **16.22** calibrated in order to weigh up the interests at stake in the enforcement of trade mark rights, particularly in view of the complex questions that may arise. Lord Walker has well described the No Man's Land in which elements of distinctiveness and descriptiveness overlap.[52] Some of the most difficult cases, for example, concern the denominative use of trade mark on goods such as books or compact discs, situations that cannot easily be resolved without a suitably nuanced test. In such cases, courts prudently err on the side of caution when determining liability for trade mark infringement, particularly where claimants have other causes of action open to them. In such cases the real basis of the claim by an author or performer clearly lies in the realm of copyright law.

B. Expansionary Pressure on Descriptive Marks: Leaving Marks Free for Others to Use Contrasted with Registrability Acquired through Use

At the upper end of the spectrum where trade marks are arbitrary, fanciful or **16.23** suggestive in nature, the effects on the public may be relatively inconsequential.[53] However, when a descriptive word becomes the subject of trade mark protection the effect on the public at large and would-be competitors may be consequential, depending on elasticity within the relevant market. The open-ended definition of a trade mark in TRIPs Article 15.1 means that the kind of pressure formerly placed on the characterization of what may constitute a trade mark now somewhat problematically rests on the concept of trade mark use.[54] Both the ECJ and the US Supreme Court have expressed

---

[52] *R v Johnstone* [2003] 10 FSR 748 per Lord Walker at 776–777.

[53] *Abercrombie & Fitch Co v Hunting World Inc* 461 F2d 1040 (2nd Cir 1972) describes a spectrum ranging from marks that can never be registered (generic), to marks that can be placed on the Principal Register upon additional investment (descriptive), to marks that can be placed on the Principal Register immediately (suggestive and arbitrary).

[54] Very little is reserved as subject-matter that is ineligible for trade mark protection. Compare Paris Convention art 6*ter* which creates obligations to refuse trade mark registration for state flags and symbols; geographical indications and the German doctrine of *Freihaltebedürfnis* and *Windsurfing Chiemsee Produktions- und Vertriebs GmbH v Boots- und Segelzubehör Walter Huber and Franz Attenberger* Joined Cases C-108/97 and C-109/97 [1999] ECR I-2779, [1999] ETMR 585. Further, art 15.1 specifically refers to signs distinguishing 'services' as being subject to registration. This is a significant change from art 6*sex* of the Paris

concern over applicants securing rights in a colour or combination of colours which should be left free for other traders to use.[55]

16.24 Although international filings are expedited under the Madrid Agreement and the Madrid Protocol, the principle of territoriality remains the cornerstone of international trade mark law.[56] The entitlement of nation states to determine the effect of an application under national law was recently affirmed by the Appellate Body (AB) in *US—Havana Club*, ruling that, following an international filing, trade mark offices of Member States are not obliged under TRIPs to accept applications automatically if, because of their national trade mark laws, the mark might prove contrary to public order.[57] At issue was the interpretation of Article 6*quinquies*, Paris Convention, the so-called *telle quelle* (or 'as is' rule). This rule provides that, with respect to international filings, the trade mark registration authorities of Member States must accept for registration a mark in the same form in which it has been previously registered in the trade mark holder's country of origin. The EU proposed an expansive interpretation, arguing that not only must the mark be accepted for registration in the same form, but the mark must also be accepted for registration 'as is', thereby considerably narrowing the scope of Member States' capacity to determine the conditions of registration.

16.25 Rejecting the EU's argument, the AB's interpretation limits the *telle quelle* to the form of a trade mark. This means that, consistently with Article 6(1) of the Paris Convention, WTO Member States are free to determine 'the conditions for the filing and registration of trade marks' by means of their domestic

---

Convention, which requires states to provide protection for service marks, but does not mandate that they be subject to registration.

[55] Compare *Libertel Groep BV v Benelux-Merkenbureau*, Case C-104/01 [2003] ECR I-3793, [2003] ETMR 63, trade mark protection of colours *per se; Heidelberger Bauchemie* Case C-49/02 (newly reported); *Qualitex Co v Jacobson Products Co* 514 US 159 (Sup Ct 1995).

[56] Madrid Agreement Concerning the International Registration of Marks of 14 April 1891, as revised 1979 and the Protocol Relating to the Madrid Agreement Concerning the International Registration of Marks, Adopted at Madrid on 27 June 1989. Art 4 of the Paris Convention provides a six-month right of priority in respect to the filing of trade mark applications outside the country of first application. TRIPs arts 15 and 16, and the Paris Convention as incorporated therein, is premised on the principle of territoriality, concerning which see *Bourjois & Co v Katzel* 275 F 539, 543 (2nd Cir 1921) rev'd 260 US 689 (Sup Ct 1923). See generally WJ Derenberg 'Territorial Scope and Situs of Trademarks and Goodwill' [1961] 47 Va L Rev at 733, 734 and DE Long 'Unitorrial Marks and the Global Economy' [2002] 1 J Marshall Rev Intell Prop L 191.

[57] *US—Havana Club* (n 23) para 360.

legislation. The AB therefore concluded that the provisions of the Paris Convention would be eroded if Article 6*quinquies* required Member States to accept both the form of a foreign mark and another state's substantive conditions for the filing and registration of trade marks. This rule was designed to prevent trade mark registration authorities from requiring translations or other adaptations of marks to meet local preferences or rules.[58]

Consequently, the fact that a trade mark satisfies the requirements concerning distinctiveness under TRIPs Article 15.1 does not impose on Members the obligation to provide automatically for the registration of such mark. Consistently with Article 6*quinquies* B of the Paris Convention as incorporated, Members may deny or invalidate registration in cases where the trade mark is of such a nature as **16.26**

> to infringe right acquired by third parties in the country where protection is claimed

or where the mark consists

> exclusively of signs or indications which may serve in trade to designate the kind, quality, quantity, intended purpose, value, place of origin, of the goods

or marks that are

> 'customary in the current language or in the *bona fide* and established practices of the trade' in the country where protection is claimed.[59]

Nonetheless, requirements concerning 'intention to use' and 'non-use' remain decisive in the case of descriptive marks. *Prima facie* marks such as VOLKSWAGEN depend upon the ordinary meaning of the words to identify the goods or services. In their ordinary meaning, the terms do not distinguish between undertakings. Instead, they describe the goods of the business, albeit obliquely. Where there are 'absolute grounds', that is, grounds that are related to the inherent nature of the mark, for objecting to its registration, those objections may be overcome by evidence demonstrating that the mark has acquired distinctive character through use. In speaking of 'distinctiveness acquired through use', TRIPs Article 15.1 allows Members to condition **16.27**

---

[58] GHC Bodenhausen *Guide to the Application of the Paris Convention for the Protection of Industrial Property* (BIRPI Geneva 1969, reprinted as WIPO Publication no 611 (Geneva 1991)).

[59] See further art 6*quinquies* B, art 6*bis* and 6*ter*. Art 6*bis* establishes an obligation to refuse third party registration of well-known marks.

registration of 'descriptive' marks on their having achieved some level of distinctiveness in the minds of consumers so as to associate the goods with the enterprise in question. Consistently with Article 6*quinquies* C(1) of the Paris Convention as incorporated,

> in determining whether a mark is eligible for protection, all the factual circumstances must be taken into consideration, particularly the length of time the mark has been in use.

As we are dealing with questions of fact, the test for when sufficient use has been achieved may vary between WTO Member States.[60]

16.28 Intense competition in mass market goods, as well as new business models and forms of promotion in electronic commerce, have given rise to expansionary pressure on law's characterization of certain marks as 'descriptive'.[61] Recent case law from the ECJ points to the continuing demand by multinational enterprise for trade marks comprising descriptive words or sensory and other non-conventional signs.[62] In a setting of deep economic integration, such a situation has the potential to result in a dispute of international proportions.

16.29 Let us suppose that, following the ruling of the Appellate Body in the *US— Havana Club* case, trade mark examiners in a hypothetical jurisdiction, the Union of Transitional Economies (UTE) have increasingly objected to marks on absolute grounds. The UTE registry requires the applicant to make what it considers to be a satisfactory showing of distinctiveness. Further, certain foreign trade mark owners are required to transform their marks into a form that is more acceptable to the local culture. For example, they may be required to provide a translated version of descriptive terms. UTE justifies

---

[60] Wrigley registered the word mark DOUBLEMINT with the US Patent and Trademark Office in 1915, then unsuccessfully sought to register the mark in the EC as trademark for chewing gum (see immediately below).

[61] Consider, for example, how the practice of searching the internet using the genus of goods or services (eg hotels.com) helps fuel the demand for such marks: J Litman 'Breakfast with Batman®: The Public Interest in the Advertising Age' [1999] 108 Yale L J 1717. The ECJ broadened the definition of 'descriptive' in *Wrigley v OHIM* (DOUBLEMINT) Case C-191/01 P [2004] ETMR 9 and upheld the refusal to register by the OHIM Appeals Board.

[62] See eg *Procter & Gamble v OHIM* (BABY-DRY) Case C-383/99 P [2001] ECR I-6251, [2002] ETMR 3; DOUBLEMINT (n 61); *DKV Deutsche Krankenversicherung AG v OHIM* (COMPANYLINE) Case C-104/00 P [2002] ECR I-7561, [2003] ETMR 20; *Henkel KGaA v OHIM* Case C-457/01 P (3-dimensional marks) 456/01P, judgment 29 April 2004 (unreported).

this measure in accordance with TRIPs Article 8, which provides that Members may adopt measures necessary to promote the public interest in sectors of vital importance to their socio-economic and technological development. The development-oriented objective of the requirements is to ensure that some trade mark recognition is established in favour of a local enterprise and production.

Multinational enterprise LOGO Inc., having exhausted local remedies in the **16.30** state of UTE,[63] has requested its home state, Superstate, to take its complaint before the WTO. Failing the successful outcome either of consultations or of the panel process, the Appellate Body might then be faced with having to adjudicate a dispute based on (i) the scope of protectable subject matter in TRIPs Article 15; (ii) the interpretation of Article 20 concerning 'unjustified encumbrances' on trade marks; (iii) Article 8 concerning Members' ability to regulate in the public interest and (iv) the non-discriminatory principles of national treatment and most favoured nation treatment contained in Articles 3 and 4 respectively.

C. Trade Mark Use and the Impact of WTO Jurisprudence

As the UTE scenario reveals, the inclusion of intellectual property within the **16.31** regime of the WTO brings a new perspective to the characterization of trade mark use. While the content of trade mark use continues to transcend definition, the parameters of the concept are now qualified by the wider constraints that underpin the jurisprudence of the WTO. Membership of the WTO requires governments to impose restraints not only on tariffs, subsidies and safeguard measures governments may introduce, but also on regulations relating to the production of goods and services. To this end the WTO imposes regulatory requirements with respect to services and trade-related investment measures, as well as subsidies and countervailing measures, safeguards, technical barriers to trade, and sanitary and phytosanitary measures. This regulatory network is subject to the further superordinate discipline of national and most favoured nation (MFN) treatment, which serve to reinforce conditions for worldwide market access. Non-discrimination in

---

[63] For a state to take a case under principles of international law, local remedies should be exhausted: Brownlie (n 25).

international trade is the basic 'principle' of WTO; it is given expression in TRIPs in the 'most favoured nation' and the 'national treatment' rules.[64]

(1) Article 20: unjustifiable encumbrances involving trade mark use

16.32 In addition to claiming that UTE is in violation of its obligations under Article 15 in respect of protectable subject matter, Superstate may, in the alternative, claim that UTE is in violation of Article 20, which provides that

> The use of a trademark in the course of trade shall not be unjustifiably encumbered by special requirements, such as use with another trademark, use in a special form or use in a manner detrimental to its capability to distinguish the goods or services of one undertaking from those of other undertakings.

16.33 TRIPs Article 15.3 permits members to make registrability dependent on use. It is however arguable that, in the event the UTE places the burden of proof for trade mark registration on the applicant who relies on a foreign registration to show that it has used the mark in a foreign country, that this may indeed constitute an extra requirement in violation of Article 20.

16.34 Prior to conclusion of the TRIPs Agreement, it was not unusual for the national trade mark legislation of developing countries to contain requirements concerning the manner in which trade marks could be used. Despite the *telle quelle* rule regarding registration in the same form, foreign trade mark owners might be required to transform their marks into a form that was more acceptable to local society, including the provision of a translated version of descriptive terms. Alternatively, the domestic licensee of a foreign trade mark might be required to use its own trade mark alongside that of the licensor.[65]

16.35 The measures taken by UTE as outlined above appear to be contrary to the object and purpose of Article 20, which is precisely to prevent Member States from imposing such special requirements. The phrase 'special form' might thus be interpreted as referring both to the requirement for a translated version of descriptive terms and to the apparent need for a case-by-case

---

[64] See TRIPs arts 3 and 4.

[65] TRIPs and Development: *Resource Book UNCTAD/ICTSD Capacity Building Project on Intellectual Rights and Sustainable Development* (2003): see Trademarks Part Two: Substantive Obligations and Part Five: Interpretation; see especially 5.1, Methods of Interpretation under the DSU: available at http://www.iprsonline.org/index.htm.

determination by a trade mark authority of the extent of trade mark use. While reference to the familiar legal expression 'use in a manner detrimental to its capability to distinguish' would allow considerable breadth in interpretation, it again appears that UTE is in violation of Article 20. If, for example, trade mark owners are required to reduce the size of their marks or to place the generic name of a product alongside a trade mark, this might be said to diminish the mark's capacity to distinguish.

On the other hand, Article 20 is expressed not to   **16.36**

> preclude a requirement prescribing the use of the trade mark identifying the undertaking producing the goods or services along with, but without linking it to, the trade mark distinguishing the specific goods or services in question of that undertaking.

Thus, UTE, in keeping with its developmental objectives, would be permitted to indicate that a local producer is in fact the supplier of the goods with a view to giving local consumers and business confidence in the capacity of local suppliers. Nevertheless, the proviso concerning linkage ostensibly requires that local suppliers do not 'free-ride' on the goodwill of the foreign trade mark.

Article 20 was at issue in *Indonesia—Certain Measures affecting the Automobile* **16.37** *Industry*,[66] a WTO case in which Indonesia, as part of its National Car Programme, required a joint venture or national company to acquire and maintain an Indonesian-registered trade mark intended for that purpose. Under the National Car Programme of February 1996, 'pioneer firms' had to be 100 percent Indonesian-owned, use a unique Indonesian trade mark, be developed with national technology and reach 60 per cent local content within three years. The USA claimed that the ineligibility for benefits under the National Motor Vehicle programme of firms using an established or foreign-owned trade mark constituted a special requirement on the use of a trade mark in the course of trade that was prohibited by Article 20 of TRIPs.[67]

---

[66] Report of the Panel, WT/DS54/R, WT/DS55/R, WT/DS59/R, WT/DS64/R, 2 July 1998.

[67] The USA (joined by the EU and Japan), asserted that the 1993 and National Car Programmes were inconsistent with Indonesia's obligations under the GATT 1994 and the WTO Subsidies and Countervailing Measures (SCM) and Trade Related Investment Measures (TRIMs) Agreements.

16.38 In the result, the US claim was rejected. The panel found that the developer and owner of a mark used in the programme were sufficiently aware at the outset that the subject mark would be restricted in its use and thus that the Indonesian rule did not amount to a 'requirement' for use of the mark in the sense of Article 20. The panel further found that, while only Indonesian-owned marks would benefit from the programme, this was not a fact tied to the mark as such but was rather a condition of participating in the programme. Consequently, it concluded that the measure did not constitute a 'requirement' regarding the use of a mark of foreign origin.

16.39 While the Indonesian programme clearly favoured local trade mark holders, at least to the extent that they were able to participate in the programme, this does not necessarily mean that such a broad interpretation of Article 20 may be adopted in future. In the particular facts of the *Indonesia—Auto* dispute, the panel were cautious of allowing the USA to transform a dispute which was successfully based on violation of the Agreement on Subsidies and Countervailing Measures into a dispute concerning Indonesia's violation of the TRIPs Agreement.

(2) National treatment and MFN

16.40 As part of the WTO Charter, international trade mark law is subject to the non-discriminatory principles of national treatment and MFN treatment. The MFN provision contained in TRIPs Article 4 means that any favour, in the form of enhanced trade mark protection or concession, must be accorded 'immediately and unconditionally' to nationals of every other WTO Member State. While the original 1883 text of the Paris Convention contained an obligation to accord nationals of any country of the Union trade mark protection, the provision in Article 3 of the TRIPs Agreement incorporates not only the Paris provision but also the jurisprudence of international trade law from the inception of the original GATT of 1947. Adopting GATT terminology, the national treatment principle in TRIPs Article 3 provides that, as a matter of internal regulation, Member States

> shall accord to the nationals of other members treatment no less favourable than that it accords to its own nationals with regard to the protection of intellectual property.

In other words, Member States must accord the nationals of other members, in respect of trade marks, treatment equivalent to that which the state accords its own nationals.[68]

In *Indonesia—Auto* the USA claimed that Indonesia violated the national **16.41** treatment obligation in Article 3 because its National Car Programme provided a preference for Indonesian nationals in the acquisition of marks. In rejecting this claim, the panel found that foreigners were entitled to register and maintain marks in the same manner as nationals, despite the fact that Indonesian trade mark holders had preference with respect to the subsidy programme at issue. The panel concluded that, while this might give rise to questions regarding the scope of use of trade marks owned by US companies on cars under the programme, it posed no problem regarding the acquisition of trade mark rights. Only certain signs could be used as trade marks for meeting the relevant qualifications under the programme. This did not however mean that trade mark rights could not be acquired in a non-discriminatory manner.

Recently, on the other hand, in *US—Havana Club*, the Appellate Body found **16.42** Section 211 of the US Appropriations Act 1999 inconsistent with the national treatment obligation of the USA under the Paris Convention (1967 text), the TRIPs Agreement and the MFN provision contained in Article 4 of TRIPs. Section 211 effectively provided that trade mark and trade name rights were unenforceable with respect to trade marks and trade names that were confiscated by the Cuban Government.[69]

In the hypothetical case of UTE above, in so far as the facts recite that certain **16.43** foreign trade mark owners are required to transform their marks into a form that is more acceptable to the local culture, it is likely that the state would be found to have also violated its obligations to accord, to nationals of WTO Member States, MFN and national treatment in the event the measures in question only apply to property interests in the hands of foreign nationals.

---

[68] TRIPs art 3 requires that 'Each Member shall accord to the nationals of other Members treatment no less favourable than that it accords to its own nationals with regard to the protection of intellectual property, subject to the exceptions already provided in, respectively, the Paris Convention (1967).'

[69] s 211(a)(2) prohibits US courts from recognizing, enforcing or otherwise validating any assertion of trade mark rights based on common law rights or registration by certain persons in respect of confiscated marks and names; s 211(b) prohibits recognition, enforcement or other validation of treaty rights in respect of such property.

(3) Article 8: exceptions for economic development and the public interest

16.44 Classic GATT jurisprudence allows for exceptions to the principles of non-discrimination. In the case of intellectual property, Article XX(d) permits derogation from the national treatment obligation which is

> necessary to secure . . . the protection of patents, trade marks and copyrights and the prevention of deceptive practices.

16.45 Consistently, TRIPs Article 8 permits members to:

> adopt measures necessary to protect public health and nutrition, and to promote the public interest in sectors of vital importance to their socio-economic and technological development . . .

16.46 Consequently, UTE may claim alternatively that in the event it is in violation of the *telle quelle* rule requiring Member States to accept registration in the same form, by virtue of Article 8, in giving effect to the trade mark provision of TRIPs in its domestic laws and regulations, it may take account of key socio-economic objectives.

16.47 However, the principles of Article 8 are subject to the proviso that such measures should be consistent with the provisions of the TRIPs Agreement. Therefore, in so far as the measures in question appear to derogate from UTE's positive obligations under TRIPs Article 15, UTE's claim is unlikely to be successful. Although Article 8 is expressed so as to allow members some flexibility in adopting measures designed to promote their socio-economic objectives, according to TRIPs jurisprudence to date, even allowing for the persuasive authority of the developmental goals expressed in the Doha Declaration of 2001,[70] it is unlikely the UTE will be successful.

16.48 Based on the Canadian Patent cases, it appears that there is in fact less flexibility in the implementation of TRIPs than is often assumed,[71] irrespective of a Member State's level of economic development. In *Canada—Patent*

---

[70] The November 2001 declaration of the Fourth Ministerial Conference in Doha, Qatar.

[71] F Abbott 'The TRIPs Agreement, Access to Medicines and the WTO Doha Ministerial Conference' [2002] 5 Journal of World Intellectual Property 15; and SF Musungu, S Villanueva, R Blasetti 'Utilizing TRIPs Flexibilities for Public Health Protection through South–South Regional Frameworks' South Centre (April 2004): available at http://www.southcentre.org/publications/ flexibilities/flexibilities.pdf.

Protection of Pharmaceutical Products[72] the EC challenged certain provisions of the Canadian Patent Act which permitted generic producers to make the drugs and begin stockpiling them six months prior to the expiration of the patent. Canada purported to rely on TRIPs Article 30 which provides for limited exceptions to the exclusive rights of the patent owner, if these do not

> unreasonably conflict with a normal exploitation of the patent and do not unreasonably prejudice the legitimate interests of the patent owner taking account of the legitimate interests of third parties.

Canada further relied on Article 8, to argue that Articles 30 and 8, when read **16.49** jointly, call for a liberal interpretation of Article 30, so that governments should have the necessary flexibility to adjust patent rights to maintain the desired balance with other important national policies. However the panel rejected these arguments, finding that such a reading of Article 30 exceptions would constitute a renegotiation of the overall balance of the Agreement. As a result, Canada's stockpiling provision was found to constitute a 'substantial curtailment' of the exclusive rights granted to patent owners under TRIPs Article 28. Subsequently, in the case of *Canada—Term of Patent Protection*, the Appellate Body endeavoured to reassure developing countries that its findings concerning the inapplicability of Article 8 did not prejudge the applicability of Article 8 in possible future cases with respect to measures that they might take to promote national policy objectives.[73]

The case of *Superstate v UTE* illustrates that the regulation of trade marks **16.50** from within the framework of the WTO Agreements imposes constraints on the ability of Member States to customize the concept of trade mark use to local conditions. It clearly demonstrates that the impact of this transnational form of regulation at the microeconomic level is to impose considerable restraints on the capacity of national legislatures independently to influence the scope of property rights in the mark.[74]

---

[72] Panel Report *Canada—Patent Protection of Pharmaceutical Products* WT/DS114/R, adopted 7 April 2000 ('*Canada—Pharmaceuticals*'); similarly see s 110(5) of the US Copyright Act WT/DS160/R, adopted 27 July 2000 ('US—s 110(5) Copyright Act') paras 7.23 and 7.24–7.26.

[73] Report of the Appellate Body *Canada—Term of Patent Protection* AB-2000-7 WT/DS170/AB/R (18 September 2000) para 101.

[74] Concerning transnational forms of regulation: see Evans (n 14) chs 4 and 5 concerning the worldwide impact of the TRIPs Agreement; see also A Newman and D Bach 'The Transnationalization of Regulation', 13th International Conference of Europeanists, Chicago, Illinois, March 2002.

D. Expansionary Pressure and Trade Mark Infringement

16.51 Such is the character of property in the mark that, without the ability to exercise rights given in Article 16.1 to prevent all others from confusing uses, the trade mark may lose its ability to distinguish and therefore may be no longer 'capable of constituting a trade mark'.[75]

16.52 TRIPs Article 16.1 prohibits the unauthorized use of the trade mark in the following terms:

> The owner of a registered trademark shall have the exclusive right to prevent all third parties not having his consent from using in the course of trade identical or similar signs for goods or services which are identical or similar to those in respect of which the trademark is registered where such use would result in the likelihood of confusion. In the case of the use of an identical sign for identical goods or services, a likelihood of confusion shall be presumed.

In view of the general terms in which Article 16 is drafted, it may justify the extension of the concept of unauthorized trade mark use, either on the basis that such use would 'result in the likelihood of confusion' or that the concept of trade mark use denoting origin includes uses that prejudice the ability of the mark to distinguish the goods. The validity of these propositions with respect to the scope of trade mark use was recently tested in *Arsenal v Reed*[76] before the ECJ.

16.53 Arsenal, an internationally known football club, brought infringement proceedings under the UK Trade Marks Act 1994 section 10(1)[77] against Mr Reed who sold club merchandise bearing signs identical to the registered trade marks of Arsenal. Reference was made to the ECJ as to whether Arsenal should be able to prevent the use of its trade marks by Mr Reed as signs of affiliation to the football team. Dismissing any defence based on the notion

---

[75] See *Bayer Co v United Drug Co* 272 F 505 (SDNY 1921) where the defendant competitor was not only selling acetylsalicylic acid but was doing so under the designation Aspirin, based on the ground that the latter had become a commonly recognized name for the drug. The claimant's failure to police others' use of the term adquately resulted in its loss of distinctiveness.

[76] *Arsenal v Reed* (n 33).

[77] Use of an identical sign in relation to identical goods and services for which the trade mark is registered (s 10(1)). Arsenal was concerned with identity of registered trade mark and sign and identity of goods. Thus infringement will occur if the alleged infringer 'uses in the course of trade' the sign: [2003] ETMR 895 CA per Aldous LJ at 901.

that the team's supporters would not perceive the signs the defendant used as a trade mark use, the ECJ ruled that Arsenal could prevent the use of signs identical to its trade marks on goods for which the mark was registered.

At this point, with a view to reconciling theory and practice, it is instructive **16.54** to return to our initial hypothesis concerning the function of the mark and the scope of property rights in it, to consider whether the ECJ was correct in upholding Arsenal's right to enforce its trade marks. Is it not the case that Arsenal's goods cost more simply because it has invested heavily in promoting the belief that the 'official club merchandise' is more desirable than that of its competitors? Is the defendant selling nothing more than counterfeit goods, which are packaged identically to Arsenal's? Is this not why, in the case of the use of an identical sign for identical goods or services, Article 16(1) establishes that a likelihood of confusion shall be presumed? The ECJ, by taking an expansive approach to what constitutes infringement and by not allowing evidence of a lack of confusion to act as a rebuttal of infringement, has taken a position that reflects the requirements of Article 16(1). If we approach these questions from perspectives of property and that of unfair competition, is it not the case that the law's failure to enforce Arsenal's trade mark rights would not only constitute a failure to stimulate investment in an international sports industry but also increase the search costs of consumers?

(1) Well-known marks and anti-dilution protection: protection for unused marks and use requirements for infringement by dilution

In 1925 the Paris Convention was revised to provide a higher level of protec- **16.55** tion for well-known marks. Article 6*bis* requires countries to refuse or cancel the registration, and prohibit the use, of a trade mark which constitutes a reproduction of a well-known mark, liable to create confusion in respect of the same or similar goods. Although Article 6*bis* addresses the subject of 'well-known marks', it does not explicitly deal with the extent of the mark's use in the territory of the state in question. Consequently, a further difficulty in protecting well-known marks in third party markets concerned the restrictive definition accorded to use of the mark.

As recently as 1999, in *Prefel SA v Fahmi Babra*[78] with respect to the trade **16.56**

---

[78] 1998–1999 (case no. 200/PDT.G/1998/PN.JKT.PST).

mark PRADA, a word and device trade mark owned by the claimant in several other countries, the Supreme Court of Indonesia found for the defendant on the ground that there had been no actual use of the mark in Indonesia in the form of sales transactions. The court based its decision on the fact that the Directorate of Trademarks did not find the mark to be well known and consequently refused Prefel's trade mark application for a similar mark. This was clearly inconsistent with the terms of Article 6*bis* since it is sufficient under that Article if the mark in question is well known in commerce in another country's market as a mark belonging to a certain enterprise.

16.57 This requirement is reinforced in TRIPs Article 16.2 which stipulates that, in determining whether a trade mark is well known, Members are to take into account knowledge of the trade mark in the relevant public sector, including knowledge obtained as a result of the promotion of the trade mark. It is now clear that having goods or services on the market in the territory of the Member State is not a prerequisite to holding interests there in a well-known mark.[79] TRIPs not only affirms Article 6*bis* but also supplements the special protection accorded well-known marks. Article 16 requires that well-known marks, in consideration of the magnitude of their reputation, be given a higher standard of protection than marks that are not well known. Article 16.2 and 16.3 require that Members not only prohibit the use and registration of trade marks likely to create confusion with well-known marks but that they extend its application *mutatis mutandis*, to services.

16.58 During the last thirty years an increasing tendency for the owners of well-known marks to engage in worldwide product diversification has given rise to a demand that protection extend the prohibited use of the mark to goods that are dissimilar to those in respect of which the mark is registered. Article 16.3 addresses the situation in which a third party uses a well-known mark in connection with goods or services that are not similar to those for which the right holder is well known. It provides:

---

[79] In view of the level of international economic integration, the TRIPs negotiators considered the notion of use in international trade as a means of establishing reputation (see Geneva Draft), but later decided to abandon the notion largely it seems from administrative perspective; for national trade mark offices, demonstrating 'international use' would involve a costly and time-consuming initial examination of marks: see further TP Stewart (ed) *The GATT Uruguay Round: A Negotiating History (1986–1992)* (Kluwer Deventer 1993) vol II 2273–2276.

Article 6*bis* of the Paris Convention (1967) shall apply, *mutatis mutandis*, to goods or services which are not similar to those in respect of which a trademark is registered, provided that use of that trademark in relation to those goods or services would indicate a connection between those goods or services and the owner of the registered trademark and provided that the interests of the owner of the registered trademark are likely to be damaged by such use.

Arguably, Article 16.3 provides well-known marks with anti-dilution protec- **16.59** tion. The doctrine of dilution, as formulated by Frank Schechter,[80] enables the trade mark owner to protect his mark against forms of use where the traditional requirement of likelihood of confusion is absent. The doctrine does not seek to protect the indication of origin, which the trade mark represents, but the distinctive quality which the mark itself embodies. Accordingly, Article 16.3 appears to give the owners of well-known marks a dilution-like right to take action against any material reduction in their value through use by third parties, even where there is no competition between them or likelihood of confusion between the marks.[81]

Since the wording of the Article is ambiguous, debate continues over the **16.60** extent to which the law should give protection to the extrinsic publicity value of trade marks as distinct from their function as indicators of origin. The emphasis in the provision on (i) the well-known reputation of the mark, (ii) the absence of any explicit reference to the likelihood of confusion of the public and (iii) the requirement that the 'interests of the owner of the registered trademark are likely to be damaged' by the use of the third party's trade mark has led some scholars to the view that Article 16.3 imports the doctrine of dilution. On the other hand, others point to the incorporation of Article 6*bis* and to the reference there to a trade mark 'liable to create confusion'. In any event, Article 16.3 is drafted conservatively, in so far as it is faithful to Frank Schechter's traditional rendering of trade mark dilution.[82] He thought the use of similar marks on dissimilar goods could give rise to the 'gradual whittling away or dispersion of the identity and hold upon the public mind' of the mark or name by its use on non-competing goods.

---

[80] 'The Rational Basis of Trademark Protection' [1940] 40 Harvard Law Review 813–833.
[81] JT McCarthy *McCarthy on Trademarks and Unfair Competition* (4th edn West Group St Paul 1996) §29:63; cf UK Government White Paper *Reform of Trade Mark Law* Cm. 1203 [1990] n 8 at 14. On the economic ground for trade mark protection on the basis of dilution see Landes and Posner (n 45) 308–309.
[82] T Martino *Trade Mark Dilution* (Clarendon Press Oxford 1996).

16.61 Recently, however, the doctrine of trade mark dilution has been considerably extended by recent developments in European trade mark law. In *Davidoff v Gofkid*[83] the ECJ concluded that it was illogical for wider protection to be granted against use on dissimilar goods than against use of similar or identical goods. Despite a clear reference to 'goods or services which are not similar to those for which the trade mark is registered', the Court held that Article 5(2) of the Trade Mark Directive is not correctly implemented unless the owner of the mark is entitled to prevent the use of an identical or similar sign, not only in relation to goods or services which are not similar but also in relation to goods or services which are identical or similar to those for which the trade mark is registered. This means that the EU in its Directive grants wider protection than TRIPs since TRIPs 'dilution' protection is apparently limited to use on dissimilar goods or services. Nonetheless, even under such extended protection, Advocate General Jacobs has submitted, in the subsequent case of *Adidas v Fitnessworld*,[84] that it is a condition of the application of Article 5.2 that the allegedly infringing sign is used as a trade mark, that is to say for the purpose of distinguishing goods or services.

E. Towards a Holistic Approach to the Interpretation of TRIPs

16.62 Given the critical role the concept of trade mark use plays in mediating the scope of property right in trade marks, it is of the utmost importance that it should be implemented in a suitably discriminating and nuanced manner. The case of *US—Havana Club* reveals that the adjudicators' approach to the interpretation of TRIPs is decisive to the nature and scope of substantive content. After reviewing the Panel's approach to the interpretation of Articles 2.1 and 16.1, the AB reversed the panel's finding that trade names were not protected under the TRIPs as it incorporates Article 8 of the Paris Convention. In the view of the AB, the Panel's interpretation of Articles 1.2 and 2.1 of TRIPs was contrary to the ordinary meaning of the terms of those provisions and is, therefore, not in accordance with the customary rules of

---

[83] *Davidoff & Cie and Zino Davidoff SA v Gofkid Ltd* Case C-292/00 [2003] ETMR 42.
[84] *Adidas-Salomon AG et al v Fitnessworld Trading Ltd* Case C-408/01 [2004] ETMR 10 (protection against use of a sign in relation to identical or similar goods or services). The ECJ did not explicitly adopt this reasoning, discussing instead whether use as an 'embellishment' counted as infringement under art 5(2).

interpretation prescribed in Article 31 of the Vienna Convention on the Law of Treaties.[85]

By virtue of TRIPs Article 64, adjudicators must interpret the Agreement in **16.63** accordance with the Vienna Convention on the Law of Treaties 1969. In complementary fashion, Article 3.2 of the WTO Dispute Settlement Understanding (DSU) directs panels to interpret the TRIPs provisions

> in accordance with customary rules of interpretation of public international law

as embodied in the Vienna Convention. According to Article 31 of the Vienna Convention a treaty must be interpreted in

> good faith in light of (i) the ordinary meaning of its terms, (ii) the context and (iii) its objects and purpose.[86]

In addition Article 32, entitled 'Supplementary means of interpretation', **16.64** defines what is meant by the 'context of the treaty' and what other elements must be taken into account within the context including: the *travaux préparatoires*, any

> subsequent practice in the application of the treaty establishing the understanding of the Parties as to its interpretation

and any relevant rules of international law.[87]

(1) Ordinary meaning: beyond the dictionary

Within the short life and narrow compass of WTO–TRIPs jurisprudence, **16.65** the trade mark cases largely involve matters of first impression. Strictly

---

[85] The Convention was adopted on 22 May 1969 and opened for signature on 23 May 1969 by the United Nations Conference on the Law of Treaties. Entry into force on 27 January 1980, in accordance with art 84(1). Text: United Nations *Treaty Series* vol 1155, p 331.

[86] ibid (interpreting Vienna Convention art 31(1)).

[87] In general the PCIJ and the ICJ refused to resort to preparatory work if the text is sufficiently clear. Sometimes the Court has used preparatory work to confirm a conclusion reached by other means: *Case Concerning Maritime Delimitation and Territorial Questions Between Qatar and Bahrain (Qatar v Bahrain)* ICJ Reps. 2001. Brownlie (n 63) 630 cautions that 'preparatory work is an aid to be employed with discretion, since its use may detract from the textual approach, and, particularly in the case of multilateral agreements, the records of conference proceedings, treaty drafts and so on may be confused or inconclusive'.

speaking, there is no doctrine of *stare decisis* and in principle adjudicators are free to deviate from interpretations applied in previously adopted panel and AB reports, but they hardly ever do so. Starting in 1948, GATT Panel reports establish a reliable and comprehensive case law. Further, Article XVI:1 of the WTO Agreement affirms the application of the jurisprudence established under GATT 1947 to the interpretation of the TRIPs Agreement.[88] The 'look and feel' of interpreting a treaty may differ from domestic legislation. However, the aim of treaty interpretation in the end, like that of statutory interpretation is to give meaning to the words, read in their context and to the fullest extent possible, for the purpose of achieving the objects which are stated or otherwise apparent.[89]

16.66 The nature of submissions to WTO Panels to date shows the pitfalls of pursuing a blindly simplistic and rigidly two-tiered approach to the interpretation of TRIPs, as exemplified by this submission based on the authority of the *New Shorter Oxford English Dictionary:*[90]

> The ordinary meaning of the terms in Article 16.1 confirms the breadth and strength of the rights that must be accorded owners of registered trademarks. 'Prevent' means to '[s]top, hinder, avoid', and '[c]ause to be unable to do . . . something'. 'All' means the 'entire number of' and 'without exception'. 'Exclusive' means '[n]ot admitting of the simultaneous existence of something; incompatible' and '[o]f a right, privilege, quality, etc.; possessed or enjoyed by the individual(s) specified and no others'.[91]

16.67 It makes little sense to negate centuries of trade mark law by opening a dictionary. It would be highly unusual if the words of a legal text were to have an 'ordinary' or 'plain' meaning, as if the words themselves had some kind of essence. Can we not usually assign meanings to words based on the context and the conventions of language within the trade mark law of our global

---

[88] WTO Agreement art XVI:1 provides: 'Except as otherwise provided under this Agreement or the Multilateral Trade Agreements, the WTO shall be guided by the decisions, procedures and customary practices followed by the CONTRACTING PARTIES to GATT 1947 and the bodies established in the framework of GATT 1947.'

[89] *Golder v The United Kingdom* (4451/70) [1975] ECHR 1 (21 February 1975) paras 34–36.

[90] *New Shorter Oxford English Dictionary* (4th edn Clarendon Press Oxford 1993).

[91] *EU—Protection of Trademarks and Geographical Indications* First Submission of the US for *Agricultural Products and Foodstuffs* (WT/DS174 and 290) 23 April 2004 para 138. Counsel can be forgiven for following the approach of TRIPs Panels: see for example *Canada—Term of Patent Protection* (n 73).

community? The idea that no interpretation is necessary when words are 'plain' is fallacious. To give words an 'ordinary' meaning is surely to give them a commonly accepted meaning within a community of discourse in a particular context. In this case technical terms belonging to the field of trade mark law should be given their technical meaning. As Wright LJ observed[92] regarding the notion of the trade mark owner holding herself out as responsible for the quality of the goods sold under her mark, the word 'origin' is used in a technical sense to denote that

> the goods are issued as vendible goods under the aegis of the proprietor of the trade mark, who thus assumes responsibility for them, even though the responsibility is limited to selection.

In point of policy the literal rule makes good sense in so far as it advocates **16.68** judicial restraint. For example, in *Davidoff v Gofkid*,[93] the ECJ might have shown greater restraint before finding that Article 5(2) of the Trade Marks Directive should not be 'interpreted solely on its face, but also in the light of the overall scheme and objectives of the system of which it is a part'. Certainly, rival traders are entitled to question the logic of the grant of wider protection against use on dissimilar goods than against use of similar or identical goods.

At the national level, common law judges apply the plain meaning of the **16.69** statute as revealed by the language of the text: they do this because they treat fidelity to legislative enactment as an overriding value. With respect to the application of Article 31 Vienna Convention, the European Court of Human Rights in *Golder v United Kingdom* correctly stated that a holistic approach was required:[94] interpretation should be

> a single combined operation which takes into account all relevant facts as a whole.

This approach accords well with modern canons of statutory interpretation, **16.70** that legislation should be read with resort to all admissible indicia of meaning from the text as a whole, from identification of the purposes of the text and after consideration of the consequences of the various possible

---

[92] *Aristoc Ltd v Rysta Ltd* [1945] 62 RPC 65, 82.

[93] *Davidoff v Gofkid* (n 83).

[94] *Golder v The United Kingdom* (n 89: see separate opinion of Judge Zekia to the effect that 'the examination of this aspect is bound to overlap with considerations appertaining to the object and purpose of a treaty'.

interpretations. In sum, although the text of TRIPs may reveal its object and purpose, assistance may also be obtained from extrinsic sources. The form in which a treaty is drafted, the subject to which it relates, the mischief that it addresses, the history of its negotiation and comparison with earlier or amending instruments relating to the same subject-matter may warrant consideration in arriving at a decision regarding the treaty's object and purpose.

16.71 Moreover, international law permits decision-makers to make reference to municipal law. According to Article 38 of the Statute of the International Court of Justice, international adjudicators may have recourse to various sources, including general principles of law common to legal systems as well as judicial decisions as a subsidiary means of interpretation.[95] We are now fortunate in having a corpus of transnational trade mark law in the juris-prudence of the ECJ, to which WTO adjudicators might reasonably have recourse in order to provide guidance in the task of global harmonization. For example, ECJ case law may assist in identifying a more nuanced set of criteria for determining whether combinations of descriptive words or combinations of colours are capable of acquiring distinctiveness through use.[96]

F. Conclusion

16.72 The foregoing analysis has sought to examine the part played by the concept of trade mark use in the global harmonization of trade mark law. Recent developments in marketing and commercial practice have created a demand for more robust protection which, in turn, has subject the law to pressures that would restrict the category of descriptive marks that have been tradition-ally reserved to the public domain, to the possible detriment of a more competitive marketplace. Equally, the expansion of industry into areas of life formerly reserved for purely social pursuits potentially serves to transform the community ties to which we have become accustomed. Moreover, we have

---

[95] art 38 (1)(c).
[96] For example, in *Heidelberger Bauchemie* (n 55) the ECJ attempts more nuanced guide-lines regarding combinations of colour to the effect that the juxtaposition of two or more colours, without shape or context will not be sufficient to secure registration since colour combination marks must be spatially limited and have a systematic arrangement.

seen that the strength of the principles of non-discriminatory trade that underpin the WTO Agreement, when linked to intellectual property, serves to impose additional levels of restraint on the policy options available to Member States.

Taking account of the expansionary pressures to which property in the trade **16.73** mark is subject and the possible socio-economic implications, I submit that it is to the advantage of continued international cooperation in the implementation of the TRIPs Agreement that trade mark use should remain instrumental in mediating the scope of property in the mark. International adjudicators might achieve this by adopting a more holistic approach to the interpretation of TRIPs that would render the concept of trade mark use capable of facilitating the more finely balanced distinctions that decision-making in such complex circumstances involves.

17

USE, INTENT TO USE AND REGISTRATION IN THE USA

Graeme B Dinwoodie and Mark D Janis

A. Introduction	17.01	C. Use as a Condition for Maintaining Rights	17.22
B. Use as a Condition for Acquiring Rights	17.03	D. Use and the Geographical Scope of Rights	17.26
(1) Actual use	17.05		
(2) Constructive use	17.17	E. Conclusion	17.33

A. Introduction

The concept of use pervades US trade mark law. Use doctrines manifest **17.01** themselves in rules governing jurisdiction, trade mark acquisition and trade mark enforcement. The use 'in commerce' requirement ensures that the federal trade mark system remains within the bounds of Congress' legislative authority under the Commerce Clause.[1] Actual or constructive use[2] by the

---

[1] The requirement that the trade mark owner use (or intend to use) the mark in interstate commerce appears in various provisions of the Lanham Act. See eg 15 USC §§1051(a) and (b) (Lanham Act §§1(a) and (b)) (owners of marks 'used in commerce', or persons having a bona fide intention 'to use a trade mark in commerce', may apply for registration). The Lanham Act defines 'commerce' as 'all commerce which may lawfully be regulated by Congress': 15 USC §1127 (Lanham Act §45); see also *United We Stand America Inc v United We Stand America NY Inc* 128 F3d 86 (2d Cir 1997) ('commerce' in Lanham Act is coterminous with 'commerce' in Commerce Clause). For an example of litigation over the jurisdictional aspects of the use requirement, see *Larry Harmon Pictures Corp v Williams Restaurant Corp* 929 F2d 662 (Fed Cir 1991) (use of mark in connection with restaurant services at single-location restaurant with small percentage of out-of-state customers satisfies 'commerce' requirement).

[2] Text to nn 32–39.

alleged trade mark owner is a condition precedent for securing and maintaining trade mark rights, equal with the other fundamental requirements of distinctiveness and non-functionality. And use is central to many aspects of trade mark scope,[3] including the geographical scope of trade mark rights,[4] the application of the likelihood of confusion factors[5] and doctrines usually styled as defences to trade mark infringement or dilution.[6]

17.02 While the concept of use thus plays a multitude of roles in the US trade mark system, the most substantial case law regarding trade mark use has developed from disputes concerning the acquisition and maintenance of trade mark rights (often in the context of priority disputes among claimants competing for the same trade mark rights), and the geographical scope of trade mark rights. This chapter focuses on those areas, taking up use doctrines in the context of acquiring trade mark rights in Part B, in the context of maintaining trade mark rights in Part C and in defining the geographical scope of rights in Part D. We conclude with some thoughts concerning the current state of these doctrines, mentioning some new contexts in which the use concept may be deployed in the near future to shape the content of US trade mark law.

B. Use as a Condition for Acquiring Rights

17.03 The US trade mark system is the paradigmatic example of a 'use'-based system, so it is not surprising that US law has long imposed a requirement that a trade mark claimant engage in use of its mark as a condition for

---

[3] Unconsented use is also a threshold requirement for trade mark infringement: 15 USC §1114(1)(a); Lanham Act §32(1)(a) (referring to unauthorized 'use in commerce'); *Holiday Inns Inc v 800 Reservation Inc* 86 F3d 619 (6th Cir 1996) (competitor's use of vanity phone number corresponding to 1–800-H[zero]LIDAY was not a use of plaintiff's HOLIDAY INNS mark).

[4] See below under D.

[5] Use concepts appear implicitly via typical likelihood of confusion factors, such as the factor that inquires as to the mark owner's and defendant's marketing channels. See GB Dinwoodie and MD Janis *Trademarks and Unfair Competition: Law and Policy* (Aspen Publishers New York 2004) ch 7, listing multi-factor confusion tests from all US federal appellate courts.

[6] The most obvious example is the fair use doctrine: see eg *Brother Records Inc v Jardine* 319 F3d 900 (9th Cir 2003), reciting tests for 'classic' and 'nominative' fair use.

claiming either registered or common law trade mark rights.[7] The use requirement performs at least three functions in this context: first, it seeks to ensure that those who will eventually hold trade mark rights first make a genuine commitment to invest in the mark, rather than merely reserving it for the future; second, it serves as a mechanism for putting the public (consumers as well as market competitors) on notice as to a claim of trade mark rights because products bearing that mark will be placed in the stream of commerce, often accompanied by a trade mark notice; and third, it serves an evidentiary function, providing objective evidence of the date when rights can properly be claimed and the nature of that claim.

Despite its theoretical centrality to the acquisition of rights, the use require- **17.04** ment has not always been applied rigidly in practice. In particular, US courts have long strained against the constraints of a strict concept of actual use. Prior to 1988, courts developed doctrines that implicitly recognized various forms of constructive use.[8] In 1989, constructive use explicitly entered the US trade mark orthodoxy through the incorporation of 'intent-to-use' provisions into the Lanham Act. We discuss actual and constructive use, respectively, in the following sections.

(1) Actual use

The post-1988 Lanham Act articulates a rigorous standard for trade mark **17.05** use, requiring that the trade mark claimant engage in

> a bona fide use of the mark in the ordinary course of trade, and not made merely to reserve a right in a mark.[9]

But judicial interpretations have largely ameliorated the apparent harshness of this provision. Most significantly, some courts apply a 'totality of the circumstances' test to determine whether a firm's activities with respect to a mark demonstrate that the trade mark claimant (i) in fact adopted the mark

---

[7] See eg *Columbia Mill Co v Alcorn* 150 US 460, 463–64 (1893), a case decided prior to the advent of modern US trade mark statutes, stating that 'the claimant of a trade mark must have been the first to use or employ the same' on goods or services.

[8] For example, courts employed the doctrine of 'token use' to ameliorate that actual use requirement. The 1988 reforms outlawed the token use doctrine. See Dinwoodie and Janis (n 5) ch 5. We discuss other examples of the implicit recognition of constructive use in the next section.

[9] 15 USC §1127 (Lanham Act §45) defining 'use in commerce'.

and (ii) used the adopted mark in a sufficiently public manner that consumers could identify the marked goods with a unique producer.[10]

17.06 The Court of Appeals for the Ninth Circuit, which has extended the totality of the circumstances test to service marks,[11] has elaborated on the types of circumstances beyond sales activities that it might consider relevant, including considerations of

> what would be a commercially reasonable attempt to market the service, the degree of ongoing activity . . . to conduct business using the mark, the amount of business transacted, and other similar factors.[12]

17.07 The totality of the circumstances approach is also presumably the governing approach for cases involving claims of common law rights, as US courts generally apply the same methodology to questions of actual use whether the trade mark claimant is claiming registered or (unregistered) common law rights.[13]

17.08 Exercising the considerable latitude allowed by the totality of the circumstances test, courts have found actual use even in the absence of completed sales, where the trade mark claimant had engaged in advertising and direct customer solicitations.[14] Courts have wisely resisted efforts to impose bright-line requirements as to the quantity of marked goods or the quantity of advertisements featuring the mark. In one case, the Court of Appeals for the Federal Circuit concluded that three newspaper advertisements for a restaurant constituted actual use in view of additional evidence that the mark claimant had used the mark in various state regulatory documents,[15] while the Court of Appeals for the Seventh Circuit concluded that actual completed

---

[10] *Planetary Motion Inc v Techsplosion Inc* 261 F3d 1188 (11th Cir 2001). In US patent jurisprudence, the US Supreme Court has derided the totality of circumstances 'test' as providing too little certainty, presumably because it does little (perhaps nothing) to constrain judicial discretion: see *Pfaff v Wells Electronics* 525 US 55 [1998] 66 n 11 which noted that the totality of the circumstances test had been criticized as 'unnecessarily vague' in the context of patent validity disputes involving the on-sale bar to patentability.

[11] *Chance v Pac-Tel Teletrac Inc* 242 F3d 1151 (9th Cir 2001).

[12] ibid 1159.

[13] *Allard Enters Inc v Advanced Programming Res Inc* 146 F3d 350 (6th Cir 1998).

[14] *New West Corp v NYM Co of Cal* 595 F2d 1194 (9th Cir 1979), cited approvingly in *Planetary Motion*, n 10.

[15] *West Florida Seafood Inc v Jet Restaurants Inc* 31 F3d 1122 (Fed Cir 1994).

sales of a few bottles of shampoo bearing the mark did not suffice to demonstrate actual use.[16]

Courts have emphasized that the determination of actual use rests heavily on **17.09** comparing the claimant's activities to commercial activities that are deemed to be typical within a particular industry. Where a software developer used a mark on email software posted to a website for free downloading, a court found actual use in view of the fact that free distribution (under the GNU public licence) had become customary in the Unix software community.[17] But where a hobbyist used a mark in connection with a car that he raced periodically at county fairs, a court found that these activities fell short of actual use in view of the standard practices for commercializing marks in the automobile industry.[18]

In addition to using the totality of the circumstances test, courts have used **17.10** other doctrinal mechanisms to ease the burden of the actual use requirement. Courts have reached instinctively towards subtle forms of constructive use in order to reach results that seem to align with the inter-party equities and (less obviously) with the purposes of trade mark law, even if the results depart from strict conceptions of actual use.

In other writings, we have employed the label 'surrogate use' to describe one **17.11** such set of cases.[19] In a case of surrogate use, courts allow a trade mark claimant to claim the benefit of someone else's actual use of the mark. Accordingly, surrogate uses lie at the margins of the concept of actual use; they may be considered a form of quasi-constructive use.

Courts have recognized surrogate uses in two primary contexts. First, courts **17.12** routinely conclude that actual use by one firm inures to the benefit of a second firm where the two firms are substantially related either as a matter of corporate structure (eg a parent/subsidiary relationship) or as a matter of contract (eg a franchisor/franchisee relationship).[20] The Lanham Act now

---

[16] *Zazu Designs v L'Oréal SA* 979 F2d 499 (7th Cir 1992).
[17] *Planetary Motion* (n 10) 1198.
[18] *Heinemann v General Motors Corp* 342 F Supp 203 (ND Ill 1972) aff'd 478 F2d 1405 (7th Cir 1973).
[19] Dinwoodie and Janis (n 5) ch 4; GB Dinwoodie and MD Janis *Trademark Use* (working paper).
[20] *May Dept Stores Co v Prince* 200 USPQ (BNA) 803 (TTAB 1978); *United States Jaycees v Philadelphia Jaycees* 639 F2d 134 (3d Cir 1981) (contractual relationship).

explicitly recognizes this concept, via the 'related companies' doctrine.[21] These concepts are particularly difficult to apply in cases in which the relationship between the actual user and the trade mark claimant is more ambiguous than that which is found in a conventional parent/subsidiary or franchising relationship. For example, a number of cases grapple with the question of whether use of a mark in connection with a musical group inures to the benefit of the group as an entity, individual members of the group or even someone else (eg the group's producer).[22] The fact that these groups tend to change membership and structure over time adds considerable complexity to the inquiry.

17.13   Second, courts employ a concept of surrogate use in some cases in which uncoordinated public uses of a mark run to the benefit of a trade mark claimant. For example, in *University of Wisconsin* a bookstore adopted and began to use a badger logo on the sale of clothing and other items in connection with the promotion of the University of Wisconsin's athletic teams. Eventually, the name 'Wisconsin Badgers' and associated logos came into widespread use as the nickname of the university's athletic teams. With little comment, the Trademark Trial and Appeal Board of the US Patent and Trademark Office (PTO) accepted the proposition that the bookstore's use (and subsequent public uses) should inure to the benefit of the university. As long as the public associated the mark with the products and services of the university, there could be 'no question' that the uses were attributable to the university.[23] In *Johnny Blastoff,* public and media uses of the phrase 'St. Louis Rams' in reference to the plaintiff's National Football League franchise established use on behalf of the plaintiff, even though the uses occurred before the plaintiff had completed its move of the Rams franchise from Los Angeles.[24] And in *Coca-Cola,* a pre-Lanham Act case, consumer uses of the term 'Coke' as an abbreviated reference to the plaintiff's COCA-COLA soft drinks established use for the benefit of the Coca-Cola Co., even though there was

---

[21]   15 USC §1055 (Lanham Act §5) providing that the use of a mark by an entity that is 'controlled by the registrant or applicant for registration of the mark' inures to the benefit of the controlling entity; see also 15 USC §1127 (Lanham Act §45) defining 'related company'.

[22]   See eg *Boogie Kings v Guillory* 188 So2d 445 (La App 1966) concluding that the uses at issue ran to the benefit of the musical group as an entity, not to the benefit of individual group members.

[23]   *University Bookstore v University of Wisconsin Board of Regents* 33 USPQ 2d (BNA) 1385, 1392 n 21 (TTAB 1994).

[24]   *Johnny Blastoff Inc v Los Angeles Rams Football Co* 188 F3d 427 (7th Cir 1998).

no evidence that Coca-Cola itself had ever promoted the name 'Coke' in connection with its products.[25]

This (perhaps understandable) emphasis on public perception, and the sub- **17.14** ordination of producer intent, opens the door for some remarkably tricky cases. For example, what should happen when the public uses a mark in connection with a firm's products (HOG for Harley-Davidson motorcycles) and the firm actively strives to disassociate itself from the mark, then changes its mind several years later and asserts rights in the mark?[26] In a related vein, concerning the maintenance of rights rather than the initial allocation of rights, suppose that one party adopts a mark (MARCH MADNESS for a state high school basketball tournament) and the public begins using the mark to refer to an event sponsored by another party (the men's national collegiate basketball tournament)?[27] As yet, courts have not developed a general rule to deal with these cases; the prevailing inclination to address use in an *ad hoc* and unsystematic way suggests that such a general rule is unlikely to evolve.

The doctrine of analogous use presents another example of a subtle departure **17.15** from the actual use requirement in the initial allocation of trade mark rights. The doctrine arises in Lanham Act §2(d) cases involving an allegation that a registered mark is invalid in view of the existence of a confusingly similar previously registered mark, or of a confusingly similar previously used mark or trade name.[28] Under a well-settled interpretation of §2(d), even the exist-ence of a prior use that is 'analogous to' a trade mark use suffices for invalidat-ing a mark under §2(d).[29] Neither the courts nor the PTO have defined analogous use precisely (or, some would say, comprehensibly). An analogous use, by definition, falls short of actual use, but must be 'open and notorious', directed to the relevant segment of the purchasing public, and carried out in a manner so as to have a substantial impact on the public.[30] These same qualities, of course, would also describe actual use.

---

[25] *Coca-Cola Co v Busch* 44 F Supp 405 (ED Pa 1942).

[26] See *Harley-Davidson Inc v Grottanelli* 164 F3d 806 (2d Cir 1999) which concluded for other reasons that the mark was generic.

[27] *Illinois High School Association v GTE Vantage Inc* 99 F3d 244 (7th Cir 1996): public's use of the mark in reference to the collegiate tournament divested the initial trade mark owner of exclusive rights, and coining the phrase 'dual use' term to describe the phenomenon.

[28] 15 USC §1052(d) (Lanham Act §2(d)).

[29] *Herbko International Inc v Kappa Books Inc* 308 F3d 1156 (Fed Cir 2002).

[30] *TAB Systems v Pactel Telectrac* 77 F3d 1372 (Fed Cir 1996).

17.16 As with all these departures from the strictness of the actual use requirement, courts must be careful not to imperil the objectives that underpin the use requirement.[31] As a result, courts seem disinclined to consolidate these *ad hoc* departures in rigid, bright-line doctrine.

(2) Constructive use

17.17 In 1988 Congress explicitly introduced the concept of constructive use into US law when it adopted an intent-to-use system.[32] Under Section 1(b) of the Lanham Act, enacted by the 1988 reforms, a trade mark applicant may file an application for a federal trade mark registration based upon a bona fide intent to use the mark in commerce.[33] Such an application constitutes 'constructive use of the mark, conferring a right or priority, nationwide in effect'.[34]

17.18 This reform might seem to attenuate the 'commitment and investment objective' of the use requirement in favour of the notice and evidentiary objectives; the availability of intent-to-use applications elevates the latter objectives by facilitating early federal registration. However, such a conclusion must be viewed in the light of both prior trade mark registration practice (which validated 'token uses' as means of obtaining registrations without commitment and investment) and the 'use' conditions which the Lanham Act imposes on intent-to-use applicants. In particular, although an application may be filed based upon on intent to use the mark, a positive response from the PTO will result (after the expiry of the opposition period) in the issue of a Notice of Allowance, which will in turn mature into a registration only upon the applicant demonstrating actual use to the PTO.[35]

17.19 In some ways, more radical departures from the use requirement are found in those provisions of the Lanham Act implementing international treaty-based

---

[31] For a fuller elaboration of the costs of a liberal concept of use, see GB Dinwoodie 'Trademarks and Territory: Detaching Trademark Law from the Nation-State' [2004] 41 Hous. L. Rev. 1885.

[32] See Trademark Law Revision Act of 1988 Pub L no 100, 102 Stat. 3935 (1988).

[33] 15 USC §1051(b). The TRIPs Agreement now prohibits the US from requiring actual use as the sole basis for filing an application for registration: TRIPs art 15(3).

[34] 15 USC §1057(c) (Lanham Act §7(c)).

[35] 15 USC §1051(d) (Lanham Act §1(d)). Moreover s 7(c) limits the ability of the intent-to-use applicant to obtain relief pending the commencement of use. See *WarnerVision Ent Inc v Empire of Carolina* 101 F3d 259 (2d Cir 1996).

registration mechanisms.[36] In particular Section 44(e), which implements the *telle quelle* provision found in Article 6 *quinquies* of the Paris Convention, permits an application for federal registration to be made based on a registration of the same mark in the applicant's country of origin. Although such an applicant must allege a bona fide intent to use the mark in commerce, it need not make use of the mark in commerce prior to the registration issuing.[37] This places Section 44(e) applicants in a better position than domestic intent-to-use applicants and is thus a greater departure from the actual use requirement of US law. Similar latitude has been afforded foreign applicants who request an extension of protection in the USA under the Madrid Protocol, which the USA joined with effect from 2 November 2003.[38] Instead, for these applicants, the use requirement is of greatest import in maintaining their US registrations. Use must be made within the statutory time-period or the mark may be treated as abandoned.[39]

17.20 Although these mechanisms represent exceptions to the actual use requirement, and might be viewed effectively as even stronger endorsements of constructive use concepts, they do at least further the notice and evidentiary objectives of the use requirements (while ignoring the investment and commitment purposes). Section 44(d) of the Lanham Act, which implements the priority rule of Paris Convention Article 4, and enables the foreign registration to claim the benefit of its foreign priority date by filing in the USA within six months thereof, additionally undermines the notice function of the use requirement by effectively according a constructive use date that precedes US filing.[40]

17.21 Thus the constructive use provision introduced into US law by the 1988 intent-to-use reforms is the most explicit derogation from the actual use requirements of trade mark acquisition. However, the most likely

---

[36] See also *British-American Tobacco Co v Philip Morris Inc* 55 USPQ 2d 1585 (TTAB 2000) (interpreting the Pan American Convention).

[37] See *Crocker National Bank v Canadian Imperial Bank of Commerce* 223 USPQ (BNA) 909 (TTAB 1984) (en banc).

[38] See 15 USC §§1141–1141n (2004) (Lanham Act §§60–74).

[39] See *Linville v Rinard* 23 USPQ 2d (BNA) 1508 (TTAB 1993).

[40] See *SCM Corp v Long's Foods Ltd* 539 F 2d 196 (DC Cir 1976). S 44(d) does offer some limited protection to unsuspecting US users; see 15 USC §1126(d)(4) (precluding suit for acts committed prior to date of US registration unless registration based on use in commerce). This rule facilitates the acquisition of multinational rights (a goal underlying the priority system of the Paris Convention).

continuation of this trend away from the requirement of actual use may be generated by international developments rather than by purely domestic considerations.

C. Use as a Condition for Maintaining Rights

17.22 Just as adoption and use (actual or constructive) is a condition for the initial allocation of trade mark rights under US law, continued use is a prerequisite for maintaining trade mark rights. Under the applicable Lanham Act definition, a trade mark may become abandoned if (i) the mark owner ceases using the mark and does not intend to resume use or (ii) the mark owner acts (or fails to act) in such a way as to allow the mark to become the generic reference for the underlying goods or services.[41]

17.23 Concerning the first part of the definition, the mark owner's cessation of use for three consecutive years gives rise to a presumption of abandonment.[42] A mark owner may attempt to rebut the presumption by showing actual use, or by showing intent to resume use in the reasonably foreseeable future.[43] In *Qashat*[44] the mark owner unsuccessfully argued actual use based upon a shipment of marked product from a US manufacturer to its own UK offices, followed by sales from the UK to the Middle East. In *Silverman*[45] the mark owner CBS fell short in arguing intent to resume use. CBS was asserting trade mark rights in the Amos 'n Andy characters, despite having dropped the characters from broadcasts some twenty-one years earlier because of concerns over their racial overtones. CBS argued that it had always intended to reintroduce the characters at some point in time, but the court found this assertion too open-ended to serve as a basis for rebutting the presumption of abandonment. Notwithstanding these examples, courts generally state that the burden of establishing abandonment is heavy.[46]

---

[41] 15 USC §1127 (Lanham Act §45).

[42] ibid.

[43] *Emergency One Inc v American Fireeagle Ltd* 228 F3d 531 (4th Cir 2000). The Fifth Circuit has insisted that a mark owner's showing of mere intent not to abandon the mark is not sufficient; the mark owner must show an intent to resume use: *Exxon Corp v Humble Exploration Co Inc* 695 F2d 96 (5th Cir 1983).

[44] *General Healthcare Ltd v Qashat* 364 F3d 332 (1st Cir 2004).

[45] *Silverman v CBS Inc* 870 F2d 40 (2d Cir 1989).

[46] *Cumulus Media Inc v Clear Channel Communications Inc* 304 F3d 1167 (11th Cir 2002) (burden is 'strict').

An emerging issue in non-use cases is whether non-use can be overcome by **17.24** evidence of residual goodwill (that is, goodwill that endures despite the lack of substantial affirmative acts of manufacture, distribution or advertising on the part of the trade mark owner). US courts have not reached common ground on whether to accept the concept of residual goodwill. In *Ferrari*[47] the court embraced the concept and concluded that, even though Ferrari had ceased manufacturing the 365 GTB4/Daytona Spyder, the company had nevertheless maintained trade mark rights in the shape of the Spyder chassis because, independent of any activities on the part of Ferrari, the public continued to associate the chassis with Ferrari. However, Ferrari had continued to supply repair parts for the Spyder and had continued to manufacture other similar designs. Based on these facts in *Stickley*[48] the Court of Appeals for the Second Circuit distinguished *Ferrari*: Stickley had offered evidence that it enjoyed residual goodwill in the 1990s for certain furniture designs that it had produced decades earlier. But Stickley had not supplied repair parts or manufactured similar designs; the court concluded that Stickley had abandoned trade dress rights in the designs, notwithstanding evidence of residual goodwill. The residual goodwill issue, like many other use issues, presents difficult questions about the relative significance to be attributed to public perception, especially in the face of apparently contrary acts or intentions by the trade mark owner. This, in turn, implicates more fundamental attitudes towards the property status of trade marks.[49]

Concerning the second part of the abandonment definition, a common form **17.25** of mark owner conduct giving rise to abandonment allegations is the mark owner's failure to control licensees or franchisees, especially by failing to include quality control provisions in license or franchise agreements.[50] Historically, control obligations have been an important component of 'use' rules because control was essential for the use by the licensee to inure to the benefit of the licensor. However, in one context—collegiate marks—courts

---

[47] *Ferrari SpA Esercizio Fabbriche Automobili e Corse v McBurnie* 11 USPQ 2d (BNA) 1843 (SD Cal 1989).

[48] *L & JG Stickley Inc v Canal Dover Furniture Co Inc* 79 F3d 258 (2d Cir 1996).

[49] For early discussion of the extent to which trade marks are property see generally *Hanover Star Milling Co v Metcalf* 240 US 403 (1916).

[50] See *Dawn Donut Co Inc v Hart's Food Stores Inc* 267 F2d 358 (2d Cir 1959) explaining the concept of 'naked' licensing; *Stanfield v Osborne Industries Inc* 52 F3d 867 (10th Cir 1995) illustrating the concept and concluding that the licensor had abandoned rights in the mark.

and the PTO have treated mark owners with notable generosity, routinely refusing to find abandonment even where a college or university has been historically lax in policing third party usages of its marks. In *University of Wisconsin*[51] the PTO concluded that the numerous third party users of University of Wisconsin marks in the Madison, Wisconsin area should be treated as operating under an implied licence from the university. This liberal approach to control obligations, while still unusual in the USA outside the context of collegiate marks, is consistent with evolving international norms that appear to place great faith on market pressures to incentivise producers to maintain consistent quality.[52]

D. Use and the Geographical Scope of Rights

17.26 The use of a mark is also relevant to the scope of rights that a trade mark owner acquires, whether at common law or through registration. Two principal components of the use of the mark define the scope of rights: the products upon or in connection with which the mark is used, and the geographical area in which the mark is used.

The relevance of the products on which the mark is used—though still important—has diminished as notions of actionable confusion have expanded and causes of action based on dilution have become available under federal law. In this part of the chapter, we discuss the relevance of the geographical variable because it is this component of use that most sharply brings into focus the complex interaction of use and registration and that is most acutely tested by the international marketing of goods and services.[53]

17.27 At common law in the USA, trade mark rights extended only so far as the areas in which the mark had been used. For example in *United Drug Co v Theodore Rectanus Co*[54] the senior user of a mark (REX) who had used the mark only in Massachusetts could not enjoin the use of the same mark by a trader in Louisville, Kentucky who had been the first to use the mark in that

---

[51] *University Bookstore v University of Wisconsin* (n 23) rejecting an abandonment argument in a PTO opposition proceeding.
[52] See Proposed Revised Trademark Law Treaty, WIPO Document no. SCT 12/2 art 20 (27 February 2004).
[53] See generally Dinwoodie (n 31).
[54] 248 US 90 (1918).

area.[55] The US Supreme Court recognized the coexistence of two trade marks, each defined by, *inter alia*, the territory in which they were used. This rule comported with the purposes of trade mark law, as two separate bundles of goodwill existed: each would be protected by the Court's geographically sensitive approach.

As trade expanded, US courts developed doctrines that enabled producers to **17.28** assert a scope of rights beyond areas of actual use. Most notably, trade mark owners were permitted to exercise rights both in the area of actual use and in a so-called 'zone of natural expansion'.[56]

In some ways, the amelioration of strict actual use standards in this context **17.29** parallels liberal interpretation of what *amounted* to use, as discussed in part A. And just as reforms of federal registration procedures reduced the necessity for such judicial innovation there, so too the availability of federal registration rendered judicial liberalization of *United Drug* less crucial.

In particular, Section 22 of the Lanham Act deems registration of a mark on **17.30** the Principal Register to be nationwide constructive *notice* of the registrant's claim to ownership.[57] As a result, a producer can obtain nationwide rights by federal registration even though it has not used the mark nationally.[58] And, as noted above, the constructive use concept introduced by the intent-to-use reforms has moved the date of this priority benefit up to the date of federal application.[59]

While the basic rules regarding the geographical scope of registered rights **17.31** thus have been well established, the availability of common law use-based

---

[55] See also *Hanover Star Milling Co v Metcalf* 240 US 403 (1916).

[56] See eg *Tally-Ho Inc v Coast Community College Dist* 889 F2d 1018 (11th Cir 1989).

[57] See 15 USC §1072.

[58] In some circumstances, use may continue to be relevant to the plaintiff's remedy. A producer who holds federally registered trade mark rights may, despite superior rights, be unable to enjoin good faith local use that commences post-registration if the producer has not used the mark in that area and has no plans to do so: see *Dawn Donut v Hart's Food Stores Inc* 267 F2d 358 (2d Cir 1959). This remedial rule has been criticized by some courts as inappropriate in a modern economy, especially in light of the internet. See *Circuit City Stores Inc v Carmax Inc* 165 F3d 1047 (6th Cir 1995) (Jones J concurring).

[59] 15 USC §1057(c) (Lanham Act §7(c)). To the extent that a junior user, such as the Louisville producer in *United Drug*, has used a mark locally prior to the senior user's federal registration, the junior user's rights will be frozen in scope by registration: see *Thrifty Rent-a-car Sys v Thrift Cars Inc* 831 F2d 1177 (1st Cir 1987).

rights under US law continues to present difficulties for US courts. In a key decision, the Court of Appeals for the Fourth Circuit held that the use of a mark in advertising within the USA of services rendered only outside the USA might (if those services were rendered to American consumers) amount to use in commerce sufficient to acquire US rights.[60] This decision conflicts with well-established case law holding that advertising unconnected to a US product or service would not give rise to US use-based rights.[61] It is also somewhat inconsistent with the spirit of efforts at the international level to urge restraints on national courts applying the concept of use in the online context.[62] And it will make it harder for US producers to search for conflicting marks that might assert priority based upon questionable US use.

17.32 The geographical scope of use thus continues to be an evolving topic, notwithstanding the bright-line rules relating to registration, especially in the online environment. And, as seen in part B above, it may be the international context that throws up the most challenging use-related questions.

E. Conclusion

17.33 In this chapter, we have discussed the concept of use in the contexts which currently are most important in US law. The advent of liberal registration mechanisms, both domestically and internationally, has resulted in modifications to the common law rules. But such mechanisms have not rendered irrelevant the concept of use, particularly in a system that continues to recognize and enforce use-based rights largely on a par with registered rights. The concept of use in the US trade mark system is neither as coherent or as settled as one might expect in a system that self-identifies as a paradigmatic use-based system.

17.34 At this point, we raise, without discussing in detail, various debates about use in US trade mark law that we see on the horizon. US trade mark law

---

[60] *International Bancorp v Société des Bains de Mer et du Cercle des Etrangers à Monaco* 329 F3d 359 (4th Cir 2003), cert. denied, 1245 Ct 1052 (2004).

[61] See eg *Buti v Impressa Perosa* 139 F3d 98 (2d Cir 1998).

[62] See Joint Recommendation Concerning Provisions on the Protection of Marks and other Industrial Property Rights in Signs on the Internet, adopted by Assembly of the Paris Union and General Assembly of WIPO, WIPO Document no 845(c) (2001).

contains, whether in statutes or case law, references to a number of different notions of use: for example, 'use', 'use in commerce', 'commercial use', 'use as a trade mark', 'descriptive use', to name but a few. Courts (and litigants) are beginning to urge the development of this set of concepts for a variety of purposes, most notably to confine the availability and scope of trade mark rights in a primarily expansionist era. These efforts, especially when taken with the existing panoply of contexts where use is relevant, raise new questions with which we finish this chapter. Should strict, actual use in the USA be required for the acquisition of trade mark rights, or instead should the nature of the use simply be folded into analysis of distinctiveness? Should 'use as a trade mark' be an independent element of the trade mark infringement claim, or merely a factor relevant to likely confusion?[63]

Is the concept of 'use' monolithic—a concept that applies in the same way for **17.35** acquisition of rights as it does for infringement? Should it be? We believe that the answer to this question of symmetry will turn on whether one characterizes the concept of use as inherent in the trade mark right, or whether one views the concept as an instrumental doctrinal tool of trade mark law. These are questions for another day. But they are important questions that we detect in US law, and which we see also in other trade mark laws.[64] We are convinced that they will persist for some time to come.

---

[63] See *Holiday Inns Inc v 800 Reservation Inc* 86 F3d 619 (6th Cir 1996), requiring 'use' of the mark; *U-Haul International v WhenU.com* 279 F Supp 2d 723 (ED Va 2003), requiring the defendant's use to be 'trade mark use' in order to make out its claim.
[64] See eg *Arsenal Football Club plc v Matthew Reed* [2003] ETMR 73 (CA, UK).

18

THE ROLE OF TRADE MARK USE IN US INFRINGEMENT, UNFAIR COMPETITION AND DILUTION PROCEEDINGS

Sheldon H Klein and N Christopher Norton

A. 'Use' in the Establishment of
   Rights   18.02
B. 'Use' in Infringement and Unfair
   Competition Actions   18.05
C. 'Use' in Defences to
   Infringement and Unfair
   Competition Claims   18.07
   (1) Defences attacking the claimant's
       rights in the mark   18.08

(2) Defences based on the defendant's
    priority   18.14
(3) Defences based on lack of
    likelihood of confusion   18.19
(4) Fair use defence   18.22

D. 'Use' in Trade Mark Dilution
   Actions   18.25
E. Conclusion   18.29

This chapter reviews the role of 'use' in trade mark infringement, unfair **18.01** competition, and dilution proceedings in the USA. In infringement and unfair competition proceedings, the nature and extent of use of a mark is central to one of the core elements a claimant must prove—senior rights in a distinctive mark—and key to many of the available defences including, for example, lack of priority, lack of distinctiveness, abandonment, fraud and fair use. In a claim of trade mark dilution, use by both the claimant and third parties is examined in order to determine whether the claimant's mark is sufficiently famous to warrant protection, but only certain uses by a defendant are deemed 'dilutive'.

A. 'Use' in the Establishment of Rights

18.02 In most countries, trade mark rights accrue by registering a mark with the national trade mark office. In the USA, however, sustainable trade mark rights can only accrue through use of a mark in commerce. Although federal registration (which is not essential) confers procedural and substantive advantages, such as a nationwide right of priority through constructive use and a presumption of validity and ownership, these advantages can only be perfected and sustained by use of the mark in commerce.

18.03 In order to obtain a federal trade mark registration, a US mark owner must first use the mark in commerce on the goods or in connection with the services listed in its application. A foreign mark owner, by contrast, can obtain a US registration based on an existing foreign registration or International Registration without prior use of the mark in the USA under the Paris Convention and the Madrid Protocol, as codified in the Lanham Act, sections 44 and 66. However, generally, both US and foreign owners of US registrations must use their marks in the US before they can obtain equitable or legal relief against infringers.

18.04 Trade mark rights accrue through actual use of a mark in commerce, in the ordinary course of trade, on goods or in connection with services. Token use, made merely to reserve rights in a mark, is insufficient.[1] The use must be 'deliberate and continuous, not sporadic, casual or transitory'.[2] The mark must be used in a trade mark sense, that is, it must be used to identify the source of goods or services and distinguish that source from other sources.[3] In addition, the use ordinarily must occur in interstate commerce in the USA, or in commerce with the USA.[4]

---

[1] Lanham Act §45. The Lanham Act is found at 15 USC §§1051ff. See also *Planetary Motion Inc v Techplosion Inc* 261 F3d 1188 1193–1194 (11th Cir 2001).

[2] *Circuit City Stores Inc v CarMax Inc* 165 F3d 1047, 1054 (6th Cir 1999).

[3] See eg *Rock and Roll Hall of Fame and Museum Inc v Gentile Productions* 134 F3d 749, 753 (6th Cir 1998).

[4] One court has held that the sale of services abroad to US citizens by a foreign trade mark owner, combined with substantial advertising in the USA, could constitute use sufficient to establish trade mark rights in the USA. See *International Bancorp LLC v Société des Bains de Mer et du Cercle des Etrangers à Monaco* 329 F3d 359, 364–370 (4th Cir 2003).

B. 'Use' in Infringement and Unfair Competition Actions

The use of names, terms, or signs that are confusingly similar to an **18.05** established trade mark creates causes of action for infringement and unfair competition under US law. Section 32 of the Lanham Act imposes liability on

> any person who shall, without the consent of the registrant—(a) use in commerce any reproduction, counterfeit, copy or colorable imitation of a registered mark in connection with the sale, offering for sale, distribution, or advertising of any goods or services on or in connection with which such use is likely to cause confusion, or to cause mistake, or to deceive. . . .

Infringement claims under section 32 are only available for federally registered marks. But section 43(a) extends infringement protection to unregistered marks, trade names and trade dress as well.[5] Infringement actions may also be based on state trade mark statutes and the common law.

Under the Lanham Act section 43(a), a defendant is liable for unfair com- **18.06** petition if it (i) uses in commerce a word, term, name, symbol or device; (ii) on or in connection with goods or services; (iii) in a manner likely to cause confusion, mistake or deception as to the defendant's affiliation, connection or association with another person, or as to the origin, sponsorship or approval of the defendant's goods, services or commercial activities by that other person. While a claim for unfair competition is generally broader than a claim for infringement, the factors to be considered are identical.[6] Unfair competition actions may also be based on state statutes and the common law. In both infringement and unfair competition actions, a claimant must prove that (i) it owns a valid mark; (ii) it has senior rights in the mark; and (iii) the defendant's use of a confusingly similar mark is likely to cause consumer confusion.[7] The same defences are generally available in both infringement and unfair competition actions.[8]

---

[5] *Two Pesos Inc v Taco Cabana Inc; Wal-Mart Stores Inc v Samara Brothers Inc* 529 US 205 (2000).

[6] See eg *Packman v Chicago Tribune Co* 267 F3d 628, 639 (7th Cir 2001); *GoTo.com Inc v Walt Disney Co* 202 F3d 1199, 1204 n 3 and 1205 (9th Cir 2000).

[7] See eg *Frehling Enter Inc v International Select Group Inc* 192 F3d 1330, 1335 (11th Cir 1999).

[8] *Soweco Inc v Shell Oil Co* 617 F2d 1178, 1190 (5th Cir 1980).

C. 'Use' in Defences to Infringement and Unfair Competition Claims

18.07 A defendant in an infringement or unfair competition action may contest any of the three elements noted above. For example, a defendant may assert that the claimant has no rights in the subject mark because the mark lacks distinctiveness or was abandoned; that the defendant has prior rights in the mark or a confusingly similar mark; or that the parties' use of their respective marks is not likely to cause consumer confusion. A defendant may also claim that its use of the mark constitutes 'fair use'.

(1) Defences attacking the claimant's rights in the mark

18.08 A defendant may contest the first element in the infringement/unfair competition analysis by asserting that the claimant does not have the exclusive right to use the subject mark. If the claimant owns a federal registration, it may rely on that registration as *prima facie* evidence of the claimant's ownership of the mark and exclusive right to use the mark in commerce on or in connection with the goods or services listed in the registration.[9] If the registration has achieved so-called 'incontestable' status, it will be deemed *conclusive* evidence of the foregoing.[10] However, a defendant may rebut that evidence and attack the claimant's claim of rights on a number of grounds. These grounds include the bringing of proof that the mark is generic, that it is not inherently distinctive and has not acquired secondary meaning (for a registration that is still 'contestable'), and that it has been abandoned.[11] A defendant may also claim that the claimant's registration was obtained fraudulently.[12]

---

[9] Lanham Act §§7(b), 33(a).

[10] ibid §33(b). A registrant's right to use its mark with the goods or services in its registration will be deemed 'incontestable' if, after five consecutive years of continuous use, the registrant files an affidavit with the Patent and Trade Mark Office attesting to that use: Lanham Act §15. But this so-called 'incontestability' is not complete, as several defences will remain, some of which are discussed herein. See Lanham Act §33(b).

[11] ibid §33(b).

[12] The defence of lack of seniority/prior rights will be discussed below.

(a) Genericity defence[13]

A trade mark owner will lose its exclusive right to use its mark, and its federal **18.09** registration for that mark may be cancelled—even if the registration has become 'incontestable'—if, through its use by others, the mark has become the generic name of the goods or services sold under the mark.[14]

(b) Non-distinctiveness ('merely descriptive') defence

A mark will also fail to indicate a particular source and cannot be used as a **18.10** trade mark if, despite its apparent use as a trade mark, it merely describes the goods or services and has not acquired 'secondary meaning'. A term acquires 'secondary meaning' when it becomes identified through use with the source of the goods or services in the minds of consumers. Once a registration has become 'incontestable', it cannot be cancelled based on its non-distinctiveness. However, non-distinctiveness can be used to show that a mark is weak and entitled to only a narrow scope of protection.

(c) Abandonment defence

A registration (even an 'incontestable' registration) is subject to cancellation **18.11** at any time on the grounds that the registrant has abandoned the mark.[15] A mark is presumed abandoned if its use has been discontinued with the intent not to resume use.[16] Non-use for three consecutive years constitutes *prima facie* evidence of abandonment but, if actual abandonment is proven sooner, a registration can be cancelled before three years have passed. 'Token use', or use merely to reserve rights in a mark, is insufficient to overcome a finding of abandonment, just as it is insufficient to support a use-based US registration.[17] A mark may be deemed abandoned for non-use even if the mark is used in the ordinary course of trade, if it is used with goods or services that are different from those listed in the registration, or if the mark is used only outside the USA.[18] In addition to the validity of the registration, the

---

[13] The American term for 'genericity' is 'genericness'.

[14] Lanham Act §14.

[15] ibid §33(b)(2); *Imperial Tobacco Ltd Assignee of Imperial Group PLC v Philip Morris Inc* 899 F2d 1575, 1578 (Fed Cir 1990).

[16] Lanham Act §45.

[17] ibid.

[18] *Emergency One Inc v American FireEagle Ltd* 228 F3d 531, 536 (4th Cir 2000); *Imperial Tobacco* (n 15) 1579.

abandonment defence may be used to attack the validity of the mark itself. Without a valid mark to protect, a claimant cannot prevail in an infringement or unfair competition action.

(d) Fraud defence

18.12 If a claimant in an infringement action has relied on a federal registration as proof of the validity of its mark, the defendant may assert fraud in the acquisition of that registration as an affirmative defence, even if the registration is 'incontestable'.[19] The defendant must prove (i) that the claimant made a false representation to the US Patent and Trade Mark Office (PTO) regarding a material fact, knew the representation to be false and that the claimant intended to induce the PTO to rely on the misrepresentation; (ii) that the PTO relied on the misrepresentation; and (iii) that the defendant was damaged by that reliance.[20] Falsely alleging use of a mark in commerce, or submitting specimens not actually in use, in order to obtain or maintain a federal trade mark registration may constitute fraud sufficient to void the registration.[21]

18.13 Foreign owners of US registrations that are based on the Paris Convention or the Madrid Protocol under Lanham Act sections 44 and 66 may be particularly vulnerable to this defence. Many countries permit broad or even full class recitations of goods and services in their trade mark registrations, without any requirement to use the mark with those goods and services. In the USA, however, a registration may issue only for those goods and services for which the section 44 or 66 applicant declares, under penalty of perjury, that it uses or has a bona fide intent to use the mark in US commerce. More critically, under Lanham Act section 8, even a registration based on sections 44 and 66 may only be preserved after the six-year anniversary date, and after every ten-year anniversary date, upon the filing of a declaration, under penalty of perjury, attesting that the subject mark is currently used in US commerce on or in connection with all or a designated subset of the goods or services recited in the registration (unless the registrant can prove special

---

[19] Lanham Act §33(b)(1). The claimant may still be able to rely on its common law rights in the mark. See *Orient Express Trading Co v Federated Department Stores Inc* 842 F2d 650, 654 (2d Cir 1988).

[20] *San Juan Products Inc v San Juan Pools of Kansas Inc* 849 F2d 468, 473 (10th Cir 1988).

[21] *Torres v Cantine Torresella Srl* 808 F2d 46, 49 (Fed Cir 1986). Falsely alleging use with respect to only some of the goods may nevertheless result in the cancellation of the entire registration. See *Medinol Ltd v Neuro Vasc Inc,* 67 USPQ 2d 1205 (TTAB 2003).

circumstances to excuse non-use).[22] Filing false declarations or affidavits is grounds for cancelling a registration.[23]

(2) Defences based on the defendant's priority

A defendant can avoid liability by proving that it acquired rights in the **18.14** subject mark or in a confusingly similar mark, for the goods or services at issue, prior to the claimant. Except as noted below, mark ownership and priority in the USA are granted to the first person to use a mark in commerce. However, the act of filing an application to register a mark constitutes nationwide 'constructive use', contingent on the issuance of a registration.[24] Accordingly, the application filing date is the date of priority.

Applications filed by foreign mark owners based on the Paris Convention are **18.15** awarded a priority date that is the same as the filing date of the foreign application on which the US application is based, provided that the US application was filed within six months of the filing date of the foreign application.[25] Otherwise, the actual US filing date is the priority date. With regard to applications filed under section 44(d), unless the resulting US registration is also based on use in commerce, the registration does not entitle the mark owner to sue for acts committed prior to the date the mark is *registered* in the USA.[26]

With requests for extension of protection of International Registrations into **18.16** the USA, a mark owner's priority date is the earlier of (i) the filing date of the international application, if the request for extension of protection was contained therein; (ii) the filing date of the request for extension of protection, if the request was filed after the international application was filed; or (iii) the date of the application for the basic national application, if the international application or request for extension of protection was filed within six months, and the request for extension of protection contained a claim of priority.[27]

---

[22] Lanham Act §§8, 9, 71.
[23] *Le Cordon Bleu SA v BPC Pub Ltd* 451 F Supp 63, 71–74 (DC NY 1978); *Medinol Ltd v Neuro Vasc Inc* (n 21).
[24] Lanham Act §7(c).
[25] ibid §44(d).
[26] ibid §44(d)(4).
[27] ibid §§66, 67.

18.17 For a successful defence based on priority, a defendant must prove that it acquired rights in its mark prior to the claimant. If the defendant owns an existing federal registration or application for its mark, and has not abandoned the mark, it should compare its dates of first use (or constructive first use) against those of the claimant. If it has prior rights, no infringement claim will lie.

18.18 If the defendant began use of the mark after the claimant, but before the claimant filed its application, and the defendant adopted its mark without knowledge of the claimant's prior use, then the defendant may be permitted to continue using its mark, but only in the geographical areas where its continuous and exclusive prior use is proved, along with a so-called 'zone of natural expansion'.[28] This is the concept of the 'intermediate junior user'. If the defendant began use prior to the claimant, but after the claimant filed its intent-to-use application, the claimant can enjoin the defendant's use, but only after the claimant's registration issues.[29]

(3) Defences based on lack of likelihood of confusion

18.19 A defendant may assert that the parties' marks are not likely to cause confusion, mistake or deception. Without a likelihood of confusion, there can be no infringement or unfair competition. In the USA, each federal circuit has enunciated a list of factors to assess likelihood of confusion. Typical factors include the similarity of the marks in appearance, sound and meaning; the relatedness of the goods or services offered under the marks; the marketing channels used by the parties; the strength of the claimant's mark; the defendant's intention in adopting the mark; likelihood of expansion into other markets; the likely degree of purchaser care; and evidence of actual confusion.[30]

(a) Distinct geographical areas defence

18.20 If the parties use their respective marks only in distinct geographic areas, without any overlap and without plans to enter the other's areas, there may

---

[28] ibid §33(b)(5); *Dawn Donut Co v Hart's Food Stores Inc* 267 F2d 358, 364 (2d Cir 1959).

[29] Lanham Act §7(c); see also *Fila Sport SpA v Diadora America Inc* 141 F R D 74, 80 (ND Ill. 1991).

[30] See eg *GoTo.com Inc v Walt Disney Co* and *In re E I Du Pont de Nemours & Co* 476 F2d 1357, 1361 (CCPA 1973).

be no likelihood of confusion.[31] Under the *Dawn Donut* rule, even if the owner of a federal registration has nationwide priority, there is no likely confusion for a court to enjoin until the registrant demonstrates a likelihood of entry into the junior user's market.[32] Under *Dawn Donut*, owners of registrations under the Paris Convention or the Madrid Protocol—which do not require use prior to registration—would first have to begin use in the USA or demonstrate a likelihood of entry into the USA prior to seeking remedies for infringement or unfair competition.

(b) Weak mark defence

Third party uses of marks similar to the claimant's can seriously affect the **18.21** likelihood of consumer confusion. The greater the number of identical or similar marks already in use on related or even somewhat related goods or services, the lower the likelihood that there will be confusion between any two specific uses of the mark.[33] If a claimant's mark is used by third parties other than the defendant, then small differences in the marks, or in the goods and services, may be sufficient to warrant a finding of no likelihood of consumer confusion.[34]

(4) Fair use defence

A defendant may claim that its use of the claimant's mark was not infringing **18.22** because it constituted 'fair use'. Under US law, a defendant may argue fair use when it uses the claimant's mark to describe the defendant's goods and services ('descriptive fair use'), or to refer to the claimant's goods or services ('nominative fair use').[35]

(a) Descriptive fair use

The fair use doctrine is based on the principle that no one should be able to **18.23**

---

[31] *Dawn Donut* (n 28). As more advertising is conducted nationally and internationally, including on the internet, there are fewer *Dawn Donut*-type situations.
[32] This concept has been recognized in the Lanham Act, through so-called 'concurrent registrations': Lanham Act §2(d).
[33] *First Savings Bank FSB v First Bank System Inc* 101 F3d 645, 653–654 (10th Cir 1996).
[34] *Freedom Savings and Loan Association v Way* 757 F2d 1176, 1182 (11th Cir 1985).
[35] A defendant's non-trade mark use of his own name in connection with his own business can also constitute fair use: Lanham Act §33(b)(4).

appropriate descriptive language through trade mark registration.[36] In order to prevail under this fair use defence, a defendant must show that (i) it used the subject name, term, or sign in a non-trade mark manner; (ii) the name, term or sign is descriptive of the defendant's goods or services or their geographical origin; and (iii) the defendant used the name, term or sign 'fairly and in good faith' only to describe or characterize its goods or services, or their geographical origin.[37] For example, the defendant should be able to use the name, term or sign to describe a desirable effect of its product, the manner in which the product is to be used or the season in which the product will be sold.[38]

(b) Nominative fair use

18.24 Nominative fair use occurs when a defendant uses the name, term or sign to refer to the *claimant's* goods or services. The non-confusing use of a competitor's marks to describe that competitor's goods and services is permissible and often beneficial to consumers, such as in connection with comparative advertising.[39] The Ninth Circuit has established a test for determining nominative fair use: the claimant's product or service in question must not be readily identifiable without use of the mark; only so much of the mark may be used as is reasonably necessary to identify the product or service; and the user must do nothing that would, in conjunction with the mark, suggest sponsorship or endorsement by the trade mark holder.[40] In practical terms, this concept can often translate into permission to use the 'block letter' form of a competitor's mark for commentary or comparative advertising purposes, but not the logo form of the mark.

D. 'Use' in Trade Mark Dilution Actions

18.25 The dilution doctrine, codified federally in the Lanham Act, section 43(c), protects famous marks from uses of similar marks that would lessen the

---

[36] *Sands Taylor & Wood Co v Quaker Oats Co* 978 F2d 947, 951 (7th Cir 1992).

[37] See eg *Packman v Chicago Tribune Co* 267 F3d 628, 639 (7th Cir 2001) and *Schafer Co v Innco Management Corp* 797 F Supp 477, 481–482 (ED NC 1992).

[38] See *Cosmetically Sealed Indus Inc v Chesebrough-Pond's USA Co* 125 F3d 28, 30 (2d Cir 1997).

[39] See eg *August Storck KG v Nabisco Inc* 59 F3d 616, 618 (7th Cir 1995) and *National Federation of the Blind Inc v Loompanics Enterprises Inc* 936 F Supp 1232, 1241 (D Md 1996).

[40] See *New Kids on the Block v News Am Publishing Inc* 971 F2d 302, 308 (9th Cir 1992).

capacity of the famous mark to point uniquely to the claimant. To establish dilution under the Lanham Act, a claimant must prove that (i) it owns a famous mark; (ii) the defendant is making commercial use of a similar (dilutive) mark or trade name in US commerce; (iii) the defendant's use began after the claimant's mark became famous; and (iv) the defendant's use dilutes the distinctive quality of the claimant's mark.[41] The parties' respective goods or services need not be related to establish dilution.

The concept of 'use' is integral to three of the four essential elements for establishing trade mark dilution under the Lanham Act. First, a claimant must prove that the defendant is using the dilutive mark or name in a commercial manner, in US commerce. Only such use will diminish, or dilute, the distinctive quality of the famous mark.[42] The Lanham Act enumerates several non-diluting 'fair uses', including using a famous mark in comparative advertising, using the mark in a non-commercial manner and using the mark in news reporting and news commentary.[43] Courts have also held that 'nominative uses'—that is, referring to or describing the famous mark owner's goods or services—are non-diluting as well.[44] **18.26**

Second, the defendant's use of the famous mark must occur after that mark has become famous. Most marks may be used by multiple parties, as long as the goods or services with which they are used are sufficiently unrelated to prevent consumer confusion. Only famous marks are granted special protection from dilution under federal law, whereby third parties can be prohibited from using the same mark with unrelated goods and services. 'Use' plays an important role in several of the factors considered when determining whether a mark is sufficiently famous to warrant protection from dilution: the duration and extent of use of the mark in connection with the goods or services; the duration and extent of advertising and publicity of the mark; the geographical extent of the trading area in which the mark is used; the channels of trade for the goods or services with which the mark is used; and the nature **18.27**

---

[41] Lanham Act §43(c). A dilution claim may also be based on state statutes. State dilution claims may be easier to establish in some states, as, for example, proof that the claimant's mark is 'famous' may not be required and a showing of likelihood of dilution, rather than actual dilution, may suffice. Thirty-five states have dilution statutes: see J Gilson *Trademark Protection and Practice* (LexisNexis/Matthew Bender New York 2003) §5A.02.

[42] See *Playboy Enterprises Inc v Welles* 279 F3d 796, 806 (9th Cir 2002).

[43] Lanham Act §43(c)(4).

[44] See *Playboy v Welles* (n 42) 806.

and extent of use of the same or similar marks by third parties.[45] Other factors include the degree of inherent or acquired distinctiveness of the mark, the degree of recognition of the mark and whether the mark is registered.[46] Determining exactly when a mark became famous and whether the defendant commenced use of the mark before or after that time are both matters of fact to be determined by the court.

18.28   Finally, a claimant must prove that the defendant's use causes dilution of the distinctive quality of the famous mark. Dilution may take one of two forms: blurring or tarnishment. Blurring occurs when the defendant's use lessens the ability of the famous mark[47] to uniquely identify the claimant's goods and services. Tarnishment, on the other hand, occurs when a famous mark is associated with an inferior or offensive product or service. For either to occur, the defendant must use the claimant's mark in a trade mark sense with goods or services not offered by the claimant.

E. Conclusion

18.29   In US trade mark infringement and unfair competition proceedings, use is central to a claimant's claims and to the defendant's available defences. The parties must establish who acquired rights in the mark first and whether those rights are still valid; whether the use requirements for the claimant's registration have been met; whether the parties' respective uses are likely to cause consumer confusion; and, finally, whether the defendant's uses are fair. Use is also central to establishing and defending against dilution claims: use figures prominently in determining whether a mark is sufficiently famous to warrant protection from dilution and only certain uses may be deemed diluting.

---

[45]   Lanham Act §43(c)(1).

[46]   ibid.

[47]   *Moseley v V. Secret Catalogue Inc* 537 US 418 (Sup Ct 2003). It is expected that the USA will consider legislation in 2005 to change the federal standard for the imposition of liability for uses which are *likely* to cause dilution of a famous mark. Some states may currently employ this looser standard.

Part H

POST MORTEM

19

CONCLUSION: WHAT USE IS USE?

Jeremy Phillips and Ilanah Simon

A. The Danger of Drawing Conclusions	19.01	D. Use: The Battle Lines are Drawn	19.11	
B. Is There Just One Type of Trade Mark Use?	19.02	E. Is Use the Centre of the Trade Mark System?	19.14	
(1) Backwards and forwards	19.04	F. The Essential Function: The Linchpin of the System?	19.17	
C. Further Issues for Investigation	19.05	G. The Future of Use	19.22	
(1) Use and the Community trade mark	19.06	H. Eine Kleine Answer . . . or five	19.26	
(2) The role of old law	19.07	(1) Answer 1	19.27	
(3) The interface between trade mark rights and other intellectual property rights	19.09	(2) Answer 2	19.29	
		(3) Answer 3	19.31	
		(4) Answer 4	19.33	
		(5) Answer 5	19.34	

A. The Danger of Drawing Conclusions

This chapter will attempt to draw together some of the strands of legal **19.01** analysis offered in the preceding chapters. In undertaking this task, we are conscious of the fact that we have set the parameters within which this study has been undertaken; we are also conscious of the fact that we approached the subject of study with fixed, if different, notions as to what some of our conclusions might be. Our comments in this chapter should therefore be read in the light of this.

B. Is There Just One Type of Trade Mark Use?

Throughout this book, we and our contributors have used a single definition **19.02** of trade mark use—use of a sign to indicate the origin of the goods or services on which the sign is used. There is one exception, referential use. This concept, which is particularly considered in Massimo Sterpi's chapter (Chapter 8), involves use of a sign by a defendant to refer to the origin of *another's* goods, rather than his own. For example in *BMW v Deenik*[1] the defendant, an independent mechanic and second-hand car salesman, used the BMW trade mark to tell consumers that he serviced BMW cars. The conceptual link with 'ordinary' trade mark use is strong because the central idea is the use of the sign to indicate the origin of goods or services. Although the idea was mooted by the European Court of Justice (ECJ) in *Deenik* (though not under the label 'referential use'), it has not been exploited further and it is open to doubt whether it serves any useful function following the ECJ's ruling in *Arsenal v Reed.*[2]

19.03 Leaving referential use aside, on the assumption that there is a single definition of use, the requirements for showing that a trade mark functions in a way that denotes the origin of the goods or services on which it is, or is intended to be, used vary depending on the context. For example, the process of proving that a Community trade mark application for a non-inherently distinctive shape mark has acquired distinctiveness is very different from showing that a defendant has used his mark in a manner which infringes a trade mark.

(1) Backwards and forwards

19.04 Whatever definition of use one adopts, one is forced to concede that there are two temporal dimensions in which use must be considered. One is retrospective, as where use turns an otherwise unprotectable sign into a fully fledged registrable trade mark; the other is prospective, as where a distinctive but unused sign gains registration on the basis of an intent to use. This is particularly relevant in the USA (as Graeme Dinwoodie and Mark Janis have explained in Chapter 17). Between those two temporal extremes there are many other species of use: for example, where a trade mark proprietor continues to use his registered trade mark in order to avoid the risk of revocation for non-use. Precisely what is the significance of the different temporal

---

[1] *Bayerische Motorenwerke AG (BMW) and BMW Nederland BV v Deenik* Case C-63/97 [1999] ETMR 339.

[2] *Arsenal Football Club plc v Matthew Reed* Case C-206/01 [2003] ETMR 19 (ECJ).

dimensions has remained a bone of bitter contention between the editors of this book, both of whom agree that it remains a matter worthy of future research.

C. Further Issues for Investigation

A number of issues have been raised (implicitly or explicitly) by one or more **19.05** of our contributors which we feel are worthy of further investigation. These include the following:

(1) Use and the Community trade mark

The Community trade mark is a unitary mark; its criteria of registrability **19.06** must therefore be fulfilled in all twenty-five Member States before registration is permitted. Accordingly, where use becomes relevant, it must in theory be proved in all Member States. However, as Arnaud Folliard-Monguiral (Chapter 4), Anna Carboni (Chapter 5) and Allan James (Chapter 14) have made clear, this is not always the case. The gap between the theory and the practice before OHIM, the Community trade mark office, is however quite wide enough to invite future exploration.

(2) The role of old law

Even though EU trade mark law has been harmonized by Directive 89/104 **19.07** and the pre-Directive UK trade mark provisions have been swept away, the spectre of the Trade Marks Act 1938 has manifested itself on a number of occasions. As has been discussed, particularly by Andreas Rahmatian (Chapter 12), the House of Lords in *R v Johnstone*[3] relied heavily on the 1938 Act for its interpretation of provisions relating to civil infringement. Robert Sumroy and Carina Badger (Chapter 10) have identified this approach as a trend running throughout the UK civil infringement jurisprudence, saying

> With the notable exception of the Court of Appeal in *Arsenal* the English judiciary seems to be operating in the jurisprudence of the 1938 Act.

---

[3] *R v Johnstone* [2004] ETMR 2 (HL).

19.08 Jennifer Davis (Chapter 3) has reached a different conclusion on the ECJ's approach to the absolute grounds for the refusal of registration. She has maintained that that Court, while not adopting the notion of the 'commons' of marks previously favoured in the UK under the 1938 Act, accepted that a role for the old law may be seen even in that area. Although the ECJ in *Windsurfing Chiemsee*[4] rejected the pre-Directive German concept of *Freihaltebedürfnis* as a bar to registrability, it did recognize that the public policy behind the descriptiveness bar to exclusion is that there exists a real and serious need to keep such marks free for other traders to use. Thus, although the court rejected the German concept in name, it imported its essence into EU jurisprudence.

(3) The interface between trade mark rights and other intellectual property rights

19.09 At a number of points, the interface of trade mark rights with other intellectual property rights has been identified. However, the reaction of the courts to this interface has varied dramatically. Certain cases have favoured granting only a single type of intellectual property protection. In a number of the denominative use instances identified by Massimo Sterpi, copyright law has been willing to step into the breach left where a sign has not benefited from trade mark protection because it has not been used as a trade mark. Similarly, in *R v Johnstone*, while the House of Lords found that no trade mark use had taken place on the facts before it, it did suggest that protection may be available under the performers' rights regime. Thomas Hays (Chapter 6) identifies a similar interest in not providing concurrent patent and trade mark protection as lying behind the functionality bar on registration of shape marks. However, in other cases identified by Massimo Sterpi, the courts have been happy to see concurrent protection under more than one intellectual property right, providing copyright protection even when trade mark use is present.

19.10 The present controversy over the relative roles of trade mark law and geographical indications in the protection of place-based appellations has not been tackled head-on in this collection of essays. However, Jeffrey Belson's discussion (Chapter 9) of the role of certification marks addresses the issue of

---

[4] *Windsurfing Chiemsee Produktions and Vertriebs GmbH v Boots und Segelzubehör Walter Huber and Franz Attenberger* Case C-108/97 [1999] ETMR 585 (ECJ).

whether trade marks and certification marks can be granted concurrently for the same appellation.

D. Use: The Battle Lines are Drawn

Certain actors within the trade mark system have clung steadfastly to pre- **19.11** conceived notions of trade mark use, particularly the idea that use as a trade mark is a prerequisite for infringement, sometimes in the face of seemingly clear authoritative statements to the contrary. Why then is the need for trade mark use considered so important by these people? Gail Evans (Chapter 16) has suggested that the use requirement somehow shows that trade marks are not as 'deserving' of protection in themselves as are other intellectual property rights. Instead, their protection is justified by reference to the role that marks play in the market, with use anchoring the protection to market-driven concerns. Another possible explanation is that judges in the UK at least are still wedded to 1938 Act notions of trade mark infringement. It is tempting though to come to the conclusion that what really drives the reluctance to dispense with use in the area of infringement is a fear of the trade mark system. Some parties see trade marks as 'monopolies' that limit the freedom of other traders and even, in extreme cases, the free speech of a wider portion of society. Imposing a use requirement is just another way of limiting the scope of such 'monopolies', one that can be disguised in the cloak of historical respectability.

On the other hand, certain brand owners may argue for as wide a definition **19.12** of infringement as possible. This wide definition would include dispensing with the use requirement. It should be remembered, though, that brand owners can just as easily end up as defendants in trade mark actions. In that situation, it would be in their interests for a narrower definition of infringement to be adopted.

The ECJ has struck a balance between the two camps in *Arsenal v Reed*. **19.13** Although it has not gone as far as to require trade mark use for infringement, it has put a brake on the scope of infringement, and hence trade mark rights, by requiring the defendant's use to impair the essential function of a claimant's mark before it is regarded as an infringing use.

E. Is Use the Centre of the Trade Mark System?

19.14 While it is certainly true that use plays a crucial role within the trade mark system, as is evinced by the many areas in which it is relevant—as many areas as there are chapters of this book and then some—one of the editors believes that it would be overstating the case to say that use is the 'centre' of the trade mark system. Protection is not granted merely because signs are used. Use only counts if it causes signs to be perceived in a certain way by consumers—as an indicator of origin. Equally well, the role of use has been sidelined in infringement with the ECJ's ruling that, at least with regard to Article 5(1)(a), use as a trade mark is not necessary for infringement. Both these instances point to another concept being of greater importance—the 'essential function' of a trade mark. That is not to say that use is not vitally important—the breadth of subjects tackled by our contributors in which it plays an important role should be enough to convince even the most cynical reader of this. However, it is not the factor on which the entire trade mark system hangs.

19.15 The other editor considers that use, in all its forms, is the central consideration that drives the registration, protection and exploitation of trade marks: its centrality is self-evident, as the historical development of the trade mark system shows. Even if it were not so, it is difficult to conceive of any justification of any facet of the trade mark system that is not directed towards use.

19.16 We leave it to our readers to determine whether these positions are incompatible or ultimately complementary.

F. The Essential Function: The Linchpin of the System?

19.17 One of the editors maintains that the essential function is the concept that brings the trade mark system together. The essential function was first defined in *Hoffmann-La Roche v Centrafarm* as

> to guarantee the identity of the origin of the trade-marked product to the consumer or ultimate user, by enabling him without any possibility of confusion to distinguish that product from products which have another origin. This guarantee of origin means that the consumer or ultimate user can be certain

that a trade-marked product which is sold to him has not been subject at a previous stage of marketing to interference by a third person, without authorisation of the proprietor of the trade mark, such as to affect the original condition of the product.[5]

It is also reflected in the tenth recital to Directive 89/104, which states that **19.18**

[T]he function of [a registered trade mark] is in particular to guarantee the trade mark as an indication of origin.

It can be seen that the main or 'essential' function of a trade mark is to act as an indication of origin and it is this role that permeates almost the entire trade mark system, including the parameters of use. Our contributors have discussed two main areas where use is relevant: (i) the role of use in determining whether a trade mark is registrable and whether it can remain on the register and (ii) the role of use in infringement proceedings. In both areas, the relationship of use to the essential function plays a determinative role.

For a mark to be registrable it must *be capable* of being used as an indication **19.19** of origin. For a mark to remain on the register it must *actually be used* as an indication of origin. Use as an indication of origin is use of a mark in a way in which the mark is carrying out its essential function. In other words, the requirements for the type of use that counts as 'trade mark use' is dictated by the essential function of a mark.

In the area of infringement, the overriding importance of the essential func- **19.20** tion is even more starkly visible. Had the ECJ in *Arsenal v Reed* found that a defendant has to use *his* sign as a trade mark to be found to be infringing another's mark, it would have given close to equal status to the ideas of use and the essential function, because it would have been saying that, in order to infringe, a defendant has to *use* his mark in accordance with the essential function. Instead, the approach it took promoted the essential function above trade mark use: instead of finding that the defendant must make use of his mark as a trade mark to indicate his goods (trade mark use as we understand it), the court found that any use that impairs the ability of the claimant's mark to fulfil its essential function can be considered to be infringing use.

---

[5] *Hoffmann-La Roche & Co AG and Hoffmann-La Roche AG v Centrafarm Vertriebsgesellschaft Pharmazeutischer Erzeugnisse mbH* Case 102/77 [1978] ECR 1139 para 7. The concept has been referred to in numerous post-Directive and Regulation ECJ cases.

19.21 The other editor believes that use is more important than essential function in any understanding of trade mark law. While essential function is a signifi-cant doctrine which has radically shaped the development of the law, use is a concept which exists above and beyond any doctrine of which it may be part: it is a fact-based concept which is part of the very DNA of trade mark law. In other words, use remains of key importance, whatever form the doctrine of the essential function may take.

G. The Future of Use

19.22 There can be no doubt that the concept of 'use as a trade mark' will remain fundamental to the trade mark system. The idea of revocation for non-use presupposes the idea of use and, in determining which marks should be barred from registration on absolute grounds, one of the determining ques-tions will continue to be 'can this mark be used as a trade mark to indicate the origin of the goods or services on which it is used?' However, the future importance of 'use as a trade mark' in the area of infringement is less assured.

19.23 In *Arsenal v Reed*, the ECJ seemingly made it clear that 'use as a trade mark' is *not* a necessary condition for infringement, at least under Article 5(1)(a) of Directive 89/104. In the UK, the Court of Appeal accepted this without question in its contribution to the *Arsenal v Reed*[6] saga. However, within the UK, there has been judicial opposition to this approach and courts continue to require a showing of trade mark use before they will find infringement.

19.24 In *R v Johnstone* (discussed by Robert Sumroy and Carina Badger and Andreas Rahmatian) the House of Lords made it plain that they required trade mark use under sections 10(1) to (3) of the Trade Marks Act. The importance of this case can be mitigated: it was, after all, a criminal rather than a civil infringement case and their Lordships did not have the opportun-ity to read the judgment of the Court of Appeal in *Arsenal v Reed* which was delivered only one day beforehand. However, these arguments are not open when considering the Court of Appeal's judgment in *Reed v Reed*.[7] There, a year after *Arsenal v Reed*, one of the most experienced intellectual property

---

[6] [2003] ETMR 73 (CA).
[7] [2004] ETMR 56 (CA).

judges in the country, Jacob LJ, required trade mark use for infringement. Others have been quick to take up his lead. For example, in *Electrocoin v Coinworld*[8] counsel for the largely unsuccessful claimant in *Reed v Reed*, Geoffrey Hobbs QC, now sitting as a Deputy Judge, imposed the same requirement of trade mark use, even managing to rely on *Arsenal v Reed* to reach this conclusion. Though it may be strongly argued that *Arsenal v Reed* drove a dagger into the heart of trade mark use in the context of infringement, the UK judiciary has brought it back from the dead and, in the UK at least, it seems to be alive and kicking.

Also open to question is the scope of the ECJ's ruling in *Arsenal v Reed*. **19.25** While Robert Sumroy and Carina Badger have assumed that the ECJ's downplaying of the importance of trade mark use applies equally to infringement under Article 5(1)(b) and 5(2), it should be pointed out that the court limited its ruling to Article 5(1)(a).[9] This could have been a deliberate limiting strategy on the court's part, though it could equally well have been brought about by the fact that the referring court's questions were restricting to that article.[10] Either way, it is difficult to see how there could be confusion that results in the public thinking that the two parties' goods or services come from the same or economically linked undertakings under Article 5(1)(b) without the defendant in fact using his mark as a trade mark.[11] However, it is less clear that trade mark use is a factual prerequisite for the harm under Article 5(2) (detriment to the claimant's mark's distinctive character or repute or taking unfair advantage of the claimant's mark's distinctive character or repute) to occur. A further reference to the ECJ may be necessary to clarify this point.

---

[8] [2005] ETMR 31.

[9] See particularly the operative part of the court's judgment. The House of Lords on the other hand, in *R v Johnstone*, stated that its requirement of trade mark use extended to ss 10(1) to (3), though they did not seek to justify this finding. Arguably, it is a dangerous one since their Lordships based their need for trade mark use largely on the 1938 Act which had no equivalent of s 10(3).

[10] *R v Johnstone* (n 3) para 27.

[11] *Canon Kabushiki Kaisha v Metro-Goldwyn-Mayer Inc* Case C-39/97 [1998] ECR I-5507, [1999] ETMR 1 (ECJ) para 29.

H. Eine Kleine Answer . . . or five

19.26 These are the five answers that the editors received from various contributors. You can draw your conclusions as to which offer Mr and Mrs Jones the best advice.

(1) Answer 1

19.27 Mr and Mrs Jones run a risk of being found liable for trade mark infringement: the law is unclear and there is no knowing what the ECJ will do. However, on a true construction of the Directive, there is only infringement if the use by the Joneses is in the course of trade in buses and in relation to buses. It is perception and not intention which matters. If the mark is perceived as being use in the course of trade and in relation to buses, then there is infringement. If it is not so perceived, then there is no infringement—it is a matter of fact which goes beyond those set out in the exercise.

19.28 The exceptions to infringement listed in Article 6(1) of the Directive do not work because the mark is not being used to identify the manufacturer of the goods.

(2) Answer 2

19.29 Mr and Mrs Jones should not worry. Their use of the sign BRIGADIER is likely to be perceived by the public as being use of the sign in relation to Tomkins' beer. The use of the sign BRIGADIER by them is use of the sign as a trade mark, but their use of the sign is 'in relation to' Tomkins' beers rather than 'in relation to' the bus. Mere physical proximity between the sign and the product for which it is registered as a trade mark does not automatically mean that the name is being used as a sign in relation to that product: see *Euromarket v Peters.*[12]

19.30 On that view of the matter, the question would be whether the Joneses have a case to answer under Article 5(2) of Directive 89/104. Assuming that BRIGADIER has the necessary reputation for buses to bring such an action (as also

---

[12] *Euromarket Designs Inc v Peters and Another* [2000] ETMR 1025 para 57.

seems likely) and that the Joneses' use, while being perceived as use of the name as a sign for beer, would nevertheless (because of the use of the bus as an advertising vehicle) also trigger a connection in the public's mind between the beer mark and the bus mark (which is more arguable), it would still be necessary for the claimant to show that such a link was detrimental to, or took unfair advantage of, the reputation or distinctive character of the bus mark. That seems unlikely on the facts.

(3) Answer 3

Mr and Mrs Jones are simply asking for trouble. Article 5(1)(a) of Directive **19.31** 89/104 confers exclusive rights on a trade mark owner which enable him to prevent all third parties from using, in the course of trade, 'any sign which is identical with the trade mark in relation to goods or services which are identical with those for which the trade mark is registered'. The mark is registered in respect of buses and only Brigadier have the right to use it on buses. The argument that the use of the BRIGADIER mark for beer on the side of the bus is not 'in relation to' the bus since that use is in relation to beer fails to consider that a use of a beer trade mark on the side of a bus may be regarded by consumers as use 'in relation to' *both* beer and buses. More to the point, the Court of Appeal in *Arsenal v Reed* made it plain that any adverse use of another's trade mark that affects the ability of the trade mark to exercise its essential function as a guarantee of the identity of the origin of goods would be regarded as an infringement of that mark.[13] That may well be the case here.

Finally, what if the alleged infringing use was the other way round, with **19.32** Brigadier putting their bus trade mark on to beer bottles? Could it be seriously argued that such a use was 'in relation to' buses and therefore not an infringement in relation to Tomkins' beer trade mark? No, Mr and Mrs Jones would be well advised to adopt the path of caution.

(4) Answer 4

Mr and Mrs Jones should proceed with caution. The Joneses will be affixing **19.33** the BRIGADIER sign to a bus. In doing so they are hoping to identify the origin of the beer that is sold on board, rather than the origin of the bus itself. The Joneses, by using a sign on a bus that is identical to the BRIGADIER mark that

---

[13] *Arsenal v Reed* (n 6) paras 48 and 50.

is registered for buses, may be at risk of infringing the bus company's mark under Article 5(1)(a) of Directive 89/104. Although their intention, and most likely the consumer perception, is to identify the BRIGADIER sign with beers rather than buses, under Article 5(1)(a) there is no need for a sign to be used as a trade mark for the defendant's goods for infringement to take place. The earlier registration is for buses and the Joneses are using the sign on a bus so the goods are identical. The signs are also identical. Therefore infringement will have taken place according to the ECJ's judgment in *Arsenal v Reed* if the essential function of the bus company's mark, ie its ability to distinguish the bus company's goods from those of other undertakings, has been damaged. The sorts of uses that cause harm to the essential function of a mark remain unclear in the absence of further case law, although the Court of Appeal, again in *Arsenal v Reed*, has suggested that a wide interpretation that would encompass almost any use of a mark will be in order, since any used will diminish an earlier mark's distinctiveness and hence its ability to distinguish the goods of its proprietor.

(5) Answer 5

19.34 Under Article 5(1)(a) of Directive 89/104 a person infringes a registered trade mark if he uses in the course of trade a sign which is identical with the trade mark in relation to goods or services which are identical with those for which it is registered.

19.35 The signs are identical; the latter sign is used in the course of trade; it is not used in relation to goods which are identical but it is applied on an identical product (a version of the *Wet, Wet, Wet*[14] scenario).

19.36 Surely when you buy a bus you can do whatever you want to do with it; the trade mark rights of the bus producer should not limit the rights of the bus owner. They can advertise the fact that they are using a Brigadier bus to transport their customers, they can use it to sell beer, they can use it to promote Brigadier beer. The mark is not used to sell buses but beer. A strict interpretation of the provision would ensure that such use is outside the scope of infringement.

19.37 Even if we have to follow *Arsenal v Reed*, their use does not affect the interests of the bus manufacturer.

---

[14] See *Bravado Merchandising Services Ltd v Mainstream Publishing (Edinburgh) Ltd* [1996] FSR 205.

INDEX

abandonment
loss of trade mark through, United States
13.24–13.25, 17.22–17.25, 18.11
acquired distinctiveness
balance with freedom for others to use
3.25–3.29
Community Trade Marks
language issues 5.53–5.54
proof of acquired distinctiveness 5.45–5.52
conclusion 4.57
decision as to when to argue for 5.55–5.56
direct evidence of
advertising and promotion 5.19–5.23
confidentiality 5.25–5.28
introduction 5.14–5.15
market size and share 5.24
sales and supplies 5.16–5.18
evidence of
conclusion 5.60–5.61
contents 5.13
direct evidence of use 5.14–5.28
introduction 5.01–5.03
legal and regulatory guidance 5.06–5.12
maximising 5.57–5.58
objective, focus on 5.05
OHIM Examination Division Practice Note
5.12
OHIM Examination Guidelines 5.11
recognition, evidence of 5.29–5.40
understanding the objection 5.04
geographical extent of use conferring
distinctiveness 4.45–4.50
introduction 3.03–3.04, 4.01–4.11
non-persuasive elements 4.55–4.56
persuasive elements 4.51–4.54
publication 5.59
recognition, evidence of
individual consumers 5.39
introduction 5.29–5.31
national registration 5.40
survey evidence 5.34–5.38
trade evidence 5.32–5.33
relevant date for proving 5.41–5.44
sign for which acquired distinctiveness claimed
introduction 4.12–4.14
juxtaposition with other signs 4.15–4.17

merger into broader ensemble 4.18–4.23
signs having a function 4.24–4.33
time of acquisition of distinctiveness
application 4.36–4.40
introduction 4.35
invalidity 4.41
when distinctiveness can be claimed 4.42–4.44
advertisements
comparative 11.49
direct evidence of trade mark use 5.19–5.23
internet 15.22–15.24
**Agreement of Trade-Related Aspects of
Intellectual Property Rights,** *see* **TRIPs
Agreement**
analogous use doctrine
United States 17.15
Arsenal **case** 8.62–8.67, 16.53–16.54
Court of Appeal decision 10.22
ECJ ruling 10.16–10.19
First High Court decision 10.14–10.15
introduction 10.12–10.13
Second High Court decision 10.20–10.21
TRIPs Agreement 16.53–16.54
Australia
certification marks
persons permitted to use 9.13–9.14
use requirement for registration 9.08
collective marks
definition 9.32
ownership and use 9.32
Austria
criminal infringement of trade marks 12.30

badges of support, loyalty or affiliation
Arsenal case, *see* ***Arsenal* case**
Barbie Girl **case** 8.07–8.16
BIANCANEVE **case** 8.36–8.37
Bodenhausen, GHC 2.04, 2.08, 2.10, 2.38
books, *see* **press products and merchandising**
brands
concept 10.04
importance 10.04–10.11
Bugge, JJ 2.24
business names
real and fictional names used in
CACAO MERAVIGLIAO case 8.42–8.45

business names (*cont.*):
    Daily Planet case 8.40–8.41
    introduction 8.38–8.39
    Lane Capital Management case
      8.46–8.47
    Nichols case 8.48–8.52

CACAO MERAVIGLIAO case 8.42–8.45
Canada
    certification marks, use requirement for
      registration 9.08
    stockpiling 2.14
    TRIPs, exceptions for economic development
      and public interest 16.48–16.49
certification marks
    introduction 9.01
    ownership and use
      authorized use versus trade mark use by
        licensee 9.17–9.21
      introduction 9.11
      licensee estoppel 9.22–9.23
      persons permitted to use 9.12–9.16
    purpose 9.02–9.04
    registration
      introduction 9.07
      use requirement 9.08–9.10
    summary 9.34–9.36
collective marks
    collective membership mark 9.06
    introduction 9.01
    ownership and use 9.28–9.33
    purpose 9.05–9.06
    registration 9.24–9.27
    summary 9.34–9.36
collective membership mark 9.06
colour marks 6.36
commercially sensitive data
    direct evidence of trade mark use 5.25–5.28
commons theory, *see* **trade mark common**
Community trade marks
    conclusion 19.06
    language issues 5.53–5.54
    proof of acquired distinctiveness 5.45–5.52
comparative advertising 11.49
competition
    trade marks as anti-competitive 10.46
    unfair, *see* **unfair competition**
concept of use
    centre of trade mark system, as 19.14–19.16
    essential function 1.07
    future role 19.22–19.25
    global concern 1.06
    importance in trade mark law 1.04–1.05
    introduction 2.01–2.05
    methodology for analysis 1.08–1.18
    single definition
      introduction 19.02–19.03

    prospective dimension 19.04
    retrospective dimension 19.04
    temporal dimensions 19.04
    US trade mark law, *see* **United States**
confidentiality
    direct evidence of trade mark use 5.25–5.28
conflicting earlier marks, *see* **earlier trade marks**
confusion
    internet
      'deep linking' 15.25
      framing 15.26
      initial interest 15.16, 15.22
    likelihood of, *see* **likelihood of confusion**
constructive use
    United States 17.17–17.21
consumers
    individual, evidence of recognition of trade
      mark 5.39
contract manufacturers
    third party use of trade marks 7.40–7.45
Cornish, W 2.01
criminal law
    Austria 12.30
    conclusion 12.35
    European jurisdictions 12.27–12.34
    France 12.32
    Germany 12.29
    honesty, concept of in UK law 11.26–11.32
    infringement of trade mark 12.02–12.07
    introduction 12.01
    R v Johnstone
      House of Lords decision 12.08–12.12
      infringing trade mark use in criminal
        proceedings as interpreted by
        12.13–12.26
    Switzerland 12.31

Daily Planet case 8.40–8.41
de minimis use 13.14–13.23
defences to infringement 10.40–10.44
    comparative advertising 11.49
    conclusion 11.58
    factual requirements not made out 11.04
    honesty
      concept in UK criminal law 11.26–11.32
      duty not to cause prejudice to another's trade
        mark, honesty equating to 11.23–11.25
      Gerolsteiner case 11.12, 11.33–11.35
      introduction 11.11
      non-use related definitions 11.20–11.22
      objective and subjective definitions
        11.33–11.40
      use-related definition 11.13–11.19
    infringing use 11.01
    legal requirements not made out 11.04
    legislation 11.06–11.10
    licensed use 11.04

other indications 11.42–11.48,
    11.50–11.51
own name and address 11.41
owner not entitled to sue 11.04
permitted exception 11.04
prior marks 11.52–11.57
terminology 11.02
types 11.04
types of infringement 11.03
United States, *see* **United States**
defences to unfair competition claims
United States, *see* **United States**
defensive marks
Germany 2.14
Denmark
earlier trade marks 14.06
genuine use 2.24
time limit for use 2.30
denominative use
conclusion 8.67–8.68
fictional characters, *see* **fictional characters**
introduction 8.01–8.03
music industry, fictional characters, *see* **fictional characters**
press products and merchandising, *see* **press products and merchandising**
descriptive fair use 18.23
descriptive marks 16.23–16.30
ECJ doctrine 3.13–3.15
dilution doctrine
extension 16.61
origin 16.59
role of trade mark use in proceedings 18.01, 18.25–18.29
TRIPs Agreement 16.18, 16.21
well-known marks 16.55–16.61
dispute resolution
internet 15.31–1.32
WTO procedure 16.06
distinctiveness acquired through use, *see* **acquired distinctiveness**
distinction between trade marks and other intellectual property rights 2.01
distinctive character
lack of 3.01–3.03
ECJ doctrine 3.16–3.17
distinctive principles of trade mark law 2.01
distinguishing use
functional use versus, three-dimensional marks, *see* **three-dimensional marks**
distributors
third party use of trade marks
    claim of ownership 7.36–7.39
    introduction 7.33
    nature of use 7.34–7.35
doing down the mark 11.03

domain names 15.03–15.11, 15.13–15.17, 15.28–15.30
Douglass, S 9.18

earlier trade marks
defences to infringement 11.52–11.57
evidence of use in opposition and invalidation proceedings
    applicant for invalidation, timing of filing of supporting evidence 14.56
    Community Trade Mark Regulation 14.09–14.11
    conclusion 14.74–14.75
    filing of proof of genuine use at OHIM, timing 14.23–14.26
    form of evidence 14.57–14.60
    form of evidence of genuine use for OHIM 14.16–14.22
    nature of proof 14.38–14.44, 14.61–14.63
    notional specification 14.69–14.73
    opponents filing of supporting evidence, timing 14.54–14.55
    period within which genuine use must be shown 14.27–14.29, 14.64–14.68
    preliminary indication in opposition proceedings 14.52–14.53
    purpose of provisions 14.01–14.08
    request to invoke use condition 14.48–14.51
    statement of use 14.48–14.51
    territorial extent of use 14.30–14.37
    timing and nature of request for proof of genuine use 14.12–14.15
    UK Trade Mark Act 1994 14.45–14.47
EC Directive
distinctive character acquired through use 4.01–4.10
sign for which claimed 4.12–4.32
earlier trade marks 14.04
limitation of effect of trade mark 11.07
meaning of notion of use 2.16–2.19
necessity to use registered mark, reason 13.02
technical features of products 6.06
use requirement 2.09, 13.03–13.05
EC Regulation
acquired distinctiveness 4.02–4.10
    sign for which claimed 4.12–4.32
earlier trade marks 14.07, 14.09–14.11
English language common 3.04, 3.06–3.11
essential function 1.07
definition 19.17
ECJ interpretation 4.05
linchpin of trade mark system 19.17–19.21
evidence of use
acquired distinctiveness, *see* **acquired distinctiveness**
genuine use of earlier marks, *see* **earlier trade marks**

exploitation
certification marks, *see* **certification marks**
collective marks, *see* **collective marks**
denominative trade marks, *see* **denominative use**
third party use of trade marks, *see* **third party use of trade mark**

fair use doctrine
United States 18.22–18.24
famous marks 16.18
dilution doctrine, *see* **dilution doctrine**
exceptions from use requirements 2.36–2.44
exploitation by merchandising, *see* **merchandising, press products and merchandising**
fan sites
Harry Potter 8.26
introduction 8.22
Paramount Pictures, policy of 8.24
real character's name and places referring to him, Elvis Presley 8.27–8.29
Star Trek 8.24
Time Warner, policy of 8.25–8.26
Fezer, K-H 2.01
fictional characters
music industry
Barbie Girl case 8.07–8.16
introduction 8.04–8.06
NELLIE THE ELEPHANT case 8.17–8.20
retailing
BIANCANEVE case 8.36–8.37
introduction 8.30–8.31
TARZAN case 8.32–8.35
websites
introduction 8.21–8.22
Paramount Pictures 8.24
Time Warner 8.25–8.26
fictional names
business names, used in, *see* **business names**
film industry
fan sites, *see* **fan sites**
fictional characters, *see* **fictional characters**
merchandising 10.07
football
unauthorized use of trade mark in press products and merchandising 10.08
Arsenal case, *see* **Arsenal case**
Juvenissima case 8.59–8.61
Super Inter case 8.57–8.58
France
criminal infringement of trade marks 12.32
fraud 18.12–18.13
freedom for others to use
balance with recognizing distinctiveness through use 3.25–3.29

ECJ doctrine
absence of commons theory 3.18–3.24
descriptive signs 3.13–3.15
introduction 3.12
signs devoid of distinctive character 3.16–3.17
introduction 3.01–3.05
functional shapes 4.24–4.33
functionality
acquired distinctiveness, essential features of shapes 4.24–4.33
distinguishing use versus, three-dimensional marks, *see* **three-dimensional marks**
three-dimensional marks, *see* **three-dimensional marks**

General Agreement on Tariffs and Trade (GATT) 16.04
national treatment principle 16.40
non-discrimination, exceptions 16.44
Panel reports, establishment of case-law 16.65
generic names
United States 18.09
genuine use
de minimis rule 13.14–13.23
earlier marks, *see* **earlier trade marks**
five year period for 13.05
interpretation of term 13.06–13.13
level of use required 13.14–13.23
Germany
criminal infringement of trade marks 12.29
earlier trade marks 14.06
enforcement issues 2.35
obligation to use as basic principle of trade mark law 2.01
time-limit for use 2.30
Gerolsteiner case 11.12, 11.33–11.35
Gregersen, PEP 2.24

honesty
defences to infringement
concept in UK criminal law 11.26–11.32
duty not to cause prejudice to another's trade mark, honesty equating to 11.23–11.25
Gerolsteiner case 11.12, 11.33–11.35
introduction 11.11
non-use related definitions 11.20–11.22
objective and subjective definitions 11.33–11.40
use-related definition 11.13–11.19

identical use 11.03
'identity products' 8.01
illustrative situation 1.01–1.03, 19.26–19.37
infringement
conclusion 19.11–19.13
criminal offence, *see* **criminal law**

defences, *see* **defences to infringement**
doing down the mark 11.03
expansionary pressure on scope of, *see* **TRIPs**
    Agreement
identical use 11.03
internet, *see* **internet**
similar or confusing use 11.03
types 11.03
United States, *see* **United States**
use in course of trade
    Arsenal case, *see* **Arsenal case**
    conclusion 10.47–10.49
    inertia in English courts, reasons
        10.31–10.36
    introduction 10.01–10.03
    merchandising and importance of brands
        10.04–10.11
    post-Arsenal cases 10.23–10.30
    R v Johnstone 10.24–10.28
    Reed Executive v Reed Business Information
        10.29–10.30
    UK Trade Mark Act 1994 10.37–10.46
intent to use
    declaration of, United States 2.27
    descriptive marks 16.27
    revocation for non-use 13.24–13.28
interface of trade mark rights with other
    intellectual property rights
    19.09–19.10
internet
    conclusion 15.35
    dispute resolution 15.31–15.32
    domain names 15.03–15.11, 15.28–15.30
    enforcement issues 15.31–15.34
    fictional characters, use of, *see* **fictional**
        characters
    ICANN 15.31
    infringement
        adaptation of trade mark law principles
            15.13–15.27
        adware 15.22
        'deep linking' 15.25
        domain names 15.13–15.17
        framing 15.26
        'free ride' arguments 15.18
        initial interest confusion 15.22
        introduction 15.12
        metatags 15.18–15.21
        pre-sale confusion 15.16
    initial interest confusion doctrine 15.16
    introduction 15.01–15.02
    territoriality issues 15.31–15.34
    warehousing 15.28–15.30
invalidity
    absolute grounds for, overcoming, *see* **acquired**
        distinctiveness
    acquired distinctiveness 4.41

proceedings, evidence of use of earlier trade
    marks, *see* **earlier trade marks**
Italy
    CACAO MERAVIGLIA case 8.42–8.45
    unauthorized reference to fictional characters in
        retailing
        BIANCANEVE case 8.36–8.37
        TARZAN case 8.32–8.35
    unauthorized use of trade marks in press
        products and merchandising
        Juventissima case 8.59–8.61
        Super Inter case 8.57–8.58
        Swatchissimo case 8.55–8.56

Juventissima case 8.59–8.61

Landes, WM 2.10
Lane Capital Management case 8.46–8.47
language
    Community Trade Marks 5.53–5.54
licensees
    certification marks
        authorized use versus trade mark use by
            licensee 9.17–9.21
        estoppel 9.22–9.23
    estoppel 9.22–9.23
    use of trade mark by
        attribution of use 7.27–7.32
        classic position 7.06–7.16
        present situation 7.17–7.26
likelihood of confusion
    internet, *see* **internet**
    US, defences to infringement and unfair
        competition claims based on absence of
        distinct geographical areas defence 18.20
    introduction 18.19
    weak mark defence 18.21

Madrid Agreement and Protocol 16.24
market size and share
    direct evidence of trade mark use 5.24
meaning of term 'use' 1.19
merchandising, *see also* **press products and**
    merchandising
    importance of brands 10.04–10.11
metatags 15.18–15.21
    infringement 10.29–10.30
most favoured nation (MFN) treatment 16.31,
    16.40–16.43
Mostert 2.40
Mueller, M 15.05
multinational enterprises
    descriptive marks, demand for 16.28
music industry
    bootleg recordings 10.24–10.28,
        12.08–12.12
    fictional characters, *see* **fictional characters**

Index

names
  business, *see* **business names**
  fictional characters, *see* **fictional characters**
  real, *see* **real names**
  use of own, defence against infringement 11.41
national registration
  evidence of recognition of trade mark 5.40
  non-persuasive elements as to acquired
      distinctiveness 4.56
need to leave for others to use, *see* **freedom for
      others to use**
NELLIE THE ELEPHANT case 8.17–8.20
Nichols case 8.48–8.52
nominative fair use 18.24
non-profit organizations
  brand, importance of 10.06
non-traditional trade marks, *see* **colour marks;
      shapes; three-dimensional marks**
non-use
  concept 2.23–2.25
  descriptive marks 16.27
  legitimate excuse for 2.33–2.34
  revocation for, *see* **revocation for non-use**
  United States, *see* **United States**
notion of use
  descriptive definition 2.15–2.16
  meaning 2.12–2.25
  negative definition 2.15
  positive definition 2.15–2.16

obligation to use, *see* **requirement of use**
OHIM
  earlier trade marks, evidence of use in
      opposition and invalidation proceedings,
      see **earlier trade marks**
  Examination Division Practice Note 5.12
  Examination Guidelines 5.11
  functional continuity between examiners and
      Boards 4.42
  means of giving or obtaining evidence in
      proceedings 5.09–5.10
opposition proceedings
  earlier trade marks, evidence of, *see* **earlier trade
      marks**
ownership of trade marks
  certification marks 9.11–9.23
  collective marks 9.28–9.33

**Paris Convention for the Protection of Industrial
      Property**
  certification and collective marks 9.34
  definition of use, absence 2.16
  maintenance of registration 2.28
  national legislation on conditions for filing and
      registration of trade marks 16.25
  non-discrimination 16.40
  use requirement 2.06

  well-known marks 2.37–2.40
*Philips Electronics v Remington Consumer
      Products* 6.12–6.21
Portugal
  non-use 2.34
Posner, RA 2.10
pre-sale confusion
  internet sales 15.16
press products and merchandising
  unauthorized use of trade mark
    Arsenal case 8.62–8.67
    introduction 8.53–8.54
    Juventissima case 8.59–8.61
    Super Inter case 8.57–8.58
    Swatchissimo case 8.55–8.56
prima facie **marks** 16.27
prior marks, *see* **earlier trade marks**
promotion of products
  direct evidence of trade mark use 5.19–5.23

R v Johnstone 10.24–10.28
  House of Lords decision 12.08–12.12
  infringing trade mark use in criminal
      proceedings as interpreted by
      12.13–12.26
real names
  business names, used in, *see* **business names**
  Elvis Presley, use of 8.27–8.29
recognition of trade marks
  evidence of
    individual consumers 5.39
    introduction 5.29–5.31
    national registration 5.40
    survey evidence 5.34–5.38
    trade evidence 5.32–5.33
Reed Executive v Reed Business Information
      10.29–10.30
referential use 8.16, 19.02
registration
  bad faith 2.14
  basis of trade mark law, as 2.01–2.03
  certification marks 9.07–9.10
  collective marks 9.24–9.27
  distinctive character acquired through use, *see*
      acquired distinctiveness
  distinguishing use versus functional use, *see*
      three-dimensional marks
  domain names 15.06–15.07
  United States, *see* **United States**
  use requirement, *see* **requirement of use**
reputations, marks with, *see also* **famous marks**
  unauthorized domain name or metatag use
      15.21
requirement of use
  conclusion 2.45
  enforcement issues, impact on 2.35
  exceptions 2.36–2.44

impact on rights in trade marks 2.26–2.35
legislative provisions 2.06–2.11
legitimate excuse for non-use 2.33–2.34
time limit for use 2.28–2.32
retailing
fictional characters, use of, *see* fictional
characters
revocation for non-use
abandonment 13.24–13.25
conclusion 13.29–13.30
genuine use
de minimis rule 13.14–13.23
five year period for 13.05
interpretation of term 13.06–13.13
level of use required 13.14–13.23
intentions of proprietor 13.24–13.28
introduction 13.01–13.05
rights in gross 16.17, 16.21

sales and supplies of goods
direct evidence of trade mark use 5.16–5.18
Schechter, F 16.59–16.60
secondary meaning 18.10
shapes, *see also* three-dimensional marks
acquired distinctiveness 4.17
functional features 4.24–4.33
signs of affiliation 16.13
Arsenal case, *see Arsenal* case
similar or confusing use 11.03
slogans 4.18–4.23, 5.19
Slovenia
enforcement issues 2.35
'stockpiling' 2.14
Super Inter case 8.57–8.58
surrogate use
United States 17.11–17.13
survey evidence
recognition of trade mark 5.34–5.38
Swatchissimo case 8.55–8.56
Switzerland
criminal infringement of trade mark
12.31

TARZAN case 8.32–8.35
technical features of products
shapes and, *see* three-dimensional marks
third party use of trade mark
conclusion 7.46–7.47
contract manufacturer 7.40–7.45
distributors
claim of ownership 7.36–7.39
introduction 7.33
nature of use 7.34–7.35
introduction 7.01–7.05
legal possibility of authorized use
classic position of trade mark use by licensee
7.06–7.16

present situation 7.17–7.26
licensees
attribution of use 7.27–7.32
distributors or contract manufacturers
7.33–7.45
three-dimensional marks, *see also* shapes
distinguishing trade marks from functional
features 6.07–6.11
marks with less than complete technical
functions 6.22–6.30
nature of problem 6.01–6.06
peculiarities of use 6.31–6.37
*Philips Electronics v Remington Consumer
Products* 6.12–6.21
trade evidence of recognition of trade marks
5.32–5.33
trade mark common
ECJ, absence of commons theory 3.18–3.24
English law 3.04, 3.06–3.11
trade witnesses
evidence of recognition 5.32–5.33
TRIPs Agreement
acquired distinctiveness 4.01
bounds of property, trade mark use and
16.13–16.22
certification and collective marks 9.34
conclusion 16.72–16.73
definition of use, absence 2.16
descriptive marks 16.23–16.30
dilution doctrine 16.18, 16.21
well-known marks 16.59–16.61
EC trade mark law, relationship with
16.08–16.11
exceptions for economic development and
public interest 16.44–16.50
expansionary pressure on scope of trade mark
infringement
Arsenal case 16.53–16.54
introduction 16.51–16.54
well-known marks 16.55–16.61
intention to use 16.27
interpretation 16.62–16.71
introduction 16.01–16.12
legitimate excuse for non-use 2.33
limited exceptions to rights 16.20
maintenance of registration 2.28
most favoured nation (MFN) treatment 16.31,
16.40–16.43
national treatment 16.31, 16.40–16.43
non-use 16.27
notion of personal property in the mark 16.16
property rights in public goods 16.19
unjustifiable encumbrances involving trade
mark use 16.32–16.39
use requirement 2.06–2.07, 2.27
well-known marks 2.40
WTO jurisprudence 16.31–16.50

362

Index

unauthorized use
press products and merchandising, *see* **press products and merchandising**
trade marks referring to fictional characters, *see* **fictional characters**
unfair competition
bounds of property 16.15
United States, *see* **United States**
United Kingdom
Arsenal case, *see* **Arsenal case**
certification marks
authorized use versus trade mark use by licensee 9.19
use requirement for registration 9.08, 9.10
collective marks, registration 9.24–9.26
ownership and use 9.28–9.31
earlier marks, proof of use
applicant for invalidation, timing of filing of supporting evidence 14.56
form of evidence 14.57–14.60
legislation 14.45–14.47
nature of proof 14.61–14.63
notional specification 14.69–14.73
opponents filing of supporting evidence, timing 14.54–14.55
period within which genuine use must be shown 14.64–14.68
preliminary indication in opposition proceedings 14.52–14.53
request to invoke use conditions 14.48–14.51
football
Arsenal case, *see* **Arsenal case**
merchandising 10.08
honesty, concept in criminal law 11.26–11.32
infringing use
anti-competitive practices 10.45–10.46
Arsenal case, *see* **Arsenal case**
broadening the monopoly 10.35–10.36
criminal offences, *see* **criminal law**
defences to infringement 10.40–10.44
implementation of Directive 10.37–10.39
inertia in English courts, reasons 10.31–10.36
post-*Arsenal* cases 10.23–10.30
R v Johnstone 10.24–10.28
Reed Executive v Reed Business Information 10.29–10.30
Trade Mark Act 1938 10.32–10.34
Trade Mark Act 1994 10.37–10.46
internet advertisements 15.23
licences 7.17–7.26
music industry, *NELLIE THE ELEPHANT* case 8.17–8.20
real names used in business names, *Nichols* case 8.48–8.52
registrations in bad faith 2.14

surveys, evidence of recognition of trade marks 5.35
time limit for use 2.30
Trade Mark Act 1938 7.13, 7.15, 10.32–10.34, 19.07–19.08
trade mark common in English law 3.04, 3.06–3.11
unauthorized use of trade marks in press products and merchandising, *Arsenal* case 8.62–8.67
well-known trade marks, registration of domain names 15.30
United States
abandonment, loss of trade mark rights through 13.24–13.25, 17.22–17.25, 18.11
acquiring rights through use 18.02–18.04
business names, real and fictional names used in
Daily Planet case 8.40–8.41
Lane Capital Management case 8.46–8.47
certification marks
licensee estoppel 9.23
persons permitted to use 9.15–9.16
use requirement for registration 9.08–9.09
collective marks
ownership and use 9.33
registration 9.27
collective membership mark 9.06
concept of use 17.01–17.02, 17.33–17.35
Constitution, authority for trade mark legislation 16.02
contract manufacturers 7.42–7.43
Corporation for Assigned Names and Numbers (ICANN) 15.06, 15.08–15.11, 15.31
defences to infringement and unfair competition claims, use in
abandonment 18.11
attack on claimant's rights in the mark 18.08–18.13
defendant's priority 18.14–18.18
descriptive fair use 18.23
distinct geographical areas defence 18.20
fair use defence 18.22–18.24
fraud 18.12–18.13
genericity 18.09
introduction 18.07
likelihood of confusion, defences based on lack of 18.19–18.21
merely descriptive mark 18.10
nominative fair use 18.24
non-distinctiveness 18.10
secondary meaning 18.10
weak mark defence 18.21
dilution proceedings, *see* **dilution doctrine**
distributor's claim of ownership 7.38
domain names, adaptation of trade mark law principles to 15.07

establishment of rights 18.02–18.04
famous marks 16.18
geographical scope of rights 17.26–17.32
infringement proceedings, role of trade mark
    use
  conclusion 18.29
  defences 18.07–18.24
  introduction 18.01, 18.05–18.06
Intent of Use declaration 2.27
internet advertisements 15.22
licensing 7.09, 7.14–7.15
meaning of notion of use 2.20
music industry, *Barbie Girl* case
    8.07–8.16
notion of use 2.20–2.21
non-use 17.22–17.25
stockpiling 2.14
unfair competition, role of trade mark use
  conclusion 18.29
  defences 18.07–18.24
  introduction 18.01, 18.05–18.06
use as condition for acquiring rights
  actual use 17.05–17.16

analogous use 17.15
constructive use 17.17–17.21
introduction 2.02, 17.03–17.04
surrogate use 17.11–17.13
use as condition for maintaining rights
    17.22–17.25
use requirement, *see* **requirement of use**

websites, *see* **fan sites; internet**
well-known marks 16.21
  domain names registration as 15.30
  exceptions to use requirement 2.36–2.44
  Paris Convention 2.40, 16.55–16.56
  TRIPs Agreement 2.40, 16.57–16.61
  WIPO Joint Recommendation 2.41
wholesalers, *see* **distributors**
WIPO
  internet, dispute resolution 15.32
  well-known marks, Joint Recommendation
      2.41
World Wide Web, *see* **internet**
World Trade Organization (WTO)
  TRIPS Agreement, *see* **TRIPs Agreement**